Frank Bowling

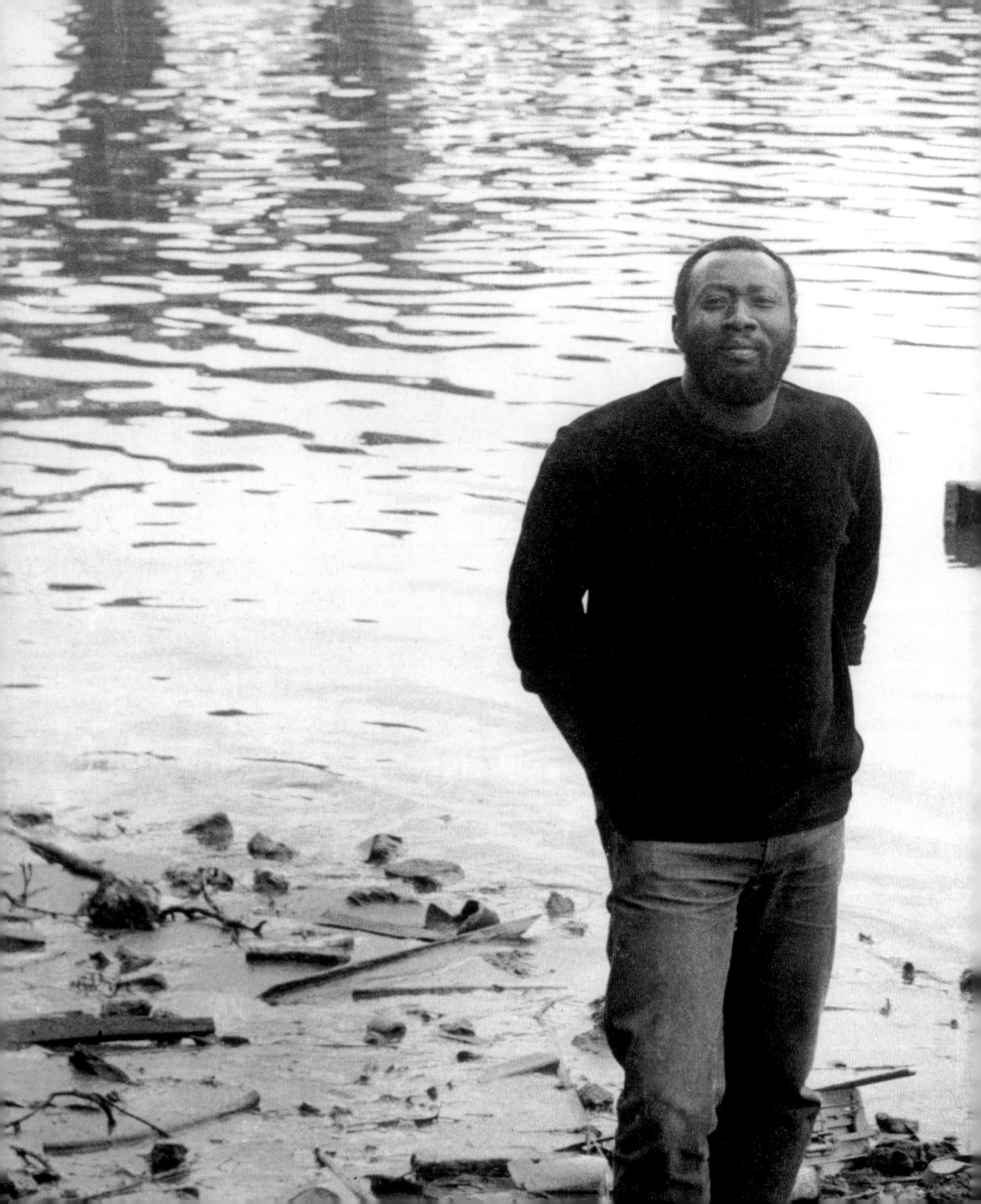

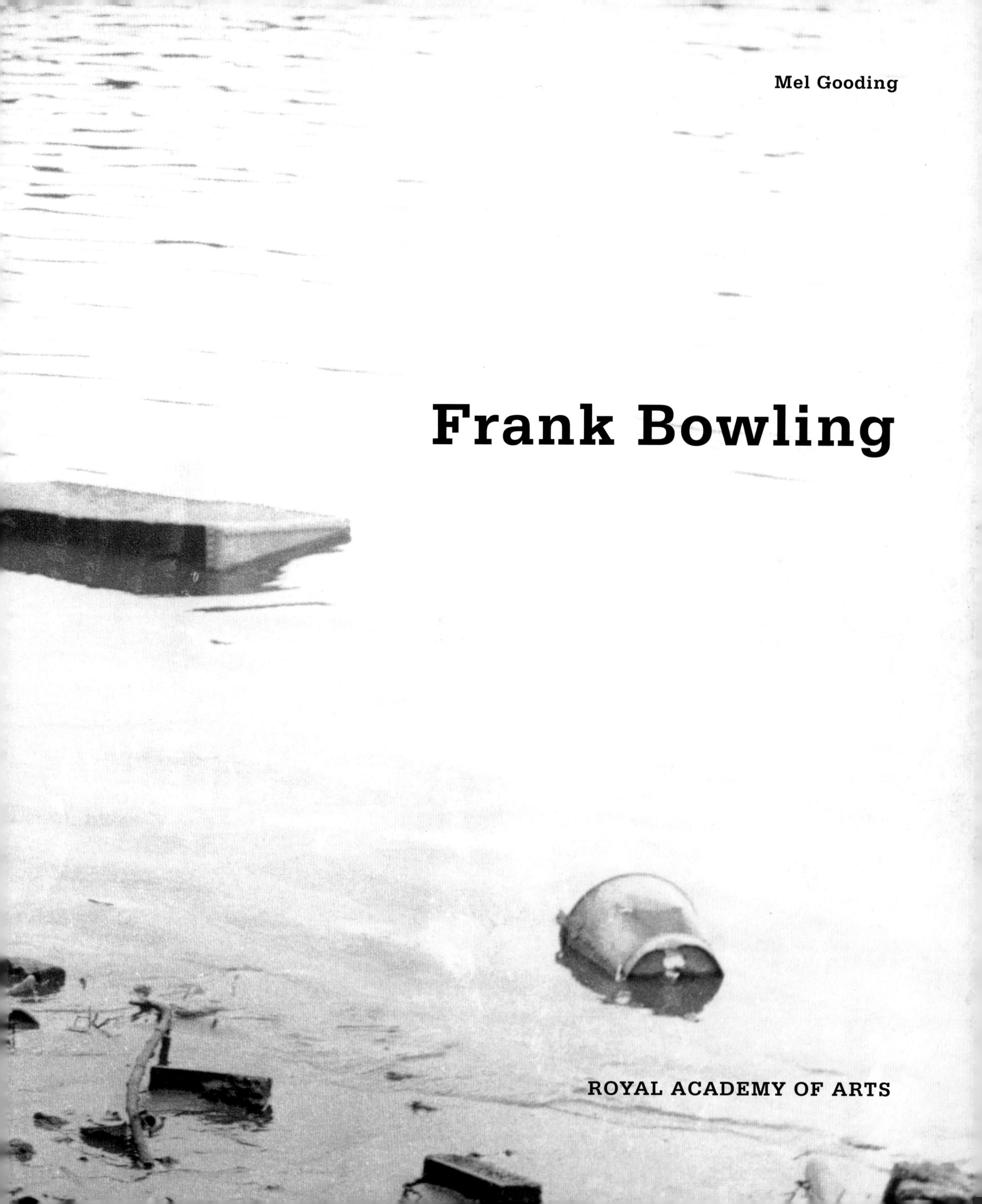

Mel Gooding

Frank Bowling

ROYAL ACADEMY OF ARTS

ROLLO

ROLLO Contemporary Art 51 Cleveland Street London W1T 4JH
info@rolloart.com + 44 (0)20 7580 0020 www.rolloart.com

SPANIERMAN MODERN

53 EAST 58TH STREET NEW YORK, NY 10022-1617
TEL (212) 832-1400 WWW.SPANIERMANMODERN.COM

British Library Cataloguing-in-Publication Data
A catalogue record of this book is available from the British Library

ISBN 978-1-905711-96-3

Distributed outside the United States and Canada by Thames & Hudson Ltd, London

Distributed in the United States and Canada by Harry N. Abrams, Inc., New York

ROYAL ACADEMY PUBLICATIONS
Beatrice Gullström
Carola Krueger
Sophie Oliver
Peter Sawbridge
Nick Tite

Editor: Jill Hollis
Designer: Maggi Smith
Colour origination: DawkinsColour

Printed in Belgium by Die Keure

Author's Acknowledgements
I owe thanks to Simon Gillespie and Emily Johnson at ROLLO Contemporary Art, and to Nick Tite and his staff at Royal Academy Publications. Martha Campbell at Spanierman Modern, New York, has been wonderfully efficient and helpful; the exhibition at that gallery in 2010 helped in no small way to shape my view of a crucial aspect of Bowling's development as an artist. Rose Jones has been helpful in many ways, and her film on Bowling's life and work will greatly add to our understanding of his career. To Spencer Richards I owe a special debt for his many kinds of insight, and for his practical help; five days with him in Brooklyn deepened my game. Above all I must express my appreciation of Frank Bowling and Rachel Scott for their continuous generosity of response to my thoughts and enquiries, and for over twenty-five years of friendship and critical discussion. Jill Hollis has been, as ever, the most exacting and scrupulous editor. My wife, Rhiannon, knows how much she has contributed to this project.

Photographic Credits
Most of the images in this book have been reproduced from photographic material owned by the artist, who wishes to thank the photographers of works on the following pages for their kind assistance: Matthew Collings p.96 (above); Adger Cowans p.61; Sean Cunningham pp.85, 128-129, 135; Tony Evans pp.48-49; Joe Grant pp.59, 68 (above); Rose Jones pp.19, 22, 23 (both), 24 (above and below), 25 (left and right), 29, 32 (above), 36, 41, 42, 43, 55, 80, 89, 101, 104-105, 106, 106-107, 107, 112, 114, 118, 119, 120-121, 122-123, 125, 127 (right), 138-139, 140 (left), 141, 146 (both), 147, 148 (all), 149; Henry Klimovitz pp.10-11, 88, 112-113; Paul Lipscombe p.105; Graham Mileson p.71; David Parmiter p.126; Spencer Richards pp.30, 56, 57, 60, 62 (both), 73, 74, 75, 76, 124; John Riddy pp.9, 104, 108-109, 116-117; Marcia Scott p.52; Tina Tranter pp.14 (both), 16, 40.

The photographs on the following pages have been reproduced by courtesy of: Aljira, A Center for Contemporary Art, Newark, New Jersey pp.65, 66; Iniva, London pp.63, 64, 65 (left), 69; Poussin Gallery, London (photographer, Paul Minyo) p.127; ROLLO Contemporary Art, London pp.130, 131, 133, 136 (above and below), Royal Academy of Art, London pp.132, 141; Serpentine Gallery (photographer Eileen Tweedy) pp.96 (below), 98, 99 (below), 100, 102-103, 122; Spanierman Modern, New York pp.77, 78, 79 (both), 81, 85, 90, 91, 92, 134, 142, 143; Tate, 2011 pp.110-111; Dennis Toft FRPS (from *The Painter RAs*) pp.152-153; University of Liverpool p.45.

CONTENTS

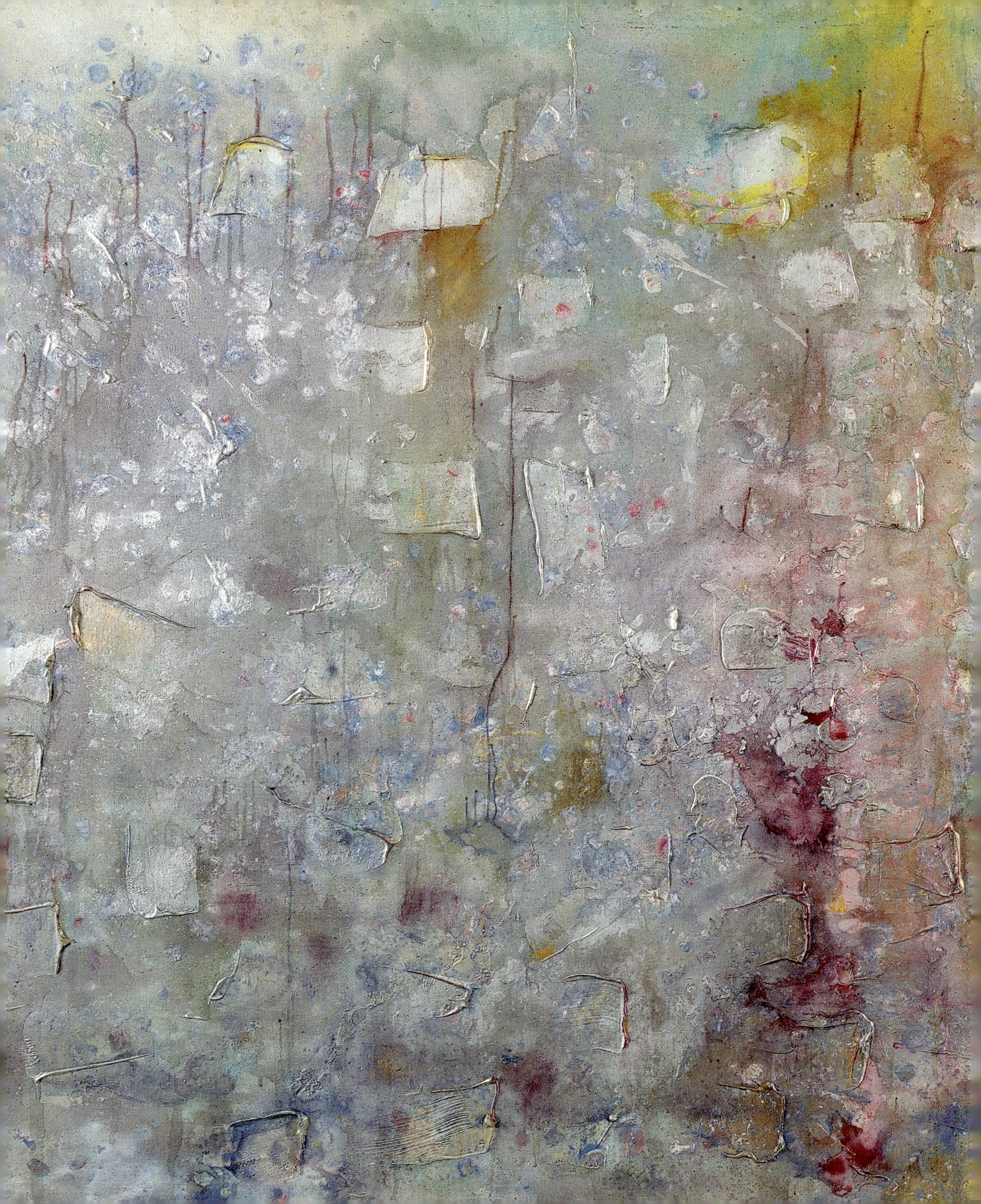

Two Studios / Two Lights: By Way of a Preface

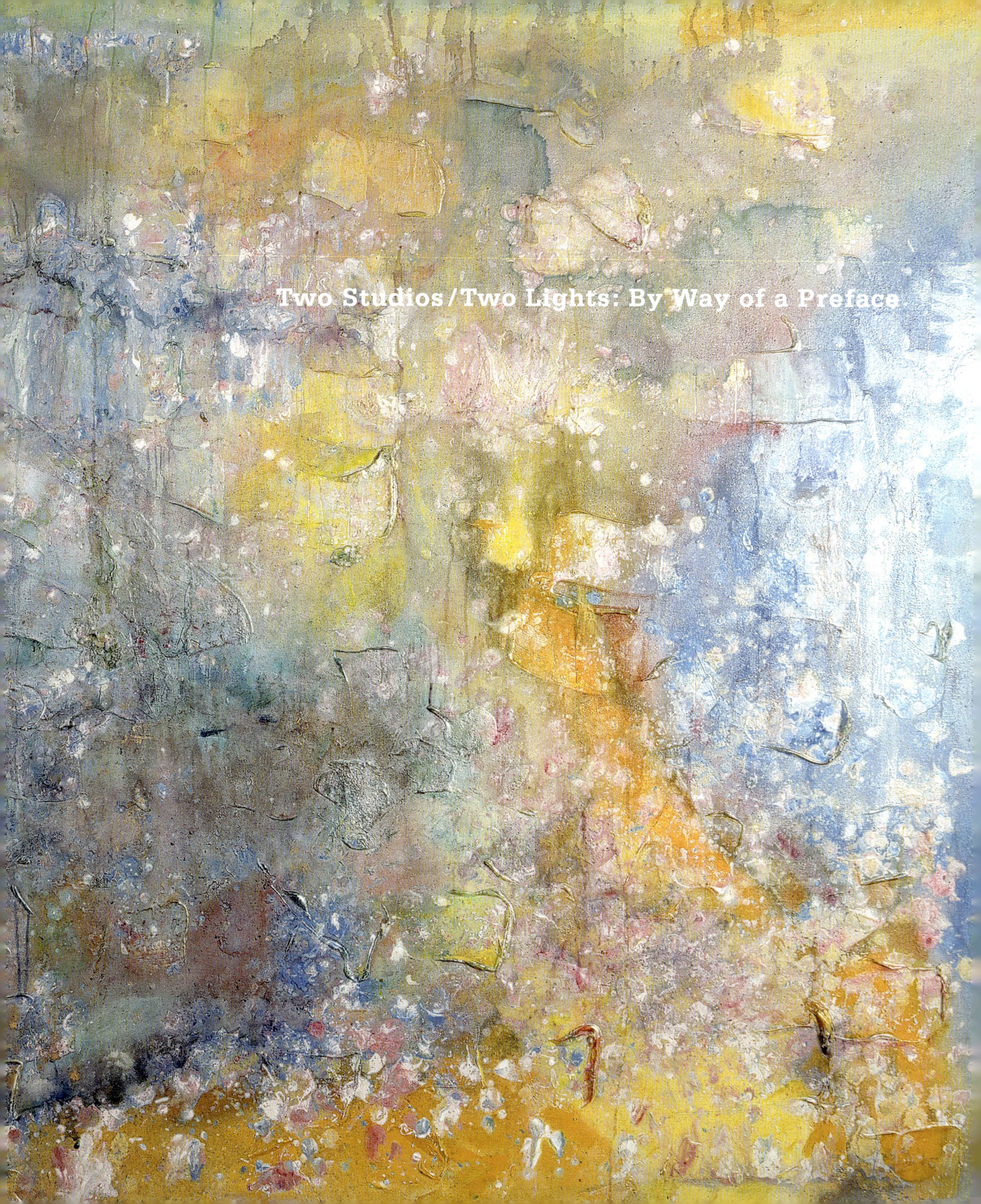

LONDON

Blue-green iridescence, deep blues, shimmering greens, metallic bronze, silver and gold: the brilliance of colour and spectacular optical effects of the peacock's plumage are created by the combination of pigments and structural elements that interfere with ambient light in a complex interaction of absorption, refraction and reflection. I have always found it strangely apt that Frank Bowling's London studio should be located in Peacock Yard. A cobbled cul-de-sac of workshops in Kennington, the yard is a charmed survival in an enclave of handsome but run-down 19th-century working-class dwellings, a product of Victorian philanthropy, ready for gentrification as smart modern blocks rise all around. Each day, on his way to the studio and back, Bowling crosses and re-crosses the shining Thames, which flows at the bottom of the street in Pimlico where he lives.

The studio itself is a modest workshop, its space cramped by stacked and racked canvases, some of them very big, which encroach on the small working area, and block much of the natural daylight entering through dusty windows on the yard side. They face west, and the light is enough at certain times of the day – afternoons, mostly – to give the artist the information he needs to judge how well a painting is progressing. He studies at such moments the interaction of daylight with the complex surface structures and textures, pigments and chemical mediums of the painting he is making. Although, much of the time he works by artificial light, natural light will be the final arbiter of a painting's success. Bowling is not interested in the stability or predictability of a studio 'north light'. Circumambient daylight changes by the minute, and his paintings respond dynamically: their surfaces catch it, absorb it, reflect it, refract it; they partake of its mutability.

To look at the bigger paintings properly it is necessary to manoeuvre them outside with a subtle turn and swing to get them past racks and through the narrow door so that they can be brought to rest against the outside wall of the studio. Now the variegations of the light, determined by the time of day, the height and position of the sun, and modulated by passing clouds, can play freely across their surfaces; and the spectator can move in relation to them, in a kind of dance that recalls the artist's own movements in the rhythm of making, viewing them head-on or sideways from right or left, stepping close up or further away; seeing them with each move in a different light. Now their vitality as dynamic objects becomes apparent: in light they come to life.

I recall once looking in just such a way, in morning light, at *Great Thames III*, and at that moment remembering it, almost finished, on another morning some years before in a borrowed studio-room in a disused factory (now demolished) at the end of Cable Street in Wapping, a few hundred yards from the shining stretch of the great river for which the painting is named. In the studio light flooded in at a high window behind the artist, and I knew that it was the light of the river that was finding its way into the colour and light of the great painting. 'I know I've got to deal with that light', Bowling had said then. Now in the morning sun in Peacock Yard the painting shone out, refulgent in the daylight: iridescence and blue and silver river-light suddenly manifest in a cobbled workaday yard. At that moment, it was not simply a picture but in itself a phenomenal reality: art became nature, nature became art.

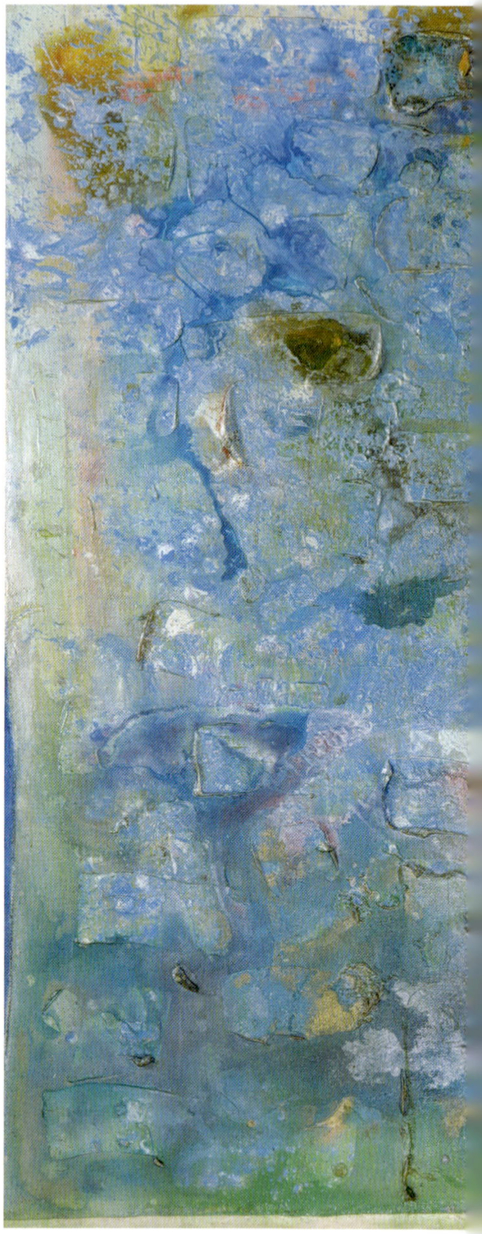

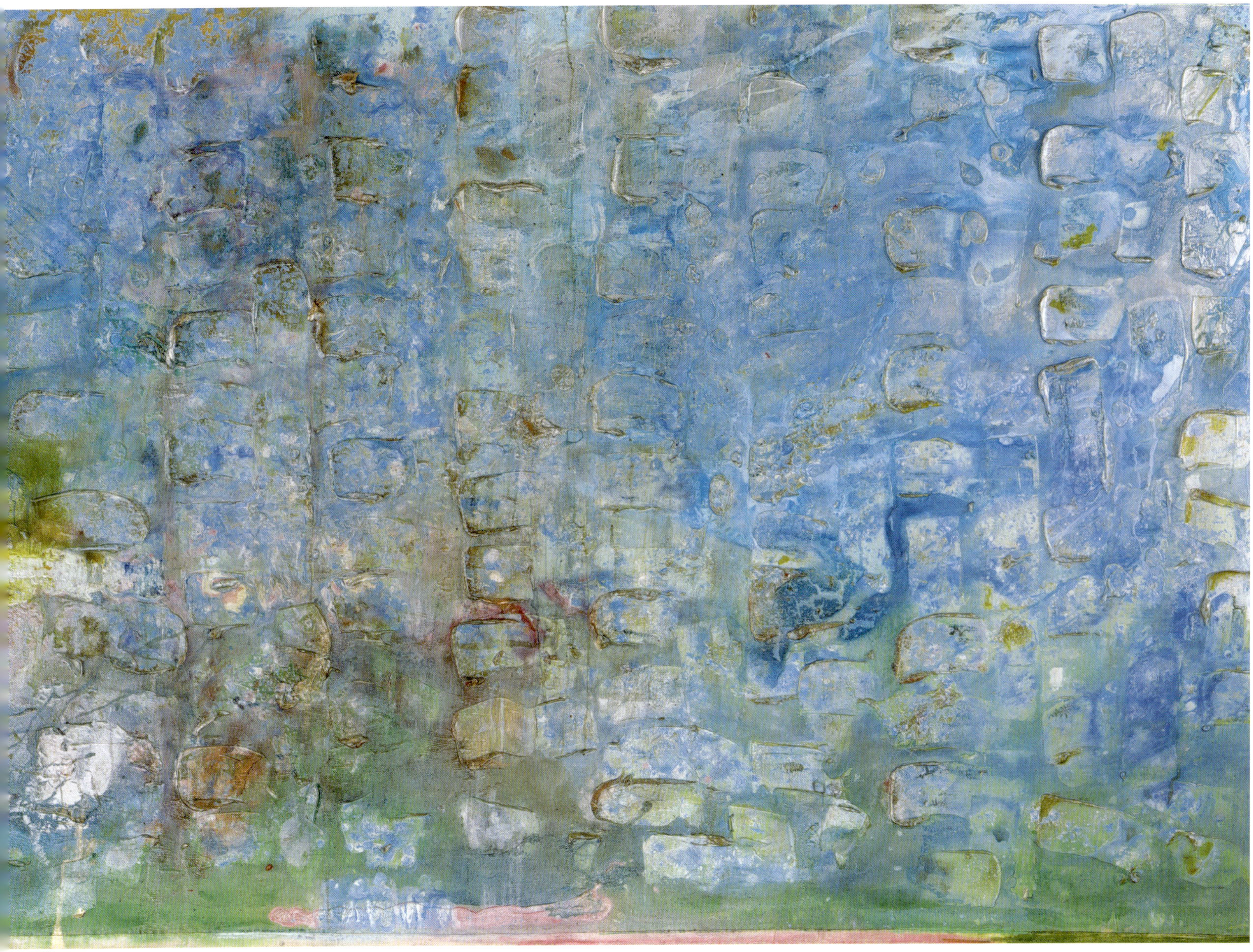

Great Thames III, 1989
Acrylic on canvas, 180 x 321 cm

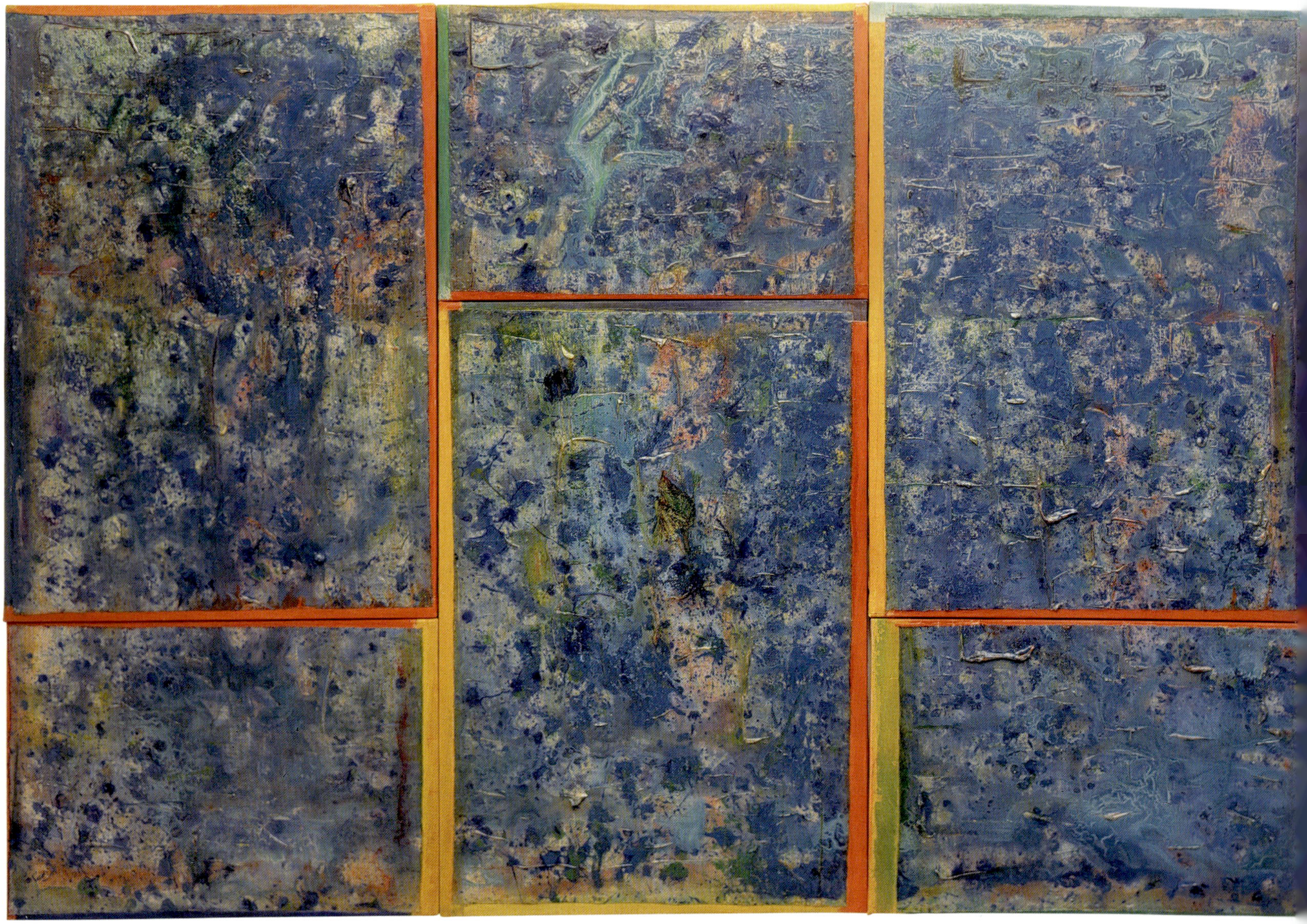

Jamsahibwall, 1990
Acrylic on canvas, 188 x 355.5 cm

NEW YORK

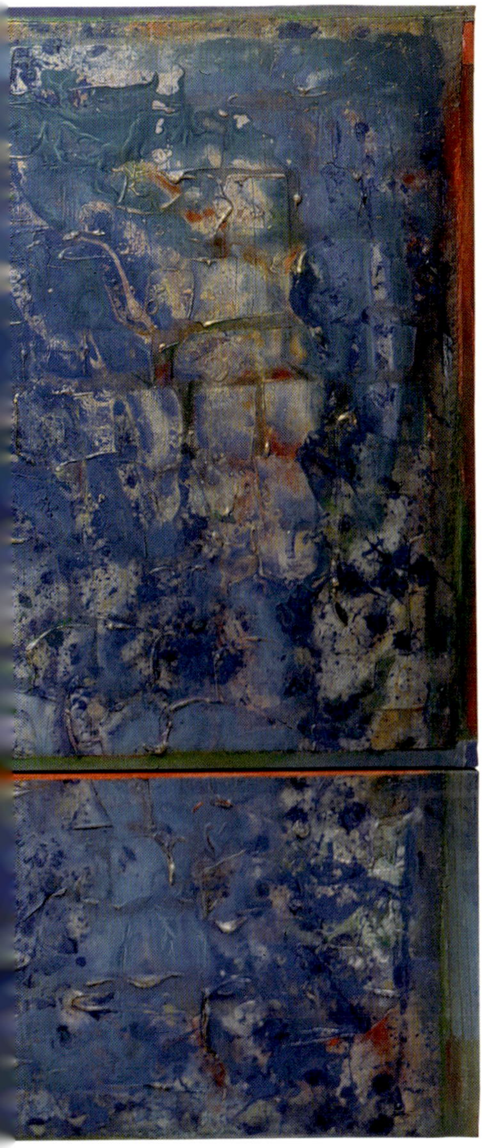

Down under Manhattan Bridge overpass in Brooklyn, a scruffy red-brick-faced factory building has thus far survived the process of gentrification, as the once-industrial dockland area becomes a place to be, with its smart apartments, cafés and bars, bookshops, health-food shops and all. The studio on the third floor is a cold-water loft, big, industrial in its simplicity, stripped for action, with minimal comforts. All day long it reverberates to the crash and rattle of the subway trains approaching or exiting the great suspended span of the bridge by way of the awesome structure of the overpass which carries it to earth somewhere inland away beyond the building. From the loft's windows you can look directly up into the high metal structures of the overpass. This is Frank Bowling's New York studio, where he has lived and worked, spring and autumn, for the last twenty years.

The four windows, facing south-west, their wooden frames painted respectively a now-faded green, red, yellow and blue, look out on to the East River at the point where it curves under the majestic Brooklyn Bridge, and across its reflecting waters to the dark silhouette skyline of the Financial District in downtown Manhattan. Morning light is therefore indirect; the afternoon is bright in the hour or so before the sun lowers and then streams for a short while directly into the studio space, briefly illuminating at an angle the studio's windowless east-facing wall.

A painting on this wall – on the day I have in mind it was the magnificent *Jamsahibwall* – registers the light in these diurnal phases, and itself changes by the hour, by the minute, as the sun moves slowly from behind the building and then across the south-western sky above the river and the bridges. At a certain moment the painting catches the afternoon splendour directly; its blue-green-bronze-silver surfaces and textures irradiated, it achieves a complex and variegated radiance: dull glimmer, reflective shine and refractive iridescence. Its seven rectangular sections, divided by strips of matte canvas (fragments retrieved from the cropping of old paintings), are windows on to blue-silver painterly light; their frames are green, red, yellow.

Marine light (just beyond the Brooklyn Bridge the river flows into New York Bay) has its own radiance. In the afternoon, the river, seen against the sun in the space between the bridges, glitters with surface agitation, and glimmers and shines in bright sheets of white light with grey shadows, changing as the currents and breezes determine. 'Look!' Frank once said to his friend Spencer Richards: 'That is the light I want my paintings to have!' The river and its ever-changing circumambient lucency are an ever-present actuality in this studio. On my first visit I was reminded, as I had anticipated, of the Cable Street studio, and of that long-ago glimpse, through industrial buildings, of the bright Thames. (Every encounter with a painting brings with it such memories, and memories of memories.) I think of the natural light that finds its way into the paintings: in every case it is its own thing, an abstract manifestation, concrete, actual; in each case, for the viewer, ineluctably, an evocation and a recollection.

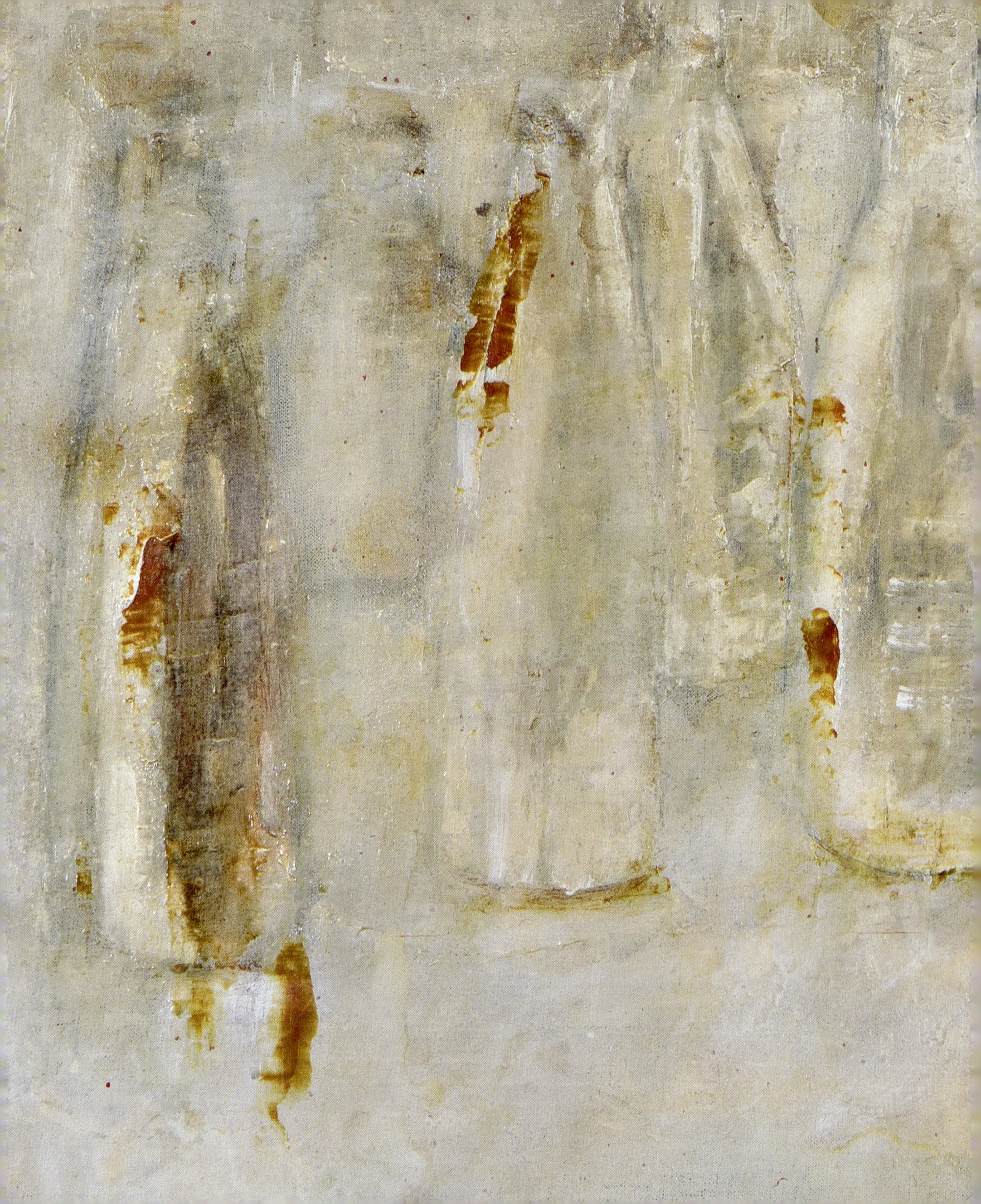

PART ONE

Bartica Born Londoner

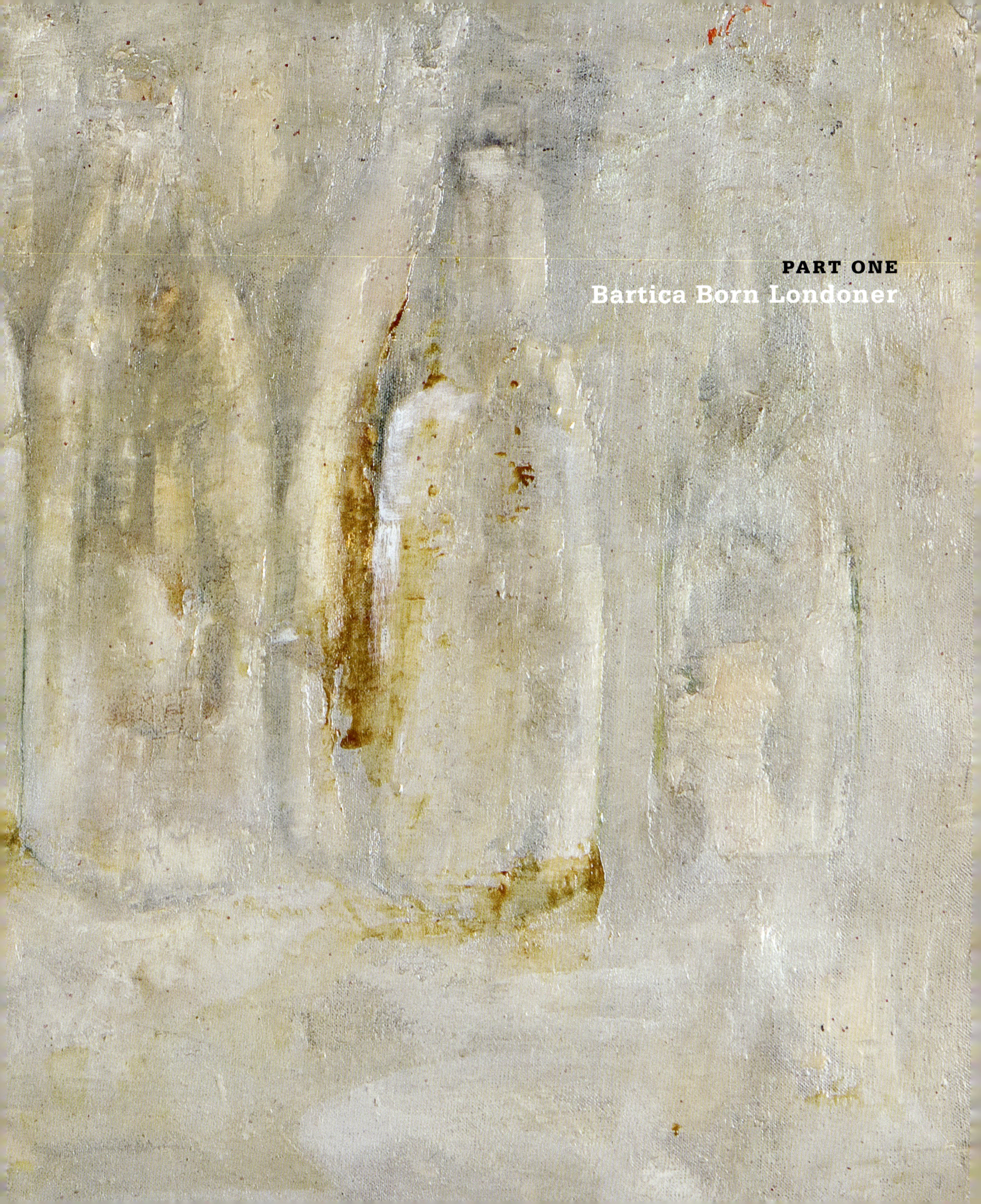

1 'MOTHER'S HOUSE': NEW AMSTERDAM

'Home is where one starts from.'
T.S.ELIOT

Bowling's Variety Store, situated on Main Street, New Amsterdam, in British Guiana, was owned and run by Agatha Elizabeth Franklin Bowling. Born in New Amsterdam on a Christmas Day, and therefore known to all as Chrissie, she was a formidably forceful and wilful woman. A highly skilled seamstress, dressmaker and milliner, she had, by dint of native wit and an iron will, created her business from scratch when her husband, Richard Sheridan Bowling, moved the family to New Amsterdam to take up his post as accountant and paymaster in the local police force in 1940. Frank Bowling is their eldest son.

Chrissie Bowling began with a small establishment in Pope Street, off the main thoroughfare, supplementing the income she made from the shop by doing property deals. Soon, she was able to move to Main Street, where she built a grand three-storey clapperboard building, with a boldly lettered fascia that proudly proclaimed its business as a general store, from which she also ran her specialist trade in clothes and hats, and saris for the local Indian community. Driven, tireless and domineering, she was a force not only in the family but in the town, managing the finances of her own family but also handling the financial affairs of others, supervising her apprentice seamstresses, cannily giving credit and famously dispensing Christian charity – bread and prayers – to local beggars. 'You know,' her son recalls, 'she ran the lives of everybody.'

Frank Bowling (whose principal forename, to his father's chagrin, was chosen to commemorate his maternal grandfather, Caesar Augustus Franklin) was born on 26 February 1934 in the county of Essequibo in Bartica, a small trading town inland from Georgetown, British Guiana's capital. Situated at the confluence of three rivers, the Mazaruni, Cuyuni and the majestic Essequibo, Bartica is a place of wide, flowing waters, extensive wetlands and mud flats, surrounded by tropical rain forest. Its name has haunted Bowling's imagination and

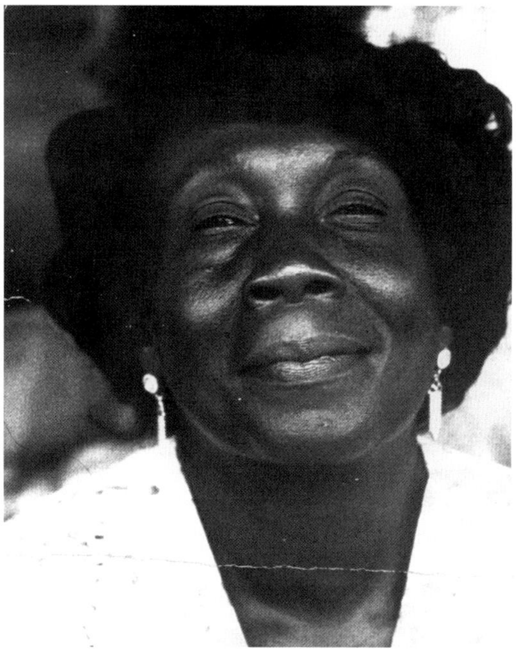

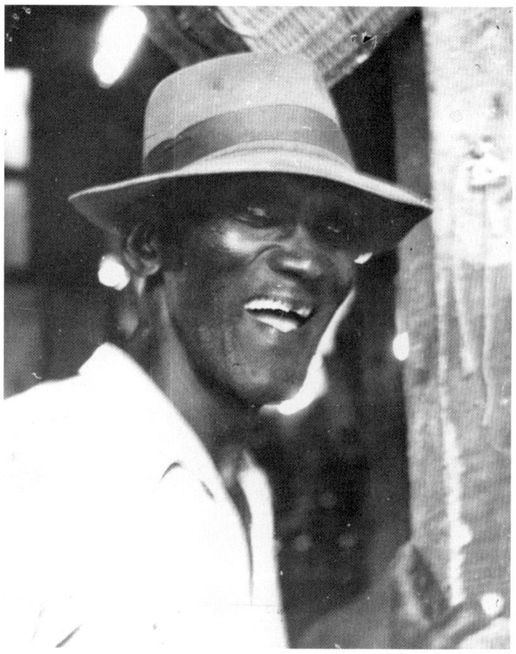

Agatha Elizabeth Franklin Bowling, Frank Bowling's mother, photographed in New Amsterdam in 1968.

Richard Sheridan Bowling, father of Frank Bowling, c.1968.

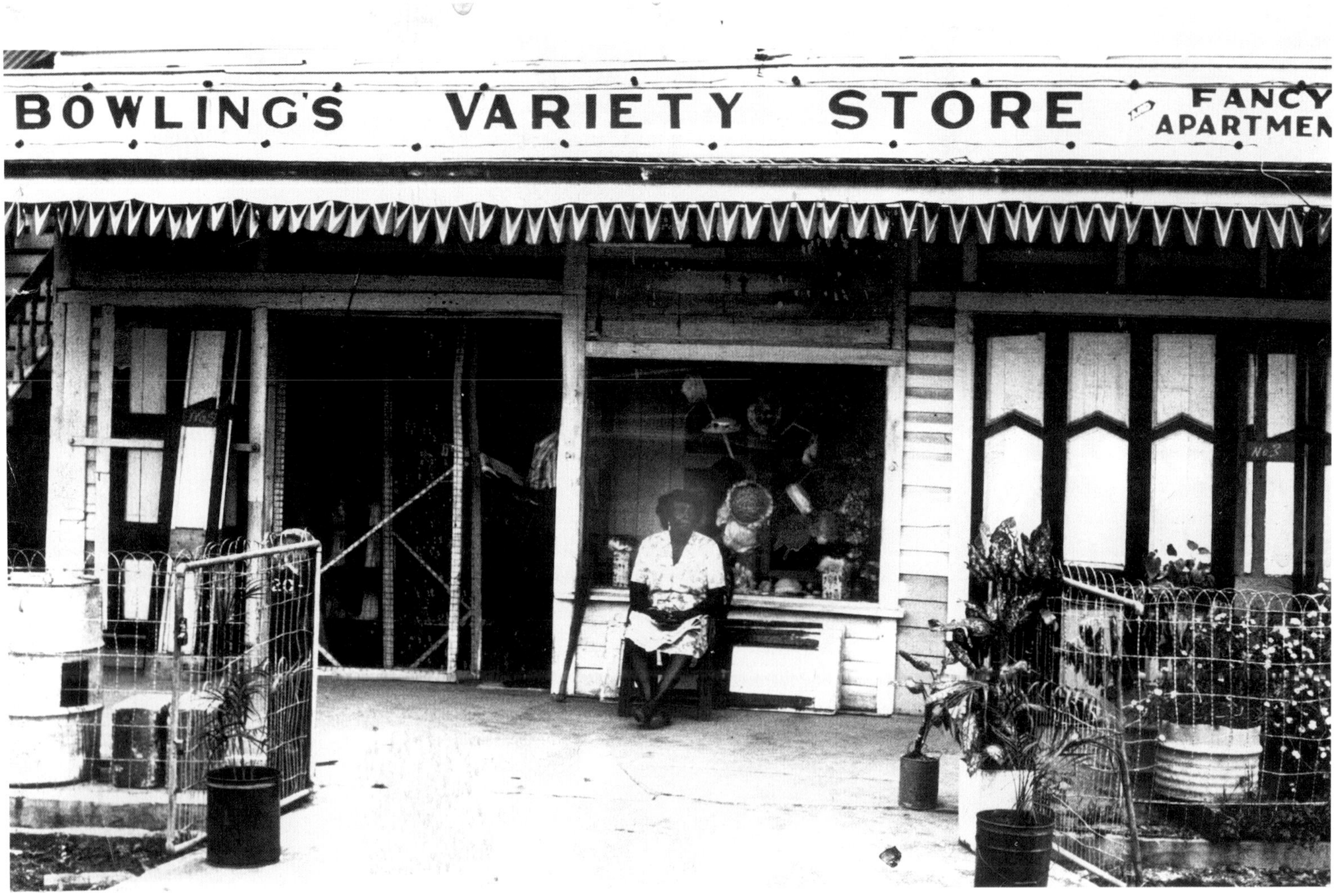

Bowling's Variety Store, Main Street, New Amsterdam, British Guiana, 1953.

recurs, as a kind of sign or reminder, in the titles of many of his paintings. Before long the family moved to Georgetown, where his father completed a police-force requirement to work for a specified period in each of the three major provinces of the colony. It was after this that the Bowlings settled in the small port of New Amsterdam, 60 miles east of the capital, on the broad estuary of the Berbice. Throughout his life, great rivers have flowed close to Bowling's successive places of habitation and work.

New Amsterdam, too, continues to recur in Bowling's reveries: '...apart from London, which is more important in my life than any [other] place I've been in, and perhaps New York, New Amsterdam is the most important place, and it reappears all the time ... in my quiet moments it reappears. It was a town that was full of terror, and at the same time it was marvellous, marvellous ... It was easy to negotiate, and certainly by the time we moved to Main Street it belonged to me.' It is the town in which

Bowling enjoyed, or endured, the terrors of what he remembers as 'a tumultuous childhood', marked by constant and sometimes extreme violence at the hands of his father.

His father was, by Frank's account, a sadistic martinet for whom his son felt little empathy, an estrangement that reflected the hostility expressed by his father. This brutal style of parental authoritarianism was not uncommon in the culture of the African-Caribbean community in Guiana; Bowling considers it an aspect of the violent inheritance of slavery. Whether it was disappointment at encountering limitations (imposed on racial grounds) to advancement in his chosen career or frustration at the unbending and unaccommodating ethos of the police force (which prohibited his participation in his wife's successful commercial activities), Richard Sheridan Bowling became a reclusive, irritable and unapproachable man, whose children's talk and play were forbidden whenever he was in the house.

In the early 1950s, at just about the time that Frank was preparing to leave New Amsterdam and British Guiana, Chrissie bought a separate house and shop for her disaffected husband, now compulsorily retired, whose disinclination to work in commerce guaranteed the failure of the business. 'He was and remains a mystery to me,' Bowling was to remark many years later. 'I can't remember ever having a conversation with him. I didn't know him at all. He never spoke. He was the most silent man I've ever met.'

As often happens when a child is subjected to frequent violence, Frank was difficult and unruly at home and at school. Lively, intelligent and headstrong, he was compelled to assert his independence, and he became used to paying for his intransigence. He was very young, for example, when, wanting to be like many of his childhood friends, he decided to become a Catholic. After many altercations and the beatings that invariably followed, his Anglican parents reluctantly allowed him to convert. At school, he was singled out by his teachers as especially troublesome, and beatings there were reinforced by savage beatings at home. 'So it was like, trouble, trouble, trouble during my childhood.' Not surprisingly, perhaps, Bowling proved as an artist to be ambitiously self-motivated, energetically original, resourceful and resolute of spirit; and when mood and circumstance have suited, he has been incisive and combative as a critic-polemicist.

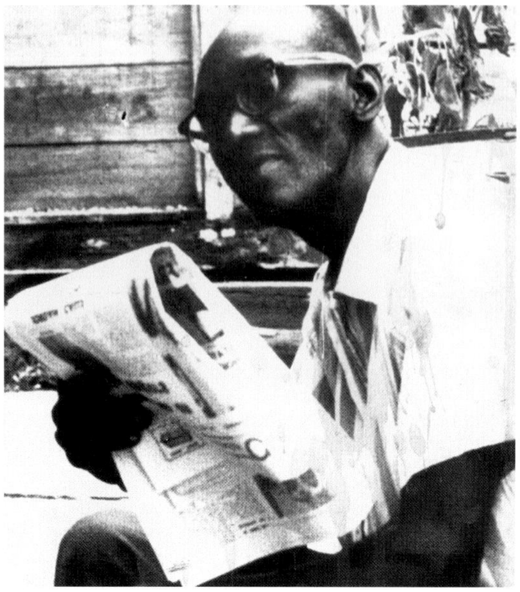

Richard Sheridan Bowling, c.1968.

His mother was not averse to adding her own cruel chastisements to those of Frank's father and teachers, but she favoured her eldest son, and he grew up very much in her thrall. 'My memory of my mother is very coloured by the fact that she was the most ambitious woman in town … and she was always being talked about.' From early on she took young Frank with her on business and when acquiring stock, and kept him close by her, sometimes until nearly dawn, while she worked at her dressmaking and millinery – as much as anything to protect her son from his father. Clearly recognising his initiative and energy, by the time Frank was fourteen she employed him as a representative for the Variety Store, selling lace and other small items, and taking orders for dresses and saris.

For two years thereafter, he rode his carrier bike along the dirt roads to and from the small town of Skeldon, some 70 miles east of New Amsterdam, or west towards Georgetown, carrying sample swatches and pattern books, happy to be free of the pressures of family and school, earning commission, and with his mother's approval making profits from his own sales. For the youthful Bowling this was an enterprise with a hidden purpose, however, for he was already determined to leave Guiana, and he was saving assiduously to that end. He nursed in these years a precocious longing 'to just get out and go to London. Part-time work, study hard, and maybe get lucky, get a scholarship. And show them that I really could do it.'

Bowling was not alone in his ambition to leave. Among his friends (many of them companions from the wild schoolboy days of the self-styled 'Rum Drinkers Club'), there were Indians and Chinese as well as African Caribbeans: all were aware that there was no possibility of advance beyond the Senior Cambridge certificate, examinations designed specifically for the young subjects of the Empire and the colonies, which ensured a uniformity of shared academic culture from India to Africa to the Caribbean. There was no university in Guiana, and emigration to England (or less commonly, the United States) was necessary for any kind of advanced academic or professional education. Many working-class West Indians were migrating from the Caribbean at this time simply to find work. These were the years of the 'Windrush generation', and certain service industries in the UK – public transport, the Post Office and, most notably, the National Health Service – had since 1948 been actively recruiting from this welcome source of much-needed immigrant labour.

In Frank's circle of teenage friends there was at this time little overt political consciousness, though the older boys who had completed their Senior Cambridge and were beginning to work in the colony's administration were well aware of discrimination, limitation and injustice as defining aspects of a specifically colonial reality. For their parents – as for Bowling's father – these were the ever-present constraints and restrictions of everyday life. Following the recommendations of the British government's Waddington Commission in 1951 (in favour of universal adult suffrage and electoral reform), the early 1950s was a period in British Guiana of intensive political agitation towards genuinely democratic self-government. Notwithstanding the evident apathy among Frank and his young contemporaries, the political landscape in the country was about to change dramatically.

A month before Bowling left New Amsterdam for good in May 1953, the People's Progressive Party (PPP), under the leadership of Cheddi Jagan and Forbes Burnham, triumphed in the first democratic election ever held in the colony. Independence was on its way. In New Amsterdam itself, the young poet Martin Carter campaigned for the PPP, and spoke at political rallies on Main Street which he referred to as 'the university of the streets'. All this, perhaps somewhat surprisingly, passed the young Bowling by. As he recalls, the Catholic Youth Organisation (CYO), where he and his young and vaguely ambitious friends talked and dreamed of a world beyond British Guiana, was 'more a hotbed of naughtiness than of political activity … We just wanted to flee and make a life for ourselves.'

It had been clear to Bowling since his early teens that he must leave his country of birth. Bowling was an avid reader, but restless and inattentive to academic things. He had completed his Junior Cambridge school course without seeking to find out his results,so busy was he making money, saving and spending it.

More than anything else the irksome and unhappy conditions of his family life predicated his earliest possible departure. In England he could perhaps get the education he needed and wanted, and prove himself. Or simply find himself, and discover in due course what he would do. He had no specific vocational ambitions, no plan beyond finding work and getting an education. London was where this would be possible. The ambition was not strange: for many intelligent and ambitious young men in the colonies, who were after all British by nationality, London was simply their capital, the place where the action was, the natural destination for those seeking adventure and a career.

Sometime in late 1952, Frank had accompanied his mother to the rural police station where his father was working out his last posting before retirement, when he overheard his father say, 'Chrissie, what you bring this boy here for? I don't want to see him.' That moment was one he did not forget: 'At that point I realised, you know, bye Guiana, bye Dad, bye…' Soon after this, he travelled from New Amsterdam to Georgetown, where he stayed briefly with an uncle before quitting British Guiana for Trinidad on a ship captained by a distant relative and owned by Booker's, the sugar and trading company that had virtually run the colony since the late 19th century, to the extent that it was even, sometimes, ironically referred to as 'Booker's Guiana'. From Port of Spain, Trinidad, in May 1953, Bowling sailed on a French ship east across the Atlantic to Europe. Of his migration Bowling has remarked: 'Well, it could be summed up in two words, *I left*', quickly adding: 'and I didn't return.' When he arrived in England, Frank Bowling was just nineteen years old.

2 STARTING OUT IN ENGLAND

'London is the place for me
London this lovely city.'
LORD KITCHENER

When he first disembarked in Europe, in Spain, Bowling found himself briefly having doubts about his journey. 'But the moment I arrived in London, I knew I was home.' He had known for some time that London was his destination, as it was for most of his friends in the CYO: '…we always saw London as the place.' It was early June 1953, the city was in the throes of Coronation fever and the young Bowling was amazed by both the scale and the energy of the city. He went to stay in a flat near the Finchley Road with an uncle, who registered him with a doctor, got him a ration book and signed him on at the local labour exchange. Frank was quick to initiate the next part of his plan – to get an education – by acquiring a copy of *Floodlight*, the directory of academic courses and vocational opportunities. in London. He enrolled immediately at Westminster College of Commerce to study for A-level English, and promptly purchased texts by Chaucer and Milton.

At the labour exchange he was offered inconsequential jobs, and there he discovered that as soon as he registered as employed he would become automatically liable to conscription for National Service. Pre-empting this certainty, Bowling went to the RAF recruitment office in Queensway, and, being assured that he would receive an education, he immediately joined up. By the early autumn of 1953 he was a regular serviceman, opting to serve as a mechanic. He quickly became noticed as an athlete, but although he enjoyed his training as a sprinter and the outings to athletics meetings, Bowling's time in the RAF was unhappy and unfruitful. Restive under discipline and restless as a result of constantly changing postings, chafing at officer-class arrogance, irritated by casual racism, he was constantly in trouble for insubordination and general unruliness. Asked once 'where were you posted?' he replied: 'Jankers, mostly'. Neither the promised education nor the training for a skilled trade materialised. Early in 1956, somewhat short of the period he had signed up for and feeling he had wasted nearly three years, he was demobbed with no more than the terse formula: 'service no longer required'.

One event in his first year of service was, however, to have the most profound long-term consequences for Bowling: he was befriended by the brilliant Keith Critchlow, who was just completing his National Service, and was about to begin his studies in architecture and art at St Martin's and the Royal College of Art. One day, arriving at Charing Cross Station having travelled up with Bowling from RAF Kenley in Surrey, Critchlow suggested that they go to the National Gallery, just across Trafalgar Square. It was the first glimpse of what was to be an unfolding and never-ending revelation. Critchlow, who was to become one of the most extraordinary polymaths of his time – among other things, a painter, an architect, an architectural theorist and a world expert in Islamic architecture, geometry and design – proceeded to introduce him to his student and artistic friends in Soho and Chelsea, and Bowling began to comprehend the possibilities of another way of life. On leaving the RAF, he was invited to lodge at Critchlow's parents' house in Redcliffe Gardens, Chelsea, and a new life began.

Critchlow's mother worked as a journalist with the principal Labour-supporting popular newspapers, the *Daily Mirror* and the *Daily Herald*; his father was a portrait painter. They encouraged Bowling, who was now twenty-two years old, to write rather than fight: to turn his experience to positive creative account. Rosalind corrected his writing and helped him stylistically, and he sat for Jerry. He also sat for Royal College student friends of Keith, including Anthony Whishaw and his wife, Jean, and gradually began to make a small amount of money in this way, augmented by casual jobs as a waiter and building-site worker. Before long, Bowling was sitting, for six-week stints, at the Royal College. In those silent hours he watched and listened, soon becoming aware of the on-occasion dubious levels of talent and commitment of certain of the students blithely attending the life classes, until he thought that if they could it, perhaps he could do it better?

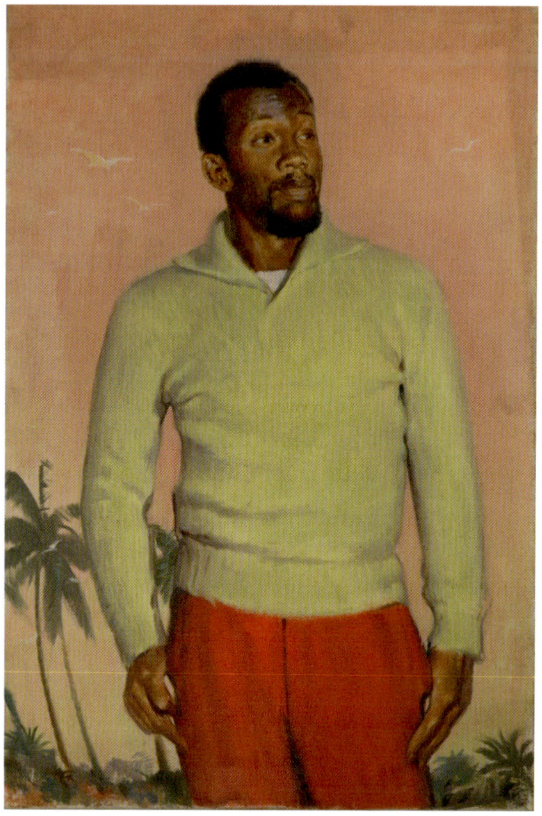

Portrait of Frank Bowling
by Jerry Critchlow *c.* 1956-57
Oil on canvas, 76 x 51 cm

Between leaving the RAF and finally getting into art school, Bowling became deeply confused as to his direction; for two years he lived a somewhat rackety London life of pubs, odd jobs and false starts. He is, however, gifted with an acute ear for language and a love of words. During this time, he became committed to becoming a writer of poetry and stories, and was attempting in a desultory way to write a novel. He read contemporary poetry, novels by Somerset Maugham and Joseph Conrad, and, among other works of fiction, the aptly titled *London Belongs to Me* by Norman Collins. In all this he was encouraged by Rosalind Critchlow (and at one crucial moment by the novelist Laurie Lee), to persevere in spite of the accumulating publishers' rejection slips. For many months, he continued to move in a lively creative circle which included not just the multi-talented Critchlow but art students from further afield – notably Jerry Pethick, a Canadian at Chelsea, and Bill Culbert, a New Zealander at the RCA. Soon the idea germinated and gradually took root that he might himself become an artist.

Bowling began to draw and paint, teaching himself from manuals borrowed from the local library. Keith Critchlow showed him how to mix paints, and taught him the rudiments of technique. His first faltering efforts were mostly studies of lonely figures in pubs. Realising before long that he needed instruction, in painting and in life drawing, he boldly applied to Chelsea School of Art, and in the autumn of 1958, thanks to the generosity of Harold Williamson, the Principal, he started his training as an artist. Williamson was already familiar with him as a young habitué of the Kings Arms, Fulham Road, close to the School. Known to all as 'Finch's', the pub was at this time the principal haunt of the extensive bohemian network in Chelsea of artists, writers and poets, including the painters Francis Bacon, Lucien Freud and William Thomson, sculptors Lynn Chadwick, Hubert Dalwood and Elisabeth Frink, and Henry Williamson, the author of *Tarka the Otter*. Regularly holding court in cap and cape was the aged, deaf and perennially libidinous Augustus John. Invited by Bowling, some time later, to come to Finch's, the savvy stylist David Hockney declined on the very grounds of its bohemian artiness: 'even the women wear beards in there', he remarked.

Asked by Williamson, in a letter, to provide funds to support her 'talented' son, his mother refused to send more than the fee for half a term, and suggested he get a grant. Too late in the academic year to do this, Bowling found himself unable to go back to Chelsea after the Christmas vacation of 1958-59. He had in the meantime, however, applied for a place at the Royal College, and in February he was invited for interview. His portfolio was original, but naïve in its diversity: 'They were intrigued ... What it probably looked like was a bit of Giacometti or a bit of Cézanne, you know, tic-tac, whatever ... If I knew you could do it by numbers, I would probably have tried that too, but luckily for me I didn't get to that!' The panel turned him down. Desperate now to study painting, he was bitterly disappointed.

Carel Weight, the Head of Painting, a man of great insight and kindness, much loved by generations of students at the College, arranged for Bowling to attend at the City and Guilds of London Art School in Kennington, where he was to undertake an intensive study of painting and work in the life room, returning to the Royal College in the summer for a second bid. Bowling had neither funds nor a place to live: '[Weight] sensed that I was serious ... So he put his hand in his pocket and gave me twenty quid. "Have you got any digs?" "No." "Go and find somewhere." ' The spring of 1959 was a time of bliss; at last Bowling had found with certainty what he wanted to do. He worked with concentration and energy in the life room, and, under the direction

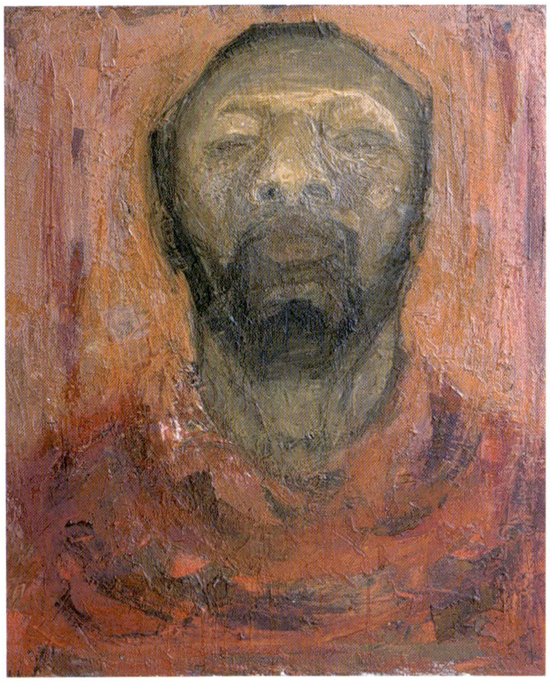

Self Portrait, 1959
Oil on canvas, 91.5 x 61 cm

of sympathetic teachers (most notably the painter, Rodney Burn), he began to paint with purpose and direction.

The still-life studies of bottles that he worked on at Kennington mark the true beginning of Bowling's career as a painter proper. He also made a series of head-and-shoulder portraits of a model at the college, a local down-and-out whom the principal had taken on as a model out of the goodness of her heart. Presenting these paintings at the Royal College at the end of the summer term, Frank won the scholarship that he so desired. It was an astounding achievement. His contemporaries were some of the brightest and best students of their generation to emerge from the provincial art schools, after training for several years; Bowling had had no advanced academic education to speak of, in art or in anything else.

The summer of 1959 found him working in one of the empty studios at the Royal College Painting School in Exhibition Road, adjoining the Victoria & Albert Museum in South Kensington, preparing for his studies there. Next door, Richard Smith, a highly successful recent graduate of the College, was working on the large 'environmental' canvases he was to show in the celebrated *Place* exhibition at the ICA later that year. Quite simply, Bowling's entry to the Royal College placed him in an intensely competitive arena with the most exciting young artists of the time. Smith, Robyn Denny and Peter Blake, who had pioneered aspects of pop art at the RCA in the years preceding his arrival, were very much on the scene, and among his contemporaries were David Hockney, Derek Boshier, Peter Phillips, Patrick Caulfield, Bill Culbert, Jerry Pethick and Ron Kitaj. This was an extraordinary galaxy of future stars, many of whom attracted critical attention even before they had left the College, beginning at the *Young Contemporaries* show in February 1961, when they hung their work as a group, as if to signal a new 'Royal College' style. It was impossible to be part of such a cohort and not be on your mettle. To survive and maintain self-respect, commitment and excellence in performance was essential. It could not have suited better the needs and aims of a fiercely ambitious but inexperienced and largely untrained student.

3 THE ROYAL COLLEGE AND AFTER

Bowling's Royal College career did not follow a smooth trajectory. He could be headstrong and difficult. Certain teachers were supportive, particularly the painter Mary Fedden, who became his tutor (she was also Hockney's), and the ever kindly but rigorous Carel Weight, who could be sharply critical when he thought a student was self-indulgent or the work unduly derivative. A major crisis occurred before the end of Bowling's first year, which had nothing to do with painting. The College Principal, Robin Darwin, was outraged when his much valued assistant and College Registrar, the redoubtable future novelist Paddy Kitchen, fell in love with Frank and promptly married him. Discovering (or inventing) a rule against liaisons between staff and students, Darwin insisted on expelling Bowling, who, with help from Weight, was placed for the autumn term of 1960 at the Slade School of Fine Art.

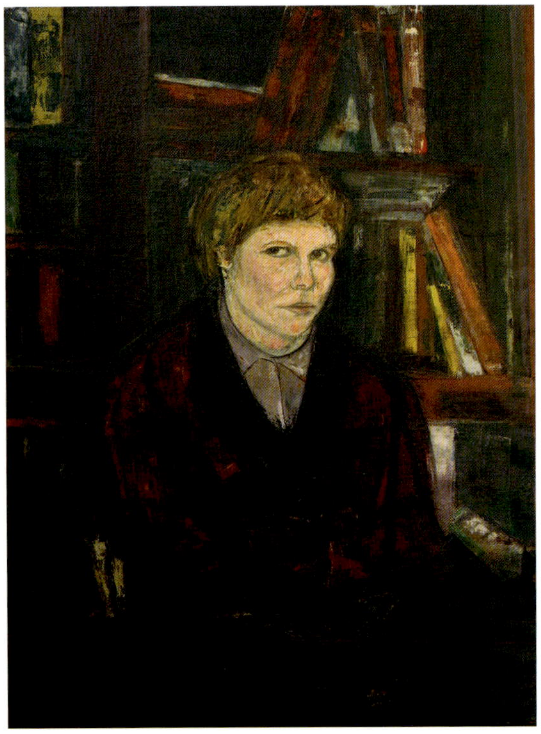

Portrait of Paddy, 1961
Oil on canvas, 122 x 91.5 cm

Bowling was unhappy at the Slade and felt uncomfortable in an environment steeped on the one hand in the heavy-duty charcoal drawing and tonal painterly expressionism of the Bomberg school, and on the other by the formulaic exactitude of figure painting (once described by the painter Terry Frost as 'dot and carry') associated with William Coldstream, the School's director. When Kitchen left the RCA to become Lawrence Gowing's secretary at Chelsea School of Art, Bowling was relieved to be allowed to return to the College for the spring term of 1961, and to complete his course there.

It is not too much to say that at the Royal College Bowling quickly transformed himself from a novice with a dream into a fully fledged painter. From the beginning he made paintings that survive critical scrutiny well enough to be considered as serious items in his life's work. At the City and Guilds Art School in Kennington, he had concentrated on painting still-life compositions of bottles and drawing from the figure, and these exercises were for years to provide the creative bases of his painting at the College. The work he made at this time is remarkable for its confidently sensuous handling, its instinctive feel for painterly *passage*, and a focused attention to paint as a natural chemical compound, a complex and subtle substance susceptible to variations of medium, pigment, glaze, density and viscosity, capable of a marvellous diversity of tactile and visual effects. It was this feeling for paint as a substance both volatile and subtle, for paint as such, that was to characterise all Bowling's future work.

What makes the *Sheep's Head* and *Birds* still-lifes of 1960-61 much more than remarkable descriptive exercises is this essentially reflexive and experimental approach to the medium. They demonstrate that Bowling was from the beginning deeply interested in the expressive effects of paint itself. It is, of course the intensity

Sheep's Head I, 1960
Oil on canvas, 51 x 63.5 cm

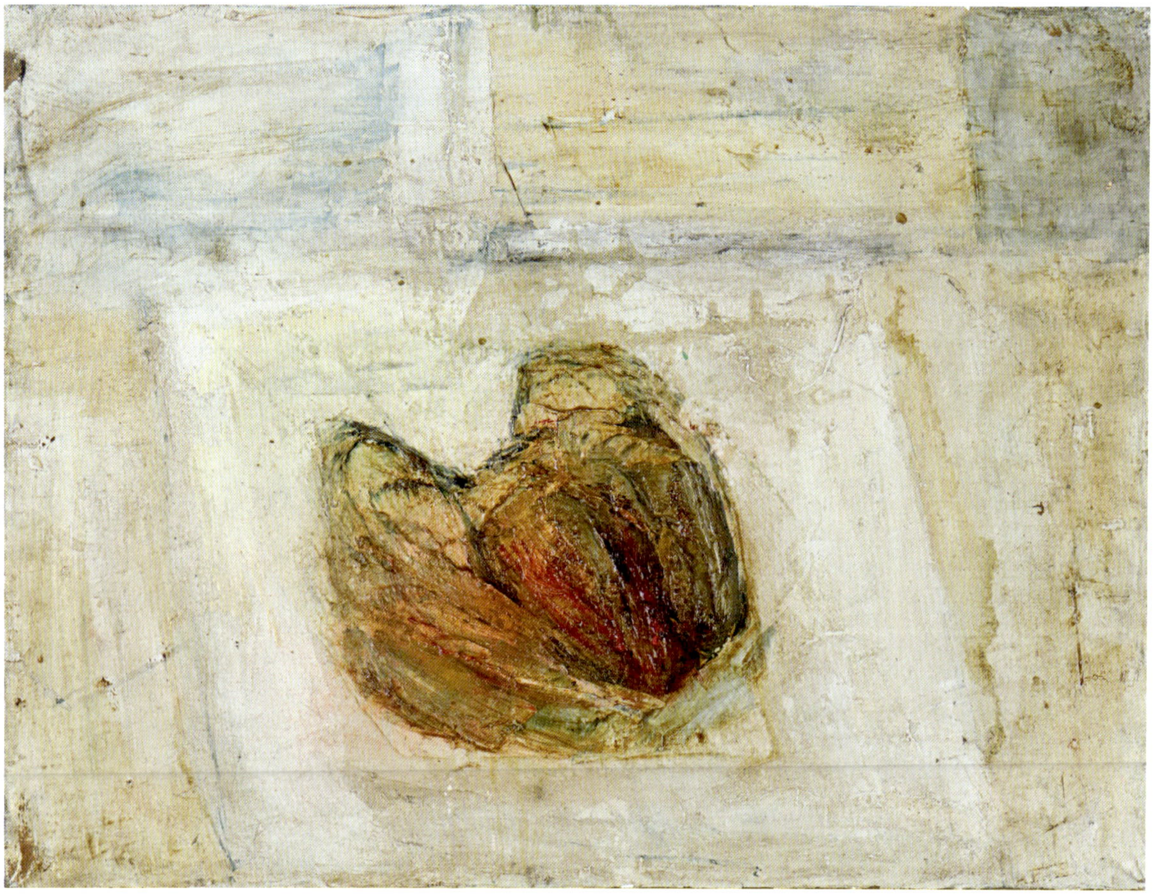

Sheep's Head II, 1960
Oil on canvas, 30.5 x 71 cm

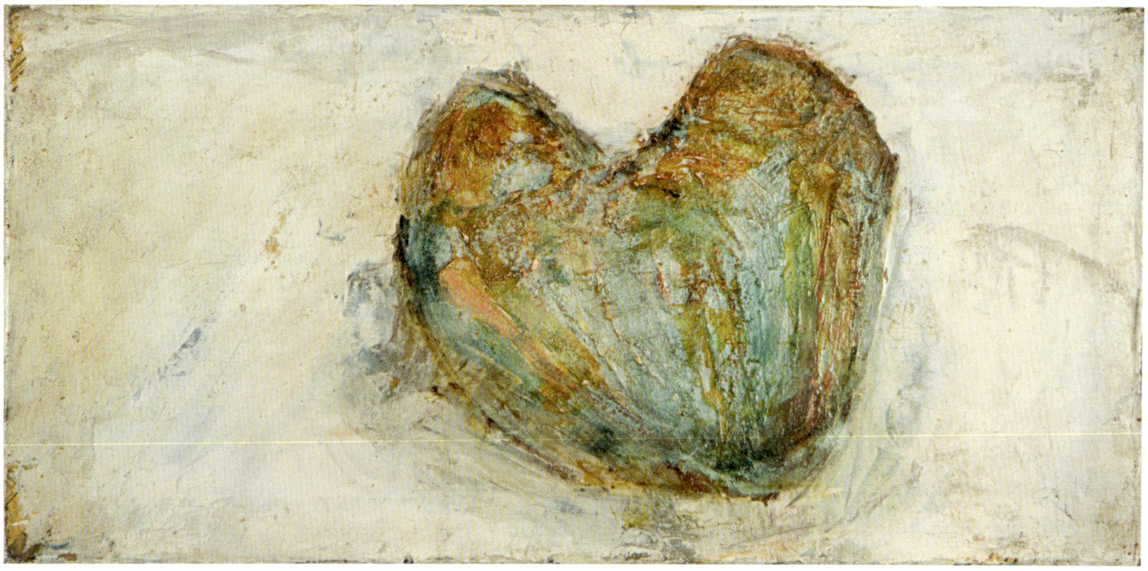

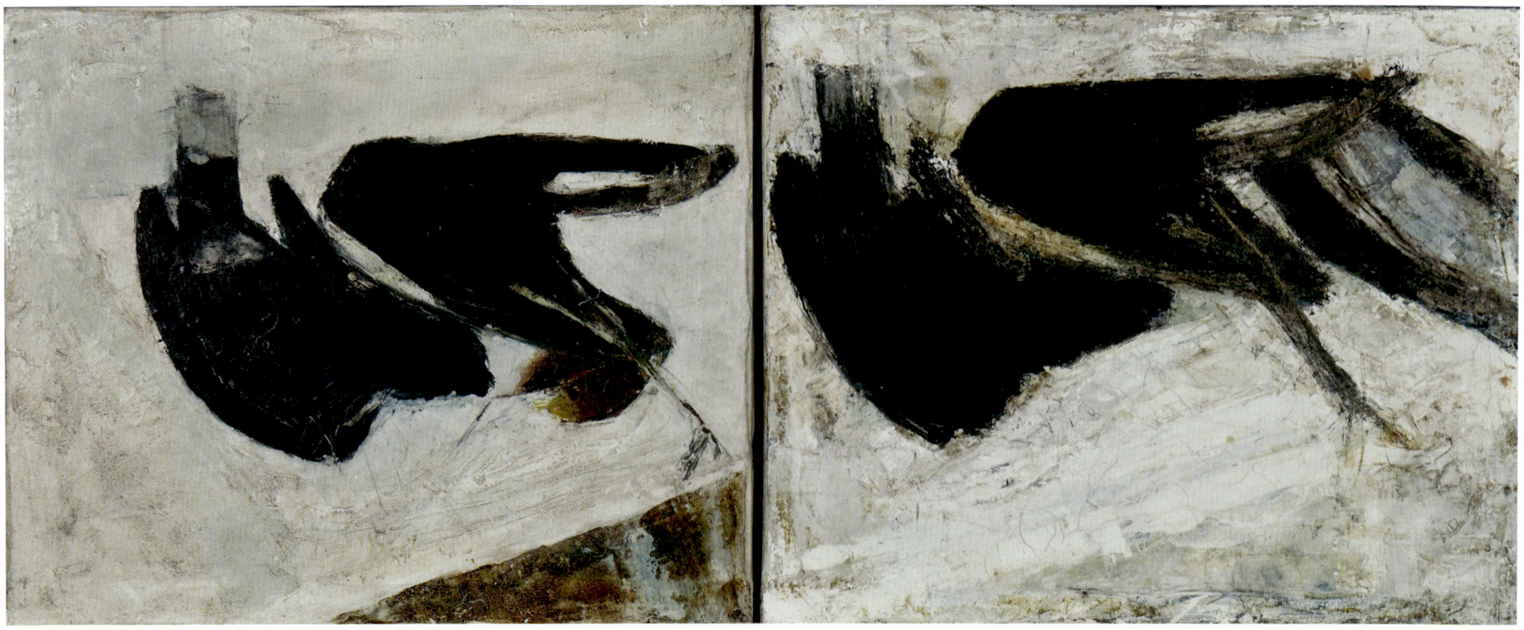

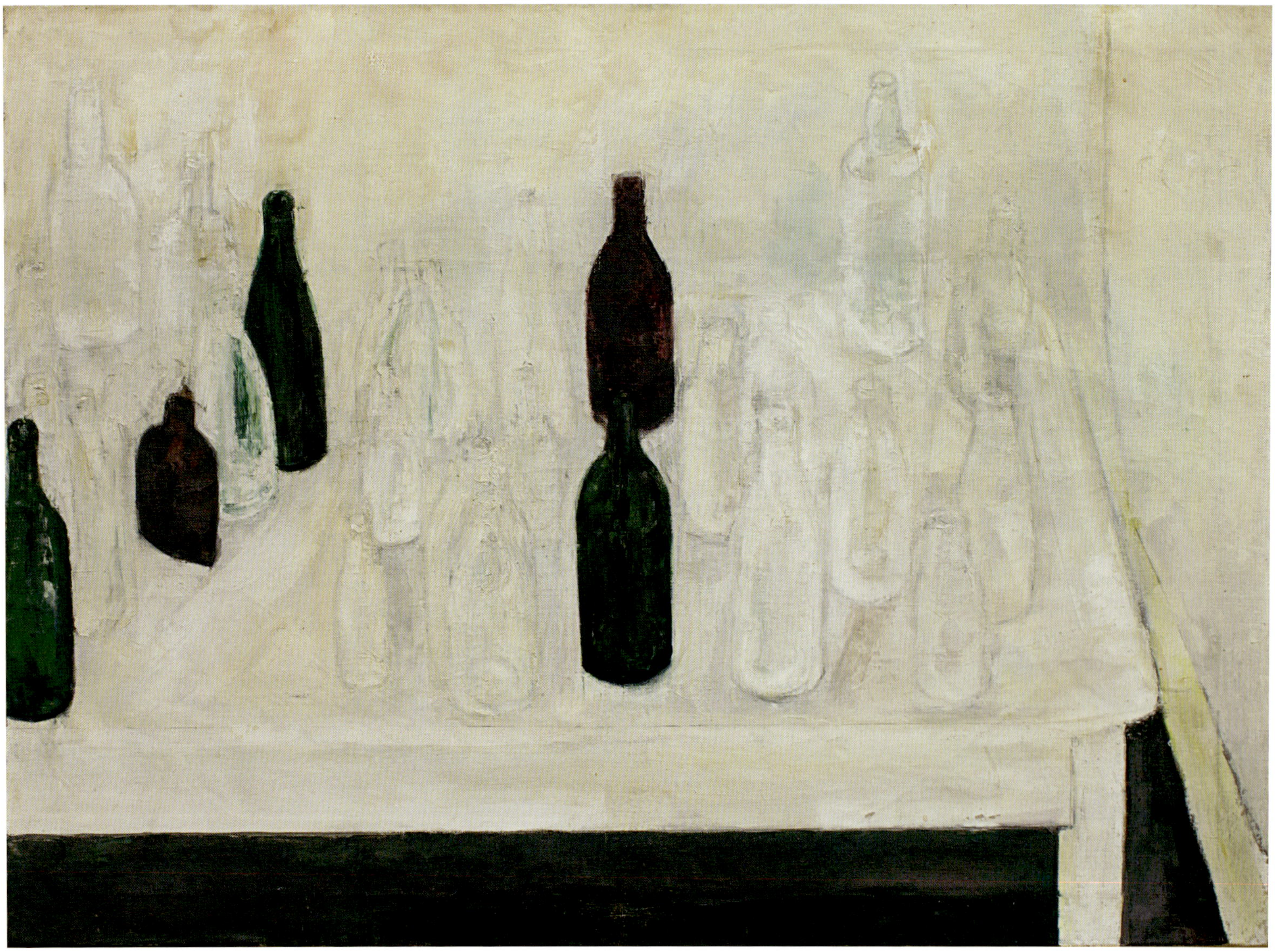

of presentation that gives these paintings their emotive charge. This might also be said of the 1959 series of self-portraits in which painterly variations of colour and texture are expressive aspects of an intense self-appraisal. Bowling had realised that a concentration on the processes of painting allowed subtle explorations of feeling leading to unpredictable revelation. It is violence of colour and the drama of light and shadow that give the 1960 *Portrait of My Father* its psychological edge, for example. There is far more to these early essays in naturalism than an effort to capture likeness.

The *Sheep's Head* paintings were made in the autumn of 1960, during the term spent by Bowling at the Slade, when he was working mainly at home in the flat that he and Paddy Kitchen had taken in Cedars Road, Clapham. (The butchered heads were kept from decomposing in a bath of formaldehyde.)

These paintings have a closely painted intensity that is more reminiscent of the silence and concentration of Morandi's bottles than of, say, the bravura of Goya's still-life studies of dead and flayed creatures, or the *grand guignol* of Bacon's sides of beef. Bowling recalls no such engagement with the work of the Italian master, however. The theme was simply a pretext for exercises in style, manner and purpose: *Bottles* (1960), for example, is a deliberate, musical *étude* in rhythm and interval, dark and light counterpoint; *Bottles* (1961) presents the ranked objects as the occasion for the play of white on white and an evocation of the palely ethereal.

In the *Sheep's Heads*, space is neutral, almost aerial: there is nothing documentary in the realisation of the subject, which is scrutinised with a mesmerising, purely painterly intensity. Death has gone out of these heads; it is absent from consideration, just as it is from the

opposite, above
***Birds Diptych*, 1960**
Oil on canvas, 51 x 122 cm

opposite, below
***Bottles*, 1960**
Oil on canvas, 91.5 x 122 cm

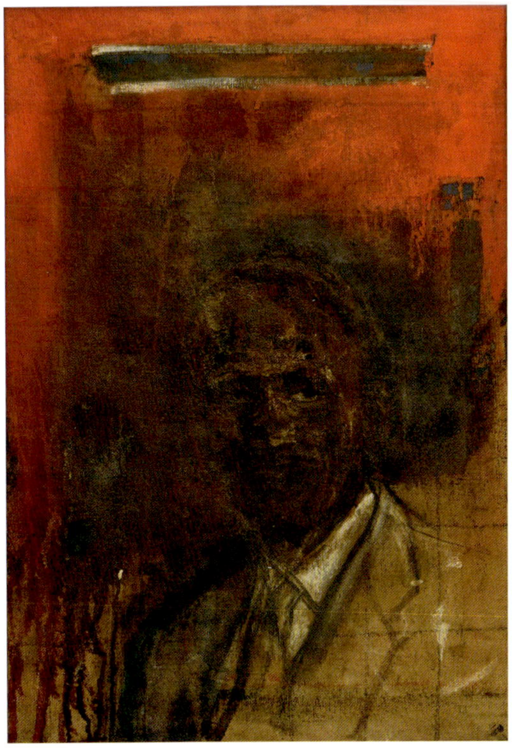

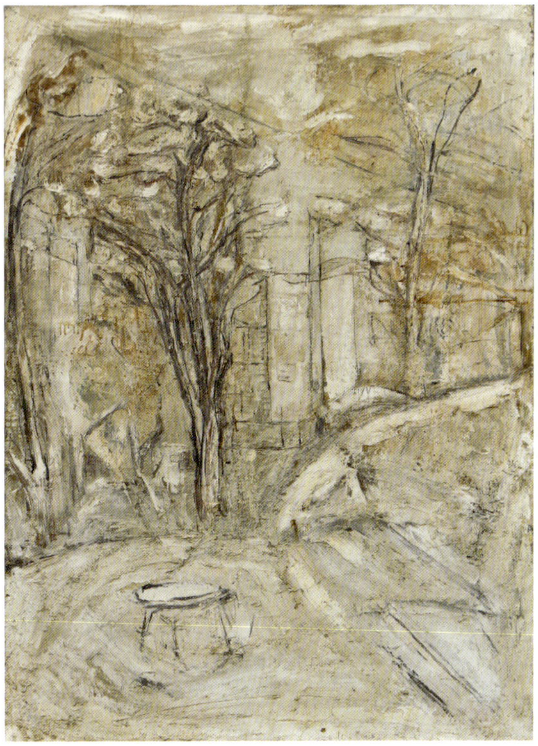

far left
Portrait of my Father, 1960
Oil on canvas, 84 x 58.5 cm

left
Snow Painting, 1962
Oil on canvas, 168 x 122 cm

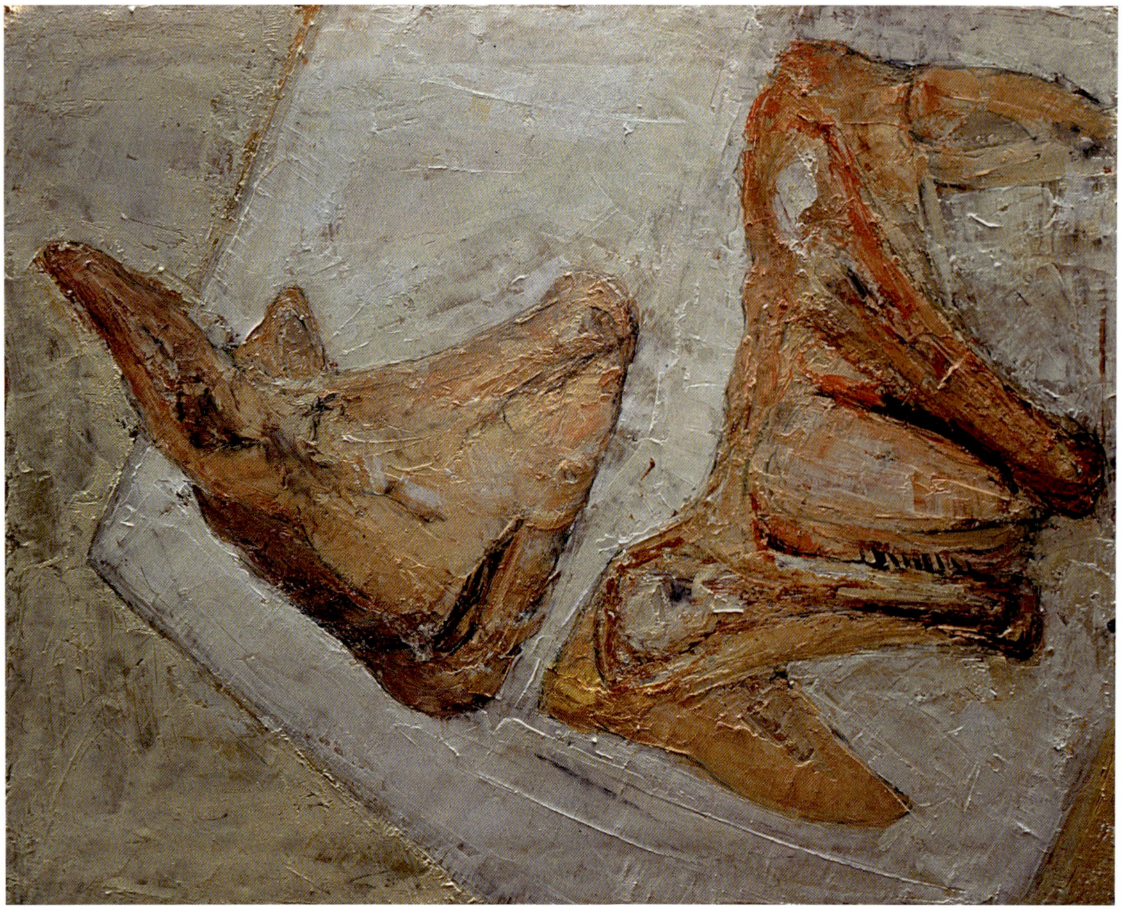

Still Life (Pig's Head), 1961
Oil on canvas, 61 x 76 cm

contemporaneous *Birds Diptych* (1960), whose models were in fact empty 'skins' of the sort used by taxidermists and ornithologists. There is, then, a disconcerting economy, if not a complete lack, of incidental poignancy in these pictures: space in them is painterly and abstract, not naturalistically contingent. As with the *Bottles* paintings, the subjects are merely pretexts for the work, providing an intense focus for the unpredictable painterly discovery of something other. What makes these striking, and moving in another way than that occasioned by the subject matter, are the gleam and sheen of the surfaces, the faceted pearlised light of the spatial whites, the silver, sienna, ochre and matt blacks that define figure and ground. This concentration on richness of facture and subtleties of tone and colour is a crucial aspect of the treatment of other still-life subjects of this period, even when they are set in a recognisably naturalistic space: *Still Life (Pig's Head)* of 1961 is a typical example of this type of painting.

By the summer term of his first year, in 1960, Bowling was forging ahead with astonishing energy. A series of paintings titled *Athletes*, dynamically asymmetrical in composition, with diagonal viewpoints and drastic truncations at the picture edges, owes something to Van Gogh's use of Japanese prints, and is characterised by vivid chromatic colour. Bowling's deployment of the striking effects of dramatic angles of view and stark cropping were a direct response to a set of sports photographs given to him by a photojournalist friend. Bowling would not at the time have seen Alexander Rodchenko's ground-breaking formalist photographs, but the influence of the great Russian innovator was clearly visible in contemporary sports photography. Bowling was himself, moreover, a keen athlete and footballer, someone who had experienced sport from inside the action. These paintings register a growing imaginative range in the artist's use of visual and experiential sources.

In 1961-62 Bowling was in his late twenties, nearing the end of his time at the Royal College, and married with a son (born in January 1962). He was ambitious and in a hurry to be a great artist. He had from the beginning 'thought

clockwise from top left
Three paintings from
the *Athletes* series, 1960
Oil on canvas, 183 x 122 cm
122 x 183 cm
91.5 x 183 cm

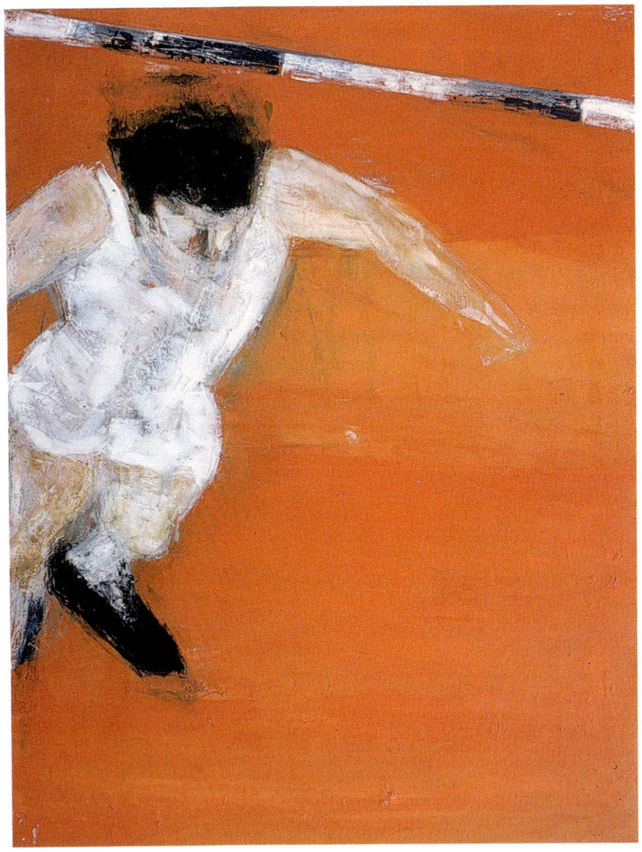

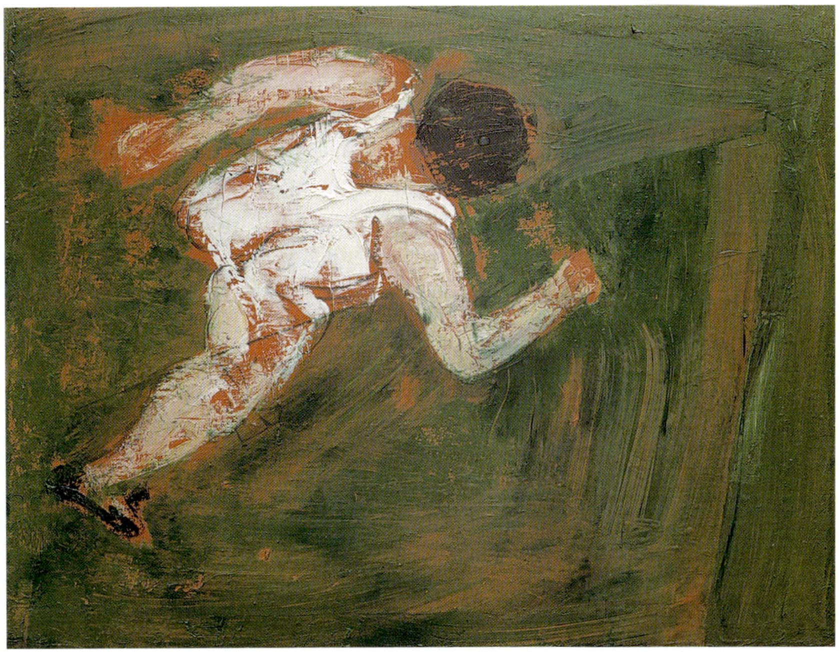

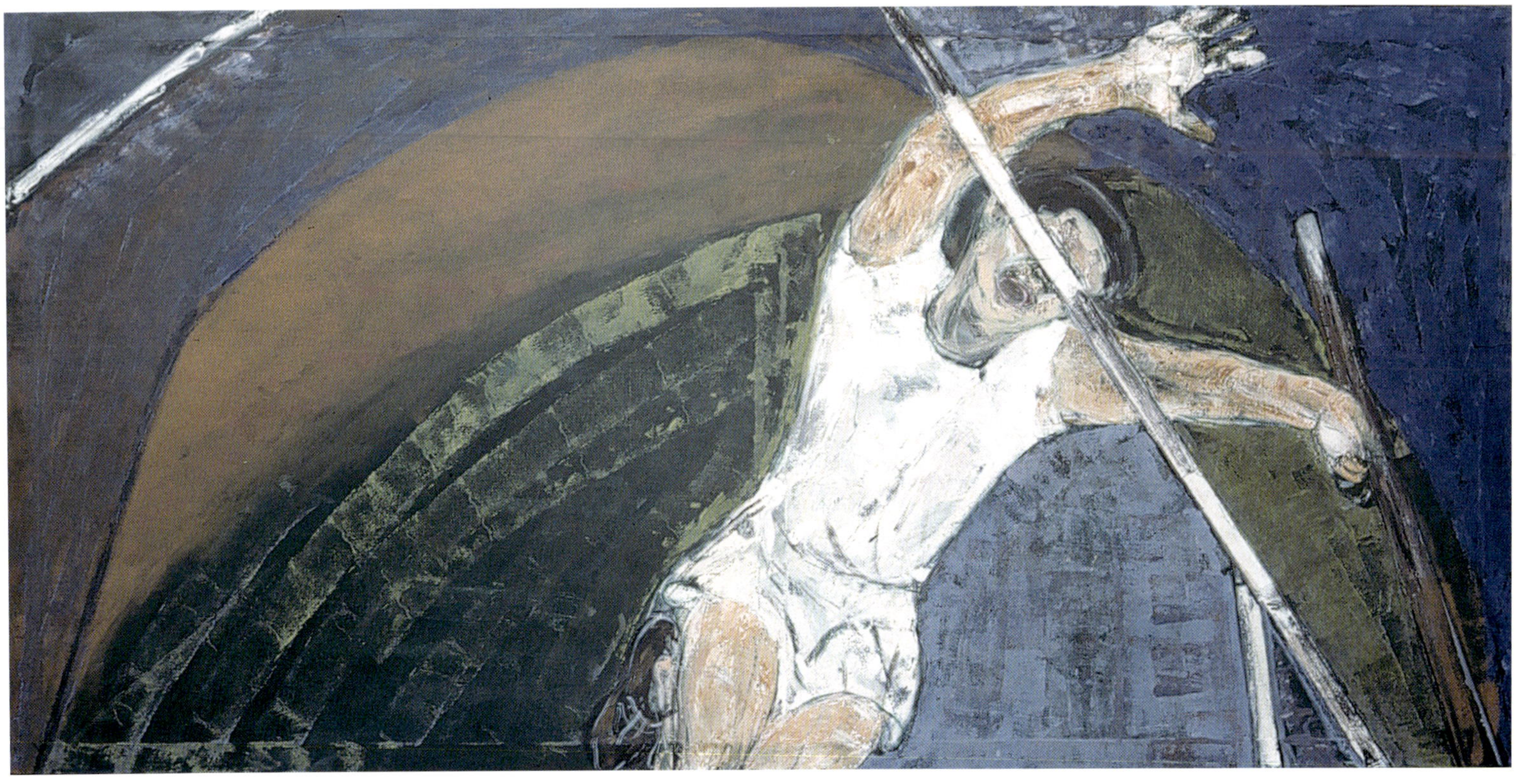

continually of the truly great' – of Rembrandt, Goya, Van Gogh – not as distant masters but as living mentors and models for artistic emulation. And without question the dynamic presence of Francis Bacon in London at the time had its own effect. A late-starter with barely sixteen years of sporadic work behind him, yet already a major figure, Bacon was a free spirit whose extraordinary ambition predicated a direct address to the greatest of the masters, Titian, Velasquez, Van Gogh, Picasso. His was also, of course, a magically hypnotic presence in Bowling's everyday and night life, as it was for many others in the pubs and clubs of Chelsea and Soho.

'It's fairly certain', wrote David Sylvester in *The New Statesmen in* April 1962, 'that the modern British artist most talked about among young painters over the last ten years has been Francis Bacon.' He added: 'the Bomberg cult has been intense but not widespread.' (In his brief time at the Slade, Bowling had been unimpressed by that cult.) Sylvester suggested that Bacon's influence had been 'nothing like proportionate to the interest he's aroused – maybe because a sense of self-preservation has made painters ward off an influence so hot to handle.' But now, he implied, certain painters were working in ways that assimilated Bacon's extremity into a distinctive personal style. Referring to a series of Bowling's paintings he had seen at the *Young Commonwealth Artists* exhibition, Sylvester remarked that '[he] has obviously seen in Bacon ways to compress terror and violence into the form of painting [...] Bowling's development over the last couple of years is a living proof of the truism that, for an artist bursting with something to express, a gain in control of the medium is a gain in forcefulness of expression.'

Bowling, we should remember, was at this time still a student at the Royal College, and his first encounter with Bacon's work predated his formal training by some five years. With his friends Critchlow, Keith Cunningham and Michael Pope, he had visited the celebrated Hanover Gallery exhibition of March to April 1957, and had been deeply impressed by Bacon's fresh and free handling of paint, especially in the vitally disconcerting *Van Gogh Studies* – 'where the paint was still moving, almost before your very eyes ... Marvellous pictures ... just directly painted ...' Without his knowing it at the time, this experience was clearly formative.

During his time at the RCA, Bowling readily acknowledged Bacon as the painter whose example was most immediate to him, though it was not until well into his second year that he felt the confidence to exercise painterly freedom on a large scale, with quasi-narrative subjects and a theatrical *mise-en-scène*. By then he had seen Bacon's first highly successful exhibition at Marlborough Fine Art, in the spring of 1960. It was, incidentally, an influence not greatly appreciated by his mentor Carel Weight (a painter who had his own disquieting figurative manner), who one day expostulated: 'We don't want these Baconesque paintings in here!' Without question, Bacon is a powerful presence in the paintings Bowling made in a period of extraordinarily energetic production from spring 1961 to the autumn of 1962, when he presented his first commercial exhibition, *Image in Revolt*, at the Grabowski Gallery in London, alongside Derek Boshier, a fellow graduate of that year.

Reviewing the show in *The New Statesman* in October 1962, Andrew Forge noted that the 'deep and genuine influence' of the older painter had provided a language that Bowling 'could have found nowhere else [...] Although his style is taken directly from Francis Bacon, I have the feeling of an entirely original imagination [...] Bowling has subjects of his own to measure up to the style: births, monsters, mirrors, surgeons, beautiful girls on ornate sofas, himself as Othello. There is real pain and horror here and an explosive delivery.' Forge's list suggests a repertoire of recurrent themes and images, which presciently anticipates what was to become Bowling's lifelong tendency to paint in series.

Forge's recognition of the importance of subject is perceptive. In marked contrast to Bacon, whose amoral emphasis (an emphasis carried by style and manner) is on the dynamic inner relations of sensation to consciousness, and with subjects that will trigger a psychic and emotional energy in the viewer, Bowling's subjects had a resonance that was anecdotal or historical. The situations he depicted were affected from the start by an urgency of concern, sometimes personal, sometimes political. The murder in January 1961 of the brave Congolese leader, Patrice Lumumba, facilitated by agents of the Belgian government and the CIA, saddened and angered him deeply. A sudden, unattended birth he had unexpectedly witnessed in a squalid London flat had shocked him into a dark awareness of the most fundamental of human realities; he remembered the poverty and despair of the beggars who received charity from his mother. These real events and situations haunted his imagination. In a conversation with William Thomson, the realist painter, Bowling recalled the motivation of his work at this period:

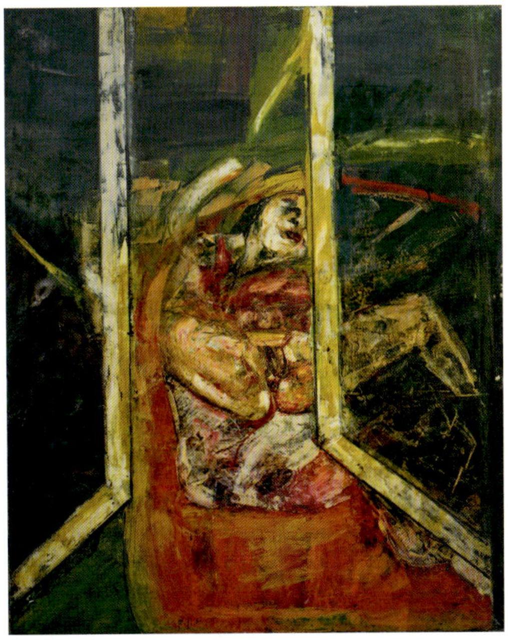

Birthday II, 1961
Oil on canvas, 127 x 101.5 cm

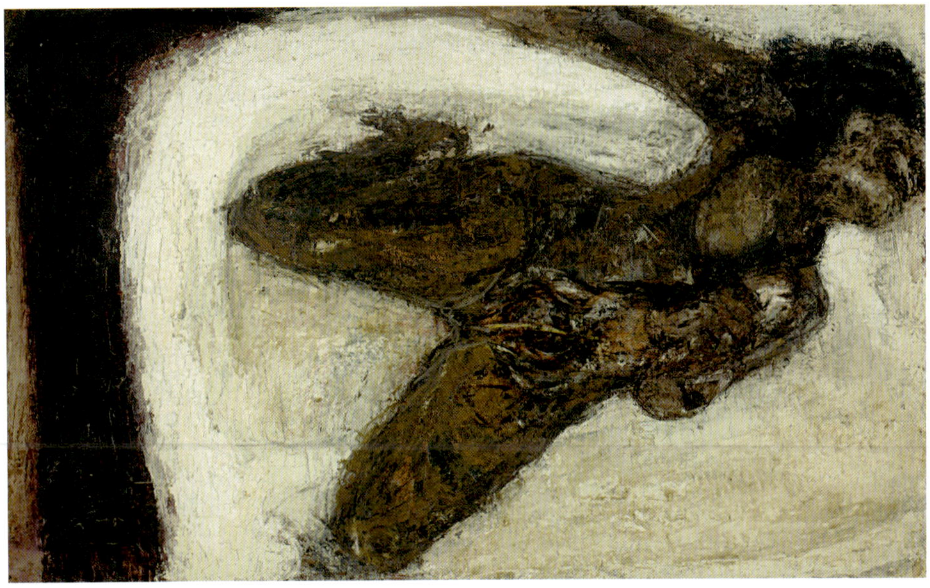

Birthday I, 1960
Oil on canvas, 101.5 x 131 cm

> What was feeding my creative energy and what I was making pictures about was life ... Distilling my drive to painting was the human dilemma and all this business about suffering; trying to put it right by showing it ... and people turned me towards examples which they thought would be important to me, but were not. Like Richard Wright and Paul Robeson, people to whose tradition I don't belong, because I am British ... What I painted was human concern. From Rembrandt through Goya I got an insight into how to paint suffering and I took it from there. Things like beggars, women giving birth, etc.: the real life example was Francis Bacon. *He* was the one who was doing all that. But I have always felt that he was doing something different from me. He was preoccupied with something that has to do with his *own* life. I was more concerned with the life *around* me.

Two powerful versions of the seminal subject, *Birthday*, painted in May 1961, were actually a response to one of two compulsory 'figure composition' topics set in the RCA Painting School in the spring term of the second year.

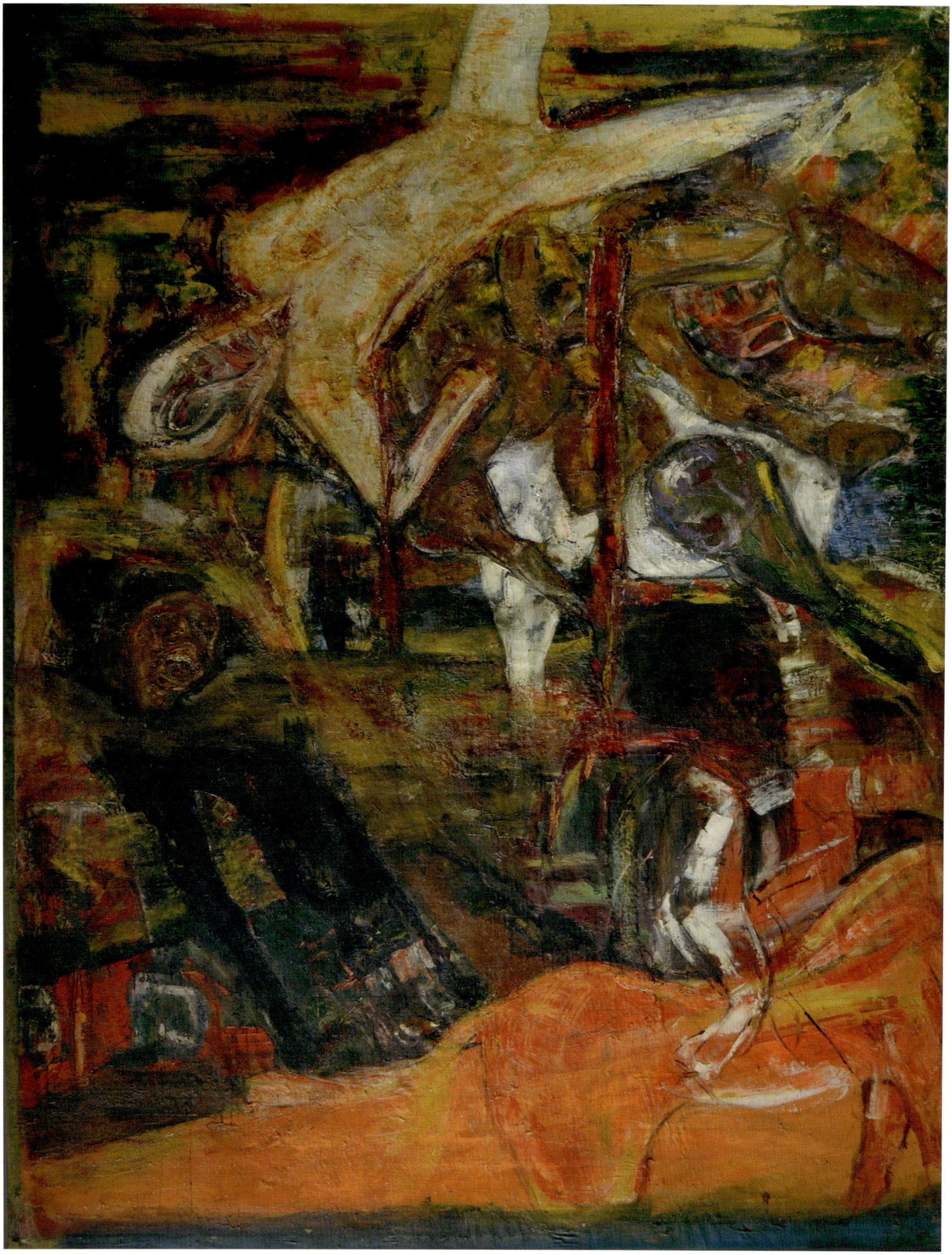

opposite
The Four Horsemen of the Apocalypse, 1961
Oil on canvas, 218.5 x 168 cm

Neither his tutors nor his classmates could have anticipated the stark drama and pathos of the images that he duly presented for critical appraisal. (Among responses from other students to the theme was a painting of a children's birthday party.) Another set topic was The Four Horsemen of the Apocalypse, and this too elicited a painting of extraordinary power, whose intractable obscurity of image, figurative complexity and painterly violence seem to hark back with a vengeance to Bacon's darkly inchoate *Figure in a Mountain Landscape* (1956), a painting seen by Bowling at the 1957 Hanover Gallery exhibition. These student works were among the paintings that so impressed Sylvester and Forge the following year.

As with other works made during this frenetically creative period, they exhibit great painterly energy and an uncompromising graphic directness. Forge concluded his 1962 review with an expression of unbridled enthusiasm: '[Bowling] uses the Bacon apparatus – drawn frames in space, empty areas juxtaposed with frenetic detail – with a real feeling for traditional deployments. It is as if he had discovered Figure Composition stripped of cobwebs – smoking and bloody on the plains of Chios.' This allusion to Delacroix may hint at Forge's 'traditional deployments', but had he been less preoccupied with the present example of Bacon (whose first major retrospective at the Tate Gallery had created a sensation in the early summer of 1962), he might well have recognised the evident importance of certain great artists from the past to whom Bowling had been paying close creative attention in the demanding and illuminating critical company of Keith Critchlow.

Bowling's engagement with the figurative tradition is sometimes quite obvious. Even when tropical *joie de vivre* is a subject, his colour is generally low-key and tonal in an old-masterly way rather than raw and chromatic as in the (disparate) modern manners of the expressionists, of Matisse and of Bacon.

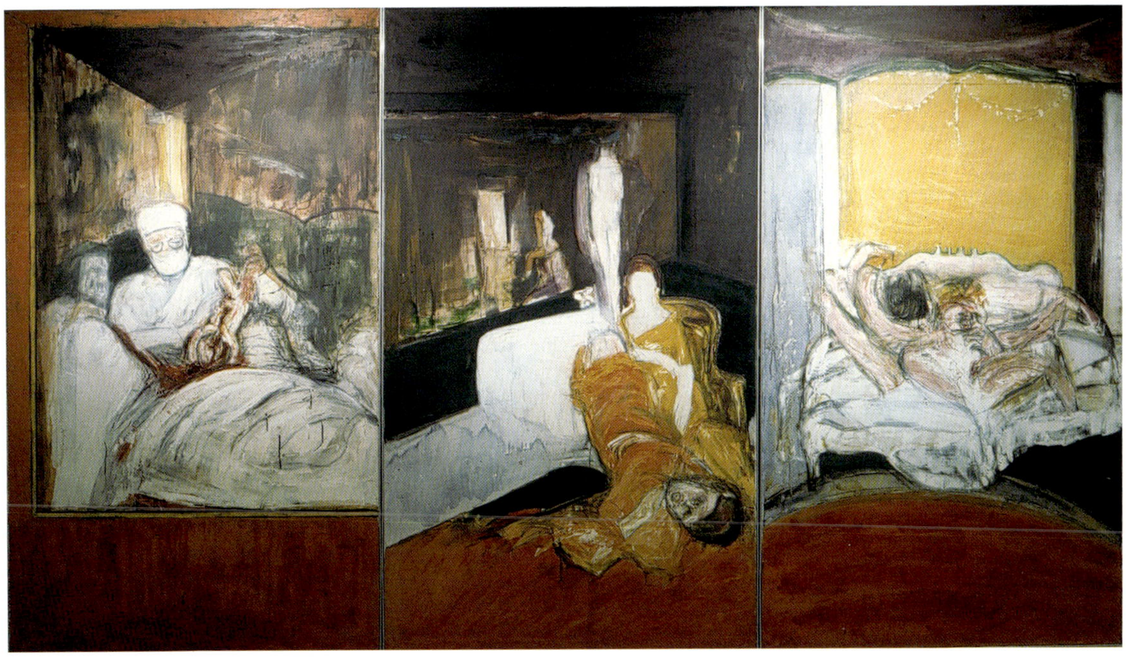

A Mirror, Three Windows, a Door, 1962
Oil on canvas, 213.5 x 368 cm

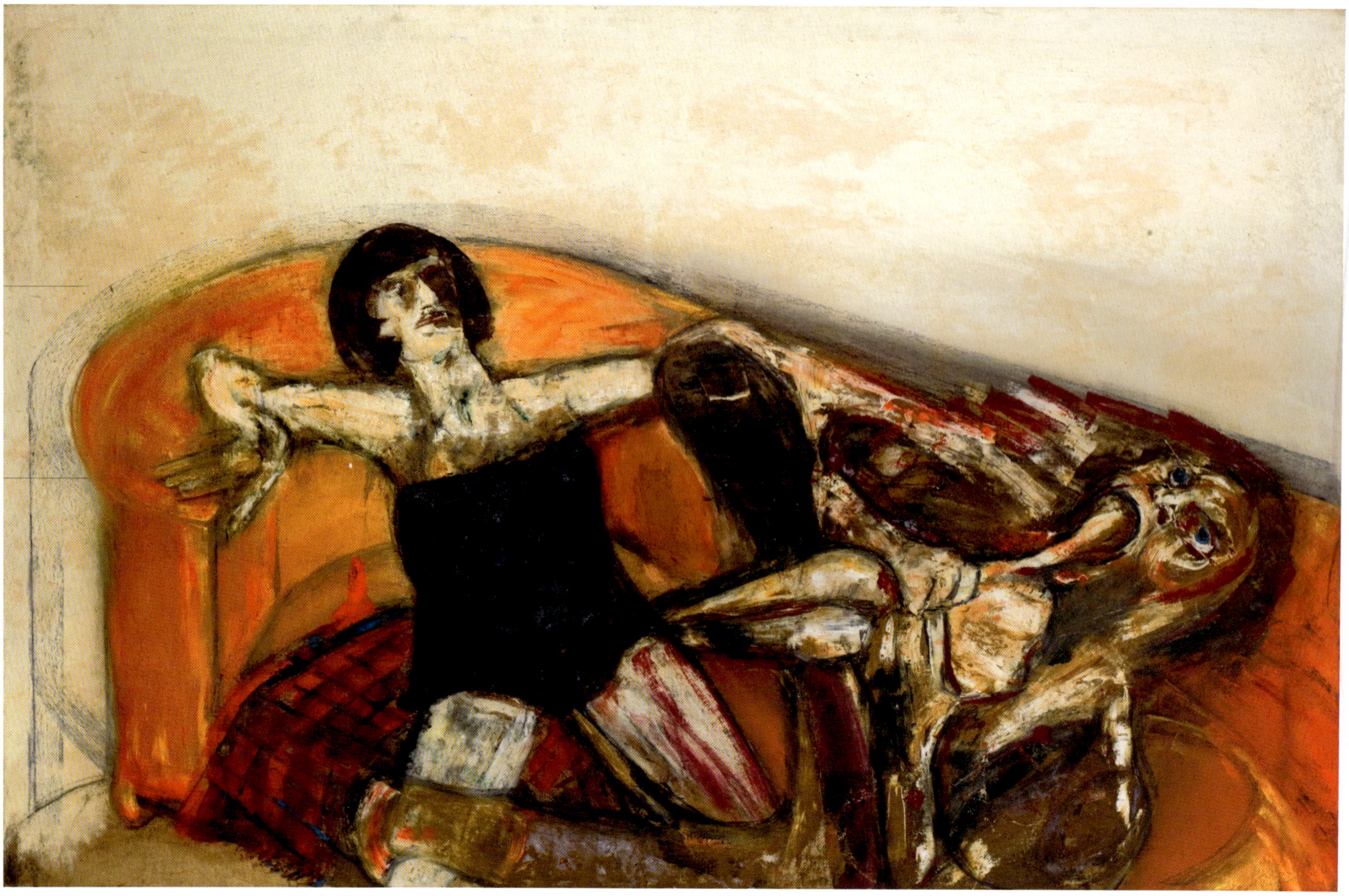

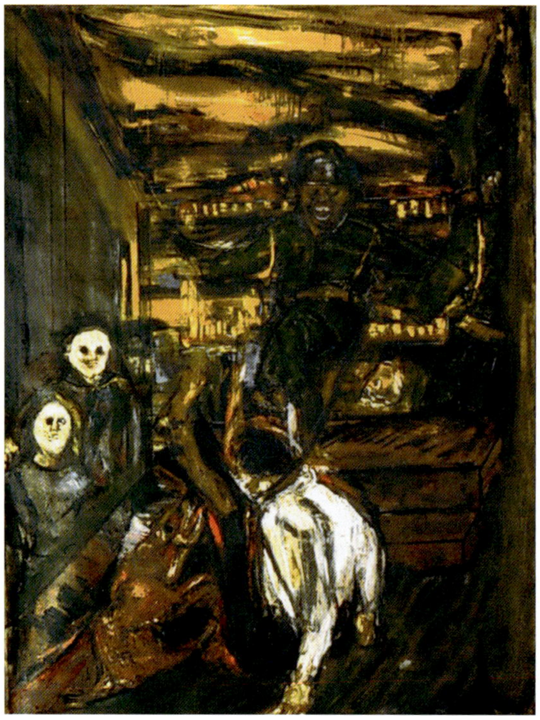

In his triptychs and panoramas – *A Mirror, Three Windows, a Door* (1962) and *Lent* (1963), the latter now lost – he was thinking of the grand multiple-figure narrative compositions of Rembrandt. In some works there is direct quotation, as in the various versions of *Afternoon Nap* (1962), in which a female character wakes to discover Goya's Saturn devouring his children at the other end of the sofa; and Goya's dramatically direct *Third of May 1808* (1814) cannot have been far from Bowling's mind when he composed the tragic *Martyrdom of Patrice Lumumba* (1961).

Even what critics discerned as the 'Bacon apparatus' in Bowling's paintings of this period is not what it seems. In *Birthday II*, for instance, the open window has a theatrical function: the splayed figure pictured at the moment of parturition is seen through it in such a way that the accidental voyeurism of the protagonist's glimpse is emphasised; the window forms part of the fictional space of the picture. In *Birthday I*

above
***Afternoon Nap*, 1962**
Oil on canvas, 122 x 183 cm

left
***Martyrdom of Patrice Lumumba*, 1961**
Oil on canvas, 183 x 152.5 cm

(1960), the space is again diegetic; we look into it as on to a stage set. In such cases, there is a deliberately domestic *mise-en-scène*, and not, as in Bacon, a purely arbitrary pictorial space objectively separated by linear devices to frame the space-and-action it isolates for the spectator's gaze.

One notable contemporary critic recognised the originality of the paintings at the Grabowski Gallery in 1962. Writing in *Art International*, Norbert Lynton identified Bowling as 'an expressionist of striking power and individuality'. He went on to define certain preoccupations of Bowling:

> He draws his material from immediate experience, and endows that material with a passionate vividness that makes self-identification unavoidable. His principal concern is sex and he has what seems to me to be the unique distinction of seeing in sex more than the crisis of intercourse: birth appears not, so to speak, as a second subject but as an inversion of the first. So a good deal of his power lies in the inevitable relevance of their content to any heterosexual observer: woman as magnet, woman as object of fear; birth as the dreadful bloodstained miracle. His mode of vision steps up to the current.

Lynton was rightly dismissive of the tendency to see Bowling as an imitator of Bacon: 'To me the differences seem so great as to overwhelm the similarities. It is true that he borrows from Bacon some manners of applying paint, but while in Bacon they are used to decorate a painting that in its essentials already exists, here they are integral parts of the subject/mode-of-vision/matter compound. Bowling's colour, though varied and, considering the violence of his paintings, surprisingly subtle, knows neither the eschatological gloom nor the brash poster brightness of Bacon's. But all these dissimilarities are subsidiary to the main one, which is really one of personality: Bowling's world is the world we know, even if we come away knowing it better.'

4 POP WITH MEMORY: A NEW BEGINNING

'...putting on the agony, putting on the style...'
LONNIE DONEGAN

Bowling was to persist for a while in confronting with painterly vehemence 'the world we know' in personal allegories and enigmatic dramas. But before long he was experimenting with other styles of presentation, and seeking an alternative to a directly expressionist engagement with personal experience and social and political *actualité*. He was looking for a cooler aesthetic but one which might encompass – with some degree of stylish indirection – the intersection of existential reality and the objective distancing of art. In late 1963 he was commissioned to make three large paintings for the 1964 exhibition at Stratford-upon-Avon celebrating the quatercentenary of Shakespeare's birth. This work demanded a completely new approach, an extension of his reach, and also precipitated a prolonged period of experiment and periodic change. The first major phase of his artistic journey had come to an end; he was poised to embark on a long creative odyssey to find new means and different purposes for his art.

At Alexandra Palace, where a great studio space was found for the project, Bowling worked into the winter of 1963 on his Shakespeare paintings, alongside Ceri Richards, Leonard

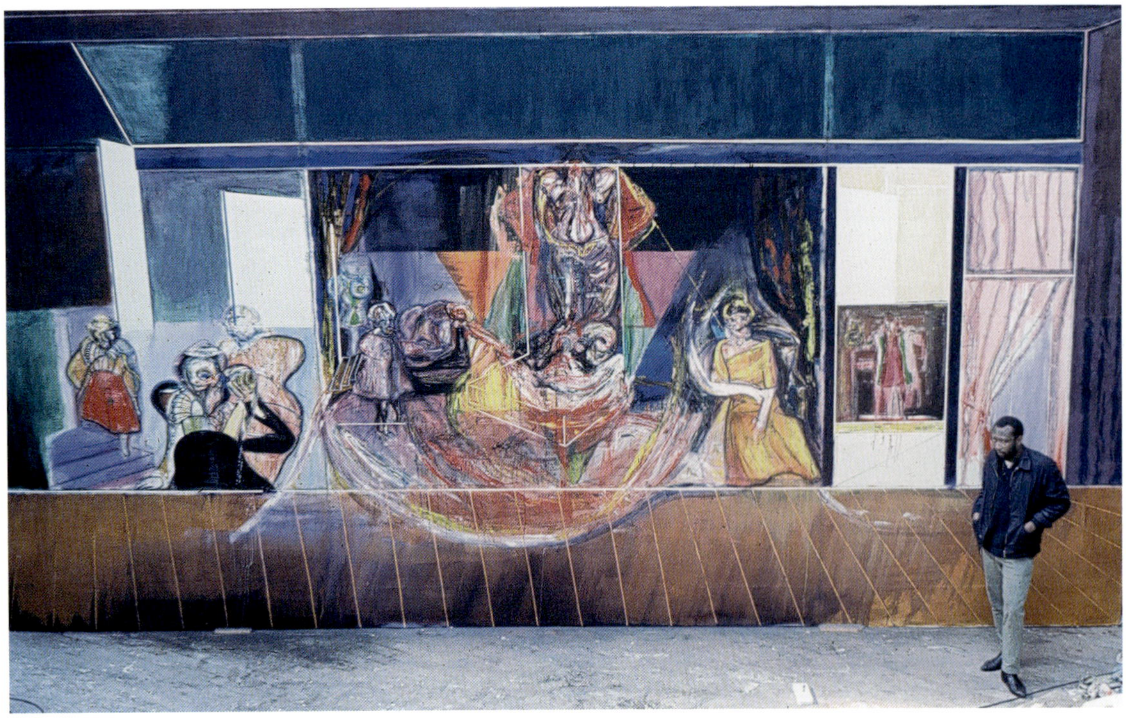

Frank Bowling with *The Execution of Mary Queen of Scots*, 1963, at Stratford-upon-Avon
Oil on canvas, 457 x 1,067 cm

Rosoman and Peter Blake, who had been commissioned by Richard Buckle, the flamboyant organiser-impresario of the exhibition at Stratford-upon-Avon, to produce mural-scale paintings on themes of their choice. Both Richards and Rosoman were distinguished and established artists who had also been highly respected teachers at the RCA during Bowling's period there. In 1962 Richards had represented the UK at the Venice Biennale, winning the major painting prize; Rosoman was famous as a war artist and had continued to maintain a distinctive career as a figurative painter not afraid to experiment with colour and elements of abstract design. Blake was one of the brightest stars of an earlier generation at the College, and was already making his name as one of the leading exponents of British pop art. The commission was an accolade, and Bowling was in exalted company.

Bowling's *The Execution of Mary Queen of Scots* was a complex, multi-compartmented panorama. After the Shakespeare exhibition, this huge painting and the two others by Bowling were rolled up and stored at Camberwell School of Arts and Crafts, where some years later they were cut up (without the artist's knowledge or permission) to provide canvas for students. The only photographic record of these paintings is an image of *The Execution* at the exhibition, but its poor quality barely allows speculation as to the success of the painting.

Bowling had begun to teach painting at Camberwell in the autumn of 1963 on the recommendation of Bryan Robertson. Robert Medley, the distinguished Head of Painting there, proved supportive and helpful, and Bowling is remembered by ex-students as intense and courteous in tutorials, and as a lively presence in the studios. Camberwell was good news for Bowling: by teaching there and at Reading (where the painter Claude Rogers created a part-time post for him), he was able to make a reasonable living, and to be in contact with many of the leading artists of his time. Kitaj, a friend from Royal College days, was also teaching at Camberwell, for example, as were Patrick Proctor, Leon Kossoff, Euan Uglow and Michael Rothenstein; Terry Frost was at Reading Univeristy. Medley deliberately encouraged lively discussion among his staff, and there were convivial lunches at the local pub. Bowling was also active in the London Group as vice-chairman (Rogers was chairman) and showed regularly in the Group's annual exhibitions.

Working on the Shakespeare paintings brought him into close creative contact with Peter Blake and Leonard Rosoman. More objective in their approach to painting than

Bowling, they both became generous mentors whom he would remember with gratitude. From Blake, especially, he learned that painting could be coolly programmatic, could use and adapt photography in an objective way, draw on contemporary popular sources, and combine styles and manners in arbitrary decorative arrangements. These ideas were to be decisively influential on his work over the next three years.

The impulse to expressionist figuration that had powered his work thus far began to ebb away. Bowling became aware of other possibilities. He discovered that he could approach the canvas in ways other than the directly painterly, that painting could work by means of stylistic contrast, visual surprise, irony and allusion. In place of the painterly rhetoric and dramatic description of his recent work, it could present images as arbitrary and enigmatic, and exploit poetic implication and thematic allusion. Titles could be cryptic, ironic or deadpan, allowing the viewer to imagine freely. He was liberated, in short, from both the expressionist manner and the expressive fallacy – the notion that painting is expressive of an artist's feelings.

The idea of integrating screen-printed images derived from photography into paintings was in the air, as was the use of photography generally. Bowling had visited New York in 1961 and again in 1962, and he was well aware of the excitement growing around Andy Warhol and the emergence of American pop art, though he was never greatly interested in it. At Camberwell sometime in 1964, not yet knowing how he would use the image-motif (or how often!), he amassed a stockpile of canvas pieces bearing the image of

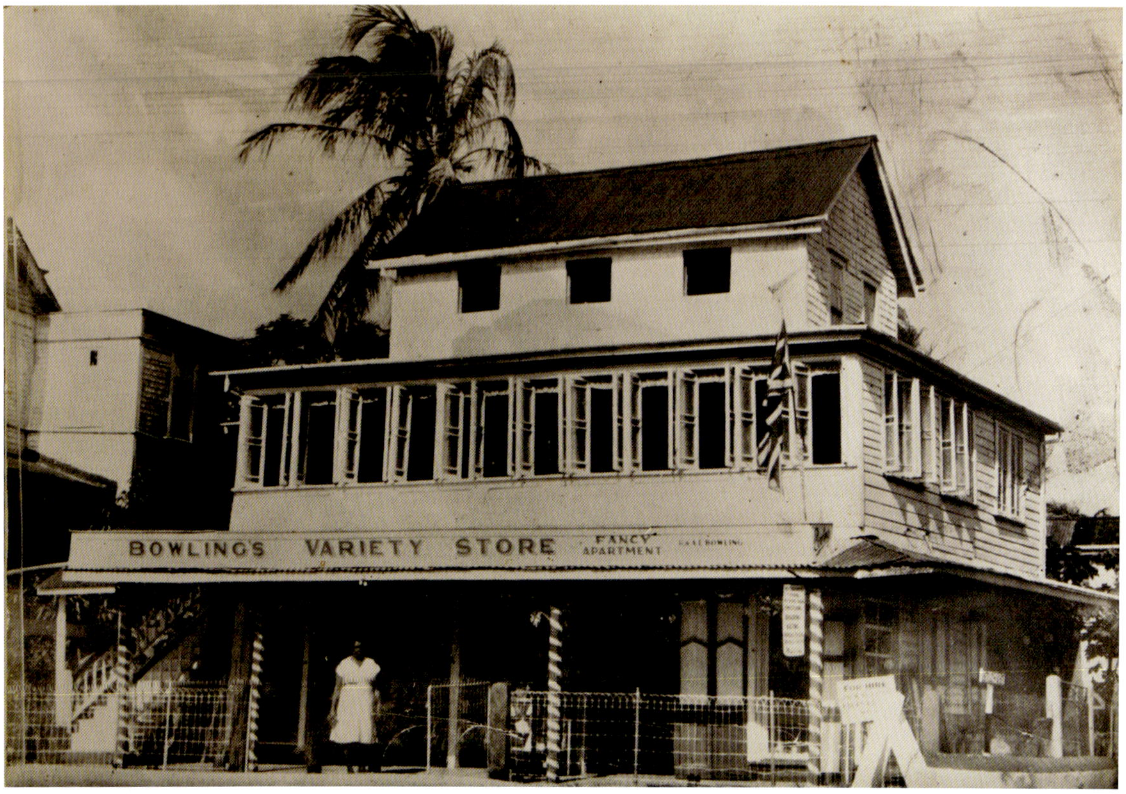

Photograph (1966) of Bowling's Variety Store showing the view used by Bowling in the screenprint, *Mother's House*, 1953.

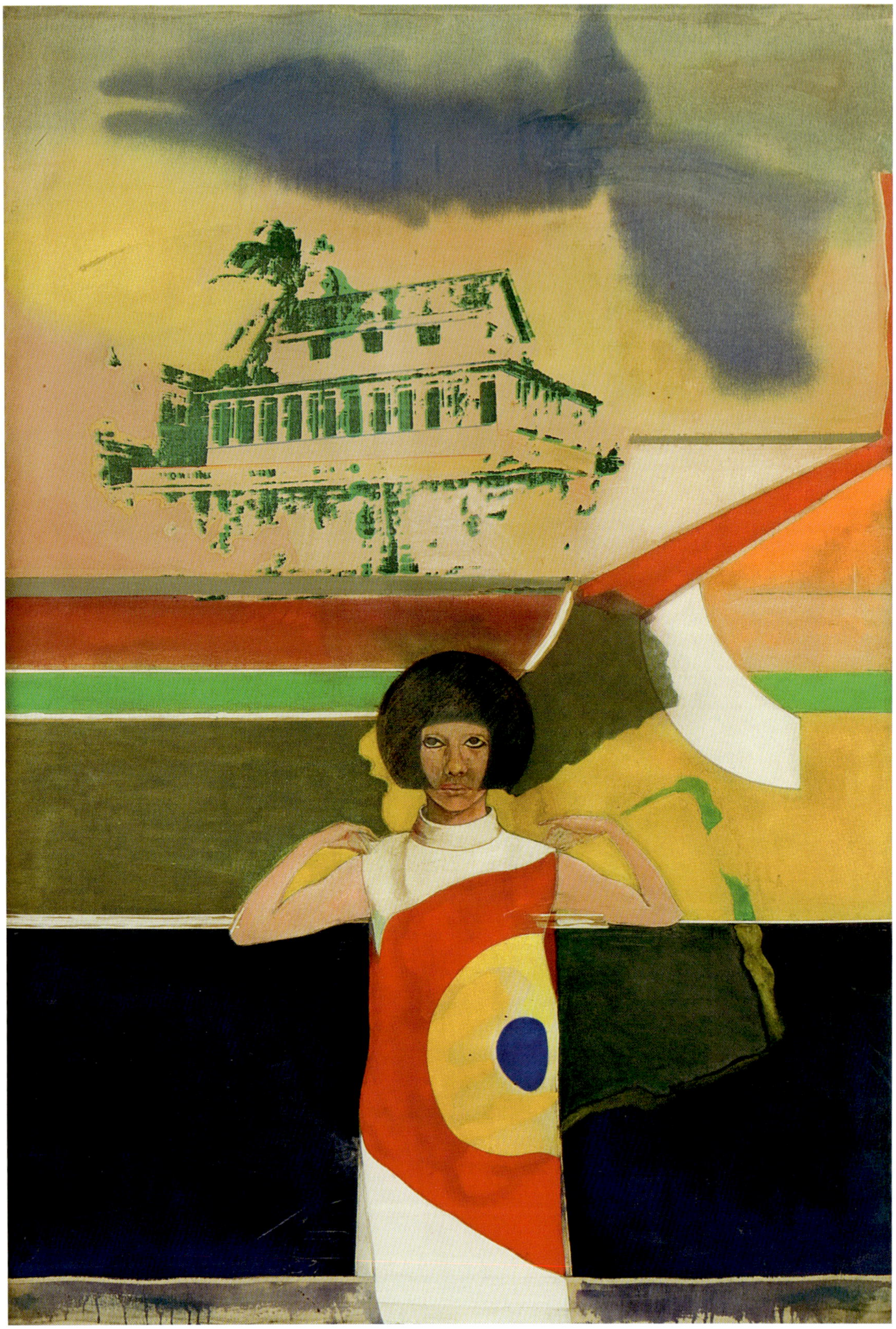

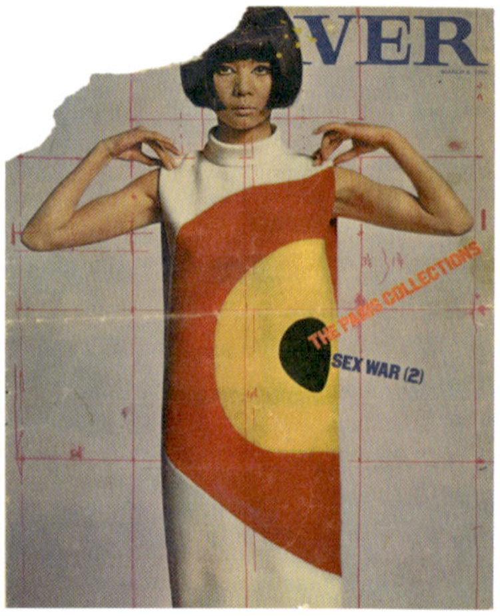

left

Cover Girl, 1966
Oil on canvas, 145 x 101.5 cm

above

The *Observer Magazine* cover (March 1966) used in ***Cover Girl***.

his mother's emporium – always referred to by Bowling as 'mother's house' – screen-printed in red or green.

For Bowling the image clearly had a powerful emotional resonance: it would become a recurring thematic reference point, a motif that carried the allusive charge of a memory of home, a signature intimation of origins. The photograph was taken, moreover, on Coronation Day 1953, the day that Bowling arrived in London. An aspect of the image that appealed to him was the appearance behind the house of a windswept palm tree, with its suggestion of a stormy emotional context contrasting with the order of colonial-style architecture and the organised economic purposes of the store.

The first painting in which the image was deployed was the strangely complicated *Cover Girl* (1966). In London the 1960s 'revolt into style' was by now at its height, and pop art colluded with pop music and young fashion to increase the excitement. Bowling's title refers, of course, to the girl with the Mary Quant-style dress and the Vidal Sassoon helmet haircut, an image appropriated directly from the cover of an *Observer* colour supplement of March 1966. Magazines like the Sunday colour supplements (first issued in 1962-63) and *Queen* were avidly promoting the new fashion styles with their characteristic target motifs, flag-like stripes and black-and-white counterchange, and at the same time holding up a photographic and journalistic mirror in which a narcissistic 'swinging London' could admire its own reflection. Peter Blake's imagery from this period – combining emblematic abstract stripes and chevrons and photo-derived images of film and pop stars – was a defining contribution to the visual *Zeitgeist*, as was the black and white op art of Bridget Riley.

Whereas Blake's enthusiastic (if sometimes gently ironic) take on popular culture had behind it a celebratory impulse, the problematic and ambiguous imagery of Bowling's *Cover Girl* suggests something more troubled, more ambivalent. The stripes behind the fashionable girl are breaking up; 'mother's house' is a mysterious presence from another place, far away, and over its shadowy emanation there hangs a darkly atmospheric cloud. There is an autobiographical tension in the painting that is quite at odds with its stylish evocation of the hedonistic vanities of contemporary London. A mood thus conflicted suggests not so much a simple critique of the coolness of pop art as an ironic juxtaposition of its apolitical narcissism with contemporaneous realities elsewhere.

The colours of the broken stripes – red, yellow, green, white and black – allude perhaps to those of the Guyanese flag, designed in 1962 in preparation for the colony's anticipated independence and renaming as Guyana. These were years of violent political stress and inter-communal conflict, a fact of which Bowling was well aware: after graduating from the Royal College in the summer of 1962 he had been awarded a travelling scholarship, and chose to travel to Barbados, Trinidad and the new Guyana. This was his first trip home. He felt no great nostalgia for the country of his childhood, no sense of belonging to its turbulent present, no loyalty to any faction in its current confused polity. But it was nevertheless his place of origin, a reality in his life with inescapable personal and political connotations. In time to come, Bowling's art would recall aspects of his early experience: the faceted gleams of the mud flats of Bartica, the clear light across the Berbice River, the intense colours of forests and skies, and the façade of his mother's house.

Bov

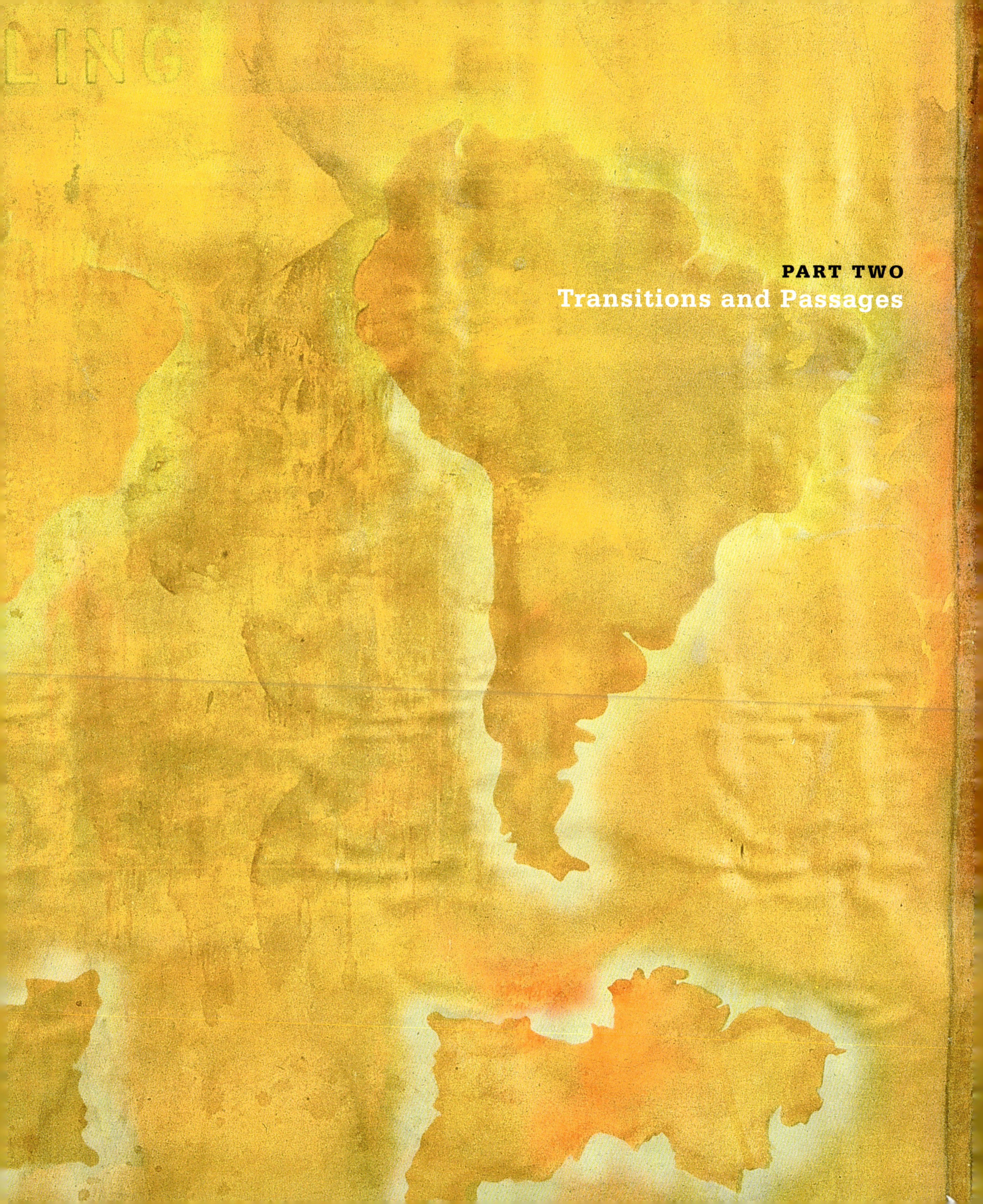

PART TWO
Transitions and Passages

5 DYING SWANS AND A SPIRAL STAIRCASE: IMAGES OF CRISIS

Bowling returned to London for his first commercial exhibition, *Image in Revolt*, at Grabowski in the autumn of 1962. By the end of 1963, in this vibrant city where he had long felt at home, Bowling, intent on making his own original and complicated uses of the colourful simplicities of Pop Art, was making a move in a new direction. A group of strangely poetic works made before *Cover Girl* contain stylistic disjunctions comparable to those evident in that painting. At some point early in 1964 Bowling had begun to engage in a highly personal manner with what might, for him, have seemed the unlikely theme of the dying swan.

Photographs taken in the summer of 1964 show Bowling on the foreshore of the Thames at Putney, contemplating a flock of those beautiful creatures. His own account makes it clear that the subject had powerful personal resonances for him, and that his treatment of it reflected repressed fears, complexities and confusions of feeling hidden behind the confident persona of the handsome, intellectually sophisticated and somewhat devil-may-care artist, teacher and party-goer. The very grace and dignity of the swan make its degradation and death the more deeply shocking and poignant.

> There was this conflict, that I felt very strongly, that I was the artist bohemian, throwing myself around, and feeling the stresses of domestic life … and the whole complexity of [a] black and white marriage was a terrible strain …
>
> I was trying to use prevailing ways of making art – Colour Field and Hard Edge painting – and incorporate them into my already established themes – the dying swan, or what [had] evolved from the interest in beggars … people who had broken lives … People would allude to the fact that if you don't straighten up and fly right, you know, you're going to end up in a gutter like those people out there …
>
> So I suppose there was quite a lot of that going on in my mind … But I was sure of my calling … that I was an artist, that I had something to say or give … I was striving to sharpen my art …

At least two 'swan' paintings of 1964 adopt the diamond-shaped supports associated with Kenneth Noland and superimpose across the centre of this cool formalist schema the agonised and twisting figure of the swan. Above this figure (or behind it, depending on the optional direction of the painting's hang), the hard-edge regularity of the colour chevrons is interrupted and dislocated by a violent incursion in which there

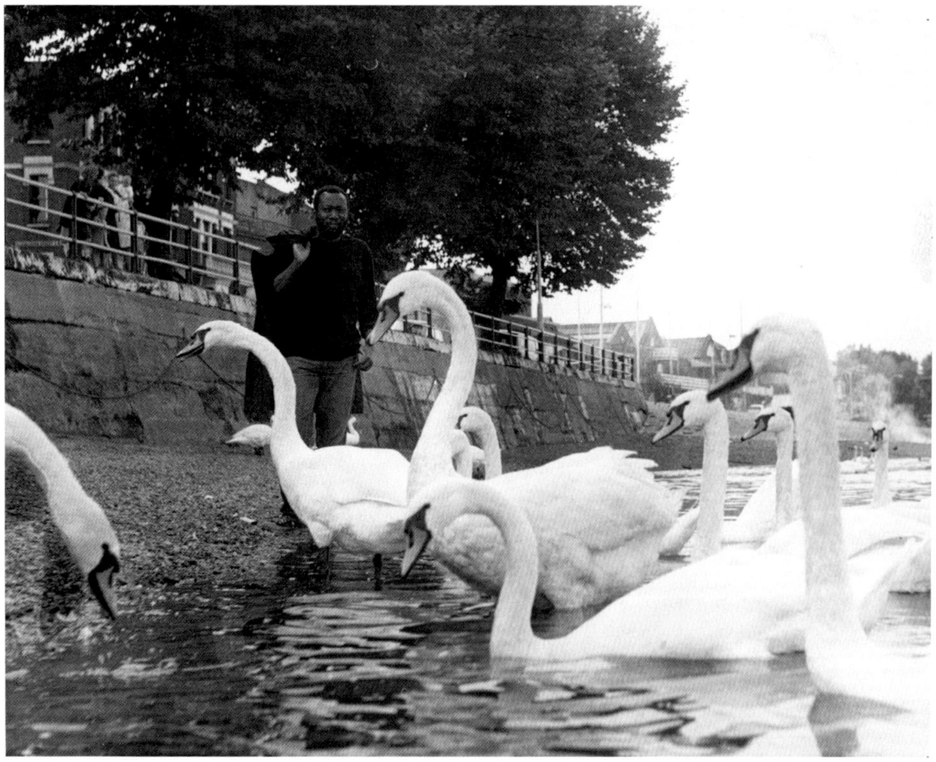

Bowling on the foreshore of the Thames at Putney, 1964.

is a confusion of references to quite different styles: painterly chaotic spatter, linear-graphic, Vasarely-Op. As in *Cover Girl*, a decorative order is disrupted and broken in ways that intimate an internal disturbance or even a kind of anger.

For Bowling, the mid-1960s were the best of times and the worst of times. His confidence in the kind of painterly expressionism that had brought him to critical notice and afforded him some degree of professional success had faltered, and he had embarked on work that in its disconcerting combination of different styles and manners seemed to signal private, political and artistic dilemmas. In the spring of 1964 he had been excluded from two important and critically significant exhibitions: the Gulbenkian-promoted exhibition *54 64 Painting and Sculpture of a Decade* at the Tate, and the Stuyvesant-sponsored *The New Generation: 1964*, selected by Bryan Robertson and put on at the Whitechapel Art Gallery. The latter was the more hurtful omission in that Bowling had been treated with great kindness, and as a kind of protégé, by the brilliantly ebullient and influential Robertson. Bowling's work was also omitted from the rapidly expanding Peter Stuyvesant Foundation Collection, put together by a team of influential selectors over two to three years to form what, in the catalogue to an exhibition of the collection mounted at the Tate, they described as 'a general picture of recent British painting'.

Towards the end of 1963 Bowling's close friendship with Francis Bacon came to an unhappy and messy end. Throughout this period his marriage to Paddy Kitchen was under acute pressure, and by 1966, after Bowling had spent some weeks in New York, he came back to a terminal matrimonial crisis. Shortly afterwards, Kitchen left him to live with Dulan Barber, the novelist and literary editor, who had been a friend of the couple for several years. A small, intensely lyrical painting, *Dulan's Swan* (1962), had celebrated this relationship in its happier days. Perhaps significantly, in 1964 Bowling turned his attention to the theme once more, with studies on paper of a swan beating the water as it tries to rise into the air: a motif that Bowling had come to associate with the coils and trammels of a complicated and troubled personal life.

A revealing installation of *Swan II* (1964) at a London Group exhibition in 1966 underlined this association. Bowling attached streamers of ribbon and chained an anchor and an iron pole to the painting, as if to suggest a false gaiety that could not disguise the drag of intractable psychic material on the struggling swan: the white bird might be thought to provide a perfect disguise for the artist. A photograph taken on the same day as

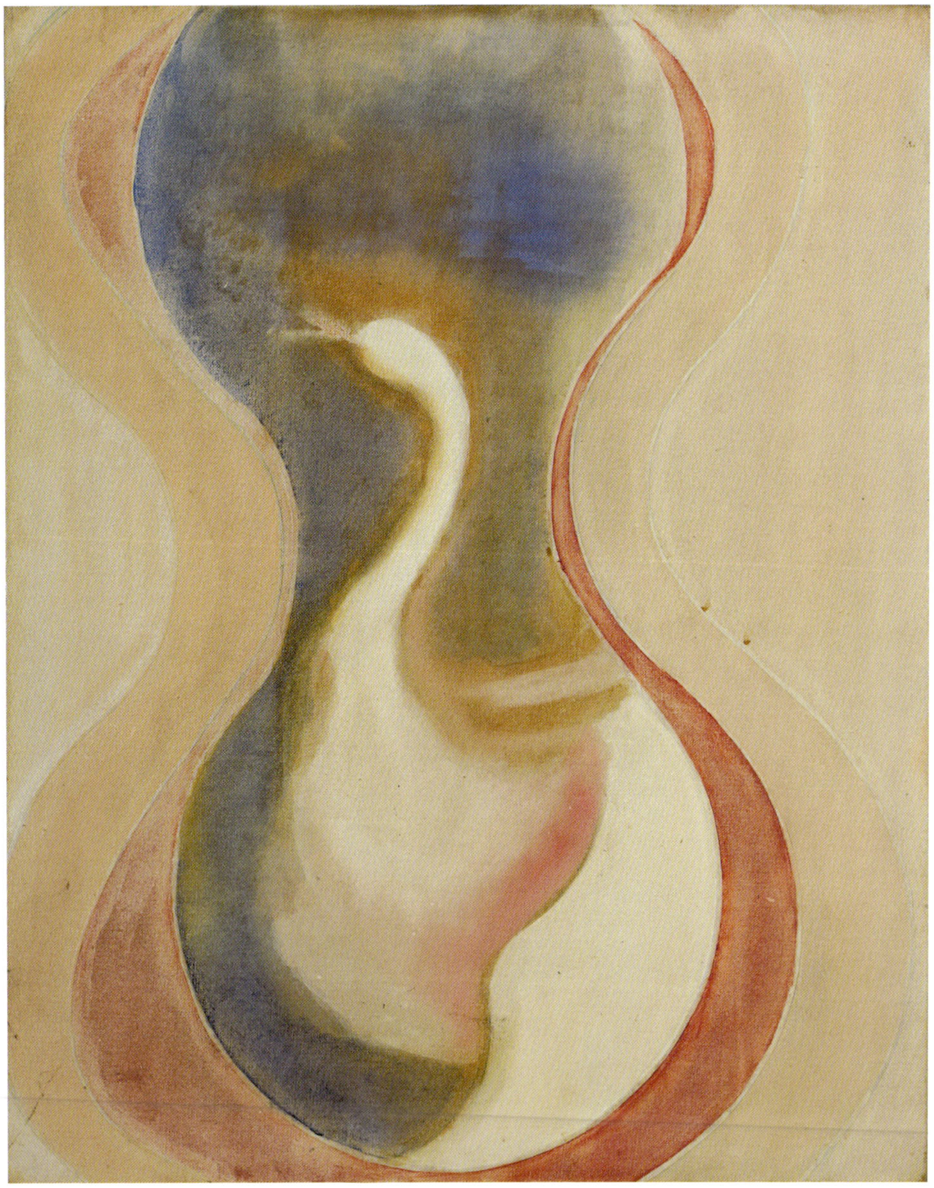

***Dulan's Swan*, 1962**
Oil on canvas, 76 x 61 cm

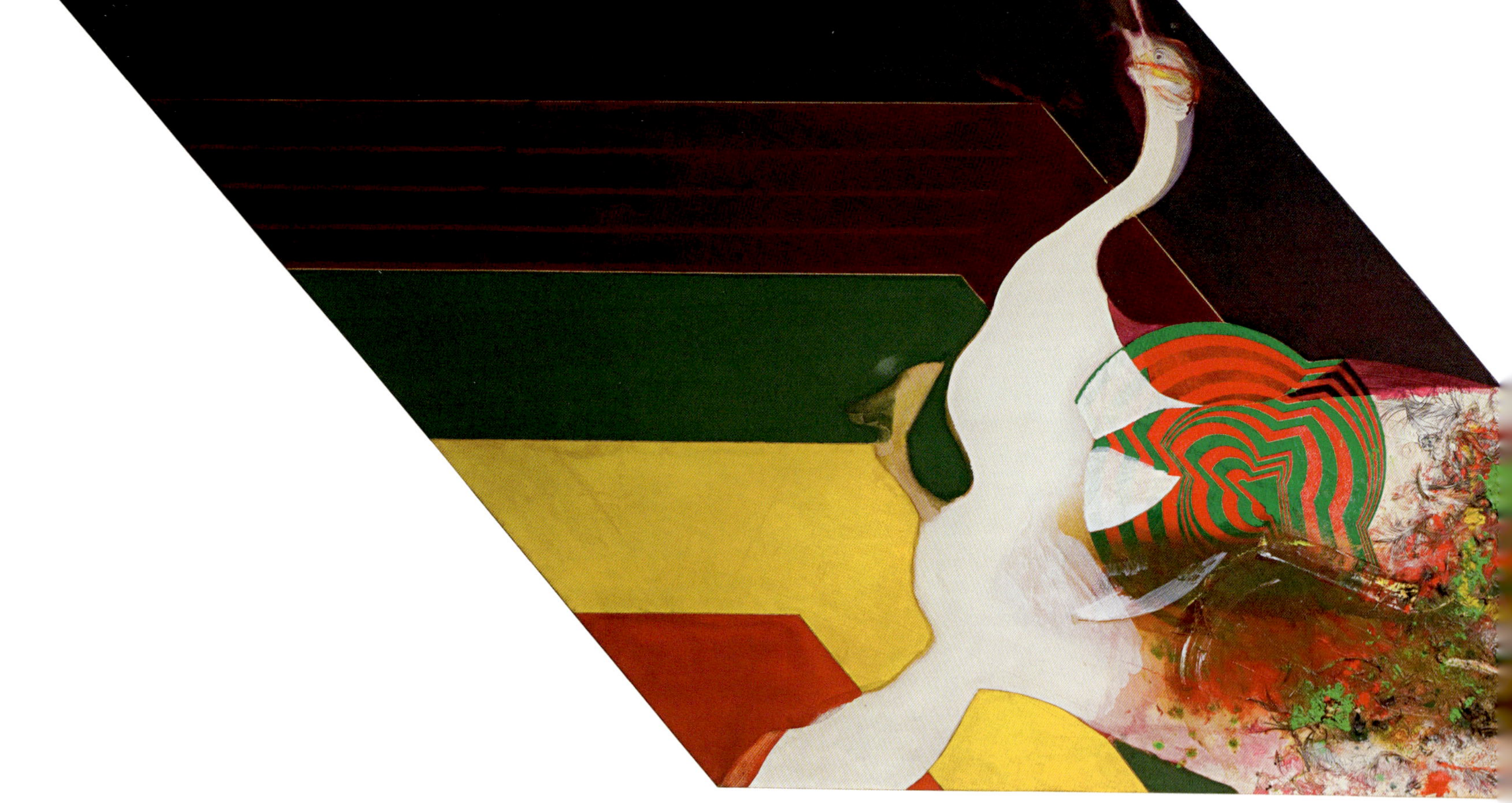

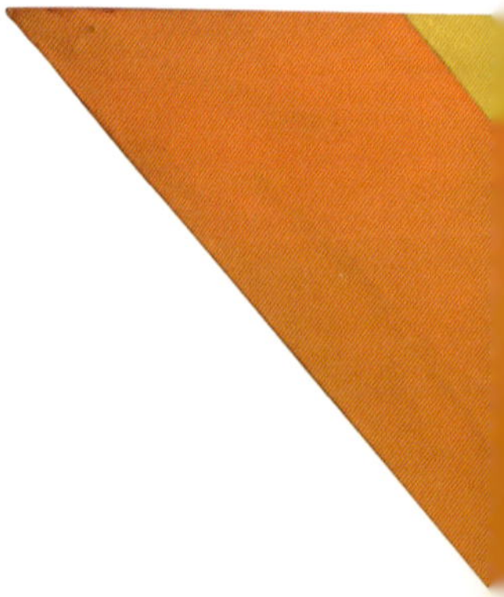

Swan I, 1964
Oil on canvas, 244 x 112 cm

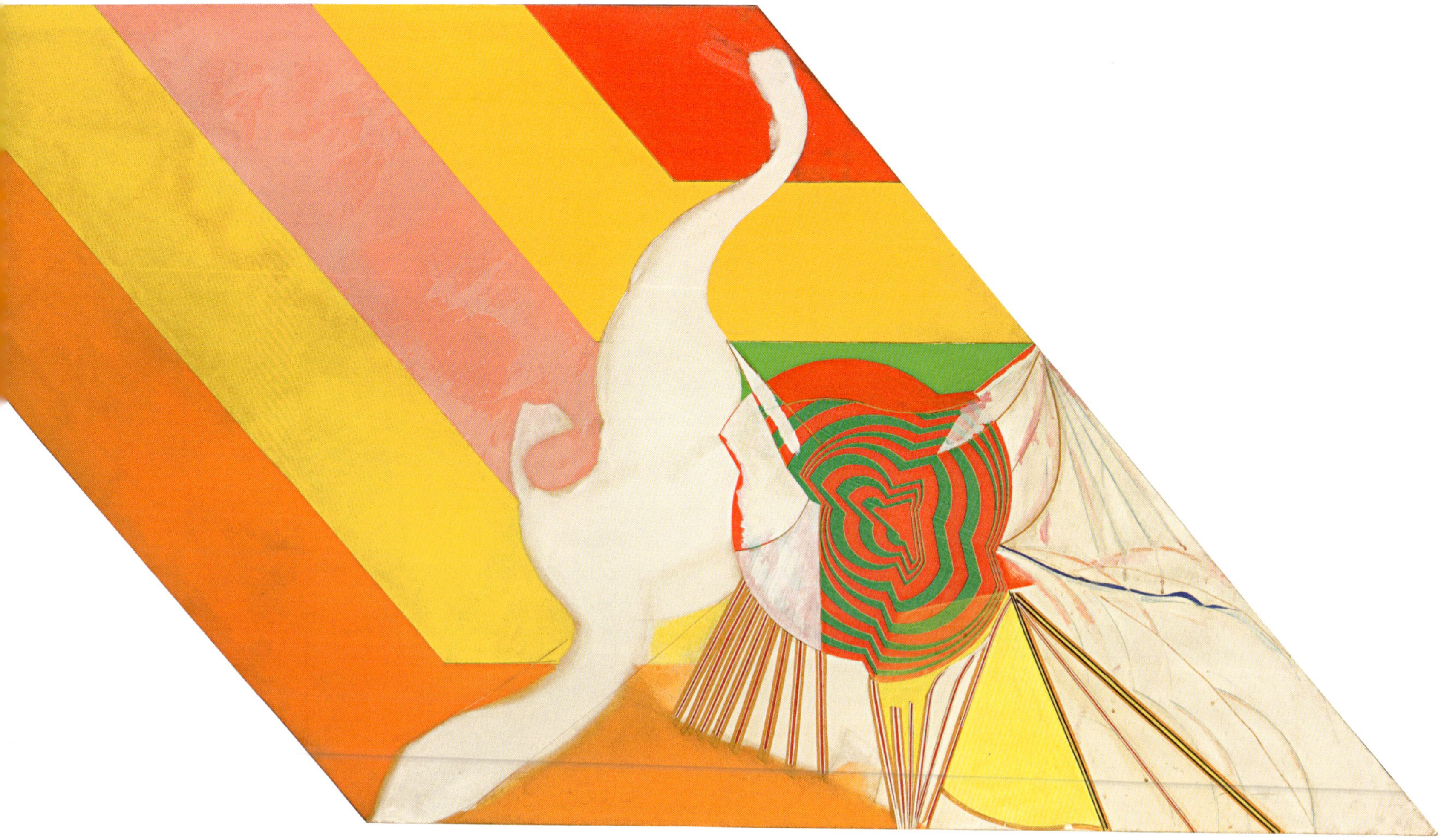

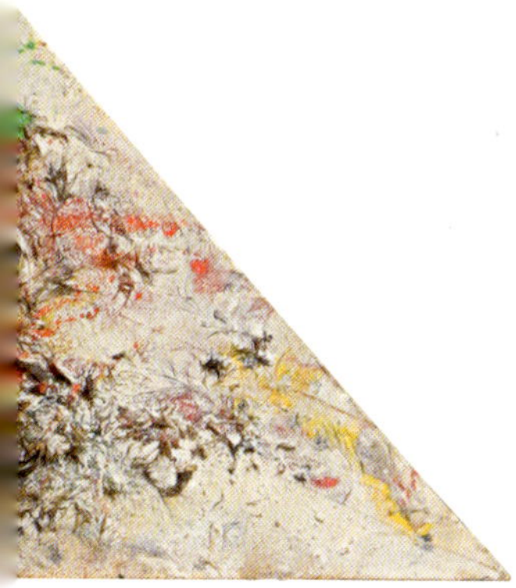

Swan II, 1964
Oil on canvas, 244 x 112 cm

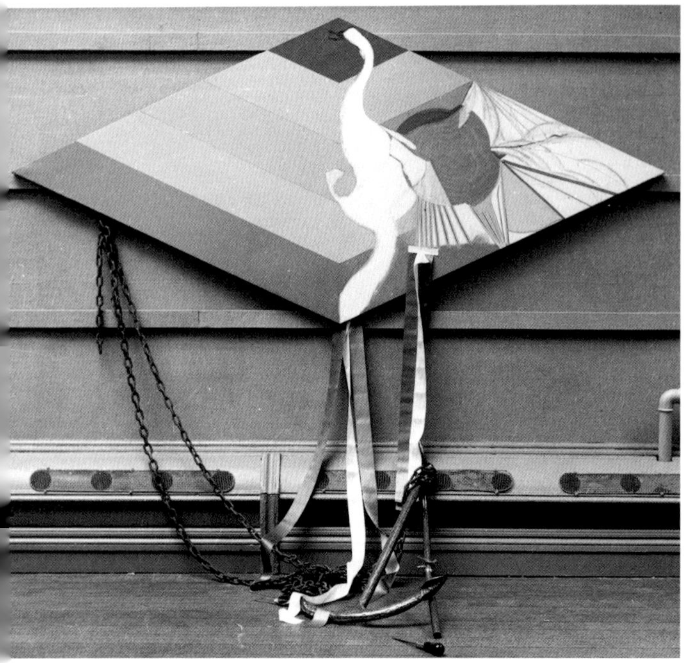

Swan II at the London Group exhibition, Society of Watercolour Painters, Piccadilly, 1966.

his encounter with the swans at Putney shows Bowling posing at the very edge of the shifting tide of the city's river, his feet among its muddy detritus – a bucket with a hole in it, rusted metal rods, etc. Bowling knew as well as Bacon (and Hockney, Warhol and, of course, Picasso) that a resonant image of the artist might be created by carefully staged, self-dramatising photographs that contain the components of a personal mythology.

The diptych *Big Bird* (1964) is a major statement of the dying swan theme. Drawings and trial impressions of projected but aborted prints featuring this motif demonstrate that in making these works Bowling was thinking of a deeper order than that proposed by the attractive shaped canvases and simple colour stripe and chevron arrangements of Noland and others. In these preparatory studies, the twisting swan-figure occupies the geometric space like an imperfect and contorted parody of Leonardo's Vitruvian Man, the perfect figure of human proportion, defining a circle inscribed within a square, conceived as a reflection of divine order. 'What a piece of work is man! How noble in reason! how infinite in faculty! … the beauty of the world! the paragon of animals! And yet, to me, what is this quintessence of dust?' Bowling is a highly literate artist of deep feeling and complexity of intelligence and spirit: he might well have thought of Hamlet's paradoxical riff as he contemplated his own condition in these deeply coded paintings of existential crisis; just as, in 1962, he had portrayed himself as Othello, invoking the torment of the deluded Moor in a blaze of joyous primaries.

Seeking other ways to 'make his art grow', Bowling had begun to think deeply about geometry as an architectonic principal in his paintings, carrying implications of a hidden eternal perfection of relations, perceptible to the mind but incapable of attainment in the material actualities of real life. Sometime in 1963-64, with his friends, Jerry Pethick, the Canadian experimental sculptor, Paul Harrison, a colour scientist, and Jeremy Thomas, an architect, he had set up a private discussion group to explore issues to do with geometry, formal architectonics and colour.

His interest in this direction dated at least from his Royal College dissertation on Piet Mondrian, an artist whose potentially infinite permutations of linear orthogonals and primary colour rectangles hint at the tragic impossibility of harmonic finality in art or life, and suggest a deeper, more troubling concept of geometry than that of simple ideal relations. Now Bowling had a surprising and disconcertingly original insight: 'I was looking at Mondrian', he recalled in 1975, 'and I thought the thing that would really make a Mondrian work was to incorporate the dying bird in all these squares. We [Hockney, Kitaj, Jones and others of that generation] tended to look at

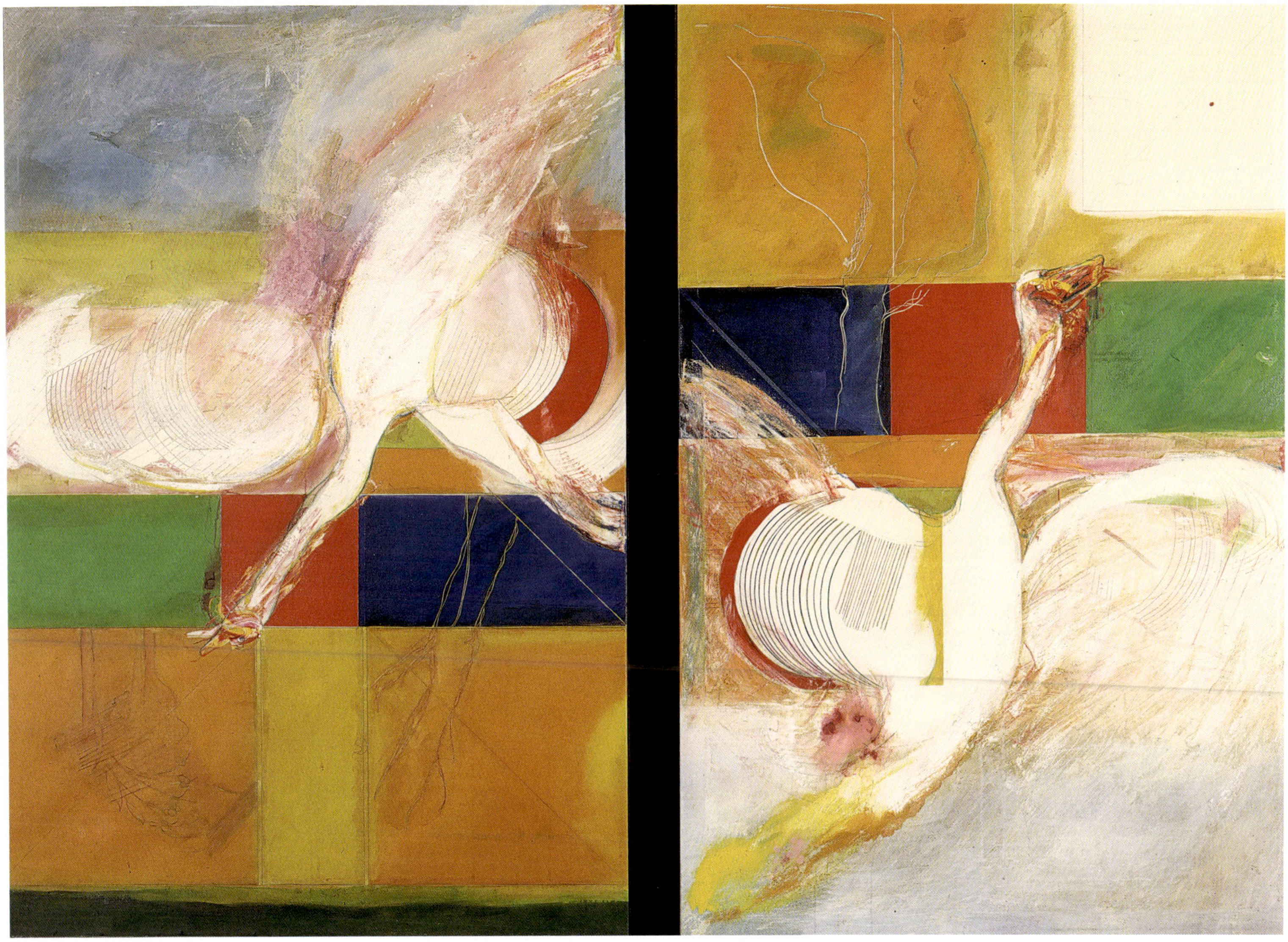

Big Bird, 1964
Oil on canvas, 74 x 144 cm

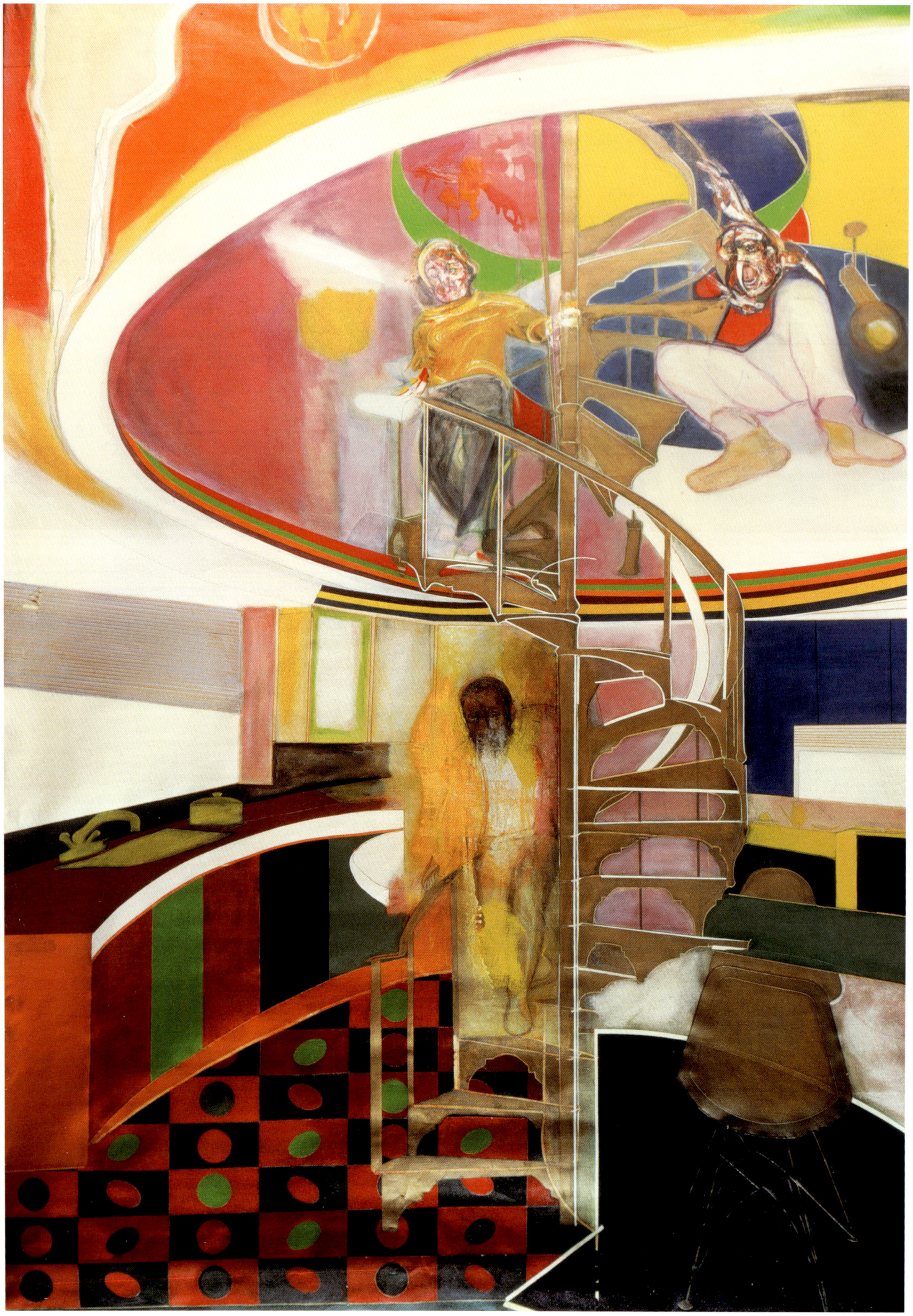

opposite
Mirror, 1964-66
Acrylic on canvas, 305 x 213 cm

abstract painting as though it was only part of the real thing.'

From this time on, Bowling avowed the importance of geometry to his work, though it is true that his uses of geometric principle have always been arbitrary: geometry may provide a formal base, a kind of ideal structure, but the contingencies of the kinetic materials, the chemical vagaries of paint and the aleatory processes of his composing invariably compromise pure geometrical principle. In the later abstract paintings, where it exists as an underlying principle, geometry is usually intimated but hidden: it is formative and constitutive rather than a matter of declarative design. And as a design principle it is based on an idea of so-called 'dynamic symmetry' rather than on static Euclidean planar geometry: that is to say, its organic principles are based on proportions and series, and on the action, reach and movement of the human body.

The titles of both *Big Bird* and *Single Bird* (1965) stress the singular subject. Each painting portrays the bloodied swan as a mirror-imaged duality in an implied double helix, each aspect being placed, as in a diptych, within its own framing rectangle. In both, the subject is set against a static geometry of sharply differentiated blocks of chromatic colour and white adumbrations of perfect circles. Thematically opposed to these colour rectangles and white discs are the swan image and a background composed of the indeterminate tonalities of clouded atmospheres, obscured in each case by a white thrashing of river water and flailing wings. These organic natural features suggest entropic dispersal and dissipation, just as the swan motif itself may be seen as an image of the divided self. (R.D. Laing's influential book, *The Divided Self*, which included vivid descriptions of psychic distress, was very much part of the *Zeitgeist* of the mid-1960s.) As in the earlier paintings, it is the life principle that is here paradoxically represented by the swans, caught up in a kinetic double helix of becoming and un-becoming – beauty *in extremis* – that contradicts the static order and clarity of Euclidean geometry. This was the very order that had so deeply troubled Mondrian. He knew only too well that the natural reality of the experienced world is messier than the abstract reality of the geometer's projections.

In 1964, the year of *Big Bird*, Bowling began work on the great summative painting described by the critic-curator Simon Wilson in an unpublished essay as 'a resounding climax to his early career … an iconic and pivotal masterpiece of British art in the 1960s.' *Mirror* (1964-66), as its title and its dates imply, is the means by which Bowling looked hard at himself and his career, without the disguise afforded by the emblematic swan, and without any suggestion of self pity, special pleading or romantic sentiment. In contemplating himself at such length, and in working and re-working the painting over a period of two years, he created a problematic poetic fable, in which a virtuosic multiplicity of styles is the reflection of circumstances at once actual and existential. In so doing, Bowling demonstratively asserted stylistic contradiction as a legitimate and effective expression of a complex consciousness and complicated external events.

From the outset, this painting has induced critical and interpretative perplexity, but Bowling had clearly decided upon the central motif of the spiral staircase as the symbolic key to its programme before beginning the work. The cast-iron spiral staircase that physically connected the creative chaos of the studios of the Royal College Painting School to the long corridor that led to the academic and historical order of the galleries of the Victoria & Albert Museum had fascinated Bowling since his first year there. It remained in his mind thereafter: 'I really found that staircase full of deep meaning… The staircase seemed symbolic, seemed to symbolise something profound in my career… I had to realise that staircase, to be able to make it real, you know, and [to] make a painting.' An earlier effort from 1964 used the central image, with the figures on the staircase, but within a simpler, less emblematically loaded geometrical space.

The descriptions and demonstrations in Jay Hambidge's *The Elements of Dynamic Symmetry* (1926), which Bowling had studied with his friends in the discussion group, were explicitly intended to provide guidance for artists. Hambidge, himself an artist, was concerned to recover the ancient design principles, or 'form rhythm', of what he called 'dynamic symmetry'. Bowling was particularly struck by Hambidge's descriptions and diagrams of the logarithmic or constant angle spiral, and though its design is not slavishly rigorous to them, *Mirror* was constructed with these diagrams in mind, and with precise regard to their symbolic or analogical potential.

To put it simply, the diagrams demonstrate that if a vertical rectangle is divided by two diagonals, one from corner to corner, creating two right-angled triangles, and the other from another corner which cuts the first at right-angles, the point at which they meet will be the pole of a (notional) infinite spiral formed by a growth principle that conforms to the Fibonacci series, as in the natural growth of a shell or in botanical phyllotaxis. It is quite simple, having drawn with exactitude this right-angled logarithmic spiral, to

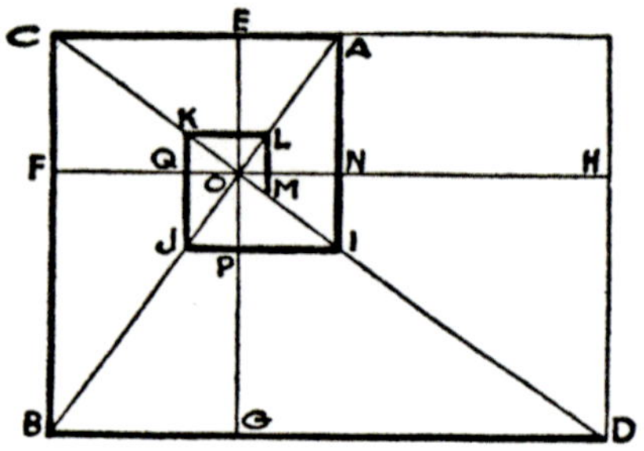

Diagram from Jay Hambidge's ***The Elements of Dynamic Symmetry***, 1926.

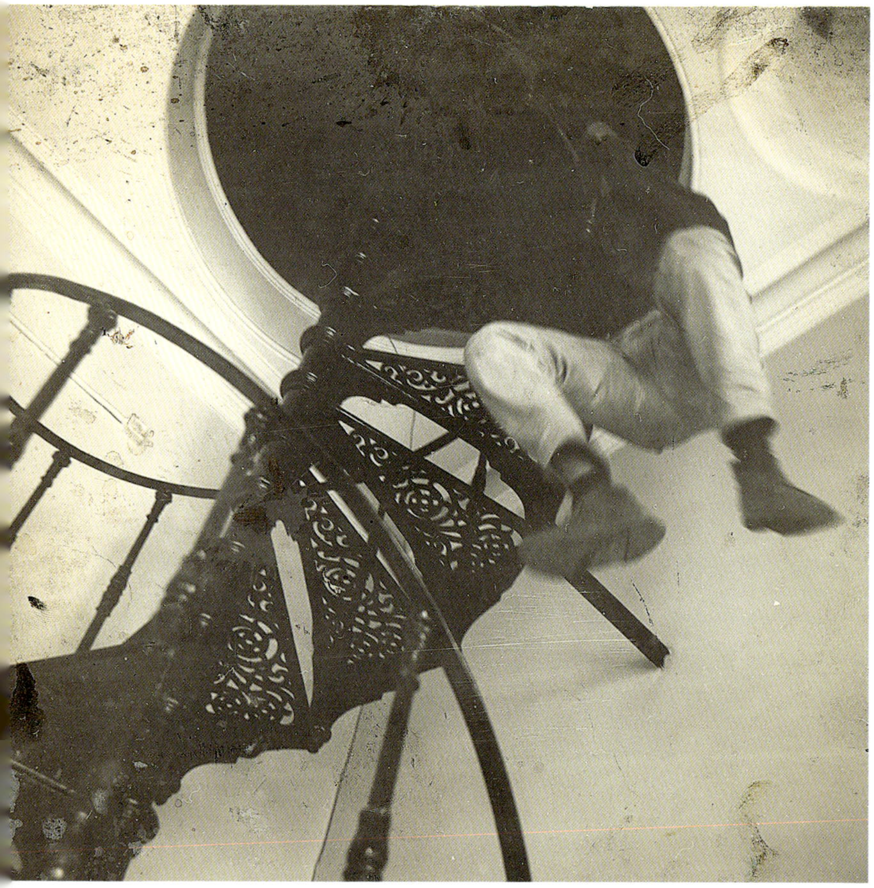

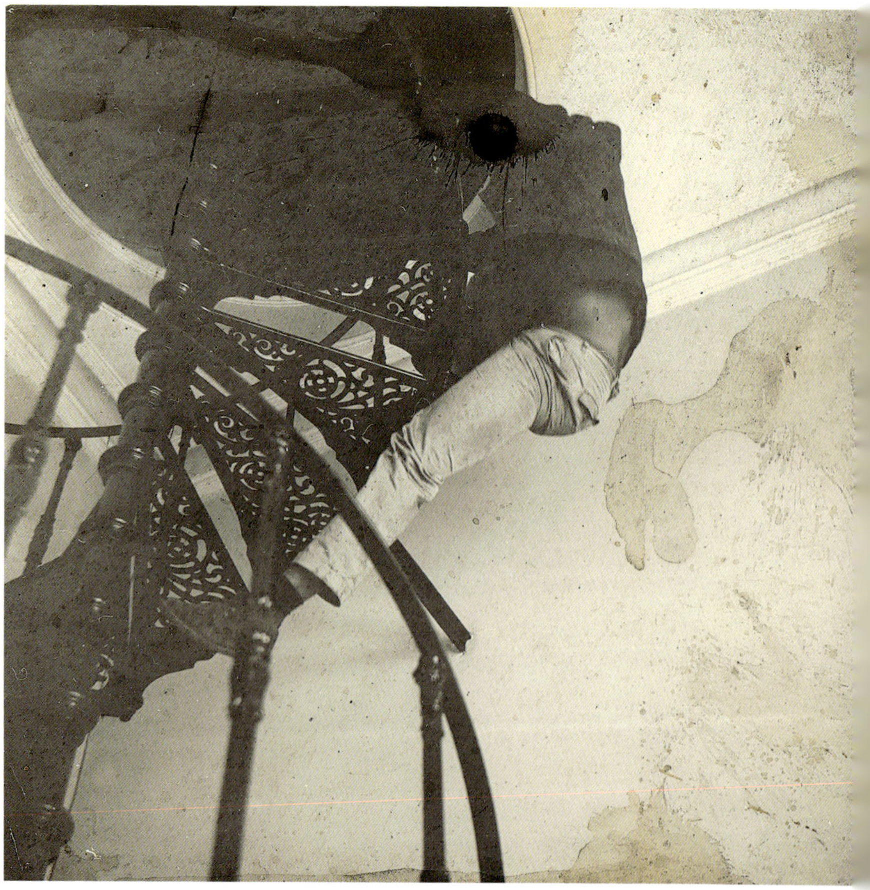

construct the curved spiral. In the painting, such a spiral is adumbrated in the exhilarating sweeping ellipse which dominates the upper section, and realised of course in the staircase itself. This central motif is schematically flattened as in a demonstrative diagram: it is a principle as well as a thing. And it is no ordinary thing: it is a golden staircase that presents the very image of dynamic growth.

Two figures are observed on the staircase, and above them a third swings out wildly into space from the handrail, close to the point at which the spiral becomes visible as it descends through the aperture in the ceiling above. This dangling man, his face angrily distorted, is a portrait of the artist. It is an image of an absurd and self-dramatising gesture of anarchic rebellion against the institutional conventions of both art and marriage, but one which must end with his clamber back on to the staircase: life goes on, just as in the spiral development of the living nautilus or plant. The figure high on the stairs, still very much in the orbit of the wayward swinger but purposefully descending on her way, is clearly recognisable as an all-too-present Paddy Kitchen.

The blurred figure at the bottom of the staircase is the artist himself at a moment of transfiguration, three steps from the staircase's arrival at the Vasarely-tiled floor of the ultra-modern, multiply styled 1960s kitchen. These three figures, in temporal terms respectively in the past, the present and disappearing into the

Photographs taken in 1964 of Bowling and Paddy Kitchen on the spiral staircase at the Royal College of Art, London.

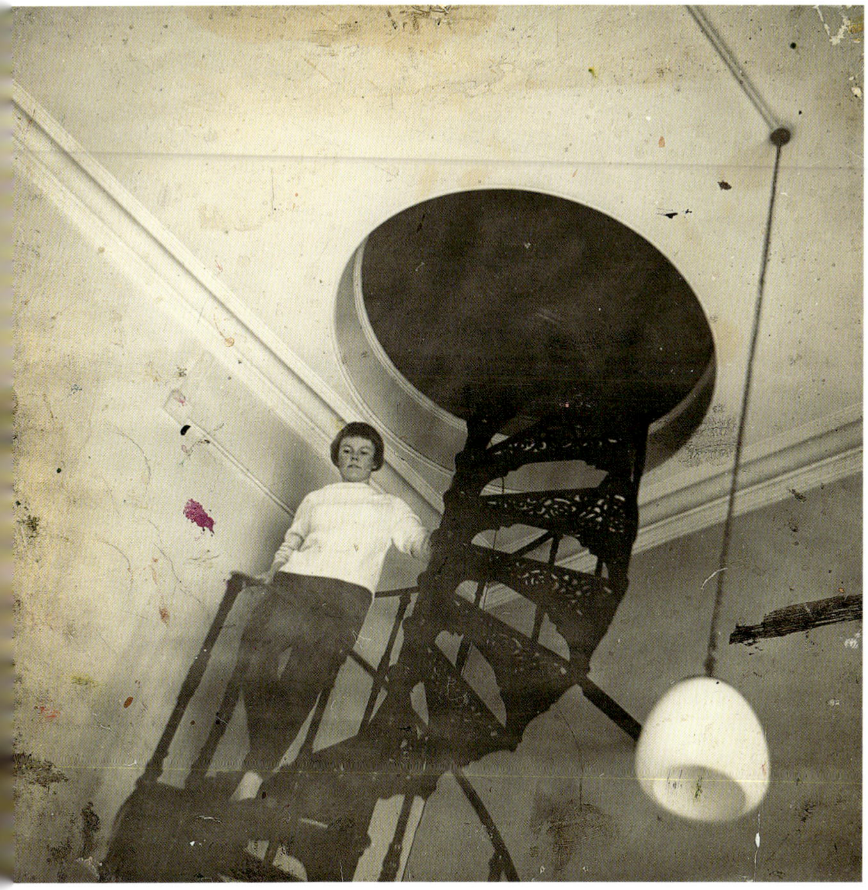

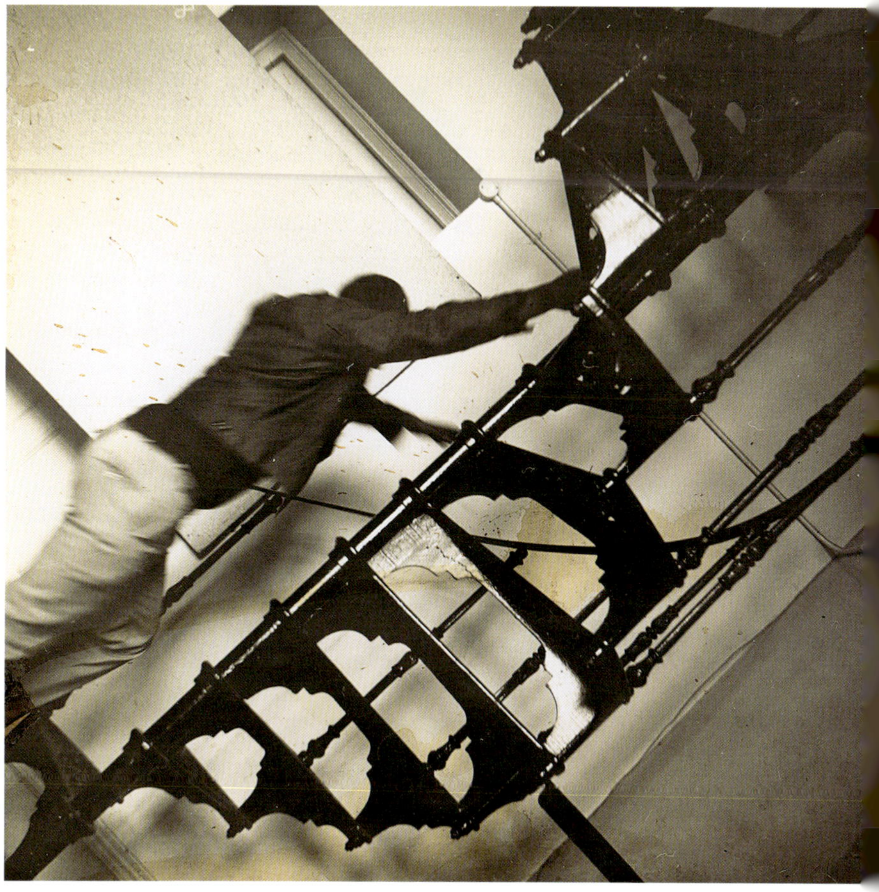

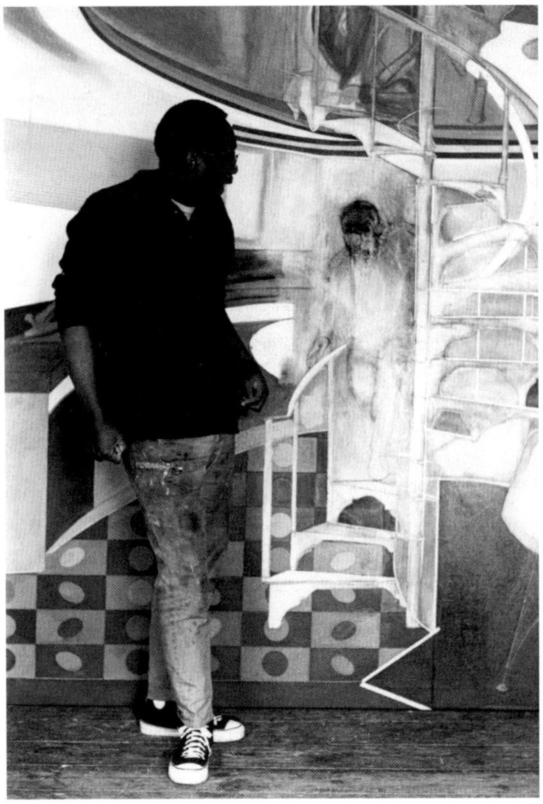

Bowling with completed ***Mirror***, 1966.

future, are rendered in the loose and painterly figurative style that Bowling is finally renouncing. This painting is its swan song.

The picture presents us with a dazzling compendium of contemporary painting styles: the dizzying range of alternatives open to an artist who at this point in the mid-'60s is opting for a non-expressionist abstract art. These stylistic elements include amorphic figure/ground abstraction (outside the upper ellipse); colour field (within the ellipse); geometric abstraction; post-painterly Kenneth Noland-like stripe painting or Peter Blake-like appropriation of commercial art; single and multi-panel monochrome painting (as in Ellsworth Kelly); op art (an extended quotation from Vasarely, rendered perfectly flat and parallel to the picture surface, without perspective); pop art (the kitchen *mise-en-scène*, sink and tap, butter dish, ceiling spotlight, the Hockney-like window and blinds at right-centre, the Charles Eames chairs, etc.).

The gold may remind us, incidentally and disconcertingly, of its iconographical significance in early Renaissance painting: this is a picture of an existential and spiritual passage, as well as of personal crisis. The concurrence within one image of events in different time frames – of things happening before and after – is another device borrowed from that earlier art.

Like a young Renaissance master, Bowling employed assistants (students from Reading) to paint the formulaic elements of the work (the Vasarely floor, for example), for this is most certainly a programmatic painting, a kind of visual manifesto. And, in keeping with earlier work, Bowling prepared for it with photographs taken quite deliberately for the purpose, though he may not at the time have known exactly what he would do with them. 'Painting from photographs was a mainstay for that generation … I began under Peter [Blake's] influence to see that I could hone my skills a great deal more. The paintings I made between 1964 and 1966 were much more tightly painted, more schematic …' Above all, Bowling was, of course, aware of Bacon's use of photographs, including those he commissioned from John Deakin of particular people in particular poses. The face and shoes of the absurd acrobat and the compositional device of the sweeping ellipse clearly parody certain aspects of the style of his erstwhile friend and mentor.

In brief, there can be no doubt that *Mirror* announces Bowling's emergence from the first London cycle of his life. The complex and contradictory *personae* of handsome, reckless, hip troublemaker, thoughtful intellectual, experimental chance-taker and troubled virtuoso are all dissolving before our very eyes. The art world of '60s London seemed perplexingly unreceptive to the paintings of an extraordinarily gifted artist who couldn't, or wouldn't, leave harsh realities – whether existential or political – out of his work. In a photograph taken when *Mirror* had just been completed, Bowling closely contemplates the image of his dematerialising, fugitive self. Shortly after, he once more departed London for New York, crossing the Atlantic with deliberate intent to make a new beginning in a new world.

opposite
Detail of ***Mirror***, 1964-66

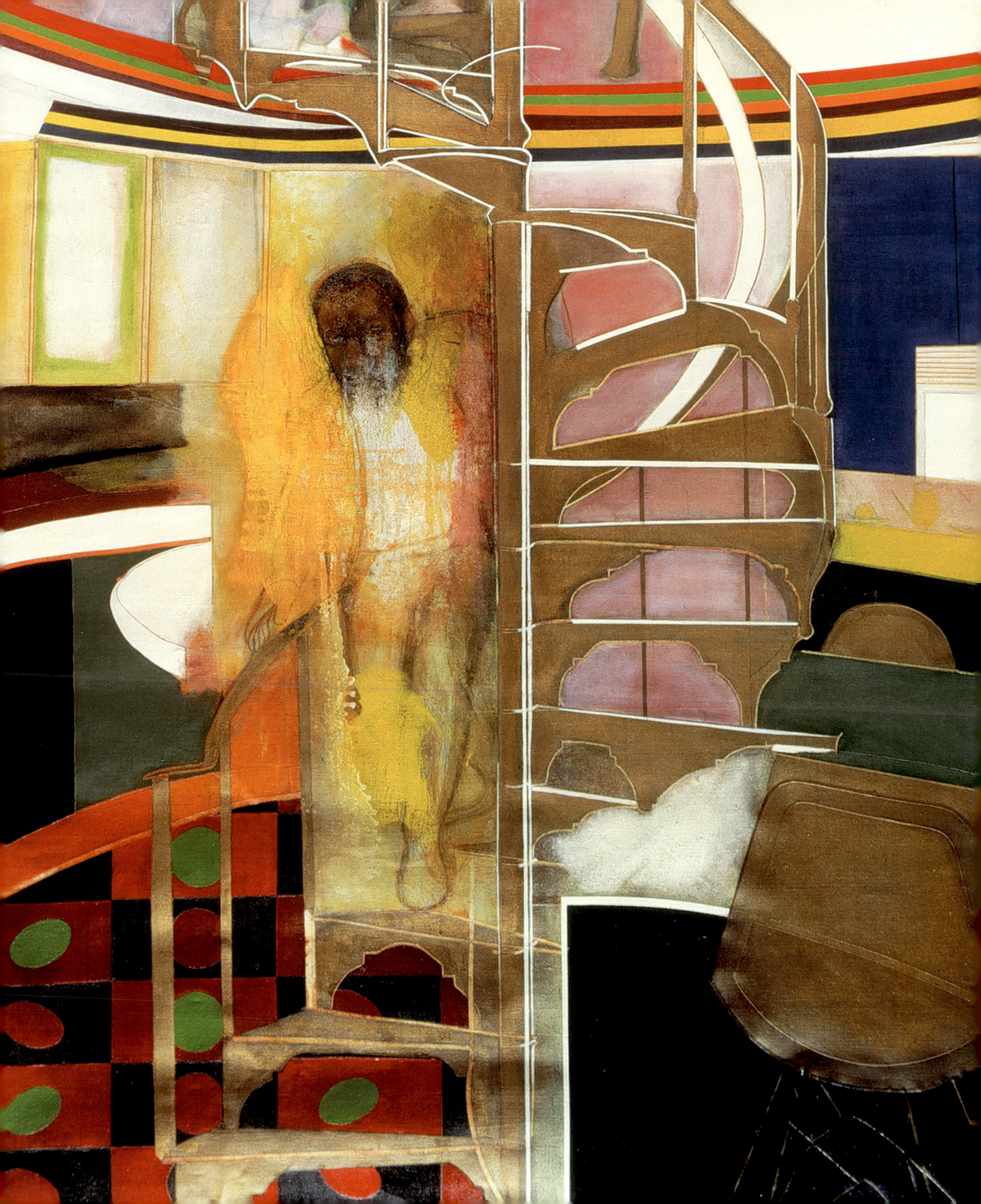

6 NEW YORK, NEW YORK!

Because he had friends there, and had found the atmosphere and the artistic camaraderie of the New York scene congenial, Bowling felt confident in 1967 about going to live and work in New York. He had already visited the city several times, staying and working at the Hotel Chelsea, a favoured venue for artists and writers and the home-from-home for a transient raggle-taggle of unconventional and otherwise displaced poets, artists, photographers and musicians. Bowling felt as at ease there, and in the New York artists' bars, as he had in the artists' pubs he frequented in London. He was nevertheless disconcerted that in New York there were distinct divisions between black and white artists and that, even in the bars frequented by both, they tended to keep apart. Bowling found, however, that his status as a black British outsider enabled him to move easily between the two groups.

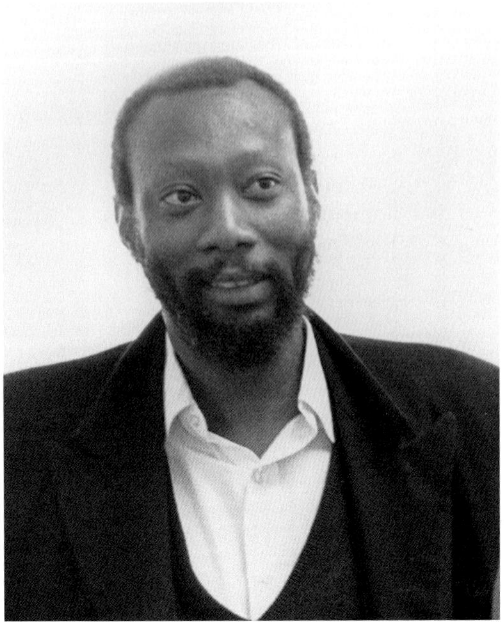

Frank Bowling at the *5+1* show, State University of New York, Stony Brook, 1969.

During an extended visit in 1965, he had been actively encouraged to migrate to New York by the poet-critics John Ashbery and Frank O'Hara (who was also a charismatic curator at the Museum of Modern Art), the poet Kenneth Koch and the painter Larry Rivers. It was thanks to a generous intervention by O'Hara that when Bowling arrived at the Chelsea in late summer 1966, Stanley Bard (the owner) was expecting him, and installed him in a room-cum-studio. 'When I asked [him] how much it cost, and he told me, I couldn't believe that anyone would think I had that kind of money. So I sat him down and told him what I could afford, and he said "Don't worry, don't worry, don't worry: we can make a trade." ' Shortly before Bowling arrived, O'Hara, at just 40 years old, died in an accident on Fire Island.

In all things an ironist and a provocateur, Larry Rivers was to be a crucial and influential mentor and a generous friend. He was a jazz musician, a poet and a brilliant and idiosyncratic draughtsman and painter who had been one of the key initiators of pop art, his own brand of which was a kind of controlled anarchy of styles in which he combined poetic juxtapositions, personal references, free-form quotation from high, low and popular art, and political parodies of big historical themes. His quick, edgy wit, his politics, his rebellious temperament, his musical and poetic gifts, his love of chance and his technical virtuosity chimed well with Bowling's inclinations and ambitions. Rivers was a quintessential New Yorker, and through him Bowling had an immediate *entrée* into the city's most lively culture. At this time, through Rivers, Bowling also met Jasper Johns, whose deep games with sign, stencilled word and enigmatic image made an impact upon a mind seeking new ways of knowing and new ways of making art.

There were, naturally, mixed impulses behind Bowling's transatlantic passage. Powerful among them was the attraction of an informal comradeship among the many artists he knew in New York 'who happened to be black' (as he ironically recalled many years later) and with whom Bowling had forged links on his earlier visits. Theirs was a solidarity intensified by their own embattled position as abstractionist modernists within a larger black visual arts community in the States which at that charged historical moment was looking for art to demonstrate a visible commitment to the civil rights movement, and expected that identification to be expressed in figurative or symbolic terms. There were also organised moves afoot to press for proper representation of black artists in public institutions such as the Museum of Modern Art, the Metropolitan Museum of Art and the Whitney Museum of American Art.

No such organised black artistic community existed in London, where Bowling had come to feel that he was regarded as an exotic. The Caribbean Artists Movement was mainly literary in inspiration and did not come into formal existence until late 1966, after his departure. Indeed it was his growing sense of exclusion and isolation as a visual artist that provided the primary negative impetus for his move. 'I thought my career path here was being blocked', he said many years later. 'If I hadn't gone to New York I wouldn't have been able to develop as an artist.'

Bowling's career in London was perhaps faltering, but for reasons it is difficult to identify with precision: it certainly seemed to be unconnected with the quality of the art he was producing or the interest it aroused. In that year, 1966, he was persuaded by Roland Penrose (who shortly after bought a painting for his own collection) and Bryan Robertson to submit the diptych *Big Bird* (1964) to represent the UK at the *First World Festival of Negro Arts* at Dakar in Senegal. At first he resisted what he felt was a subtly limiting placement, but his painting went nevertheless to the great Léopold Senghor's celebration of *négritude*, where it won the Grand Prize. At the 1966 *Summer Exhibition* at the Royal Academy, *Mirror* won the Painting of the Year award. Bowling was also a respected member of the London Group, with which he regularly exhibited.

He had, though, been disappointed not to be able to find a dealer who would operate more effectively than Grabowski within the mainstream London commercial scene, and he had noted, with troubled puzzlement, his exclusion from major exhibitions. In the polite, middle-class exchanges characteristic of English socio-cultural discourse, it is sometimes difficult to pinpoint a specific occasion of discrimination within the operations of unconscious or unspoken prejudice. But his friend Bryan Robertson had remarked sometime in 1964 (the year of the first *New Generation* exhibition) that 'England is not ready for a gifted artist of colour.'

Bowling has attested that Robertson himself (notwithstanding Robertson's exclusion of his work from the New Generation show) and several artist-administrators, Carel Weight, Robert Medley and Claude Rogers among them, had been actively encouraging and helpful to his career. He recognised moreover that neither his entry into art schools, nor his early success in the art world (which included his two teaching posts) had in any way been hindered by his background and colour. Whatever the case may be, Bowling has usually spoken without rancour of his decision to migrate west, and wryly acknowledges that it is difficult to identify any specific act of racism as responsible for the setbacks his career suffered in England during the mid-'60s.

In fact, there were powerfully subjective factors, both personal and professional, at play in his decision to relocate to New York: the crisis in his marriage; a certain personal uncertainty and complexity of spirit, reflected, as we have seen, in his creative work; above all, perhaps, the discovery that there was a raw vitality and competitive edge to the New York creative-critical scene that suited his

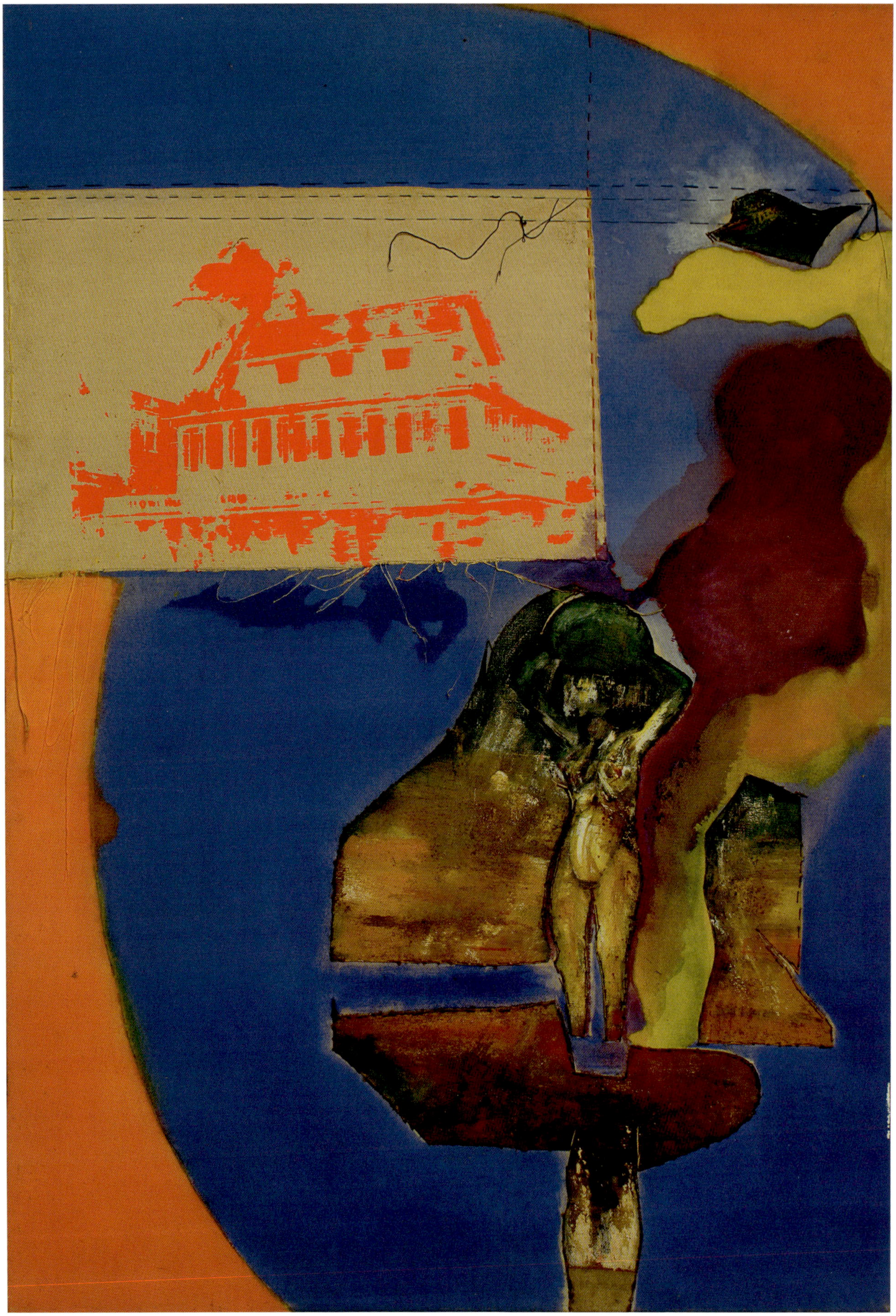

opposite
***Barticabather*, 1966-67**
Oil and stitched canvas on canvas,
148 x 102 cm

temperament. He was seeking new stimuli and a new direction, and New York seemed to offer just those possibilities. Other artists among his talented contemporaries were also responding at precisely this time to the magnetic pull of the American art world, most notably David Hockney, Richard Smith and John Hoyland. Bowling's arrival was preceded propitiously by his first solo show in New York, at Terry Dintenfass Gallery, in January 1966, which presented a number of his earlier expressionist-figurative paintings.

The critic Lawrence Alloway, who had been highly influential in promoting American abstract painting in England and was now a curator at the Guggenheim Museum in New York, had set the new critical mood in 1960: 'American art is not an exotic national style. It is the mainstream of modern art, which used to run through Paris.' For Bowling in the mid-'60s, New York was where the most interesting and challenging action was. 'New York', he later recalled, 'seemed like the centre of the modern world in terms of modernist philosophy. The best public thinkers were all there.'

Once there, he set to work to re-create himself as a painter. Paintings from his first months in the city understandably spring from pop art influences, the geometric interests and the wilful stylistic contradictions that had characterised his art over the previous two years. Paintings such as *Barticabather* (1966-67) and *My Guyana* (1966-67) combined stitched-on collage fragments of earlier figurative work with the screenprint images of 'mother's house'. It was as if he was loath to let go of the familiar and cast himself into completely unbroached territory.

Other paintings from this time, such as *Mother's House with Beware of the Dog* (1966) and *Bowling's Variety Store* (1967), contain ironically self-referential features; in these the geometry is regular and determined, and both the planes of colour and the divisions between

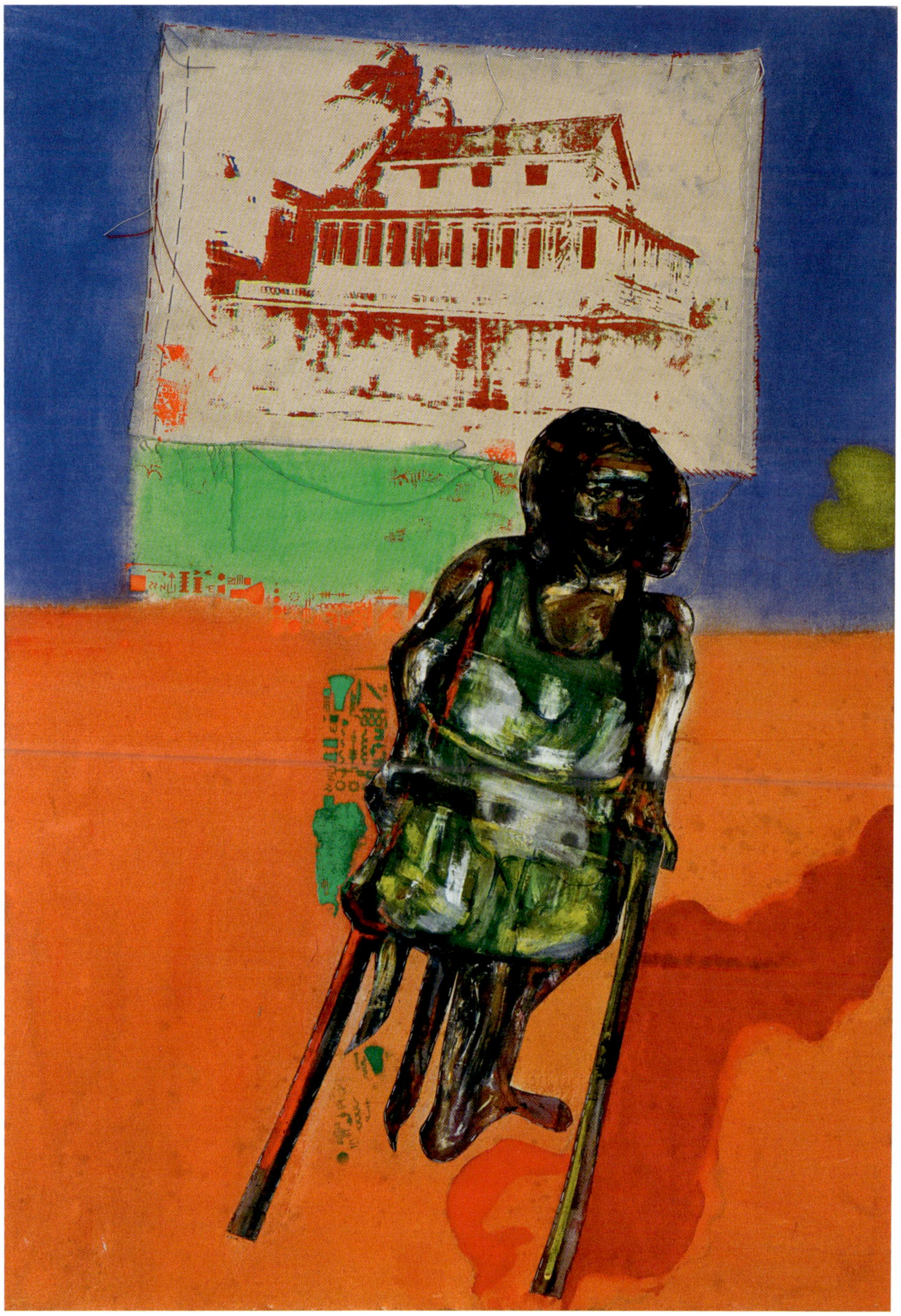

***My Guyana*, 1966-67**
Oil on canvas, 143.5 x 120.5 cm

opposite
***Mother's House with Beware of the Dog*, 1966**
Acrylic on canvas, 143.5 x 120.5 cm

them are clear and definite. Yet each painting has the feel of disguise about it, as if it is coded in some way inaccessible to the viewer. This is an aspect of Bowling's painting we have encountered before: a habit of ambiguity, a propensity for hidden meaning. It is of a piece with the striving in his work of the previous years to free his art from the literalism of any one-to-one correspondence, and to create a multivalent imagery, fruitfully ambiguous and obscure. Pure abstraction beckoned, but he was not yet ready to succumb to its call.

In *Mother's House with Beware of the Dog*, the top half is dominated by a tumultuous screen-printed image of his mother's house, its windows and the windswept palm tree in red, as if the house were engulfed in fire, while an absurd rat-like figure (a dog?) is inserted into the arbitrary geometric spaces of the lower half, and the vertically stencilled fairground lettering delivers the cheerfully multicolour *cave canem* warning. There is a kind of quasi-surreal inconsequentiality to this image; its programme (for there certainly seems to be one) is enigmatic. *Bowling's Variety Store* replaces the subject-image with its stencilled title, hinting both at the artist's own virtuosity and at his uncertainty as to style and content. Against the void of a Hockney blue sky, the lower right rectangle suggests the back of an empty canvas. What is to be the next act in this variety show?

As often happens in an artist's progress, a combination of chance and circumstance set Bowling on a course that would lead quickly to the creation of a style and imagery at once distinctive and resonant with the times. After several more paintings which juxtaposed the stencilled words 'Variety Store' with colourful if somewhat arbitrarily geometric abstractions, in the spring of 1967 Bowling's search for a new way of painting led him to experiment with thin acrylic washes flooded over a canvas spread on the floor,

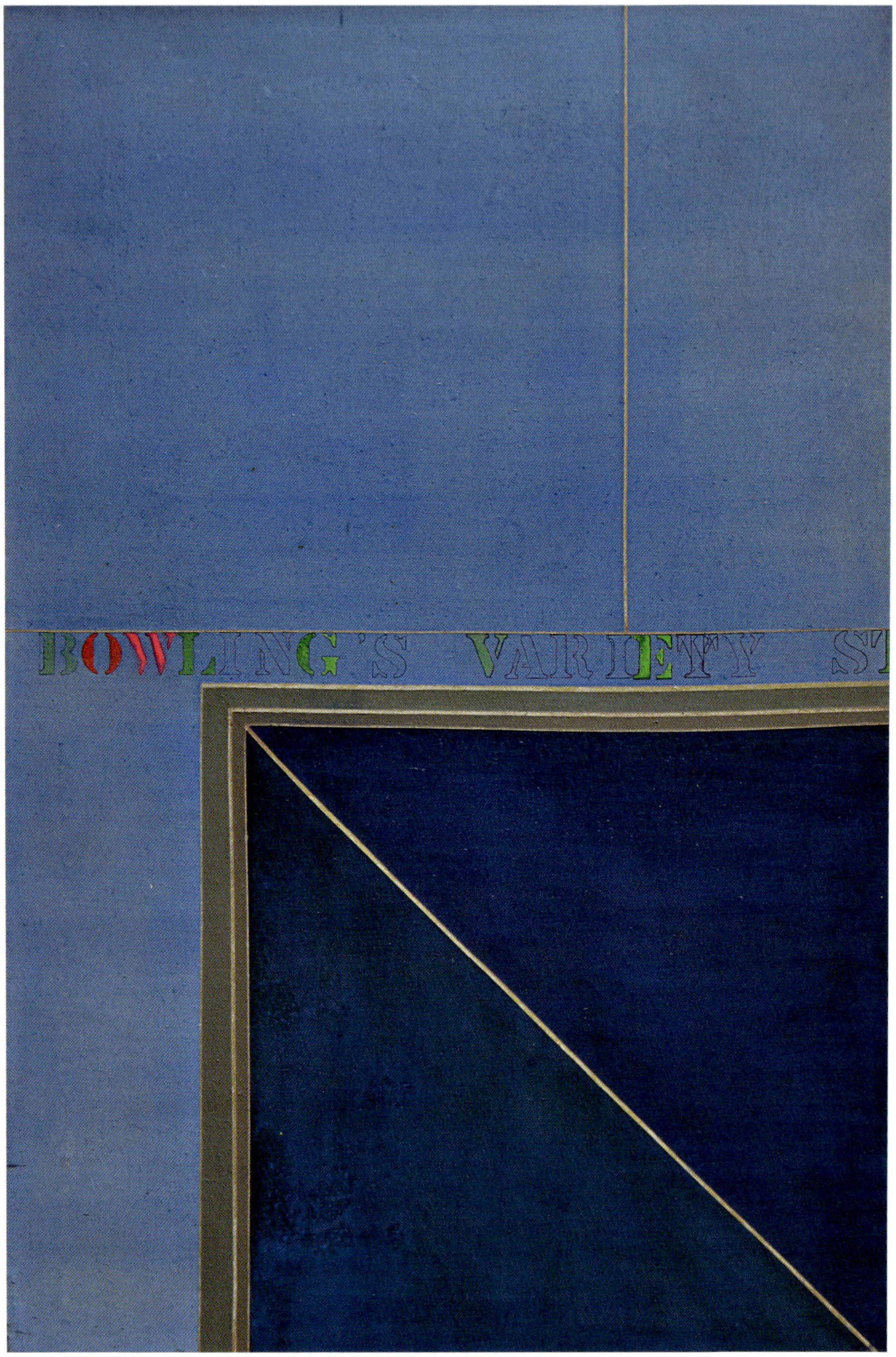

***Bowling's Variety Store*, 1967**
Acrylic on canvas, 120.5 x 79 cm

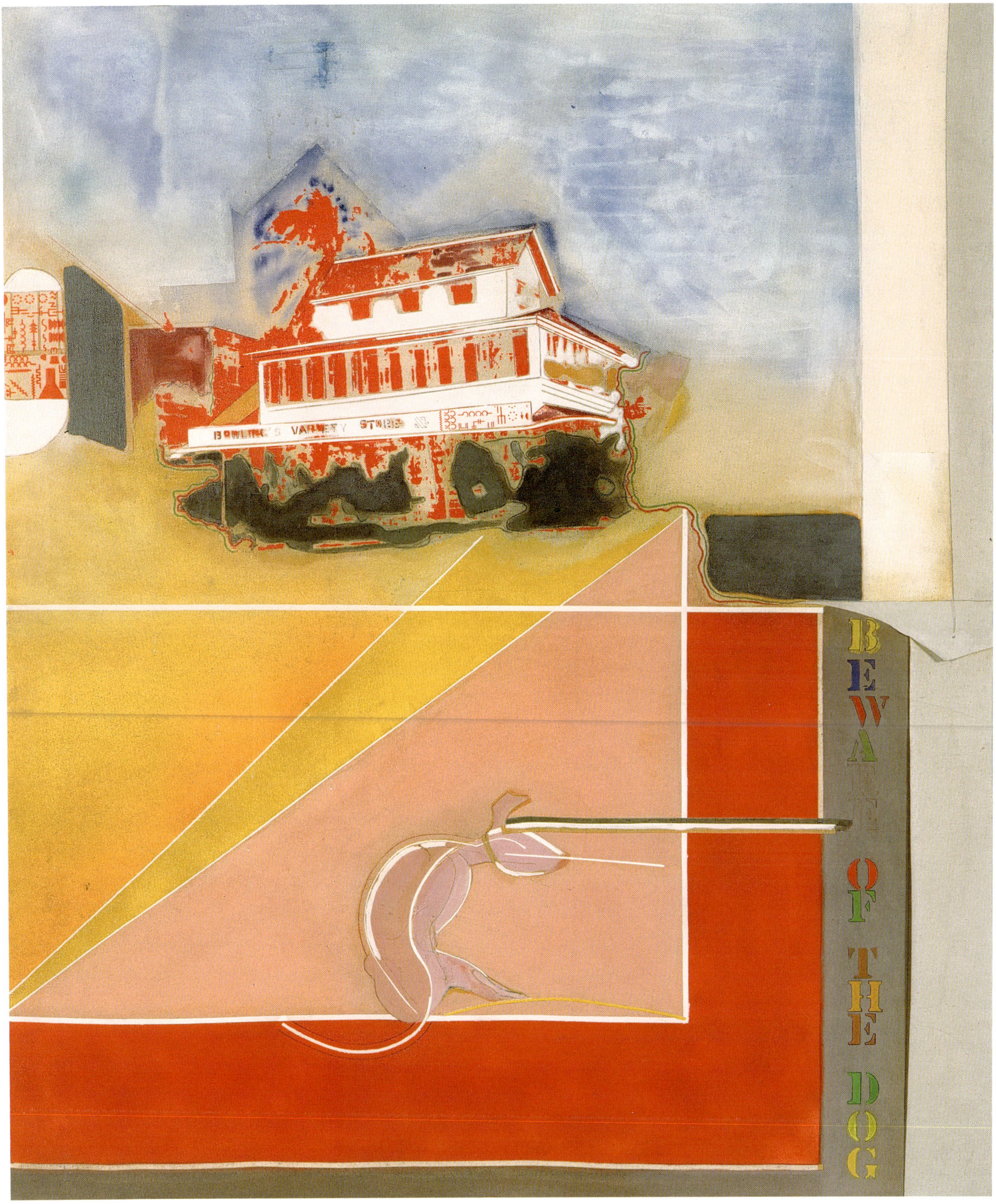
BEWA
OF THE DOG

sometimes incorporating the 'mother's house' motif, sometimes not. Using the shifting shadows thrown by the window light as a guide to shape the liquid movement, Bowling noticed how often those shapes assumed the vague look, first of General de Gaulle (then in the news over the *Québec Libre* affair) and then, more significantly, of the outline map of South America. Following this lead, he began also to create the shape of Guyana, still imprinted in his visual memory by endless drawing exercises at primary school. Later in the year Bowling was taught by Rivers to use an overhead projector to create accurate outline drawings of South America and Guyana.

7 MAPS, HISTORIES AND POLEMICS

'The origin of something is the source of its nature.'
MARTIN HEIDEGGER

With these two simple map images (he later added an outline of Africa, and then of other continents, to his repertoire of map-signs), Bowling had found a motif-idea that was not a 'subject' as such, but was charged with thematic possibilities. The image of the map had, of course, a history in recent New York painting: his friends Jasper Johns and Larry Rivers had both used maps, albeit in quite different ways. Maps are immediately recognisable; like flags or targets, they are common visual property, being, as Johns remarked, 'things that the mind already knows'. Their denotations (except in cases of dispute) are abstract, simple and value-free, but they carry connotations as diverse as the histories and world-views of those who recognise them. Johns also observed: 'Everyone is of course free to interpret the work in his own way. I think seeing a picture is one thing and interpreting it is another.'

Bowling now had to hand a number of readymade motifs. These included 'mother's house' and images of his mother and of his son Dan, and map outlines of the continent and the country of his origin. On the one hand there were microcosmic memory-signs, on the other, there were macrocosmic geo-historical signs: the former deeply personal in signficance, the latter objective and instantly recognisable as outline maps of that southern half of the Americas that was not 'American'. Repetition of these signs, especially when placed in enigmatic juxtaposition, created a kind of identity for the artist, but one whose character remained as yet indeterminate. They might seem autobiographical, suggesting a local personal history set against an impersonal continental vastness, but they have no discernible narrative, and have no tendentious political agenda.

The paintings were, of course, materially present, taking the stand, so to speak, on the gallery wall, but they did not testify, or imply a view of the world. They were art works, not political statements. They were expressive of no position except that of engagement with certain aspects of the recent histories of American painting. It was this purely artistic engagement – the need Bowling felt to find a visual style and manner of his own within what he regarded as the most vital living discourse of painting – that fired him with the ambition to make abstract paintings. If they were any good, then they would create their own dynamics of meaning within the immediate historical moment of critical encounter, whether in the present or the future.

In the late '60s, much of the potency of these remarkable paintings derived from their enigmatic ambiguity, their provocative neutrality. And that power had, undeniably, a profoundly political cast. It provided the spectacle – and these are spectacular paintings – of a black artist committed to a form of quasi-abstraction that, notwithstanding its resort to the emblematic sign, was obdurate in its refusal of any clearly figurative or symbolic expression of an overtly political kind. Their historical significance persists in this aspect of ambiguity, of neutrality. Stencilling and epidiascope-tracing are both mechanically mediated procedures which abnegate the personal mark and thereby evade any inference of autobiographical or emotive expression. The traced and stencilled signs in these paintings are purely denotative.

The map paintings do not register any directly political response to the cruelty, pity and sorrow of black history in the Americas or elsewhere within the Atlantic ambit, nor do they carry any reference to the heroics of resistance. This does not in any way preclude readings of the paintings in which that history resonates: in the quasi-abstraction of the map paintings connotation is all; 'seeing' is one thing, 'interpreting' is another. Bowling was well aware of myriad interpretative possibilities, he might even provoke them, but he did not intend his paintings to be politically declarative. The power of the map paintings, like that of dreams (and indeed they increasingly acquired a dream-like countenance), lies precisely in the freedom they confer on the spectator to invest them with meanings and values.

They most certainly succeed in acknowledging the ineluctable and motive force of history, and the significance of his own origins, both racial and geographic, in the artist's life and art. They evince the Heideggerian insight that no art can be free of its double origin: 'The artist is the origin of the work. The work is the origin of the artist. Neither is without the other.' In this sense they are almost elementally assertive in the deliberation of their allegiance to art as itself defining human existence, a living register of Heidegger's 'being-in-the-world', each such condition of 'being' having its unique origins. This is precisely what Bowling meant when he later wrote of his commitment to formalist abstraction: '[The] practice of painting within the boundaries of Formalism provides a setting in which I am able to test and ultimately prove my own freedom.'

It was during this period, more precisely from 1969 to 1972, that Bowling was most active as a critic-polemicist, engaging in a lively defence of abstract formalism as a legitimate creative option for black artists. This was at a time when there was an urgency in the call – from museums and activist artists and critics – for a recognisably 'black art' defined by overtly social and political concerns and accessible to the black public engaging in the increasingly radical and angry movement towards racial equality. Bowling's

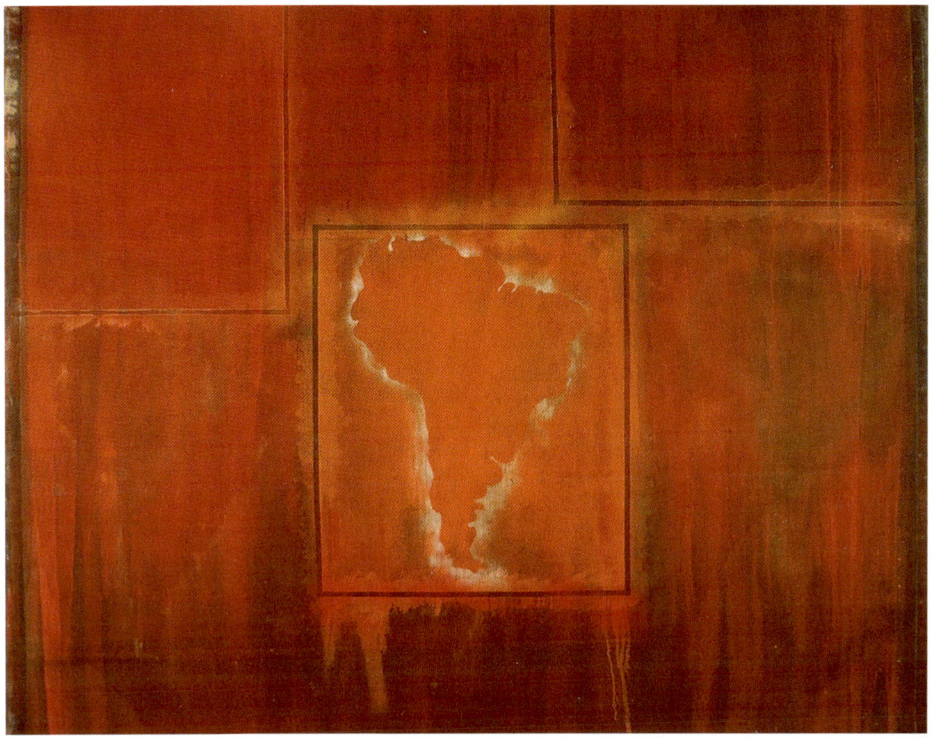

South America Squared, 1967
Acrylic on canvas, 233.5 x 269 cm

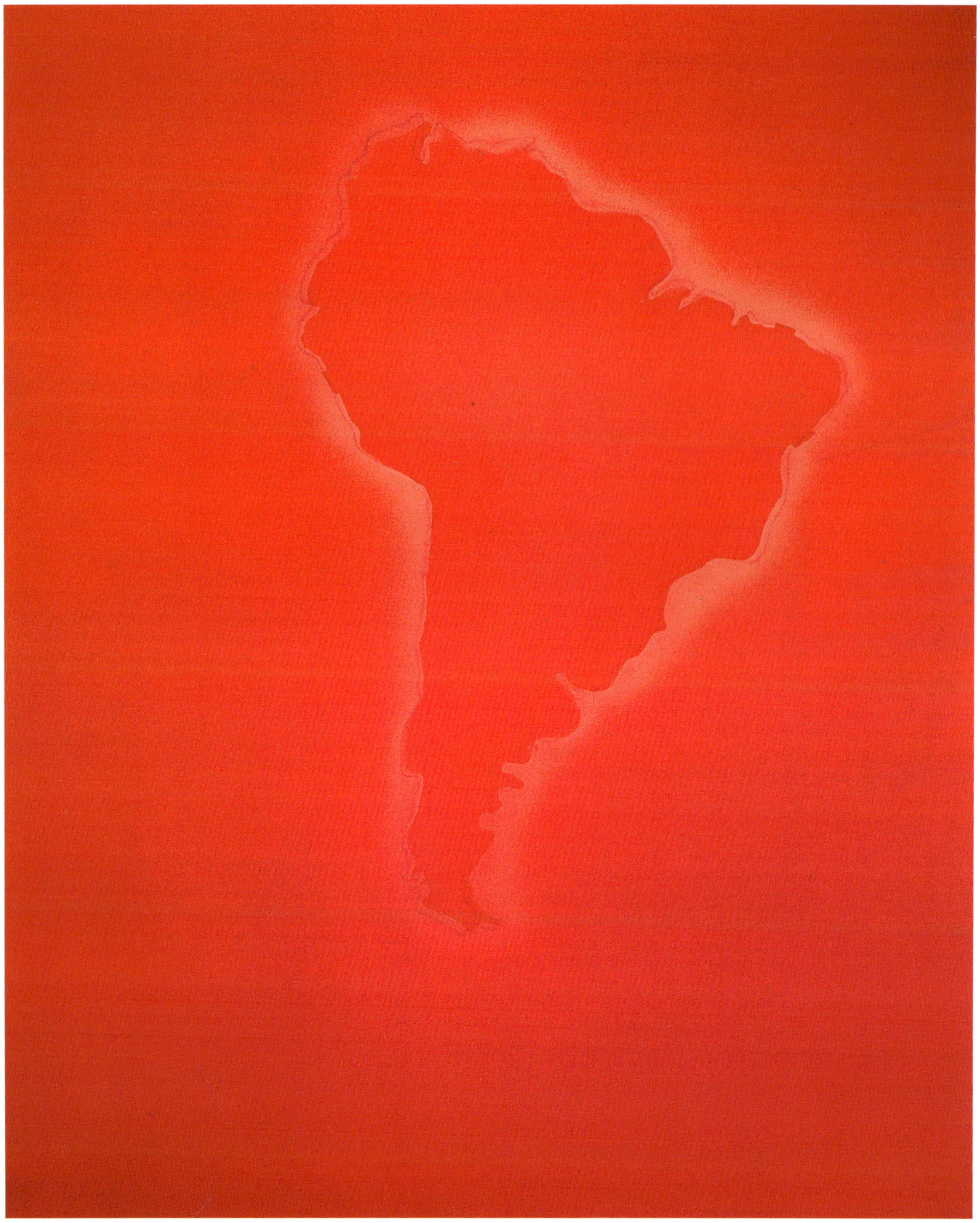

***False Start*, 1967**
Acrylic on canvas, 162.5 x 129.5 cm

writings make clear that he regarded his own practice as falling within, or moving into, the ambit of a modernist formalism, with a historical justification for abstraction reaching back beyond abstract expressionism, consisting largely of white-male existential heroics of gesture and intent, to the classic radical impersonality of European objective abstraction, and to the Russian *avant-garde*, from Malevich and suprematism to El Lissitzky, Ivan Kliun, Vladimir Tatlin *et al.* His intense admiration for Hans Hofmann was of a piece with this.

He detected similar historicity and antecedence in the work of the black abstractionist William T. Williams, for example, of whose brilliantly dynamic colour geometries he wrote: 'The influence on Williams' work, for very special reasons, was *not* Abstract-Expressionism. Instead it appears to have been European abstraction of the hard-won sort, represented by people like Albers, or even Johannes Itten. There is something (an attitude, a drive in so much of this energy) recalling the force of the Bauhaus ... More important, however, compare Williams' jazzy, jagged 1968-69 works with Lissitzky or Malevich and one gets a near equivalent of that circle-and-square tyranny dominating the intentful works of the Russians.'

For Bowling himself, as for Williams and other black artist comrades, such as Mel Edwards the sculptor and the painter Jack Whitten, the question of authenticity, of truth to origins, was not to be confused with any particular style or manner. Reflecting many years later on the greatly contentious issue of social and political (usually figurative) relevance versus abstraction, Williams said: 'For me during that period, it wasn't a question of being this or that. It was a question of this body of work that was coming out of me as a human being and as an artist. Now it's relevant to anyone who's sensitive enough to see and understand what I'm doing.' Mel Edwards (in the same discussion) responded immediately: 'I think all art is abstract. [We're] really talking about post-civil rights movement, post-1950s and '60s, the spirit and cultural work of black people. Some people were trying to be sure that it was useful, that art could be like a tool, or had a place. For me that wasn't a problem. I know that the earliest art of human beings was figurative *and* abstract. Period. So there was never a time that human beings didn't deal with both modes.'

Bowling's formal discoveries in 1967 (at precisely the moment that he was leaving behind an overtly politically engaged figurative style) released a flood of creative energies, and from that year through to 1972 it was the map theme that at last gave him the scope to find an unfettered freedom to use colour as colour, unconstricted by planar geometry, unconstrained by descriptive or symbolic purpose. He turned for inspiration to the great colour fields of Barney Newman and Mark Rothko, without regard to the purely abstract metaphysics and symbolic ambitions of the former or the lachrymose spirituality of the latter. It was as if he had taken to heart (and mind) the oddly apt words of Patrick Heron, the purest abstractionist of the previous British generation of painters, who in 1963 had declared: 'Painting has still a continent left to explore, in the direction of colour and in no other direction ... It seems obvious to me that we are still only at the beginning of our discovery and enjoyment of superbly exciting facts of the world of colour. One reels at the colour possibilities now: the varied and contrasting intensities, opacities, transparencies; the seeming density and weight, warmth, coolness, vibrancy...'

For Heron, colour as form was enough in itself – an end in itself, a subject in itself. For Rothko and Newman, it was emphatically not so; for them, it was a means to achieve mythical or spiritual expression. In his map paintings, Bowling depended on the informal scaffolding and compositional anchors delivered by the map outlines and 'mother's house' stencils to create the formal focus provided by characteristic shapes of colour in both Heron and Rothko, and by vertical elements in Newman. Not surprisingly, however, it was not long before critical responses to his work had in a sense politicised it, and Bowling himself recognised that his use of certain key motifs, and in some cases his use of colour, could indeed be read in political terms, however vague. He remained adamant, though, in his essential stance: 'It is easier to *say* than to *paint* the thesis that works from black hands and psyches have a distinct stamp. The measure of honesty an artist brings to his work cannot be too much stressed.' In the map paintings, in fact, the deployment of his motifs and use of colour proved to be infinitely flexible and various, and both could provoke for the viewer diverse connotations.

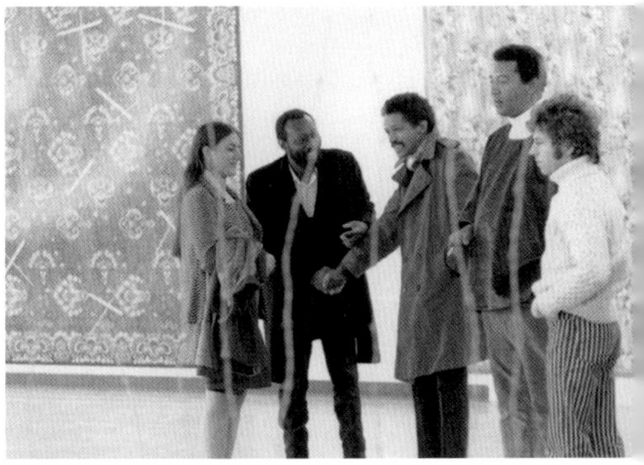

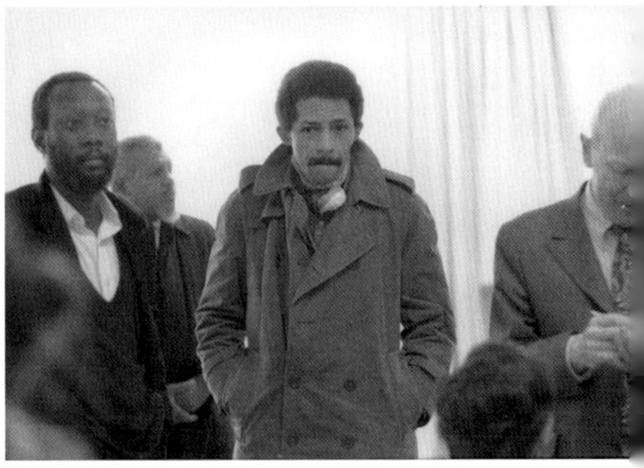

Frank Bowling at the ***5+1*** show, with Jack Whitten and Al Loving (top) and Jack Whitten and Lawrence Alloway (above), State University of New York, Stony Brook, 1969.

Sometimes a motif is isolated, as in one of the first of the map paintings, *South America Squared* (1967), in which the map is contained within a framing device that Bowling would subsequently use sparingly, sometimes almost invisibly, and which he felt free to abandon at will as he moved forward to the exhilarations of expansive, unfenced fields and undammed flows of rich and complex colour. The startling *False Start* (1967) heralds this freedom from geometric structures, as well as from any naturalistic reference. There is no constraining linear framework for the free-standing map shape and defiant, all-over commercial day-glow oranges and luminescent shocking pinks. It is pure sign, a fluorescent emblem without a moral in an open field without reference.

In other paintings the map-motifs are stepped down or repeated rhythmically across the canvas, doubled or tripled, as if to emphasise their mechanical repeatability as motifs, their schematic origins, their neutrality of intent and

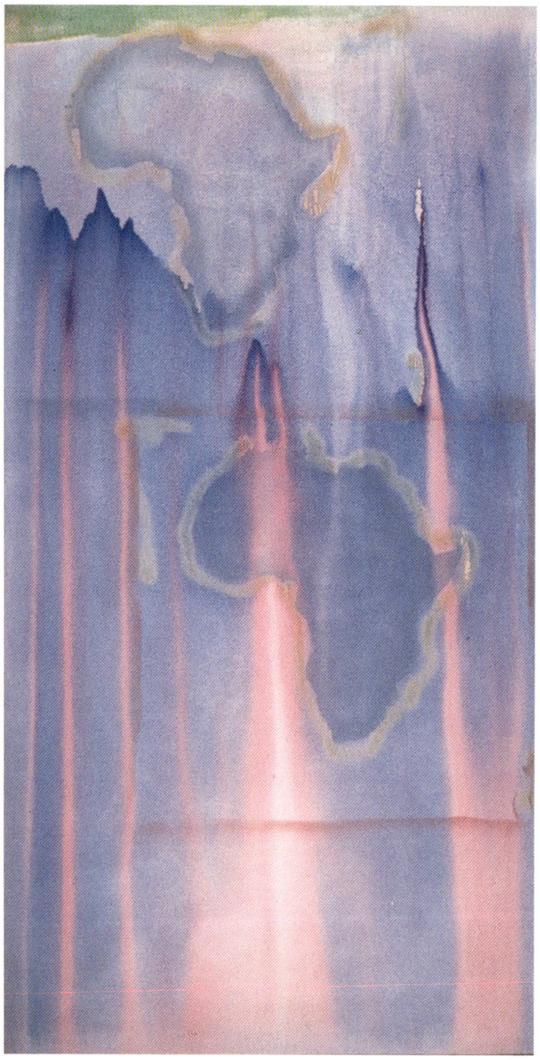

far left
***Bartica Born I*, 1968**
Acrylic on canvas, 263 x 122 cm

left
***Bartica Born III*, 1968**
Acrylic on canvas, 289 x 137 cm

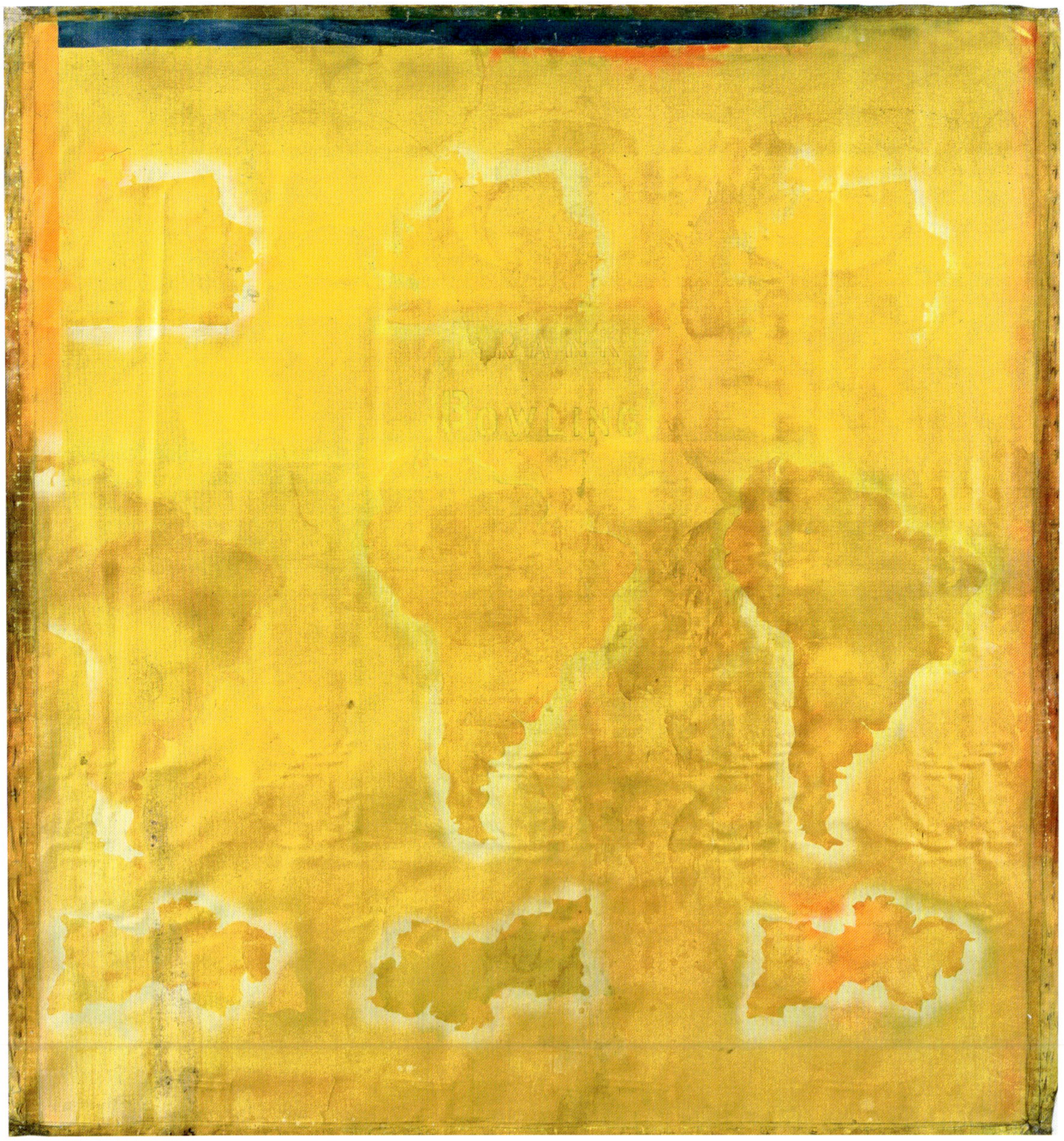

Mel Edwards Decides, 1968
Acrylic on canvas, 305 x 305 cm

their openness to unpremeditated response. In *Bartica Born I* (1968), Africa makes its first appearance: behind flowing vertical veils of blue wash over dawn pinks, the shadowy outlines of the continent shimmer like ghosts or emanations in complications of light, shadow and colour. Bowling is the Bartica-born of the title, of course, Africa an origin once-removed and dreamed of: it is an unavoidable inference, but it carries no further charge or implication.

Vertical veils of colour-wash characterise *Bartica Born III* (1968), in which the image (that is, the image presented by the whole canvas) is created out of processes of diffusion – staining, streaking, shadowing – giving these works the atmospheric insubstantiality of dreams, and the maps emerge as nothing more than a vague, intangible presence. In *Mel Edwards Decides* (1968), all three motifs – 'mother's house', South America and Guyana – regularly ranged across the canvas, are ghosts sunk in a field of gold-yellow, laid on layers of under-painting, whose richness is emphasised by the arbitrary strip of royal blue at the top of the canvas.

As time went by, Bowling hinted more insistently at possibilities of reference, both political and personal. Thus *Who's Afraid of Barney Newman* (1968) resembles a tricolour flag, its colours those of Rastafari in which red signifies the blood of martyrs, green the

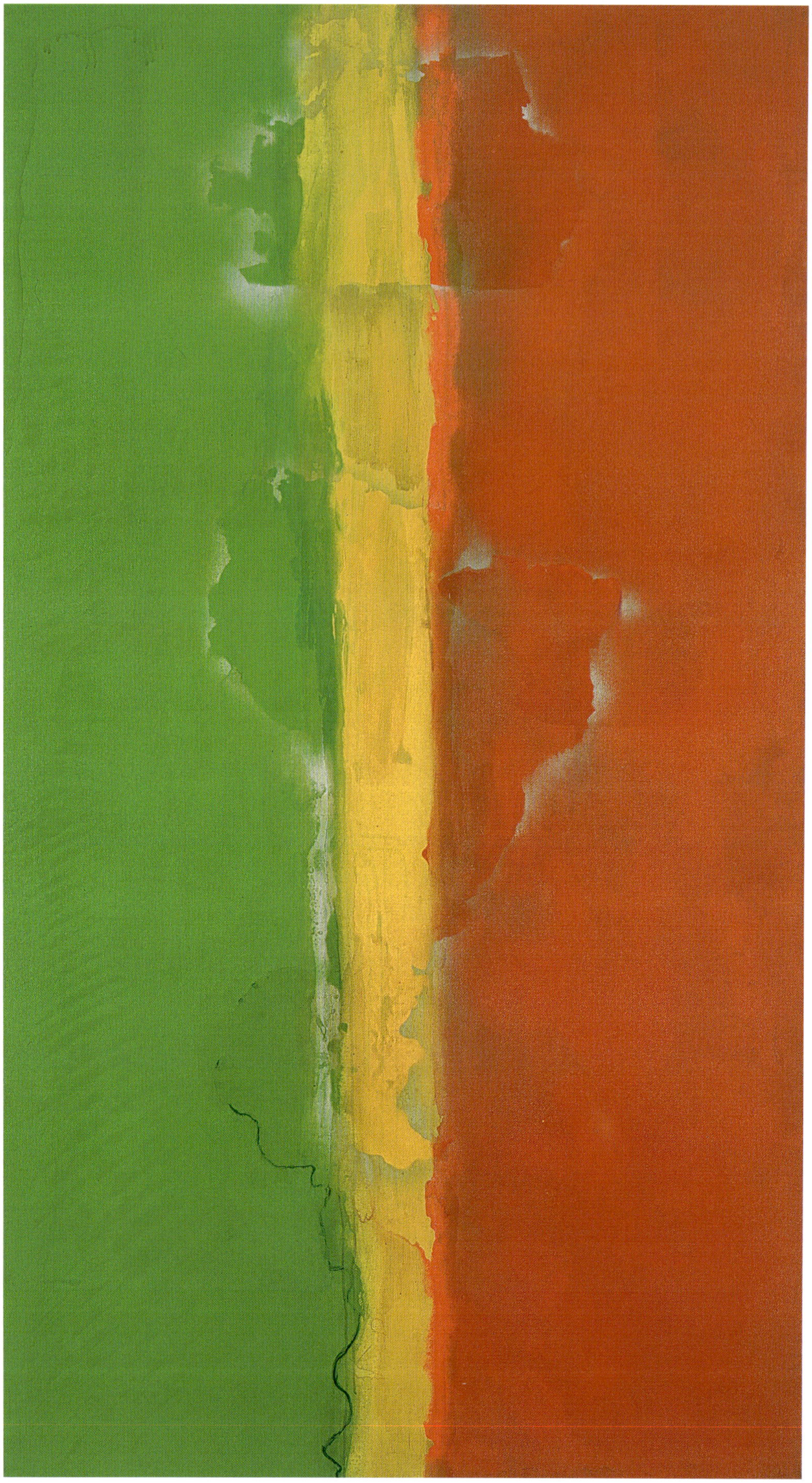

Who's Afraid of Barney Newman, 1968
Acrylic on canvas, 236 x 129.5 cm

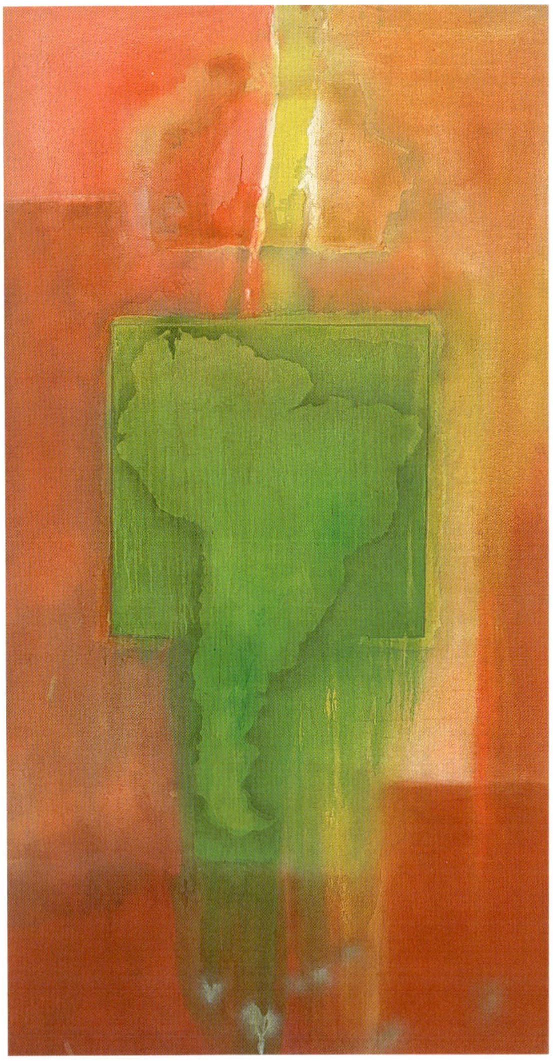

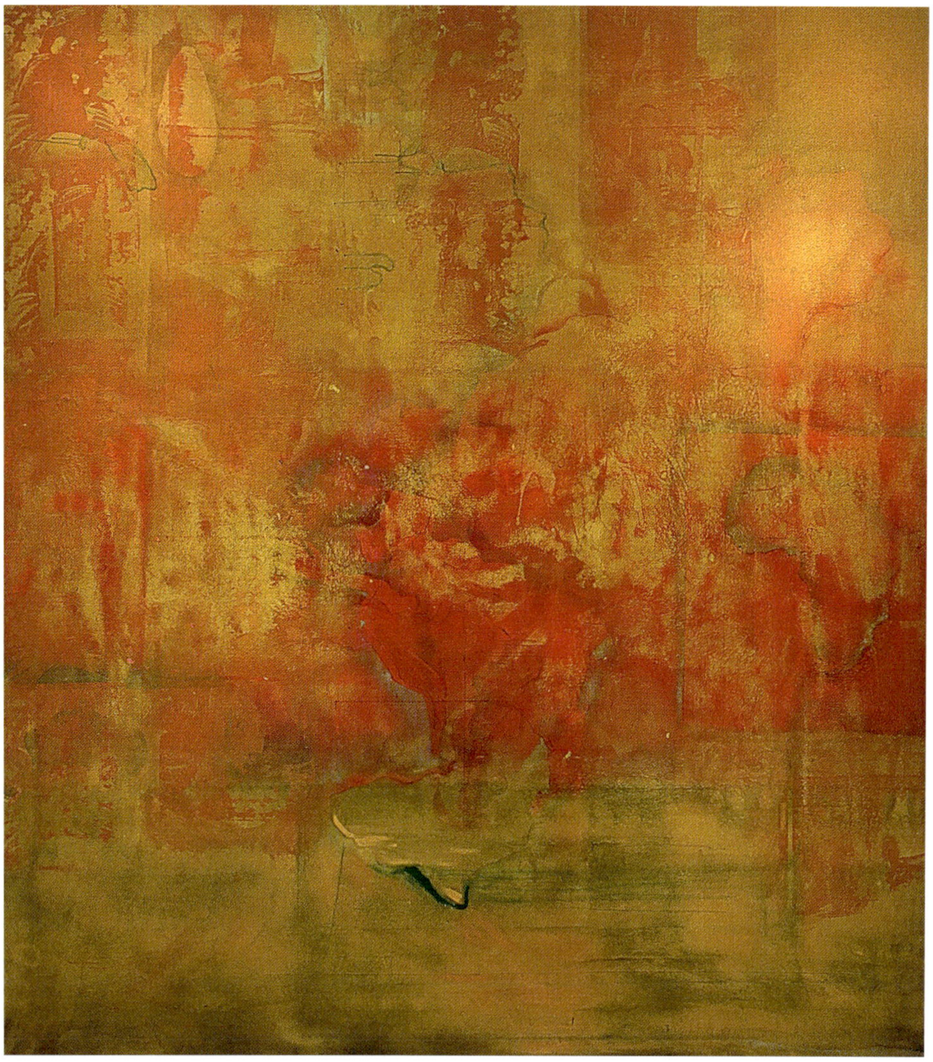

vegetation and natural plenitude of Africa, and gold the wealth of Africa (though Bowling was unaware at the time of this specificity of symbolism). They are also, as it happens, the prominent colours of the recently adopted Guyana flag. But the mischievous title hints at other connotations. The vertical composition, with its narrow ragged yellow zip, mimics the characteristic structure of early abstract paintings by Newman, especially that of the famous early breakthrough painting *Onement* (1948), and the colours are a riposte to Newman's later series, *Who's Afraid of Red, Yellow and Blue?* (1966 onwards). Newman's paintings had been conceived as a final repudiation of Mondrian's insistence on the primaries, of geometric neo-plasticism in general, and of the non-symbolic idealism of first generation metaphysical abstraction: '…only an art of no-geometry can be a new beginning' Newman had written in 1958. Bowling was proposing not only other colours (with other connotations, perhaps), but new uses for abstraction, uses less freighted with the higher symbolism or existential earnestness that characterised Newman's rhetoric.

In one of two paintings of the same period, both with the title *Mother's House on South America* (1968), Bowling used the same palette and a similar arrangement as in *Who's Afraid of Barney Newman*; in the other he deployed a spectacularly moody combination of rusty sienna reds and pale blues, with an evocative halo of white light around the stencilled motifs. These combinations may evoke thoughts and emotions, as colour in painting so often does, but they have no deliberate specificity, and any perceived political or personal significance is a matter of spectator response.

There are certain paintings in this series in which image and title may indeed invite

above left
***Mother's House on South America*, 1968**
Acrylic on canvas, 233.5 x 122 cm

above
***Middle Passage*, 1970**
Acrylic on canvas, 328 x 269 cm

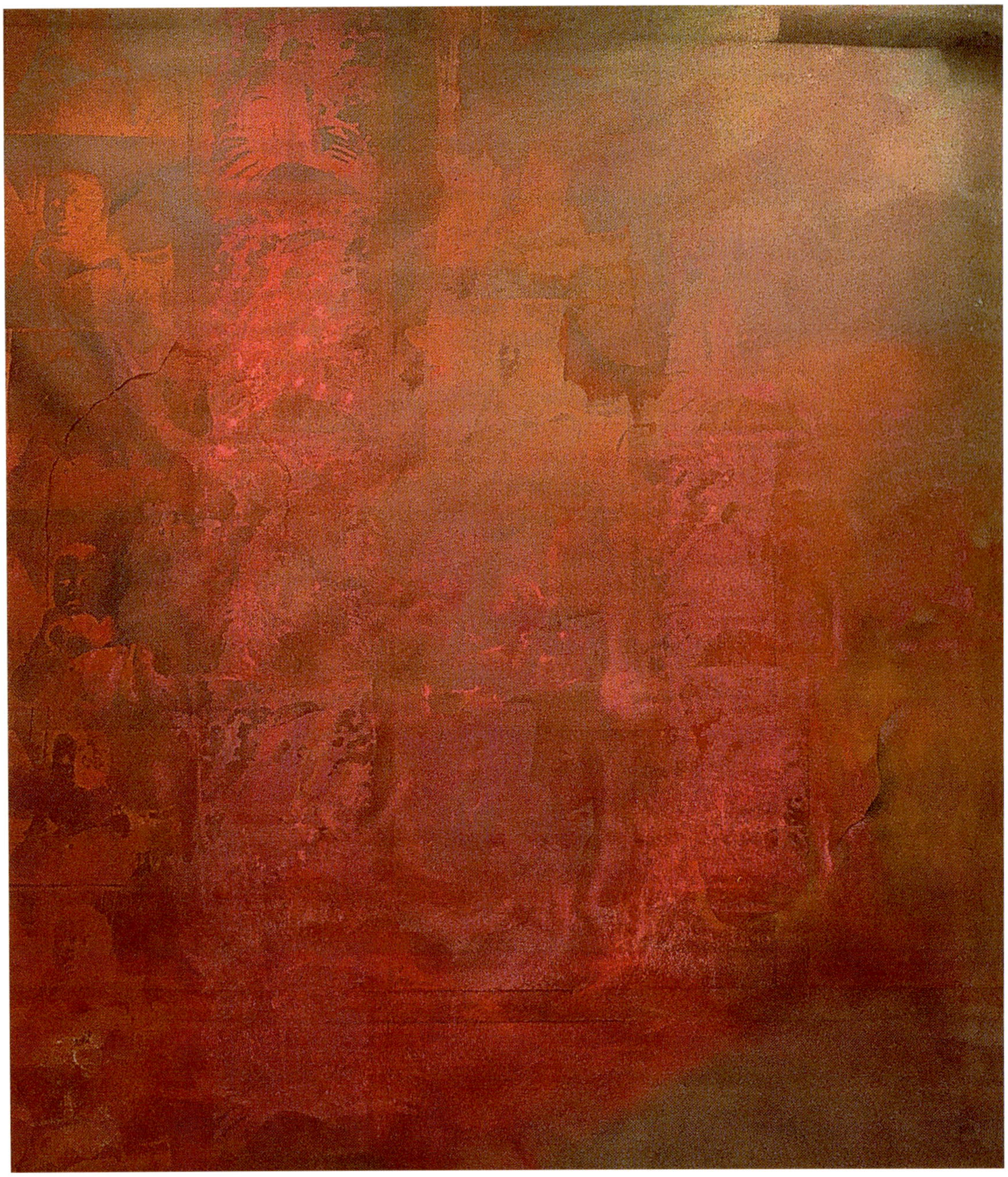

Dan + Them, 1969
Acrylic on canvas, 277 x 239 cm

more sharply focused political or historical interpretations, for example, the powerfully affective *Middle Passage* (1970), and the magnificent *Night Journey* (1968-69), in both of which a dark and dramatic relation between Africa and South America is suggested. In others, however, the relation of title to content is inconsequentially gnomic or impenetrably personal, as in *Dan + Them* (1969) and *Where is Lucienne?* (1971). That there are such distinctions between charged hints at a political-historical reality, and necessarily obscure references to the personal, intensifies the ambiguities of intention and complicates attempts to interpret them.

In 1971 the major achievement represented by the map paintings was recognised by a large installation at the Whitney Museum of American Art in one of a series of exhibitions called *Contemporary Black Artists in America* that took place over several years. This was an acknowledgement of Bowling as a New York artist, a distinguished practitioner in the American art world. He showed a range of ambitious large landscape-format paintings, mostly painted for the exhibition: in *Texas Louise* (1971) and *Polish Rebecca* (1971), he spread his

opposite
Night Journey, 1968-69
Acrylic on canvas, 328 x 269 cm

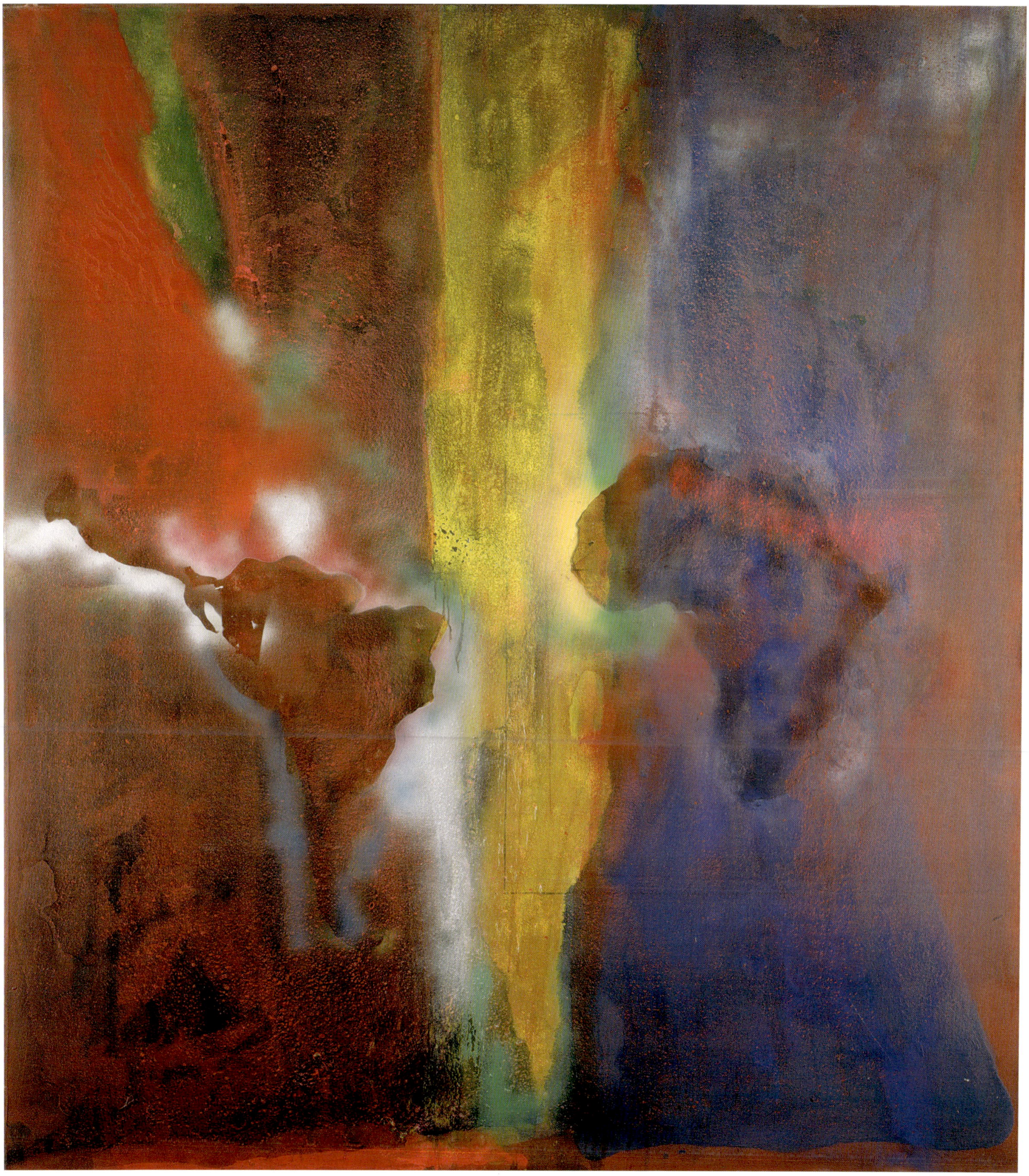

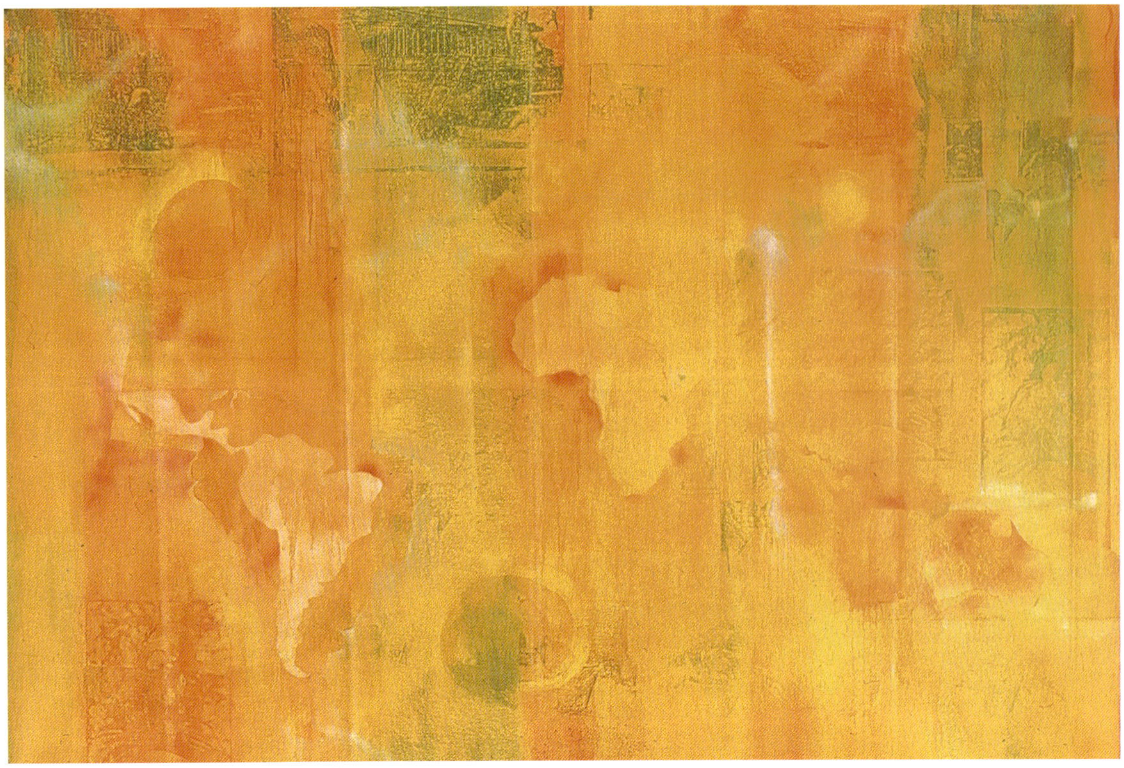

Where is Lucienne? 1971
Acrylic on canvas, 320 x 340 cm

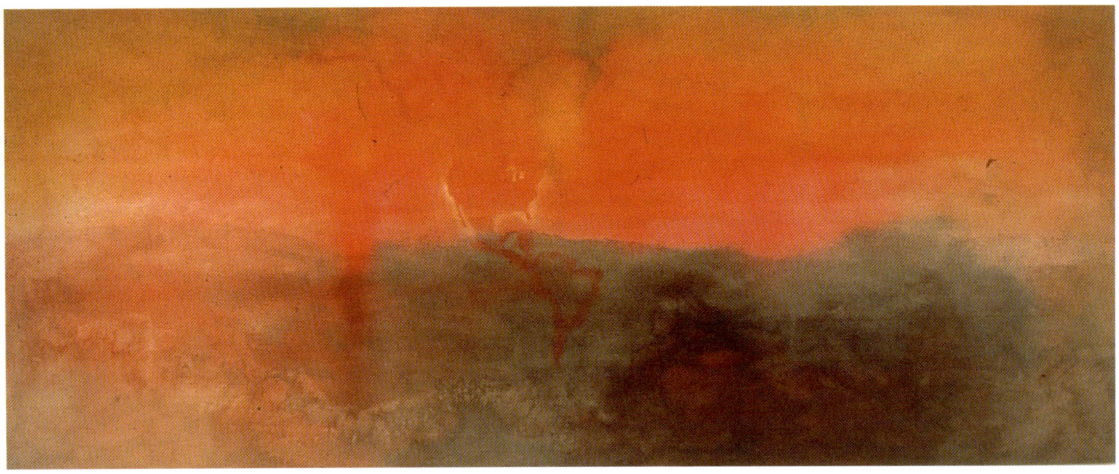

below left
Texas Louise, 1971
Acrylic on canvas, 282 x 670 cm

traced continents across extensive horizontal planes that evoked the great open spaces of the USA. It was a grand statement, but these proved to be the last map paintings that Bowling made.

Speaking to Robert Doty, the Whitney curator, at the exhibition of his work, Bowling summed up the previous five years: 'After leaving London to live in New York, I broke loose and began to get much more involved in pure painting, trying to fuse the kinds of things I was interested in with what could actually be upheld viably in a painting situation. I eventually found that the most comfortable way of actually dealing with paint and structures from the outside was by leaning on ready-made shapes and photographs. The gradual turnover of rejecting what was too complicated led me to remove much of it entirely into another medium.'

Even as he spoke, Bowling was preparing to kick away the scaffolding of the 'ready-made shapes' and operate without the 'structures'. He knew where his true interest lay: 'I'm adjusting colour almost entirely through emotional leads. Colour plays an enormous part in my work, if not the most important part.' He was poised to undertake his own exploration of the last continent 'in the direction of colour and in no other direction.'

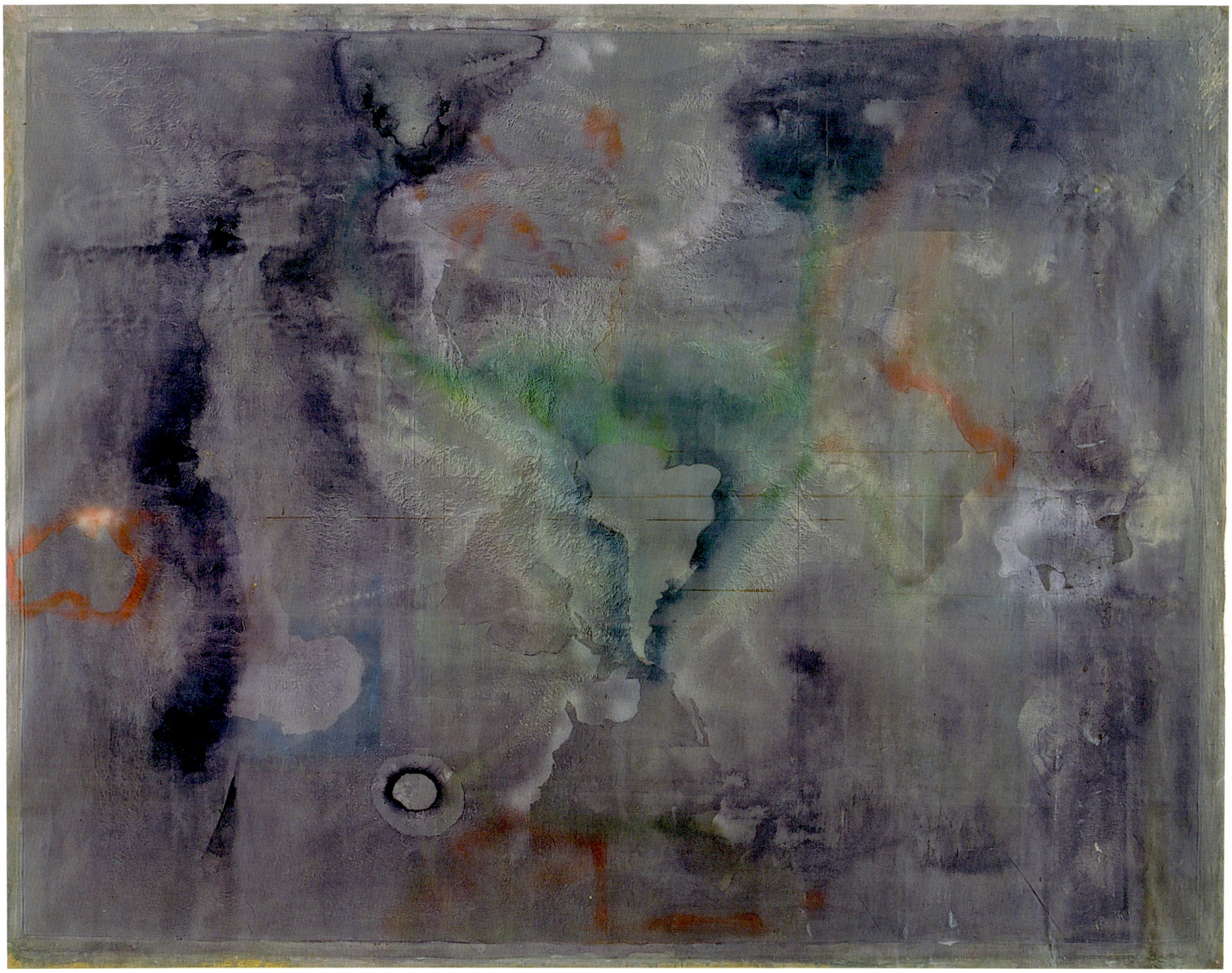

Polish Rebecca, 1971
Acrylic on canvas, 274.5 x 335 cm

8 PURE ABSTRACTIONS: BOWLING THE FORMALIST

> *'But art is not practical; it is neither philosophy nor science; it is not religion, morality, nor even social comment... It merely presents forms – sometimes intangible forms – to imagination.'*
> SUSANNE LANGER

Bowling was not alone in his realisation that colour was the true subject of his paintings in the years leading up to 1971. In 1970, he had titled a painting *Marcia H Travels*, alluding to his friend Marcia Hafif, a highly principled and committed abstractionist of luminous intelligence who had spent ten years in Italy in a dedicated study of colour in 15th-century fresco painting, and was at this time preparing to resume her painting career and embark on her own lifelong exploration of monochrome colour and surface. In December 1971 she reviewed Bowling's Whitney exhibition, correctly perceiving colour as its dominant component, recognising the map-shapes as formal devices whose purpose was to locate colour on the surface and minimise any reading of it as merely evocatively atmospheric:

> With six large, bright, stained, soaked, sprayed, masked, painted canvases in the main floor gallery of the Whitney Museum, Frank Bowling explores painterly means within what is becoming a contemporary idiom. The paintings are big, all over nine feet high and one as long as twenty-two feet. Sense of space is extended by the use of vast areas of soaked and watermarked colour, at times soft in beiges and pinks or, at others, deeply soaked acid green going into blue or fluorescent reds, magenta, yellow, orange or violet and silver. Bowling is from Guiana, studied and worked in London. Perhaps it is his concern with his native country, with South America and Africa, that makes *Texas Louise* with its upper half of pink, orange and yellow, its lower half part of soaked pink seem more evocative of sunrise over a lyric African plain than any Southwest range. When that has been absorbed, one becomes aware of the images of North America and South America fitting themselves into proper spaces within the loosely divided structure of the canvas, and at this point the space flattens out. In *Untitled I* and *II*, which are hung together, the images are even more hidden and only slowly float out, the whole world taking its place gradually before your eyes.

Turning her attention to *Polish Rebecca* (1971), Hafif perceptively puts her finger on the problem that now preoccupied Bowling, as he thought his way forward from a reliance on 'ready-made shapes'. Even as she questions the necessity of the map shapes, however, they mislead her, prompting her surmise that his colours must necessarily have allusive or specifically evocative purposes, when, with the exception of certain provocative cases, this was clearly never Bowling's intention:

> *Polish Rebecca* is a slightly earlier painting with a harder surface. Paint has slid in such a way as to make a veined pattern as in a topographical map. South America is central in this painting and North America fades above, reappearing upside-down down under. Broken orange lines join South America with Africa and continue to right and left. These and other vague horizontal and vertical divisions make a coherence out of the general floating chaos. The recognizable outlines of the continents save the viewer from being overwhelmed by the seductive mass of colour. Which brings up the question of the function of the map shapes. Their recognisibility sets up a polarity between themselves and the floating colour, erecting a tension and an interest. But couldn't unknown shapes of the same intensity carry out that work? And don't the horizontal division as in landscape and the quality of colour suggest Africa and South America and the rest of this personal view of the world? *These would be stronger paintings*

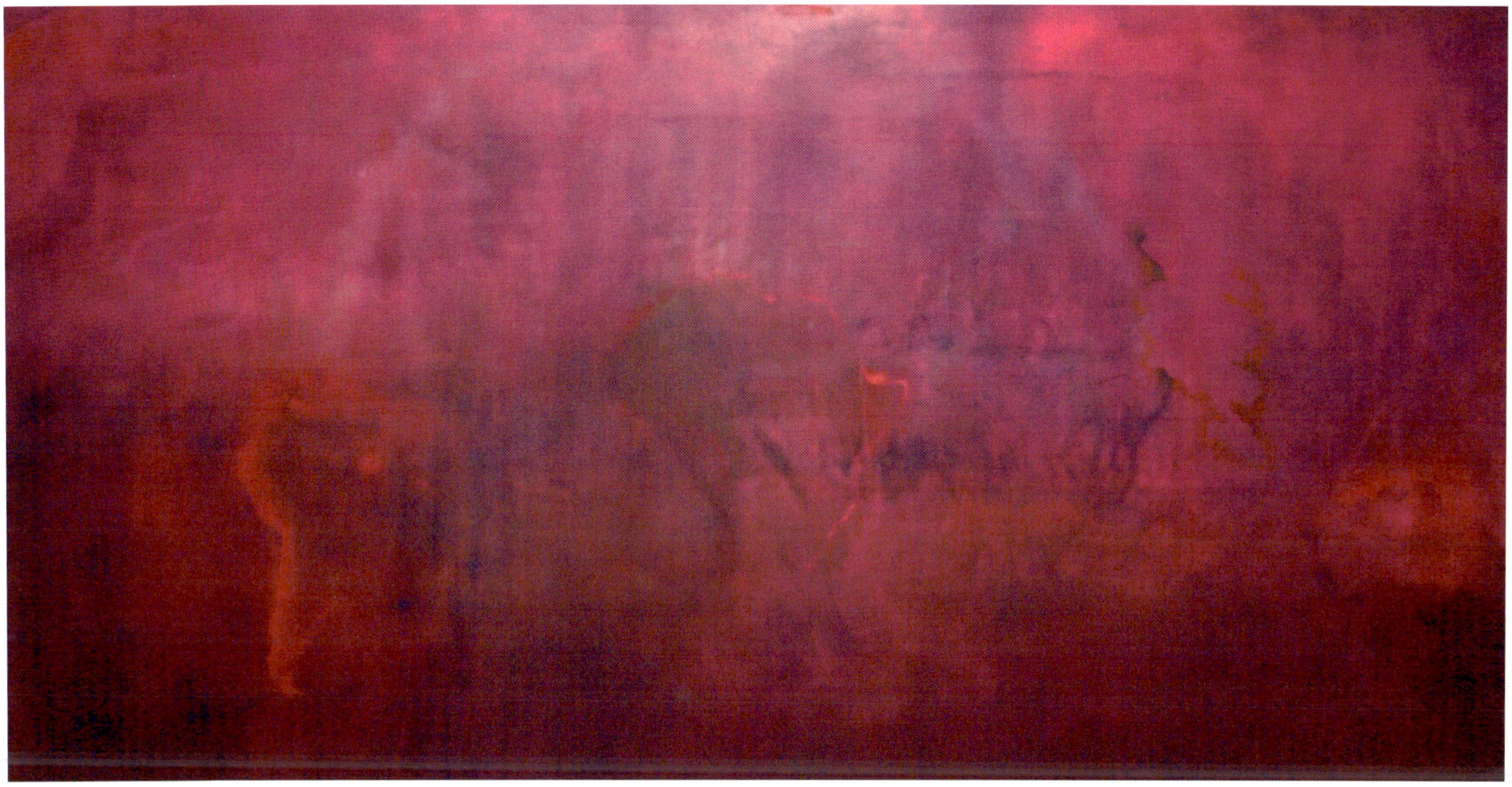

if they relied solely on the visual possibilities present within them instead of trying to deal simultaneously with the literary element of the map [my emphasis].

There is nothing particularly African or South American about the colours of a sunrise or sunset, and Bowling had long been irritated by the recurring suggestion that his colour was 'exotic' or 'tropical'. Colour is colour; and through practice and theory Bowling was developing a highly original view of the nature of that ever-present phenomenon of light and matter, and of the problem as to how a painter might engage with perceptions of it. He was also, without doubt, hyper-conscious of its affective power in art: it is impossible to respond to colour without feeling. Hafif concluded her review with this in mind:

> A viable way of painting is being searched for by painters through stain and images, through minimal organic stained shape and line, complex colour, with geometric line, thick colour, eccentric colour, systematic application of paint. Paint can be paint again and does not have to apologize for its illusion provoking qualities.

It seems strange that the energetic and influential Clement Greenberg did not see Bowling's show at the Whitney, or indeed that in five years in New York, the artist and the critic had not met. In any case, in late 1971 Greenberg visited Bowling's

***Marcia H Travels*, 1970**
Acrylic on canvas, 305 x 570 cm

studio for the first time, and was impressed by what he saw. For Bowling it was the beginning of a beneficial and productive friendship. Bowling was already taking his first steps towards a version of pure colour field painting whose antecedence went back to Rothko and Newman, beyond the cool and clear 'open' design that Greenberg admired in the 'post-painterly abstractionists' (Jules Olitsky, Morris Louis, Kenneth Noland, *et al.*) whom he had been critically promoting for the last seven years or so. Bowling had now eliminated the stencils and the maps, and with them the possibilities of connotative readings that allowed spectators to identify his concerns as overtly (as opposed to implicitly) political. In 1976 – just five years on – Bowling was adamantly clear about this in a dialogue with the figurative painter William Thomson:

> The moment I met Clem Greenberg I knew I was right. I am very unhesitating about this. He seems to come at one with a kind of moral fervour that is quite electric and you sense it, rather than know it. And working is like this. It is the first time I've been sure about something without knowing what it is. Before, it was a constant learning process. Knowing about painting arrives with doing it. Clem was able to make me see that Modernism belonged to me also, that I had no good reason to pretend I wasn't part of the whole thing.

In 1975 Bowling was still resident in New York; he was by this time painting in a radically hands-off manner that exploited automatic flow and process and abjured expressive intervention, but in which colour mixtures and fusions were determined. That is to say, he was by that time painting very much within the ambit of the current developments of post-painterly abstraction, in which objective effects, achieved by whatever programmatic procedures, mechanical, automatic or otherwise, were valued over the personal poignancies of touch and the expression of authorial thought and feeling. His current situation may well have influenced the vehemence of his recollections, and the passionate clarity of his identification with the spirit of modernism, as Bowling explained in his conversation with Thomson:

> My ambitions as a painter, and being part of the New York scene, and even to influence it are legit. You must remember that I spent from late '67 to '71 suffering through the whole nonsense about *Black* Art. I used up an awful lot of physical and psychic energy trying to get that together, and I found most of it had *nothing to do* with my real self. If I hadn't been in New York, I wouldn't have been able to get to grips with Black Art; there would have been no way of doing it had I remained in London. And it is through this that I've come away knowing that there is a something which is very distinctly Black – as there is something very distinctly Jewish, or Scots/Irish. But there is no Black Art. There is Classical or Tribal African Art, but not Black Art. I believe that the Black soul, if there can be such a thing, belongs in Modernism. *Black* people are a quite new and original people. And they're as different from any of the people that they're supposed to look like as a New Englander is from an Englishman.

This is to anticipate slightly. By early 1972, with the encouragement of Greenberg, Bowling's new formalist canvases were entirely innocent of motif and symbolic colour. These paintings, created out of washes of translucent pale blues, pinks and greens, have the aerial quality of huge watercolours, and the granularity of surface that comes (as in watercolour painting) of the distilled sedimentation of pigment on the plane, with the attendant subtleties of a crystalline interaction with light. Bowling acknowledged his masters: an early painting in this manner, *Looking at Barney and Mark* (1972), turned on its side, would have the vertical structure of a Newman zip painting (an affectionately formal irony); as it is, its landscape format (unmistakeably sand, sea and cloud) is a playful admission that any such formal structure and any colour combination must evoke memories of the world, while the blue cloud in the grey sky is an irrepressible reminder of Rothko's characteristic shimmer-edged colour shapes, and perhaps, a wry hint at their source in nature.

The titles of *Breeze* (1972) and *Zephyr* (1973) clearly indicate Bowling's sense of the invisible-aerial that these beautiful paintings summon into being by means of the spatial subtlety of indeterminate colour-tones and pearlescent textures, and of their pale or shadowed light. Both paintings could hang vertically or horizontally; in each case it is clear that Bowling has been looking at Newman's work, and in

Looking at Barney and Mark, 1972
Acrylic on canvas, 184 x 241.5 cm

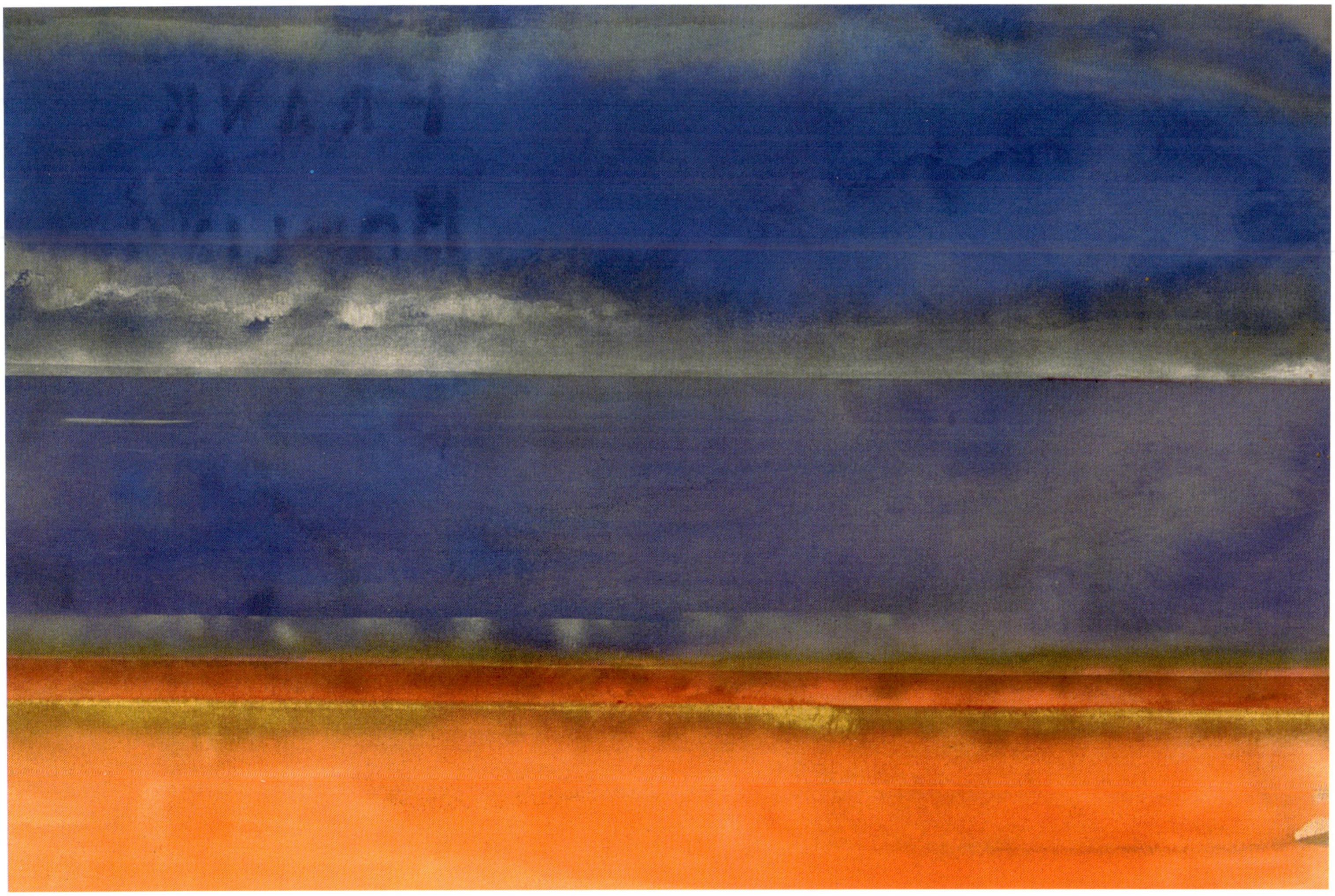

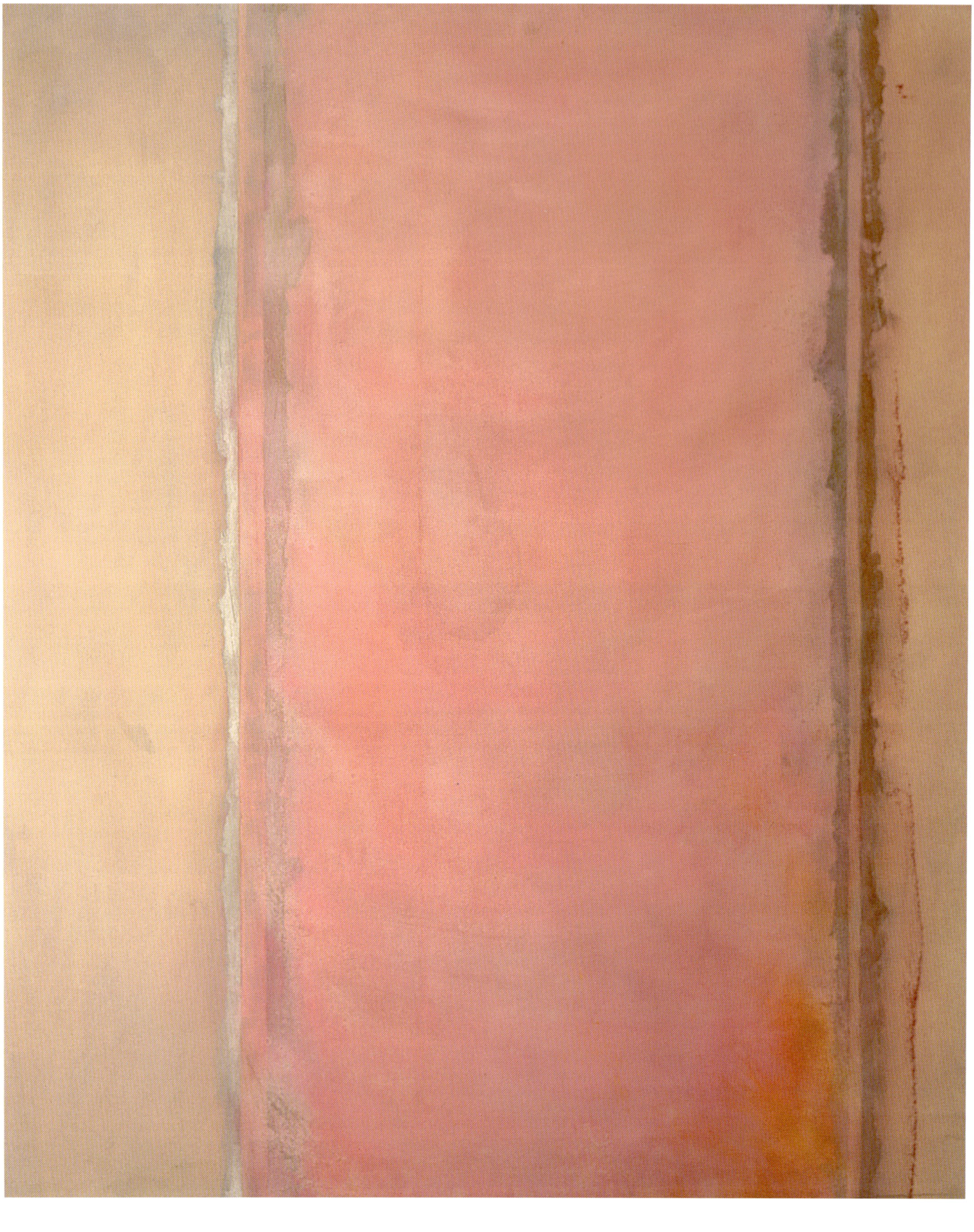

Breeze, 1972
Acrylic on canvas, 227 x 186.5 cm

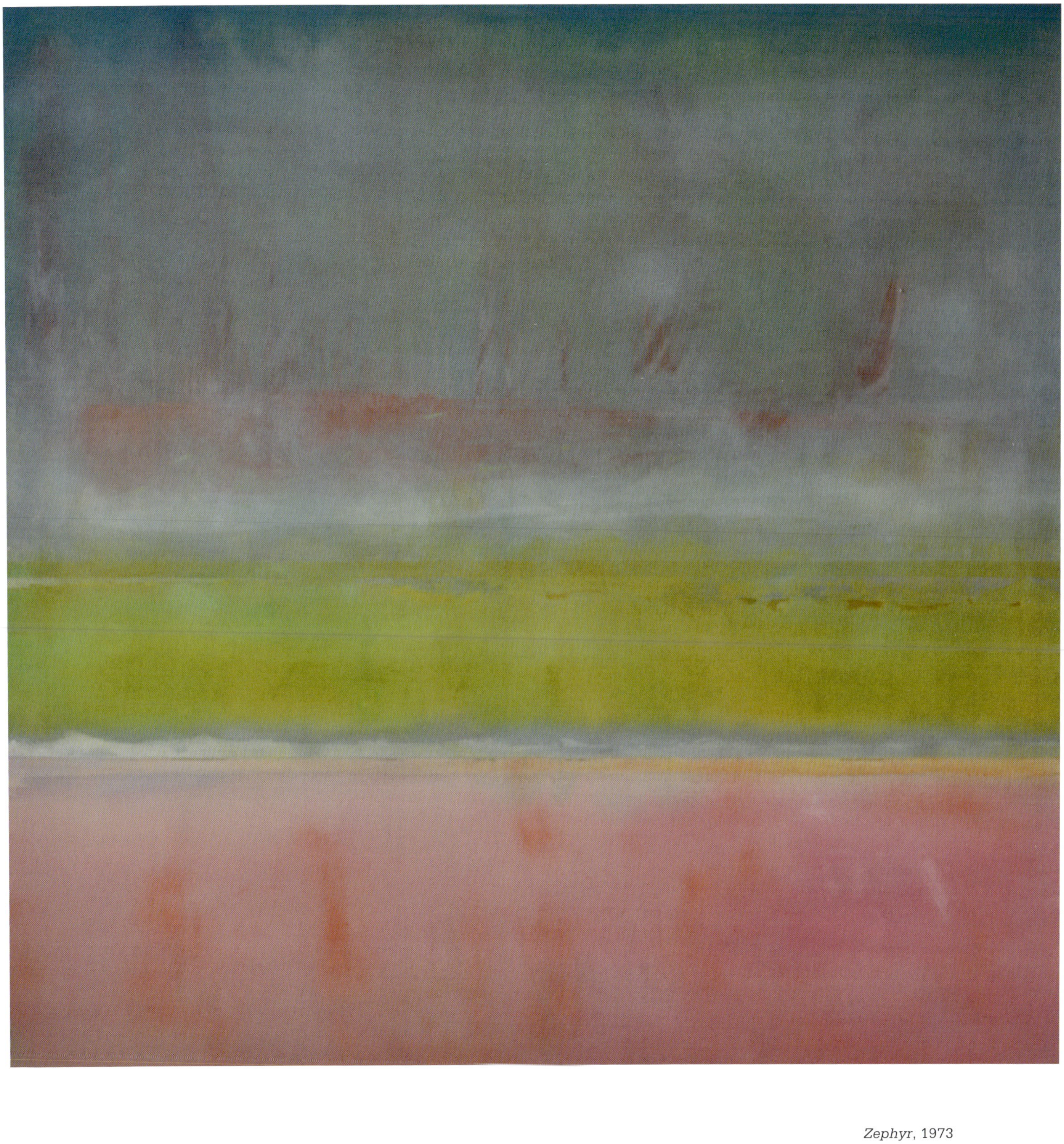

Zephyr, 1973
Acrylic on canvas, 170 x 170 cm

pondering the problem of what to do with that powerful formal example, has seen that there was more to be done, in the direction of colour, light and atmospherics. *Silverfish for Susan* (1973) changes the format, introducing rectangular divisions, and an edge strip of yellow that recalls a similarly disruptive and objectifying device in Olitski's very different spray-gun paintings of a few years before; these divisions and interventions introduce further spatial ambiguities.

These lovely paintings – Bowling's first purely abstract work – signalled a major breakthrough in his quest for a truly personal style. Thin-wash acrylic fields, translucent, diaphanous, cannot but evoke pictorial space and induce mood. Bowling became increasingly concerned, however, to create brilliant objects rather than beautiful evocative images. Atmospheric colour field had a history; it was a recognisable style. 'My ambition for my painting', he said two years later, 'drove me first to N.Y. and then to realising that what I was painting was not really my own.' His ambitions as a painter demanded something radically new.

It was perhaps ironic (given his past, not to mention his future) that the first style that was really Bowling's own was achieved by the use of a primitive mechanism of his own devising. Its purpose was to enable the production of paintings without the poignancies of direct touch by brush, hand or purposefully directed staining, soaking, spraying or masking. It took him as far as it was possible to go from expressionist gesture, the expressively stained colour field or mood evocation. It answered to Bowling's aspiration in 1974 to make paintings that were, in a sense, purely abstract objects whose impact would be immediately sensational, and altogether without intentional reference or affect. Their aesthetic was conceived as, in certain crucial respects, akin to that of natural objects whose forms and dynamics were visibly the outcomes of natural processes. In his famous 1961 essay, 'Modernist Painting', Greenberg had characteristically observed, that 'Modernism criticizes from the inside, through the procedures themselves of that which is being criticised.'

In a competitive environment, Bowling began working now with a keen awareness of the inexpressive 'post-painterly' procedures of Greenberg's protégés, Morris Louis and Olitski. Pouring, spraying, staining, masking, cropping, screening, applications of acrylic gel, unstretched canvases, shaped supports, acrylic paint applied with a self-declarative clarity of execution: these were the technical and stylistic characteristics of much of the most critically successful contemporary New York abstract painting. Bowling's own response to the challenge of modernist formalism, with its challenge to the painter to forgo the expressive touch and to discover a new reality in painting-as-painting, in what the early Russian abstractionists he admired would have called 'painting-as-such', was extreme.

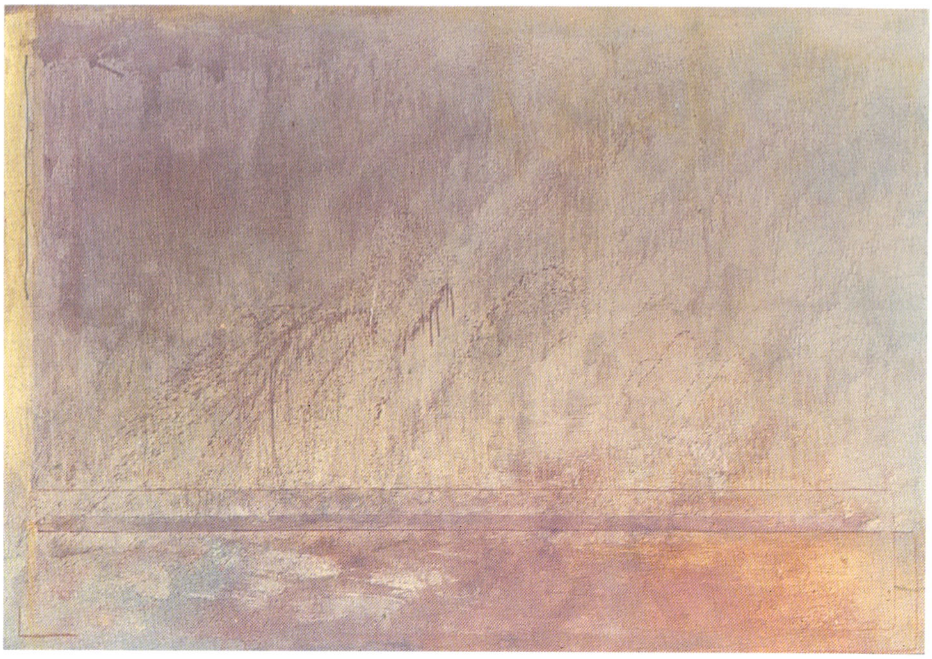

Silverfish for Susan, 1973
Acrylic on canvas, 167.5 x 213.5 cm

Corinna's Adam, 1974
Acrylic on canvas, 200.5 x 84 cm

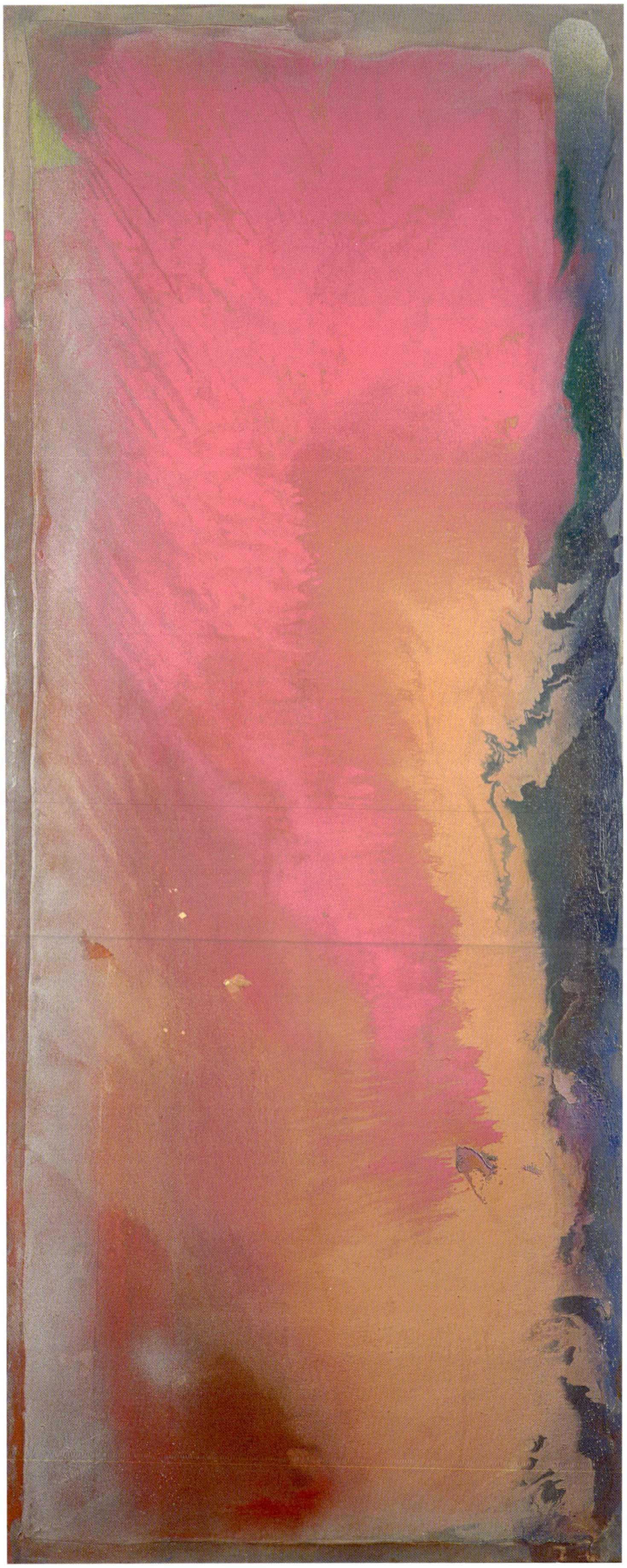

The mechanical device by means of which the poured paintings of the mid-1970s were created was a tilting board-platform, whose angle was controlled by pegs at each end, which allowed the paint to flow downwards over the stretched canvas at a determined speed, while also being susceptible to adjustment. In effect the painting made itself with a minimum of assistance from the painter. In their thrilling unpredictability, and their vertiginous disposition of the pure materials of their art, these poured paintings have about them something very close to the free-form excitement of contemporaneous advanced New York jazz, itself a brilliant manifestation of the modernist spirit. 'The inventions of the unknown,' wrote Rimbaud, 'demand new forms.'

What gives these objects their extraordinary power, their startling visual impact, is another kind of unpredictability altogether. They are images of the natural processes which made them what they are. They cannot therefore avoid resemblance to other phenomena whose forms and effects are created by similar dynamics. 'Paint can be paint again,' Hafif had predicted, 'and does not have to apologize for its illusion-provoking qualities.' The titles Bowling gave to the poured paintings – *Corinna's Adam* (1974), *Simon and Matthew* (1975), *Sunkist* (1976) – are seemingly designed to deflect immediate associations, to emphasise that these paintings are in no way descriptive of the world, and that any resemblance they may have to other (natural) things is unpremeditated, most certainly not intentional.

But the receiving imagination will work as it will, its play over things – voluntary and involuntary – determined by association, the perception of similarity, the action in the mind's eye of memory and desire. '[The] resemblance between things', observed the great American poet Wallace Stevens, '[is] one of the significant

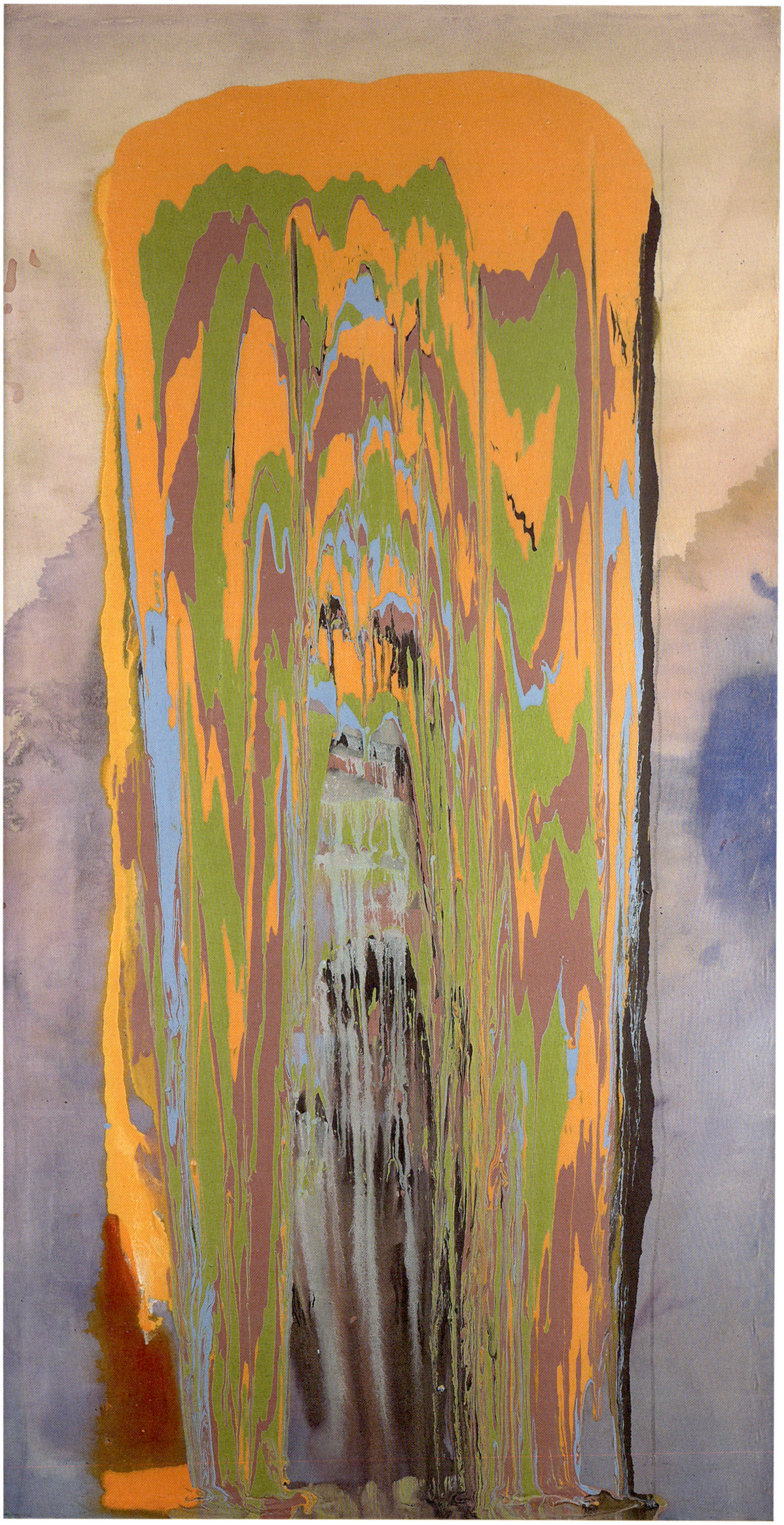

Simon and Matthew, 1975
Acrylic on canvas, 228.5 x 117 cm

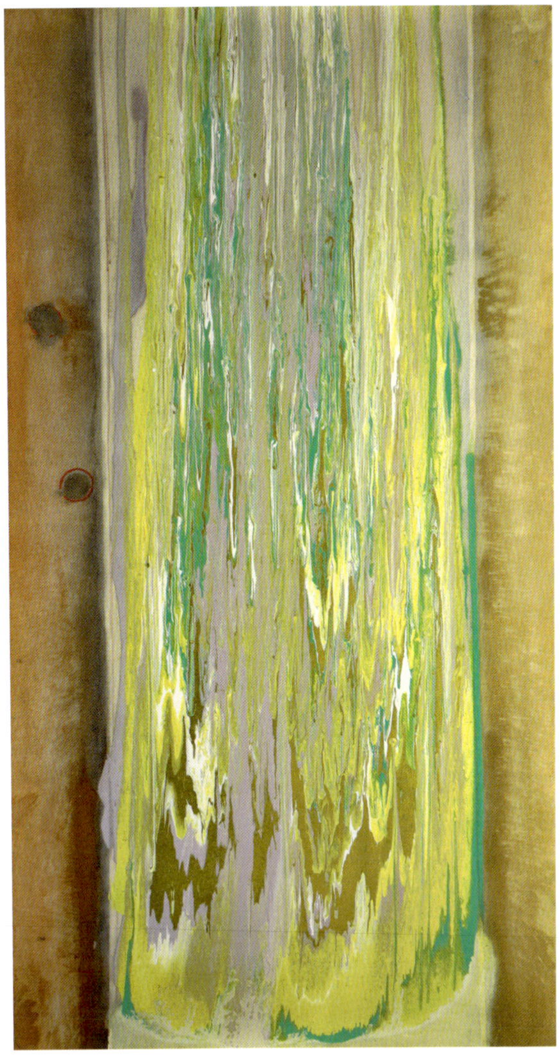

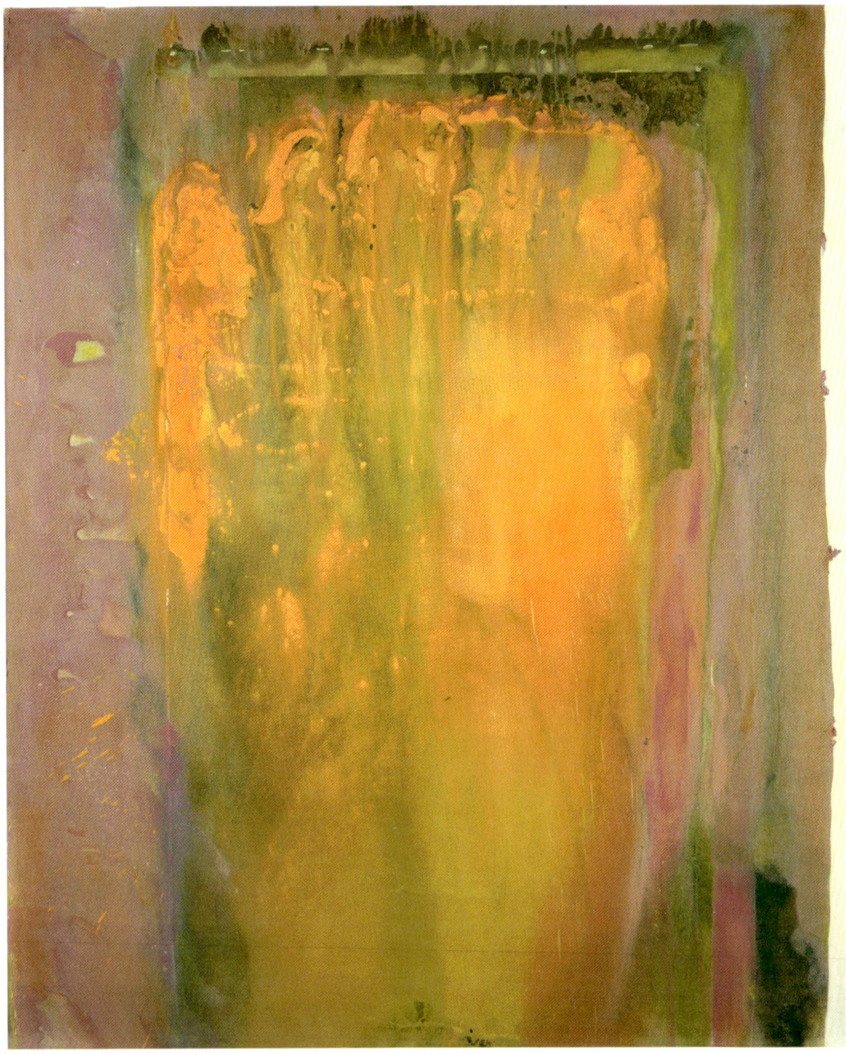

components of the structure of reality.' Resemblance may exist, he is suggesting, not only between two or more parts of reality (as one waterfall resembles all others), but also 'between something real and something imagined or, what is the same thing, between something imagined and something real as, for example, between music and whatever may be evoked by it.' Thus a similarity may be found between an inner feeling (a thrill, a mood) and an outward object (in this case a painting); or we may perceive a resemblance between a painting such as *Courteous Shade* (1974), *Irma Kurtz Visits Broadway* (1975) or *13th Hour* (1976) and a natural phenomenon such as a pillar of fire or a waterfall or a lava flow.

We may, moreover, perceive similarities between the poured paintings and other paintings, both representational and abstract. They may, for example, bring to mind the beautiful light-falls and waterfalls of the great American landscapist Frederick Edwin Church, or seem to bear a resemblance of sorts to the poured acrylic veils of Morris Louis. At the moment of such a perception of resemblance, the critical mind immediately recognises the differences, and their significance. The similarity is in the dynamic, rather than in the effect, the style or the implications and connotations of the imagery.

Church patriotically celebrates American grandeur as well the magnificence of the great cascades; Louis's veils of colour-light are translucent, diaphanous, atmospheric and moody, and they seem deeply personal. Bowling's poured paintings, on the other hand, have no referential thematic or implicit emotive or political intent; they are celebrations of their own dynamic paint-colour fusions; they present us with opaque colour as the representation of light, colour as

above left
Sunkist, 1976
Acrylic on canvas, 231 x 117 cm

above
Courteous Shade, 1974
Acrylic on canvas, 195.5 x 157.5 cm

liquid matter in motion: they are themselves of and in the world, spectacular phenomena.

With the poured paintings, Bowling had devised a method of painting that created sensational effects, and the neutrality of the pouring mechanism together with the natural dynamics of gravity and flow had made it possible to eliminate the stroke and the mark, as well as the dispositions of paint on canvas as indices of personal expression. It was a technique that could be termed 'controlled automatism'. The adjusting pegs, like those of a stringed instrument, allowed variations in pitch and density of matter and colour that produced a range of effects from the dramatic to the lyrical. The method could be infinitely productive and diverse in its effects, but it was limited in its formal outcomes. However spectacular the infinitely various fusions of colour, the mix of the chromatic and tonal, of weight and luminosity, or the speed of flow and the thickness of texture might be in different paintings, the inevitable generic resemblance of one such poured painting to another predicated a need to develop and change. By 1978, Bowling, ever restless in his creativity, was once again taking off in a new direction.

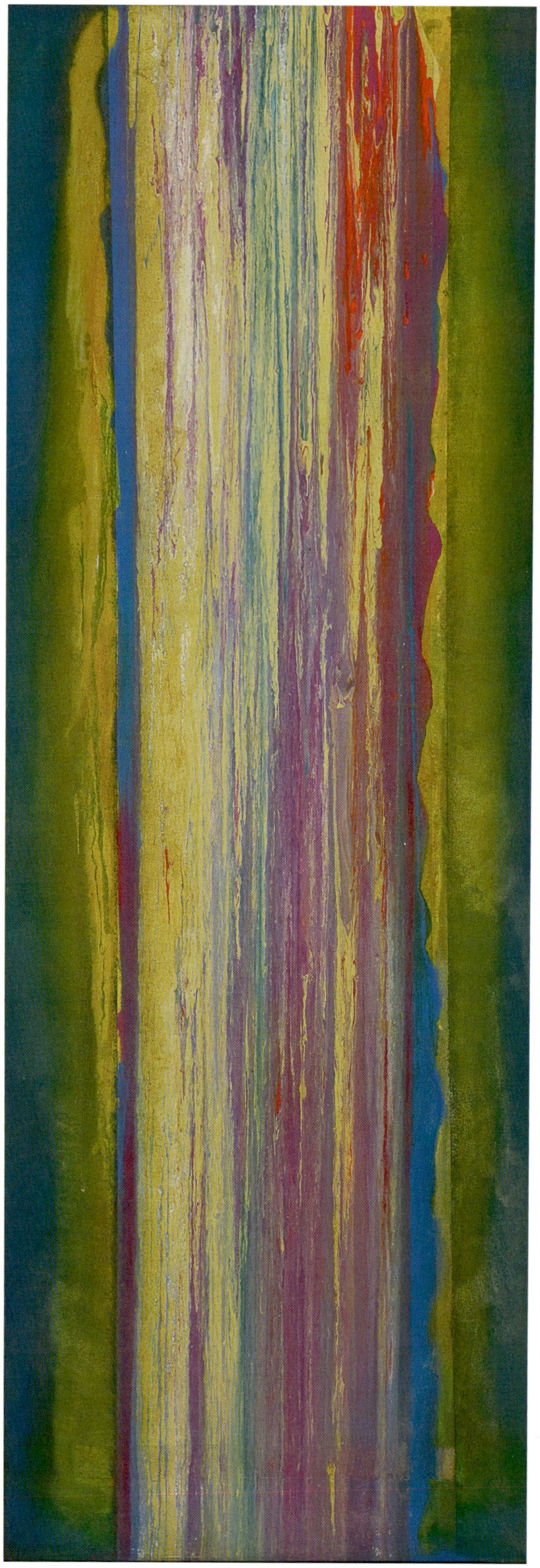

Pandora's Box, 1975
Acrylic on canvas, 184 x 63 cm

13th Hour, 1976
Acrylic on canvas, 173 x 106.5 cm

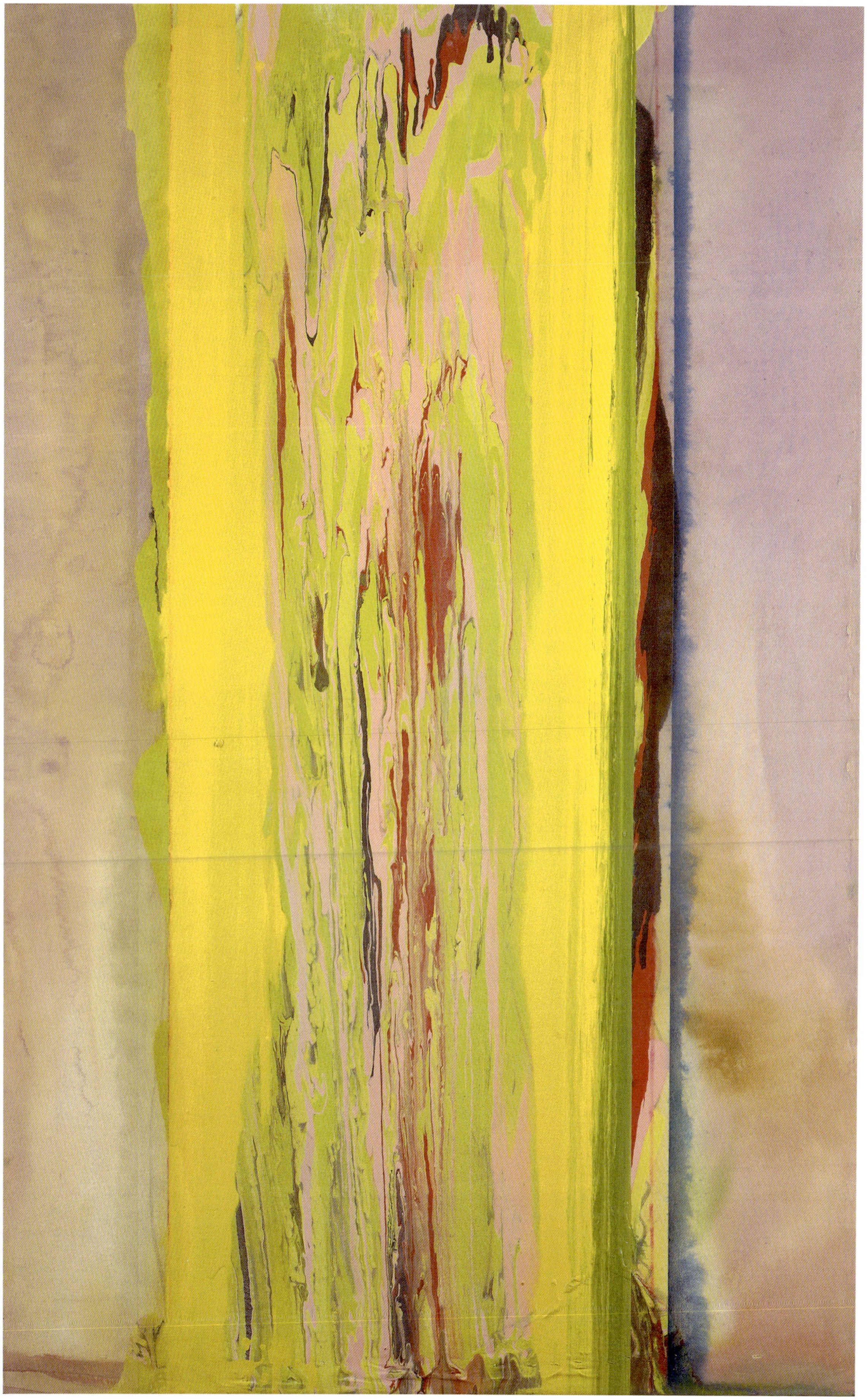

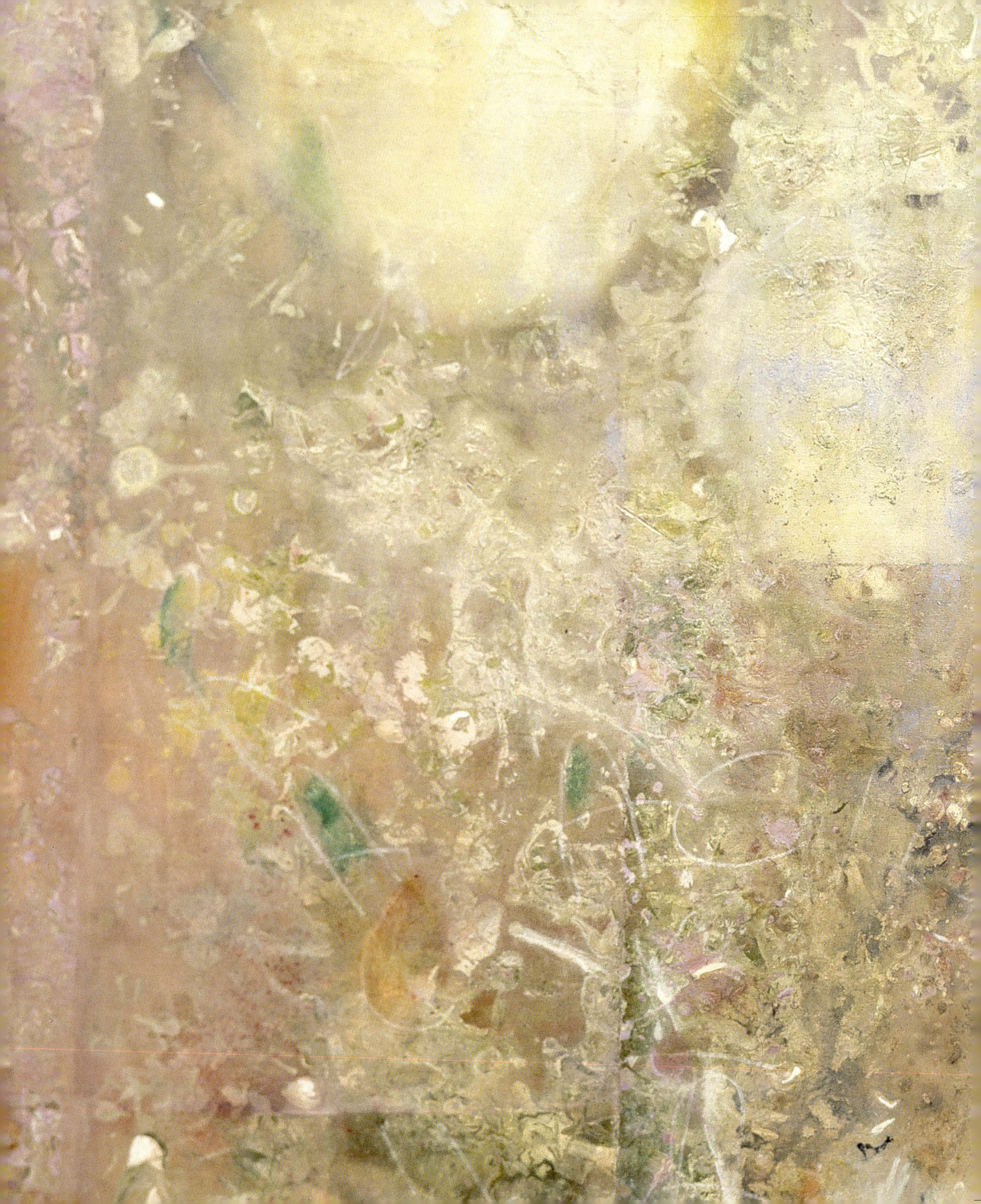

PART THREE
Painting Reality

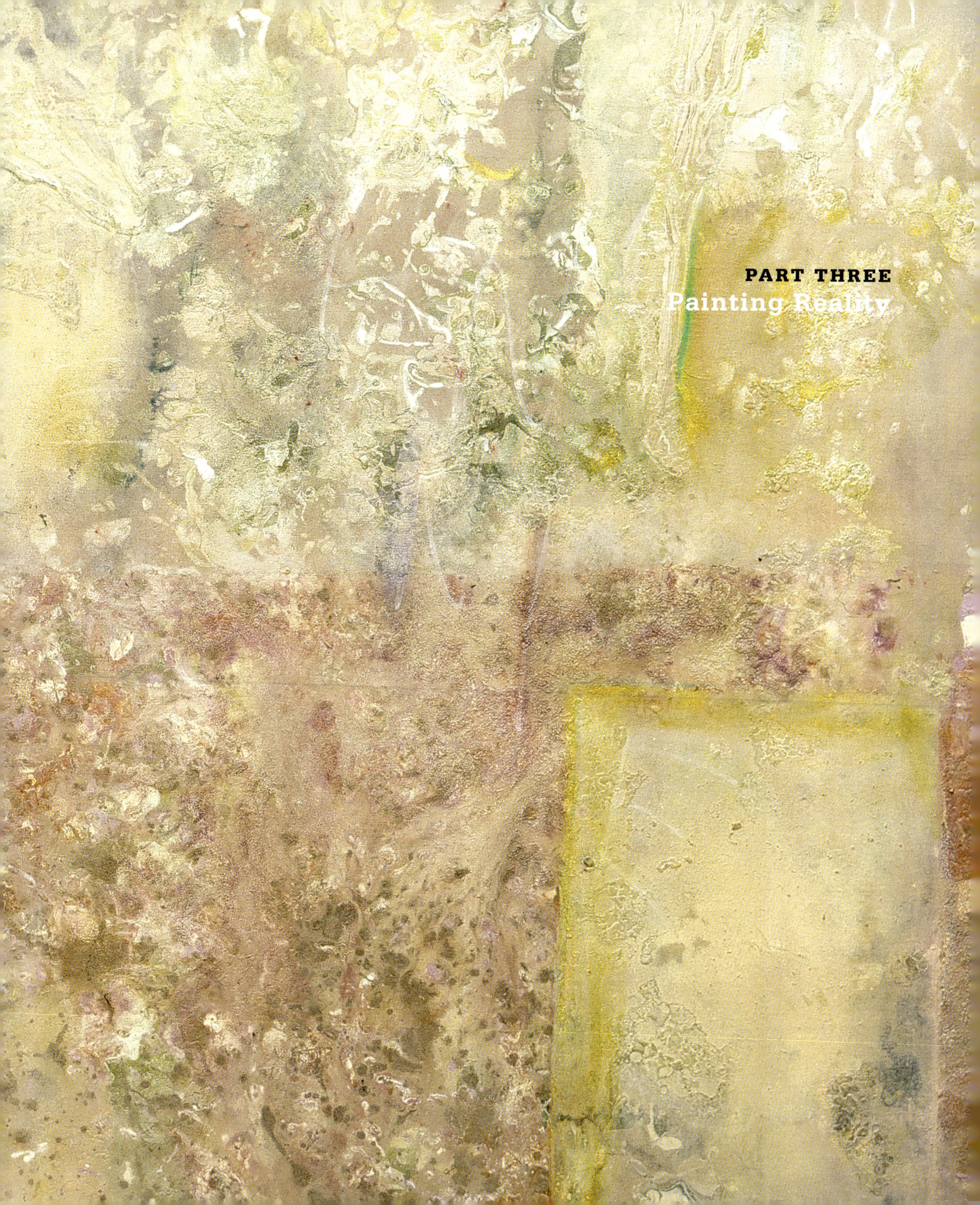

9 THE REAL WORLD: COSMIC VISIONS

In the poured paintings, Bowling demonstrated mastery of the drama of colour combination, and a virtuosic command of the dynamics of flow, density and contrast. Their pictorial structures are invariably and rigorously vertical and symmetrical, and the central paint-columns, like cascades of water or fire, or powerful upsurges, like geysers from a lava lake or a hot spring, exist in energetic contrast to an atmospheric space around them. Given the mechanical procedures of their production and the constraints they imposed on the artist's invention and intervention, they are amazingly and exhilaratingly diverse, like so many natural wonders, each as thrilling as the next.

Not for the first time, or the last, Bowling had invented an original and recognisable formal image, in this case within the conventions of New York post painterly abstraction – essentially inexpressive, declarative of its medium and infinitely repeatable in variations. In Bowling's case, every image presents an emblem of the series' recurrent dynamic: each painting is at once a marvellous object and a thrilling demonstration of the energies by means of which it has come into being. That is to say, each is at once an image (Langer's 'tangible form presented to the imagination') and a concrete thing.

Their serial consistency of structure – vertical and symmetrical and therefore essentially geometrical – gives the poured paintings a shared coherence and creates an aesthetic excitement that is provoked simultaneously by expectation of similarity and surprise at unpredictable dissimilarity. These paintings occupied Bowling for over three years, a body of purely formalistic work as exciting as any abstract painting that came out of New York – or anywhere else – in the 1970s. It is an impressive creative achievement – of painterly spectacle, of vital materiality, of motif diversity – that still awaits due critical recognition.

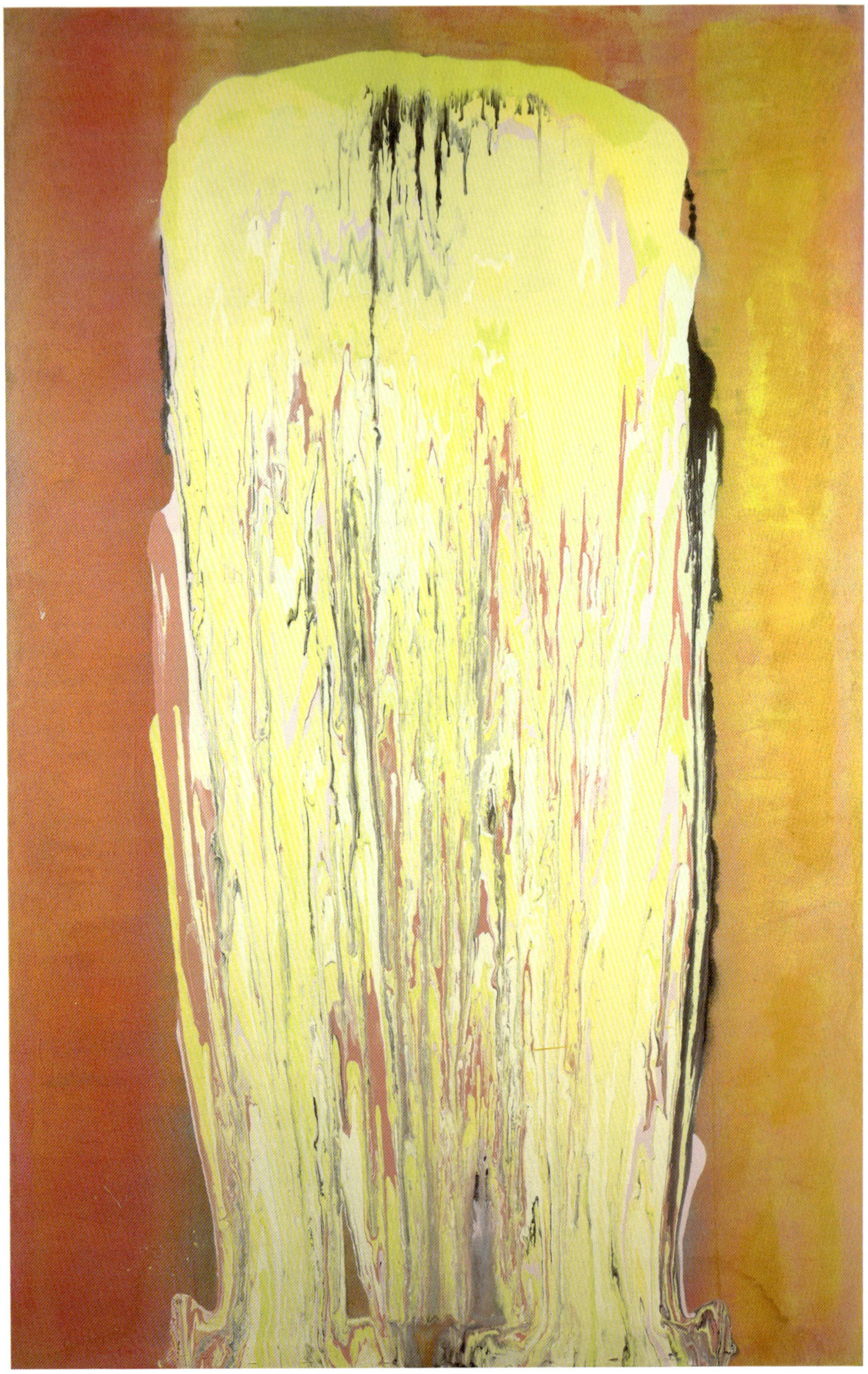

Irma Kurtz Visits Broadway, 1975
Acrylic on canvas, 203 x 129.5 cm

By 1978 Bowling was ready to explore further the possibilities of the pouring technique, and to look to more complex interventions on the surface than those that might be achieved by the formulaic manipulation of the adjustable pouring board. In *Jack* (1978), we see him moving beyond a formalistic programme towards an approach to the painted image that would produce greater variety of effect. More significantly still, it would allow the exercise of expressive intention and an exploration of the pleasures of extempore invention and discovery. The painting's compositional structure is still vertical and centralised, with a suggestion of a surrounding atmospheric field of dark blue; a residue of the poured effect is visible in the (mostly yellow) centre of a area of complex colour-textures – ranging from green to purple – across the central mass. The mode of production, however, has been modified and its mechanical automatism complicated by hand-applied splotches and chemical interventions involving the use of ammonia, pearl-essence, acrylic solutions, distilled turpentine, splatters and runs of thinned paint.

If a similar formal structure to that of *Jack* is still just visible in *Mazarunitankfeat* (1979) and *Devilssole* (1980), it has virtually disappeared in the very similar *Brassica* (1979), in which the pinks, magentas and purples of the former have been deepened to form rich clouds of colour, presenting, perhaps, a spectacle of the heavens framed as through a tall window. Colour in these paintings is no longer simply the immediately apparent property of the paint itself, as it had been in the poured works, whose various mixes, of colour, density and viscosity were pre-prepared in studio pots. It appears, rather, as an aspect and/or an image of natural light: sunlight, shall we say, filtered through translucent dawn or mists at sunset. It is no longer simply an outcome of automatic procedures and natural process; its translucent masses and diffusions have come

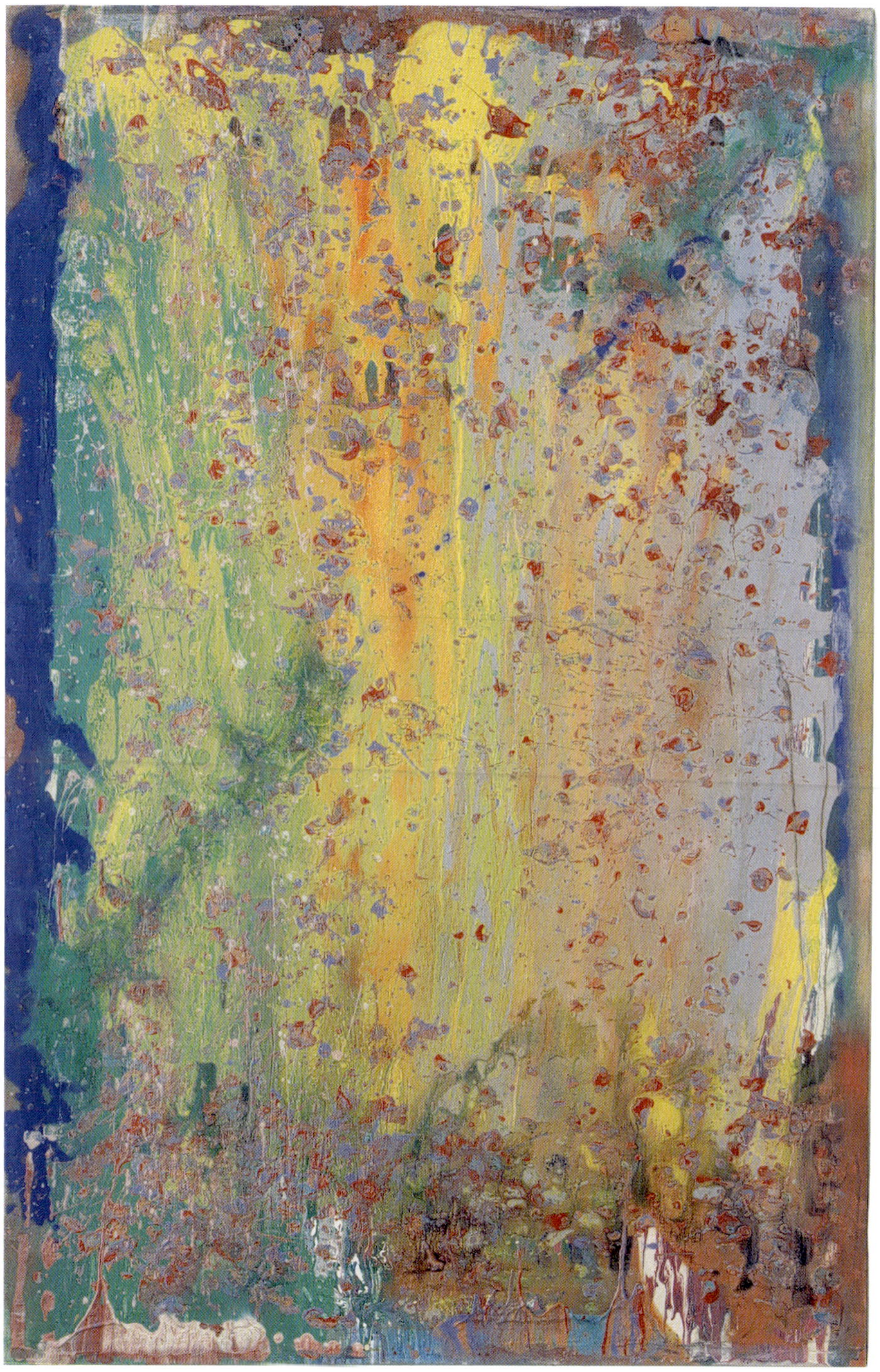

Jack, 1978
Acrylic on canvas, 198 x 129.5 cm

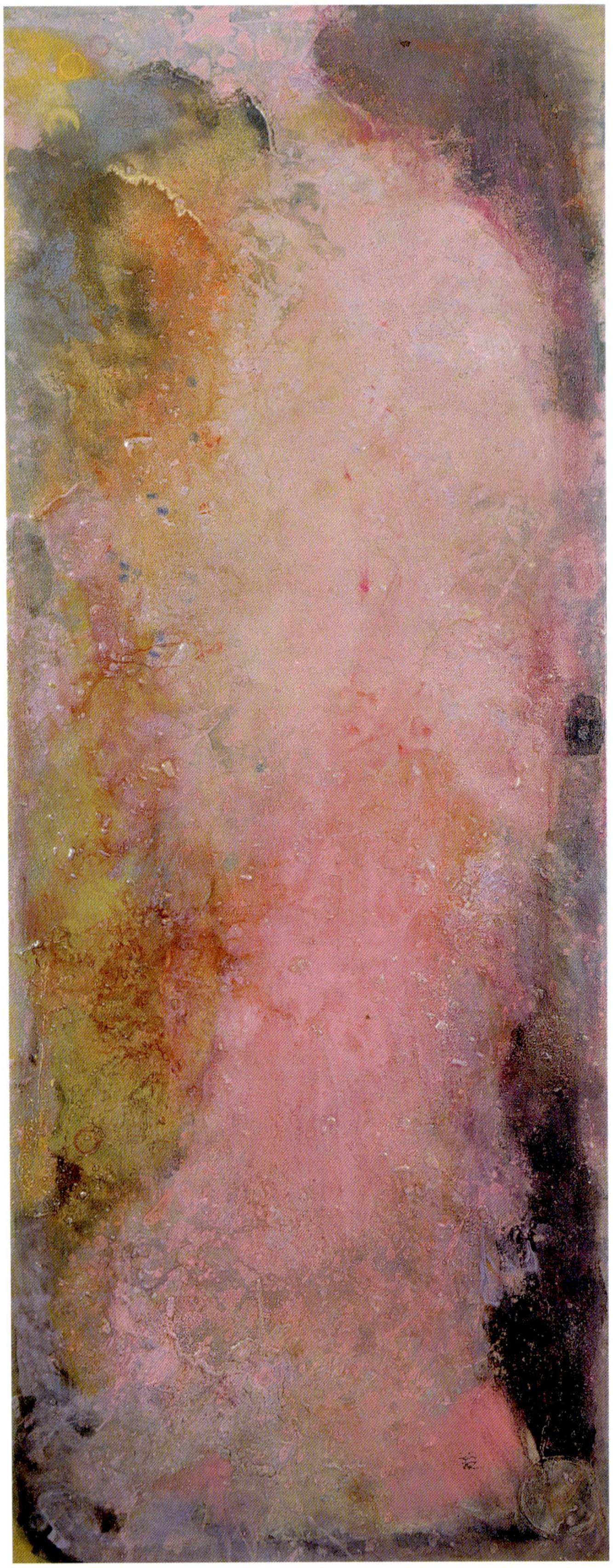

Devilssole, 1980
Acrylic on canvas, 180.5 x 71 cm

Brassica, 1979
Acrylic on canvas, 184 x 75 cm

Mazarunitankfeat, 1979
Acrylic on canvas, 180.5 x 71 cm

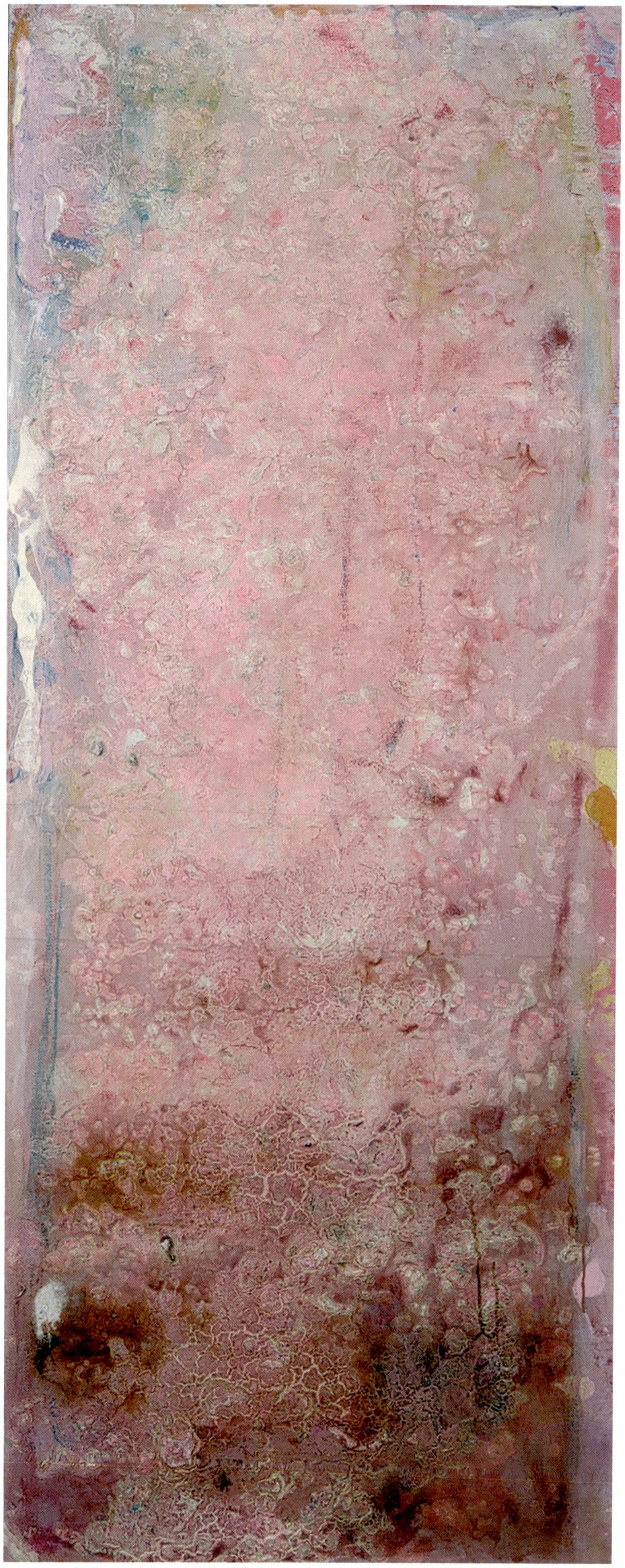

about through deliberate actions and interventions on the surface of the canvas.

Complexities and subtleties of colour are discovered in the making. Through the painting process itself, Bowling had thought his way through the presentation of brilliant objects whose structures were created primarily by process, to the representation of natural phenomena created by intentional actions including processes that manipulate the surface. The world beyond the studio has re-entered Bowling's painting in these refulgent skyscapes. Its presence is no longer a matter of arbitrary associations sparked off in the viewer as a spontaneous reaction to purely painterly effects – a waterfall! a gush of lava! fireworks! Rather, these images present a conscious recreation of natural effects by means of experimental manipulations of pigment and medium. The exhilarating reality of the perceived world – its infinite diversities of texture, colour and light, brightness, shadow and darkness, its endless variegation and constant surprise – will henceforth always be present in Bowling's painting.

Whatever the circumstances attendant on the development of this new imagery of natural light, or the mood that generated it, the fact that Bowling was once more spending frequent and sustained periods in London seems certain to have had an effect on his vision. He was living close to the Tate Gallery (as he still does), and he often visited both it and the National Gallery, to look, in particular, at the great English masters of natural light and landscape: Gainsborough, Turner and Constable. Living and working away from the urban, competitive, inward-looking, hurly-burly of the New York art world, he was bound to come back to a realisation that there were subjects other than painting itself for the painter to explore. And he could rejoice anew that the whole world of art past and present provided a marvellous prism through which the actualities of the phenomenal world might be

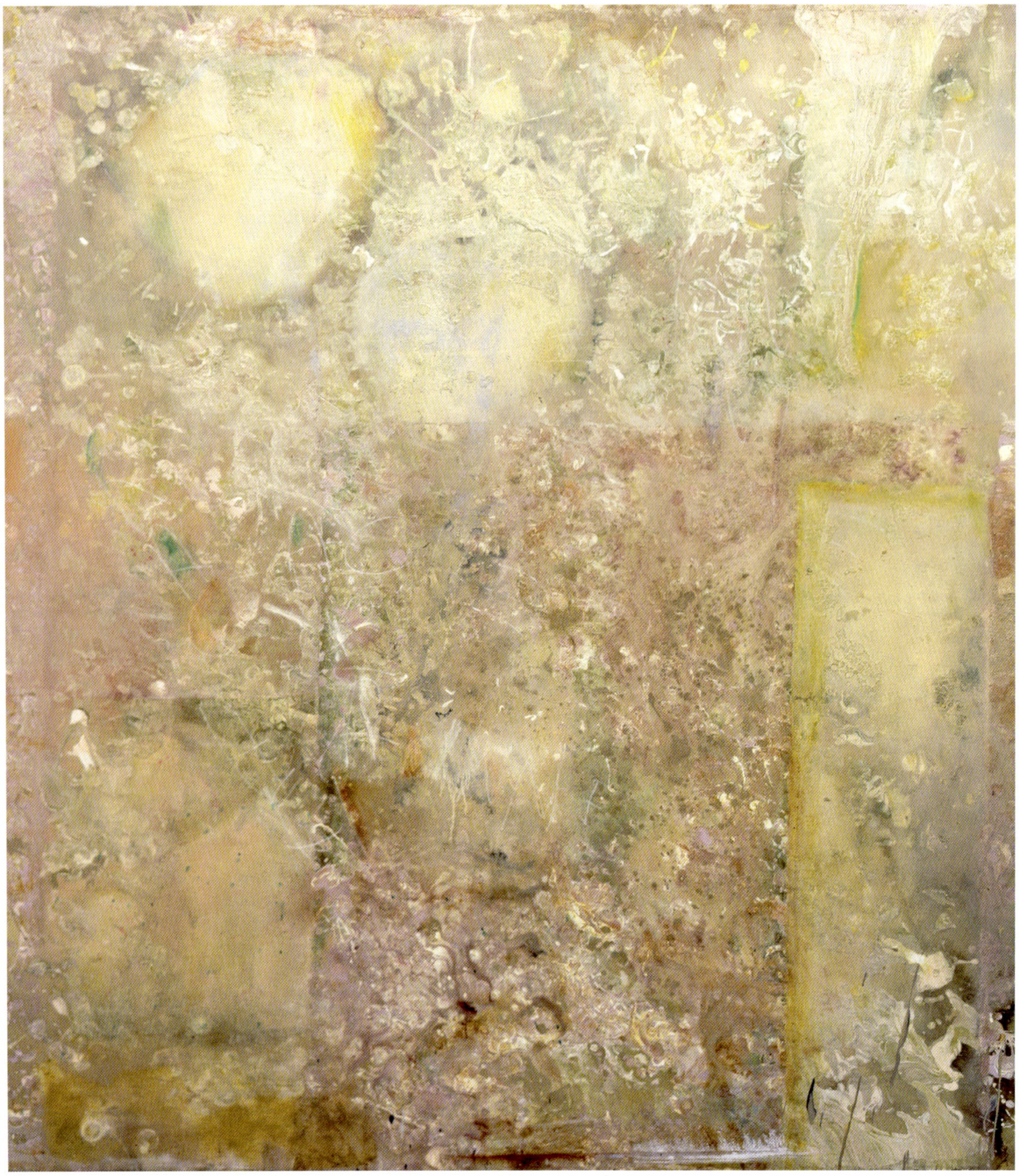

Boulder (Rocks in the Bed), 1979
Acrylic on canvas, 198 x 174 cm

refracted into a modern mind and act upon a contemporary imagination.

To speak of skyscapes and of the sunlit translucencies of clouds and mists inevitably invokes the landscape art of those major English artists of the 17th and 18th centuries, and, beyond them, the whole rich tradition of European painterly engagement with land, sea, cloud and sky. The 1979 *Boulder (Rocks in the Bed)* certainly has the look of a pale Turner sunrise, just as the pink skies of Tiepolo might come to mind when we look at *Mazarunitankfeat* and *Devilssole*, or the mysterious and clotted light of Redon (say) seem to be called up by *Brassica* (1980) and *Silenus Pisces* (1982). These associations are not arbitrary, for the simple truth is that we see in these works the beginnings of Bowling's painterly re-engagement with European painting and its traditional subject matter, albeit in a highly original, even idiosyncratic, manner.

As we have seen, Bowling had begun his career acutely aware of the histories of figurative painting and of its most vital contemporary

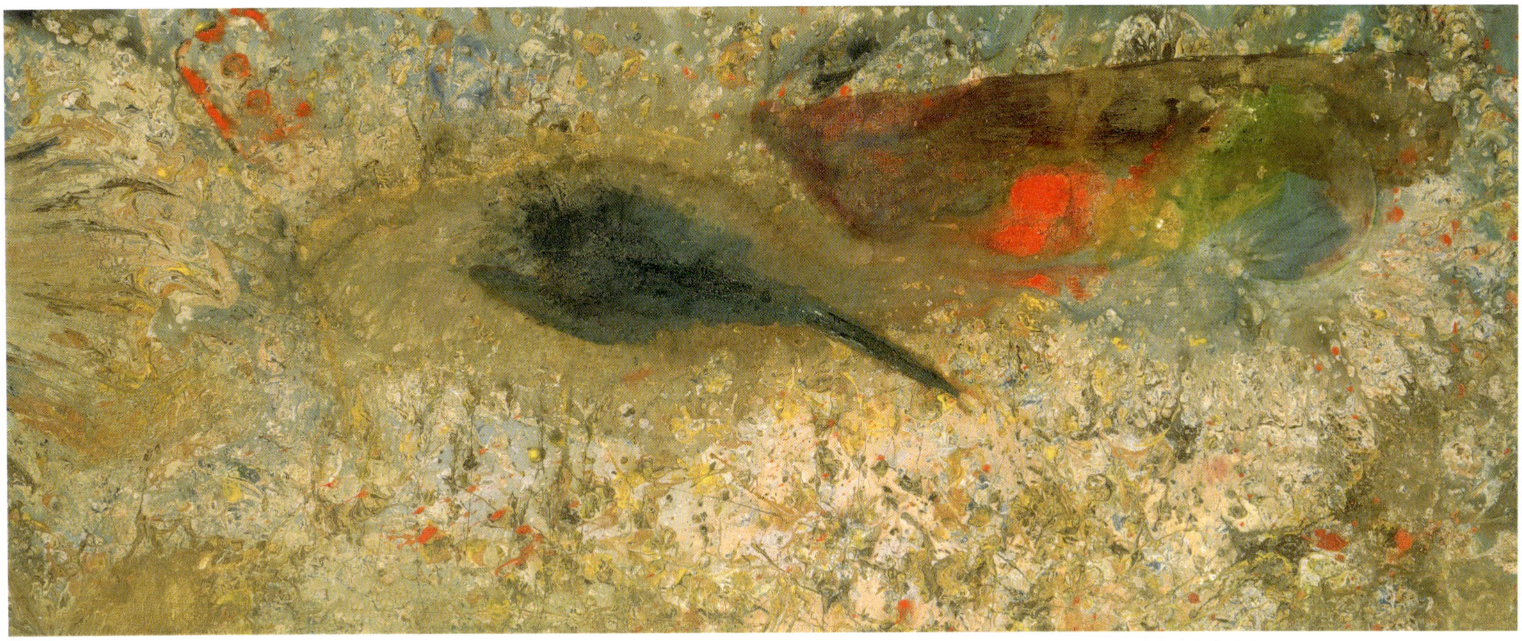

Silenus Pisces, 1982
Acrylic on canvas, 73.5 x 175 cm

manifestations. Now he was contemplating the painted landscape afresh, steeped in the vision and techniques emanating from the theory and practice of American colour field abstraction in all its diverse manifestations: painterly and post-painterly, emotionally atmospheric and coolly systematic. It is not too much to say that as a consequence Bowling was now sharply attuned to the purely abstract aspects of traditional painting. How he was to use this profound insider's knowledge would shape the future of his own art.

A number of ambitious paintings of 1981-82 triumphantly vindicate Bowling's emergence from programmatic formalism into a bold new style in which energies of material experimentation would generate an imagery of phenomenal light and matter, visions of the world and the cosmos transformed into powerfully affect-free and painterly abstractions. These paintings were created at 19 Maclise House, just behind the Tate Gallery, in the cramped conditions of a 'studio' that was no bigger than a small domestic room. Three wonderful constellation paintings, *Ah Susan Whoosh* (1981), *Odysseus's Footfalls* and *Around Midnight Last Night* (both 1982), with their wheeling galaxies and shadowy moons, demonstrate a rapid and dramatic progression in the mastery of the many varied techniques and procedures that were to serve Bowling's artistic purposes from this time on.

There was continuity in all this. Bowling carried over into his later work aspects of the objective free-form cool of his approach to the poured paintings: above all, the principle and practice of experimental improvisation in search of abstract effects capable of generating visionary excitement in the spectator. Like his free-form jazz contemporaries – John Coltrane in particular – and their great post-war bebop and cool predecessors, whose music he had heard in the New York clubs and listened to incessantly in his studio, Bowling was seeking grandeur and grace, wit and sonority. His purpose, like theirs, was to mediate the expressiveness of the medium, not

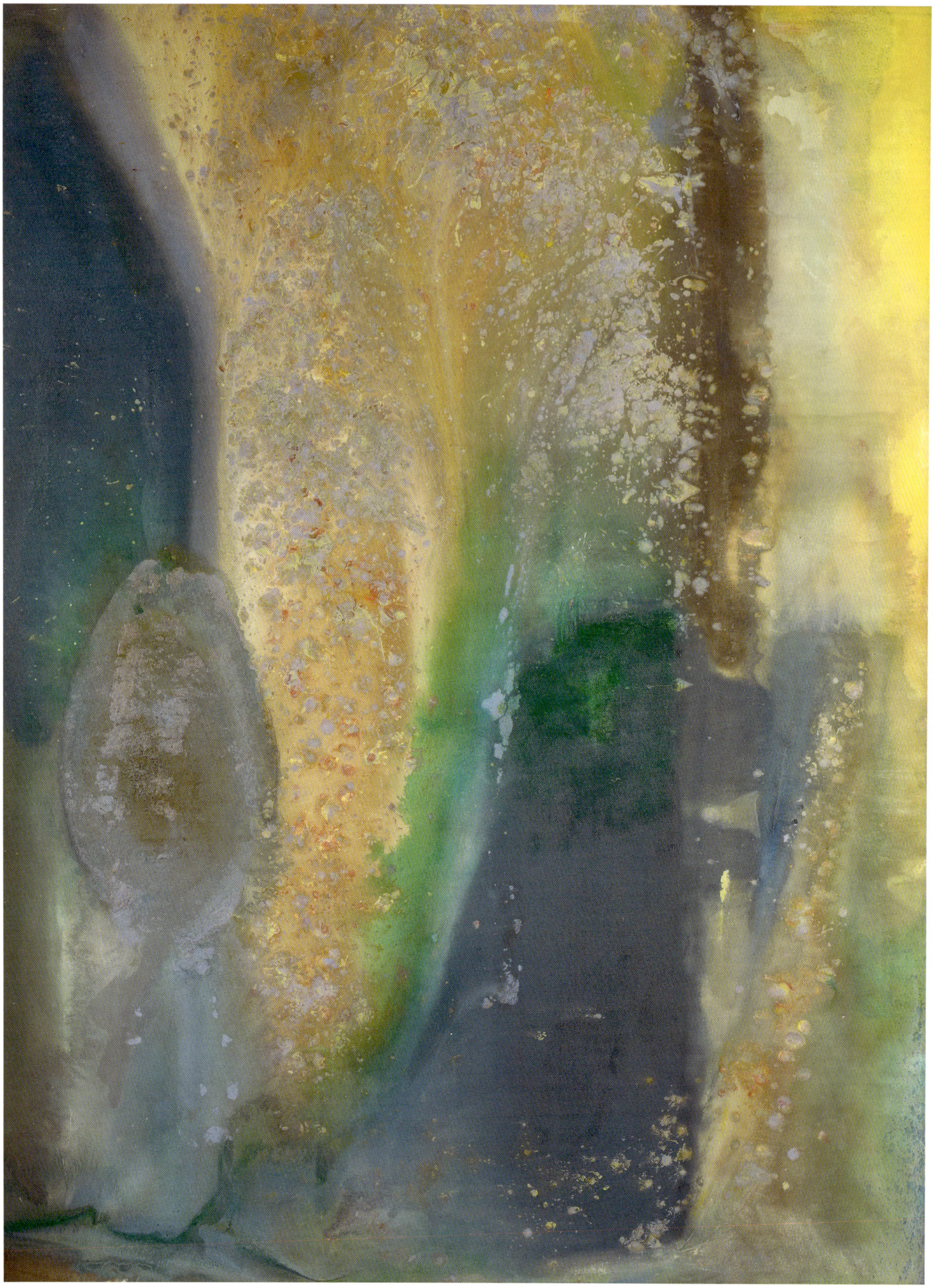

opposite
Ah Susan Whoosh, 1981
Acrylic on canvas, 241.5 x 175 cm

Odysseus's Footfalls, 1982
Acrylic on canvas, 241 x 180 cm

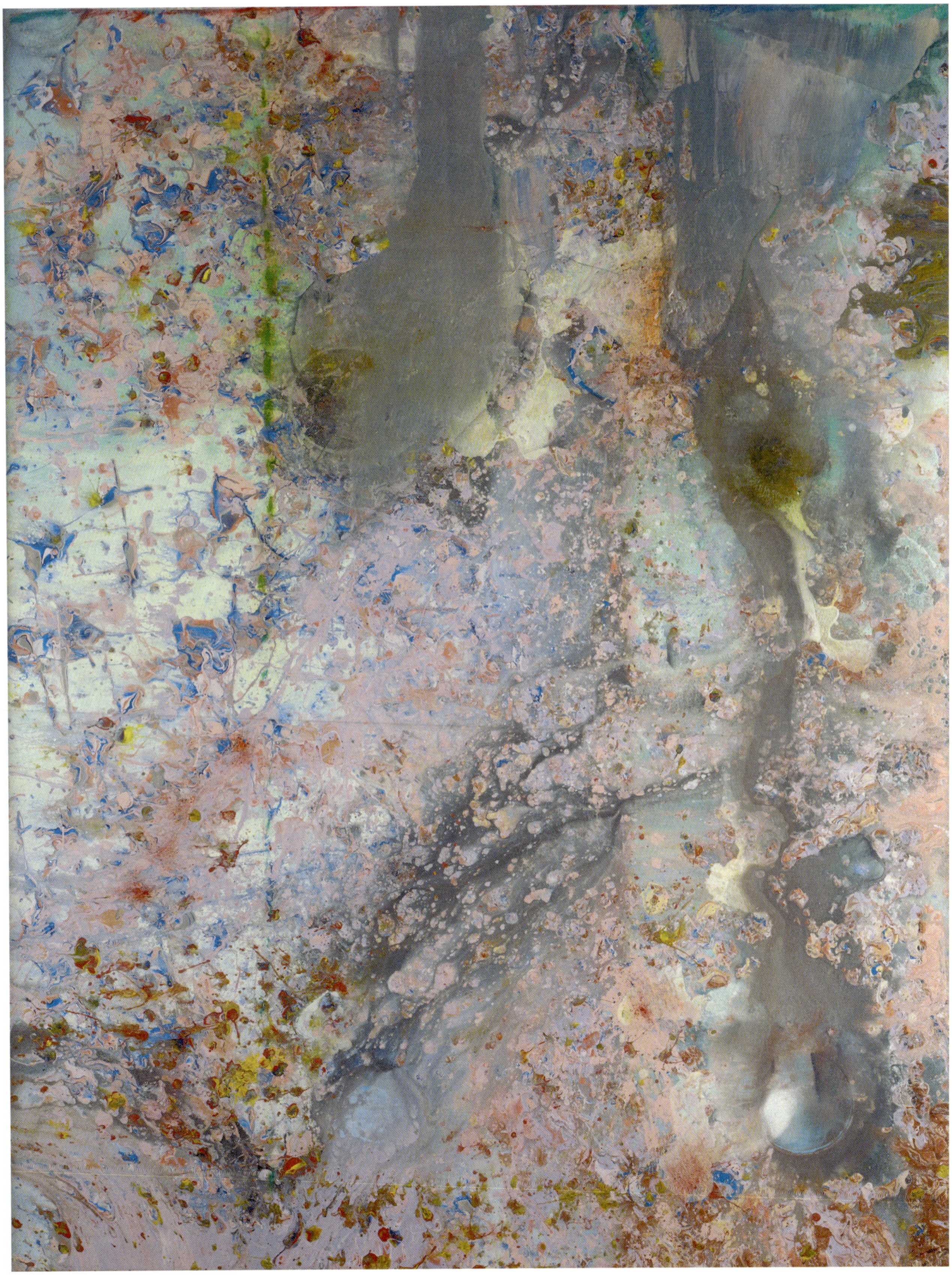

the expression of the performer, to find thought and emotion in abstract structures and material dispositions of paint, to create the painting as a resonating chamber within whose range the receiver would hear reverberations from elsewhere in the immediacy of the present.

In *Ah Susan Whoosh*, the galactic up-rush of light, which seems to fill dark skies with fiery particles and solar energies, is created out of the free play, spread and flow of chemicals across the surface of the painting, and the pitting of the surface resulting from further interventions. The combinations of process, experiment and control, of flow and halted flow, and of scattered chemicals mottling and veining the pigmented surface also characterise the creation of the cosmic effects, the vast night-sky shadows and starlit radiances, of *Odysseus's Footfalls* and *Around Midnight Last Night*. In these spectacular paintings, Bowling demonstrates the newly won virtuosity with which he would henceforth seek to bring the diversely dynamic realities of nature into thrilling visibility.

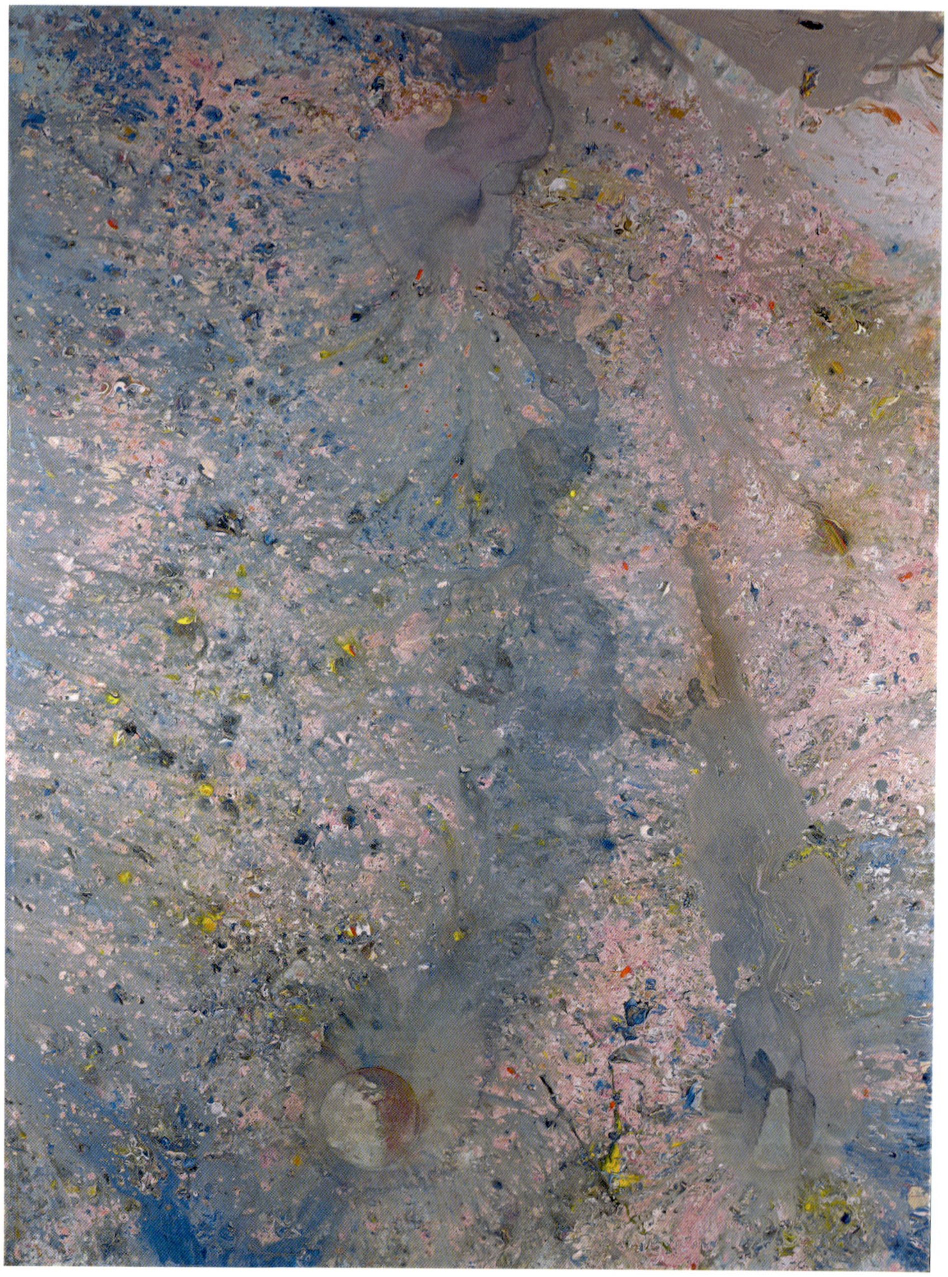

Around Midnight Last Night, 1982
Acrylic on canvas, 241.5 x 180.5 cm

10 LANDSCAPE INTO ART: COMPLEX TRANSFORMATIONS

'World is crazier and
more of it than we think,
Incorrigibly plural.'
LOUIS MACNEICE

By the early 1980s, Bowling had begun to use thick mixtures of acrylic gel in his paintings, often deploying strips of acrylic foam (a semi-rigid material used for commercial packing) to create quasi-geometric relief structures.

His approach to his painting had by now undergone a radical and ambitious development from the work of the mid-'70s. Bowling was, in fact, consciously seeking nothing less than a personal manner that would enable him to assimilate what he had learned from his immersion in New York painting, and its formalist critical discourses, with his renewed passion for historical European painting: 'I suppose, yes, my paintings changed from straightforward poured paintings … I was trying to invent ways of using the traditional ways of applying paint – spilling, dripping, marking, measuring – I was trying to accommodate [the one to the other] … I really wanted to shift the thing around so that I was always ahead of what [was] going on, I was always trying to make the work a little more than what was being done by all the others.'

A prolonged period of experimentation followed, during which Bowling found that the strips of foam tended to buckle and loop with the weight of the natural downward flow of gel. True to his experimental principles and habitual in his trusting to chance, these accidents – or, more precisely, incidents – were welcomed into the process of making: 'I would try to accommodate these things', recalls Bowling, 'it was for me a most exciting time … Having learnt how to control the gel with the structures drawn into it became part of the activity – things started to happen in unexpected ways, and I tried to hang on to those, and use them … like, make a root rectangle across the surface, and then put the diagonal, using a piece of foam, and then, of course, working from the floor on to the wall, the weight would actually make the diagonal wobble or bow … [for example,] a line for the rectangle from the edge of the painting [and] a diagonal strut might collapse into one another …'

As ever, Bowling knew perfectly well what his contemporaries in New York were doing: both Jules Olitski and Larry Poons, for example, were experimenting around this time with enriched and disturbed surfaces using acrylic impasto. But Bowling was, always, an artist on his own, with a quite distinct set of determinations and purposes. Original and idiosyncratic in his procedures, he was knowledgeable about European painting in a way that was beyond the reach of his American contemporaries, and, unlike most of the British abstractionists of his generation, he was actively aware of contemporaneous American experiment and its potentialities for presentational objectivity.

Bowling was intent on using the translucent gel in a way analogous to the use made by the classic landscapists of layered varnishes: to create, as in Gainsborough and Turner, effects of light and qualities of radiance. The hectic and broken surfaces that resulted when it was thickly applied could even, moreover, match the effects of Constable's atmospheric impasto flicker. In short, Bowling was looking with modernist eyes at his beloved English masters, to find in their work the abstract qualities of light, colour and touch that might invigorate a modernist, objective presentation of natural phenomena.

At the same time, he was committed to maintaining in his painting a formalist rigour, an all-over painterly flatness in which proposed space and its objects were never a matter of naturalistic illusion or the description of atmospheric weather and natural objects, but rather the product of the spectator's imaginative projection. The paint itself, in its textures and colours, its dispositions across the canvas surface and the affixed relief features, would provide the opportunities for such welcome speculations and imaginings. The chance buckling, breaking and

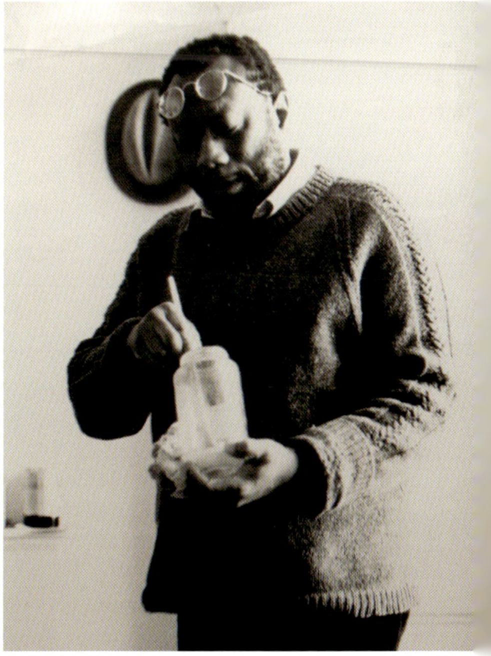

Frank Bowling working at 33 Bessborough Street, London SW1, 1981.

Towards Crab Island, 1982
Acrylic on canvas, 160 x 213.5 cm

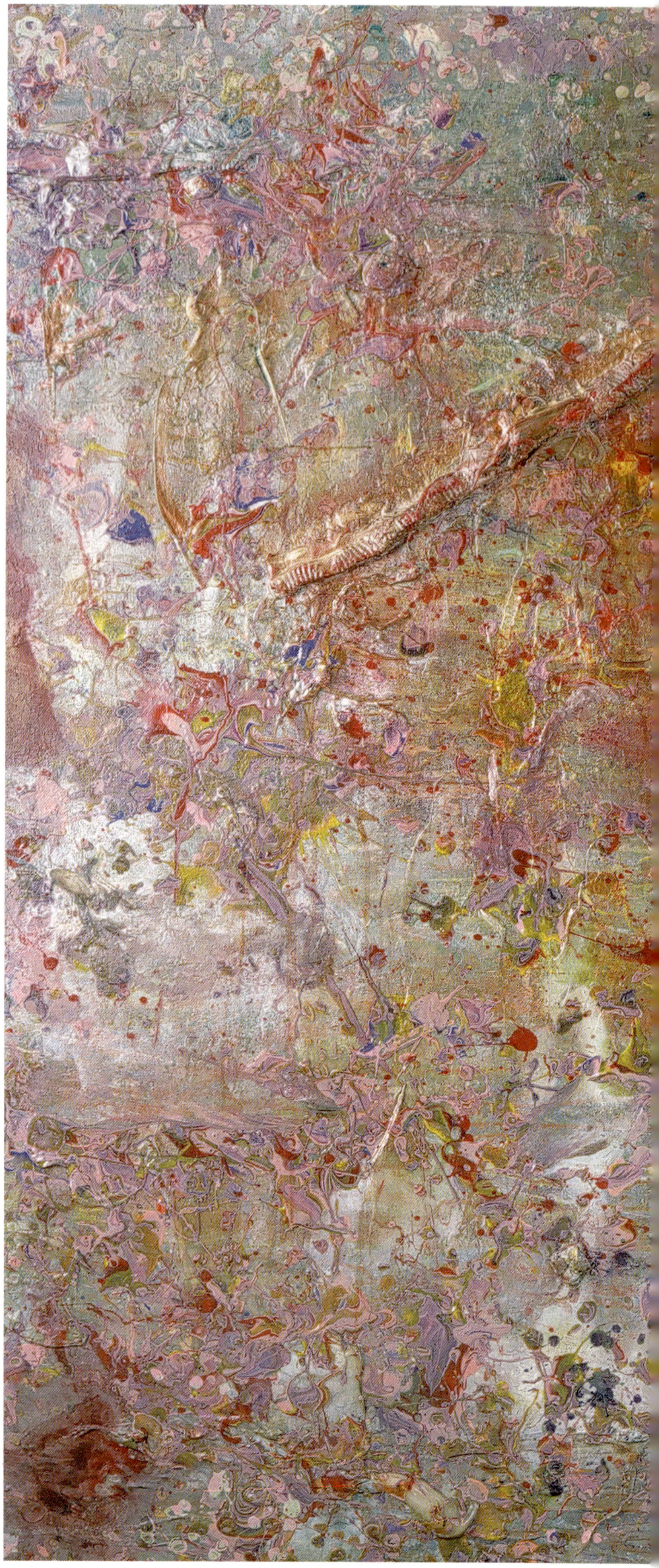

discontinuities of the 'drawn' acrylic foam geometries would bring their own affective poignancies. In paintings such as *Towards Crab Island* (1982), *Squashed Unicorn*, and *Scottscarkeysaltar* (both 1983), the action of gravity, the pull downwards of heavy gel on the structural elements of acrylic foam, can be seen to have thus played its part in the final image, with the geometries of straight line and curve broken and compromised.

The title of *Towards Crab Island* remembers an island in the Berbice estuary, and its colours suggest a watery kingdom of bright-broken greeny-blues fading into light at the right, while at the centre there is a sunset burst of crab reds, as lightly painted and brush-glazed as a Turner sky. The foam strips have lost all formal order: untethered in the alluvial flow, carried by currents of movement in the gel, they are scattered across the surface like flotsam. In the oddly titled *Squashed Unicorn* (the reference is to a tiny yellow paint detail at lower centre right), a great loop of foam, like a swing or a skipping rope, is broken at its nadir: against the vigorous horizontal sweeps of gel across dull gold and shadows of green, it is a poignant reminder of the ineluctability of natural dynamics opposed to wilful action. In each of the other paintings mentioned, there is a similarly affective disjunction between the natural beauty and richness of the colours – greens, oranges, pinks and purples – and the random dispositions of linear elements that are evidence of the dissolution of geometric order.

In the summer of 1984, Bowling spent nine weeks as a resident artist-teacher at the famous Skowhegan School of Art in rural Maine. Skowhegan was founded in 1946, and has been run and staffed by artists and writers ever since: a creative community of gifted students working each summer with established artists in residence. Its annual turnover of students and

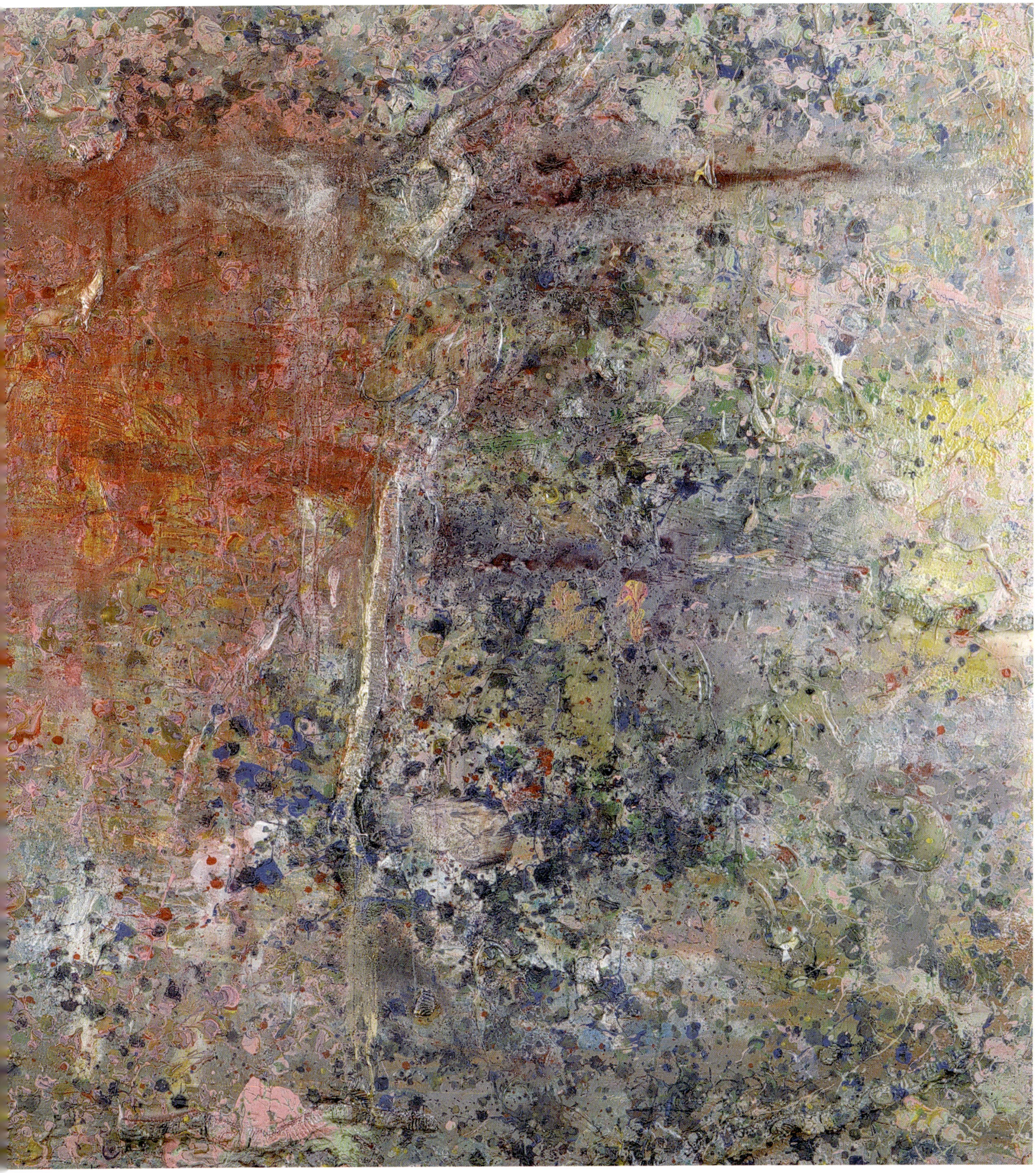

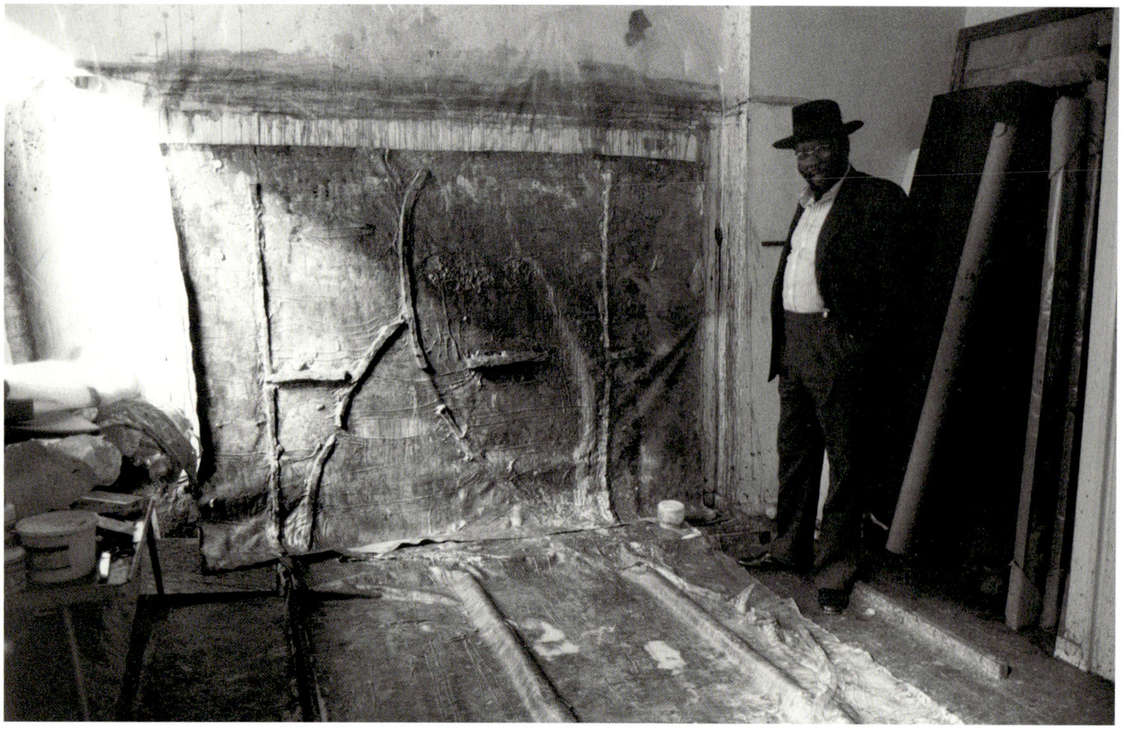

left
Work in progress at 19 Maclise House, Marsham Street, London SW1.

below
Squashed Unicorn, 1983
Acrylic on canvas, 180 x 260 cm

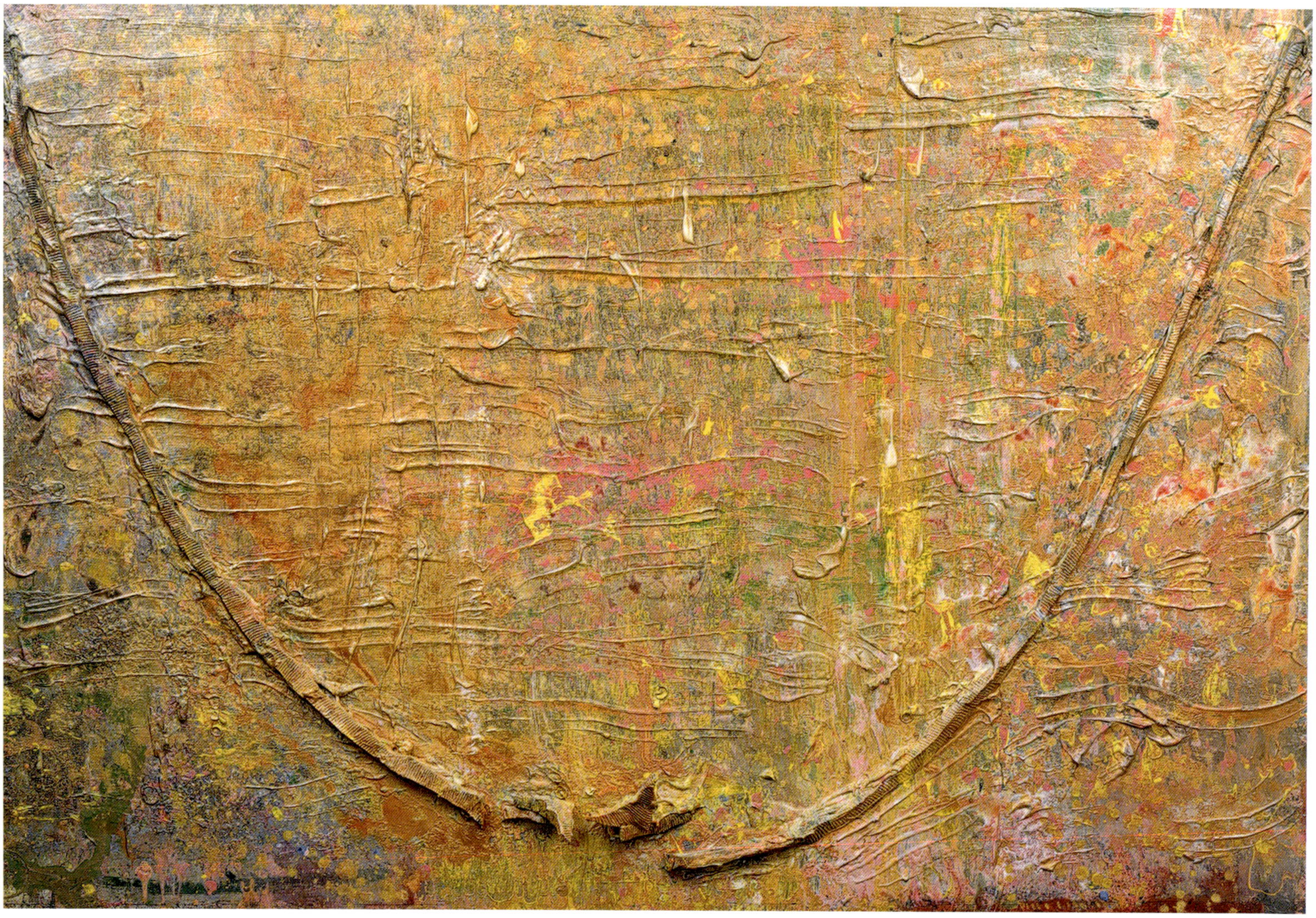

Scottscarkeysaltar, 1983
Acrylic on canvas, 180.5 x 113 cm

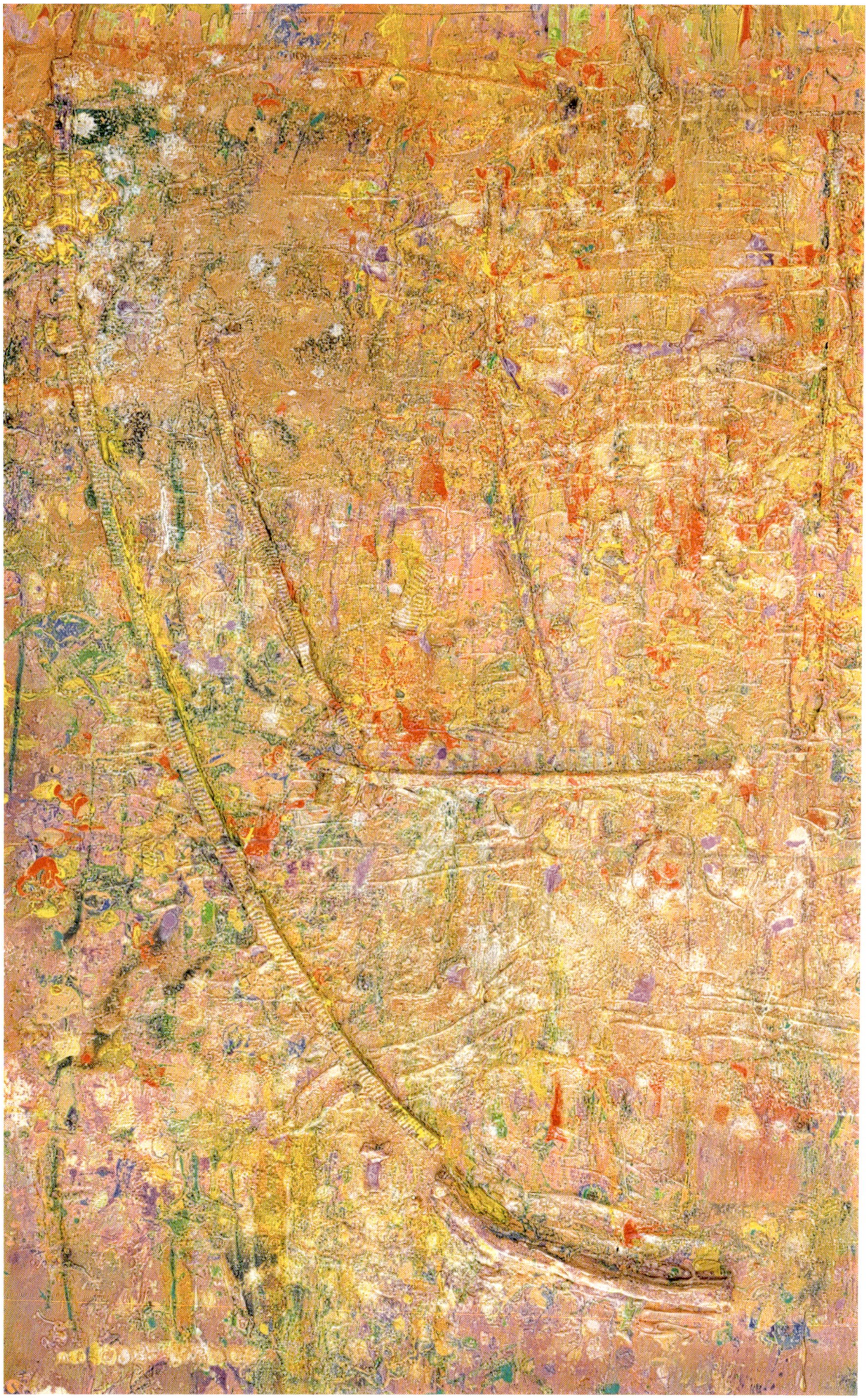

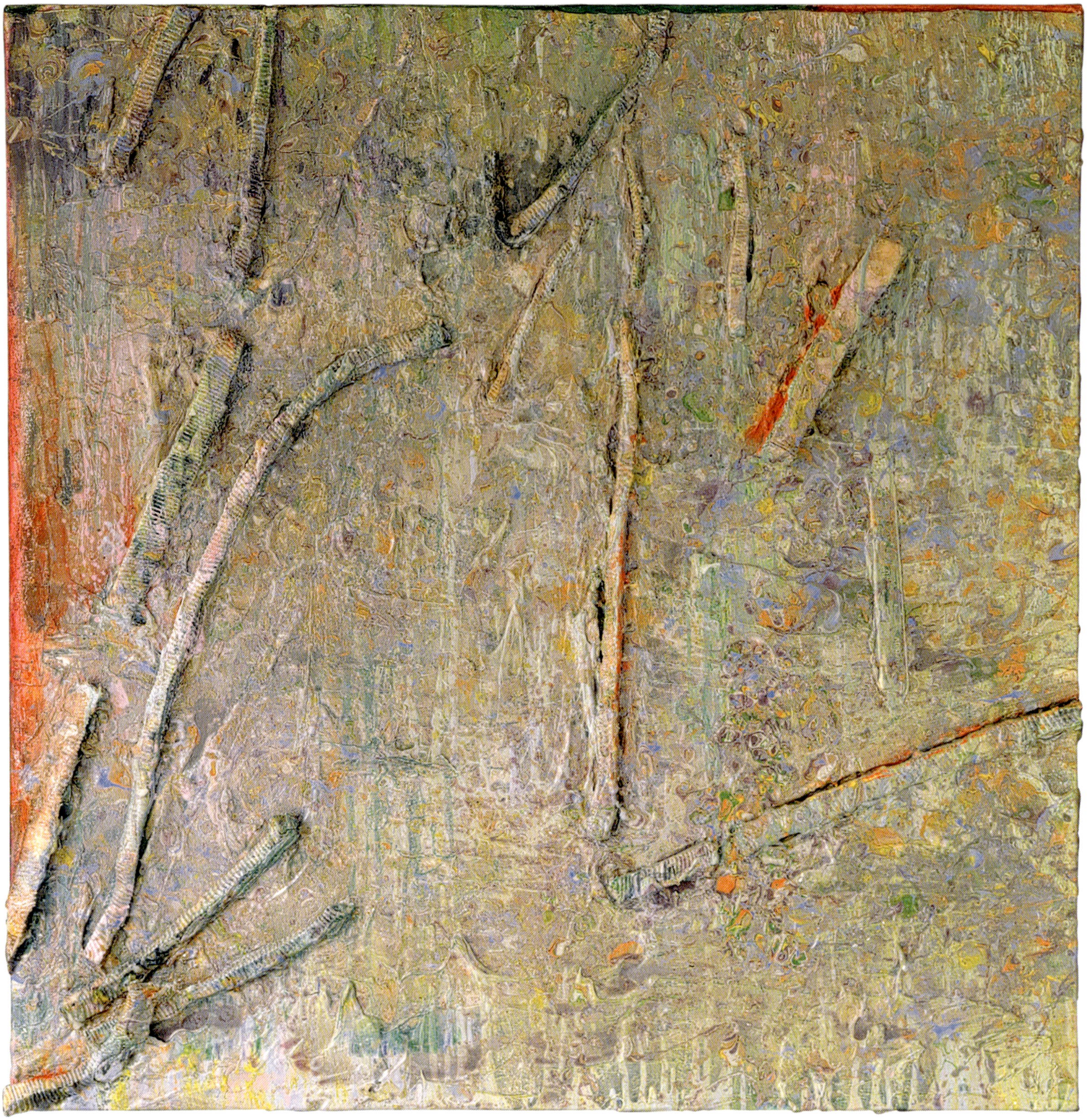

Skowhegan Green II, 1984
Acrylic on canvas, 129.5 x 145 cm

below
Enter the Dragon, 1984
Acrylic on canvas, 231 x 284.5 cm

bottom
Armageddon, 1984
Acrylic on canvas, 231 x 277 cm

visiting staff ensures a constant creative-critical vitality. Faculty colleagues in 1984 included the New York critic and art historian Leo Steinberg and the artists Richard Haas, Dorothea Rockburne and Isaac Witkin. Having the use of a large studio and comfortable quarters in Skowhegan's extensive grounds was for Bowling a marvellous opportunity for reflection, experiment and creative consolidation.

In an environment of meadows, woods and rivers, natural light and the idea of landscape became inescapable preoccupations, and his memories of classical English landscape painting informed his response to the lush greens of summer trees, the mossy greens of duckweed on pond water, the flickering complications of light on grass, the bright silvers and golds of reflected sunlight on leaves and water. The ambiguous luminosities of Gainsborough, whose feathery touch creates an effect in which, in Bowling's words, 'the surface of the work appears to hang in front of what's depicted'; Constable's broken and complicated surfaces, the material equivalent for the fragmentation of light on natural objects; Turner's varnished atmospheric and aquatic abstractions from phenomenal lucency: Bowling's paintings from the mid-'80s assimilated his remembrance of those things to the revelation at Skowhegan. At the same time they remained uncompromising in their rigorously modernist emphasis on the facture of surface, and on immediacies of optical and textural effect that deny pictorial illusion or directness of external reference.

In such grand paintings as *Skowhegan Green I and II*, *Armageddon*, *Enter the Dragon* (all 1984), *Silver Birch (No Man, No Vote)* and *Rockface* (both 1985) – all made at Skowhegan or in the months after – Bowling perfected the methodologies and techniques that have served his creative purposes ever since, albeit with diverse developments and ever-changing

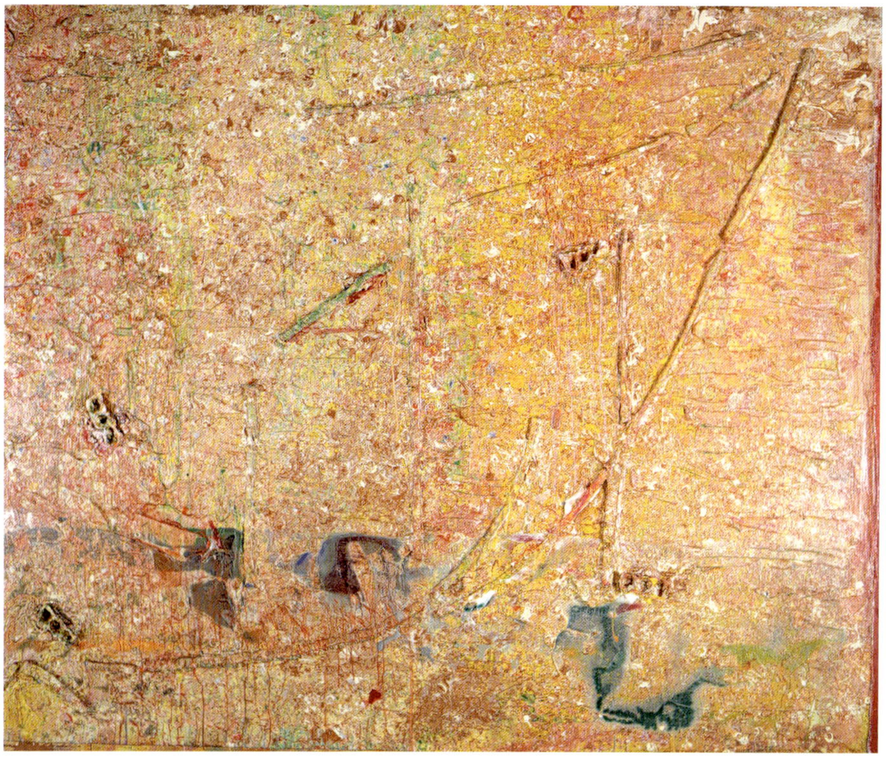

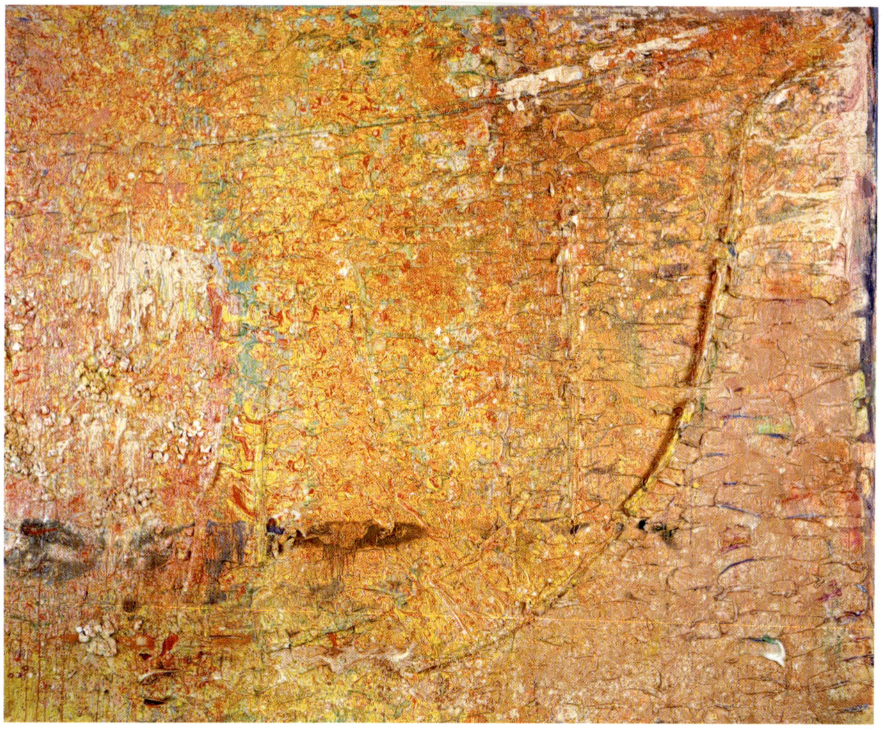

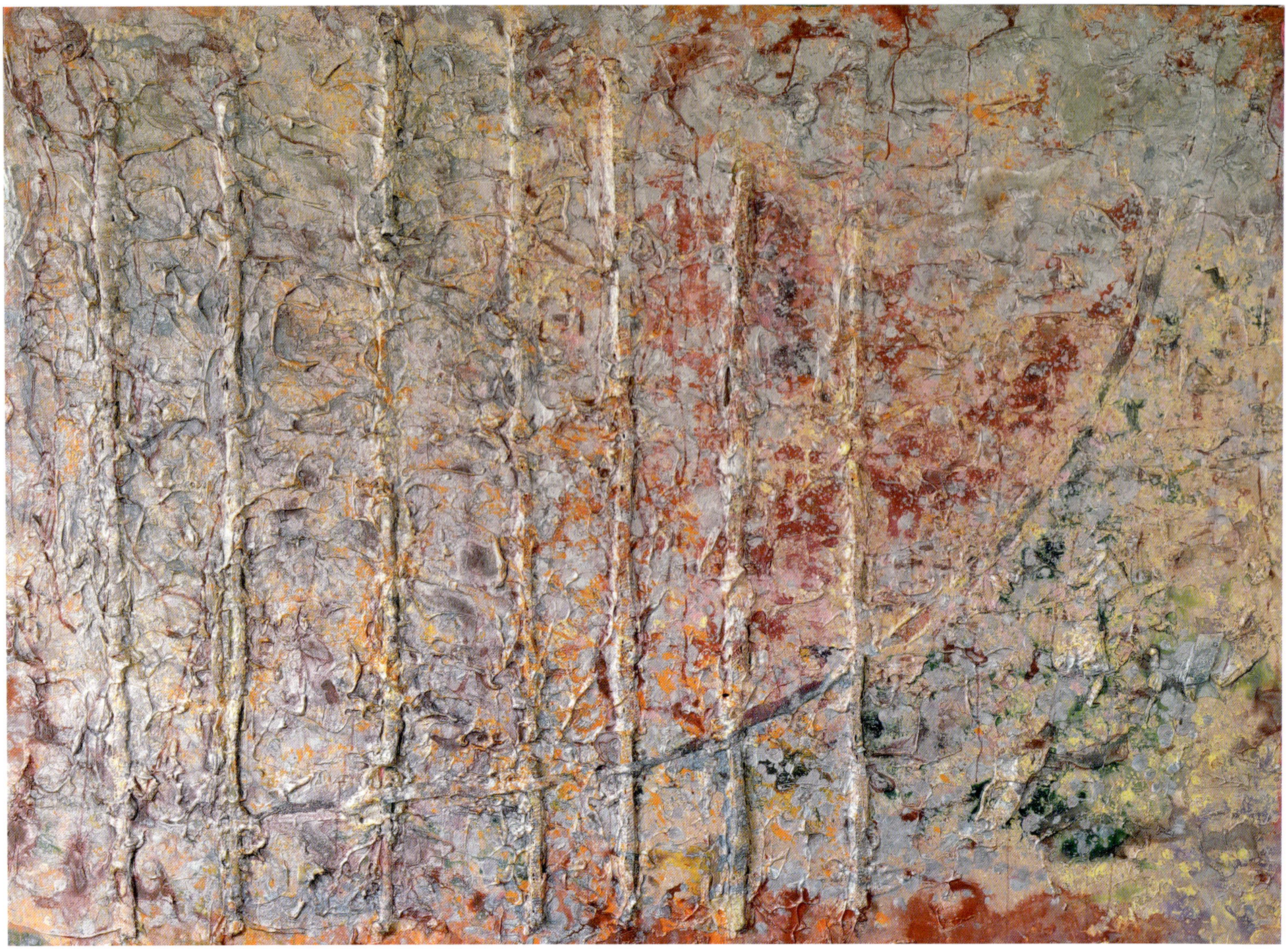

Silver Birch (No Man, No Vote), 1985
Acrylic on canvas, 179 x 244 cm

refinements of emphasis. It was at Skowhegan that he finally determined that the external world of nature, and of natural light and colour, would enter his work in terms of colour, space, texture and evocative effects, and be acknowledged, on occasion, in allusive or even descriptive titles. 'It was the first time I was faced with landscape all around; and this green: I had to wrestle with that … because I felt the green in the Skowhegan area so powerful a look that I just couldn't ignore it.' Bowling's creative mood was already receptive to nature; Skowhegan merely served to intensify this. Speaking of the Skowhegan paintings, Bowling said recently: 'I wanted to catch the light and movement of nature itself.'

Rachel Scott, his friend of many years and an indispensably resourceful facilitator and technical helpmate in all Bowling's later work, accompanied him for his first weeks in Maine. Later, he was joined by his sons, Ben and Sacha, whose superior height and reach enabled them to mark out rectangular lines and quadrant arcs on the larger canvases. Chalk and stretched cord were used in this exercise much in the manner of the early Egyptian geometers whose discoveries had inspired Jay Hambidge in his quest for the bodily origins of dynamic symmetry. Bowling had also managed to overcome some earlier technical difficulties: '... by the time I was in the studio at Skowhegan, and getting on with it, I had learnt how to stabilise [the relief drawing] more.' Using upholsterers' fixatives, he could ensure that the foam structures would adhere to the markings of the linear geometries even after they had been engulfed by the pigmented gel.

Bowling's paintings had become the product of a commitment to deliberation and technical experiment, to slow elaboration and unpredictable outcomes. Making them had become a process of contemplation, of willed chance and of arbitrary interventions creating unexpected relativities and syntheses, ambiguities of space, contrasts of light and darkness, modulations of colour, optical and textural complexities. Bowling had arrived at a creative *modus operandi*, capable of subtle variations and infinite shifts of mood, and sustainable at any scale from the miniature to the epic. Each painting presents an enthralling spectacle of simultaneities, an image coterminous with the beautiful singular object that bears it. The rich complexities of texture and colour of Bowling's painting are aspects of work done one throw at a time: 'Poetry (like craps) is managed chance', wrote the American poet Dan Chiasson. 'It is called (over the ages) by other names: inspiration, the unconscious, "craft." ' Each painting is thus the outcome of a uniquely characteristic and habitual interplay of procedure and process.

Procedures are techniques and constraints, ordered ways of doing and making, considered sequences of material application and the manipulation of the support. The total image, however immediate it is in impact, has been created slowly and carefully out of a succession of discrete actions, retractions, cancellations, reflections, additions and subtractions. These procedures incorporate aspects of routine and ritual, as in cooking, an analogy Bowling frequently reaches for when describing his methods of working. In any one painting, they may include embeddings in thick gel of linear foam-strip and of personal or found objects;

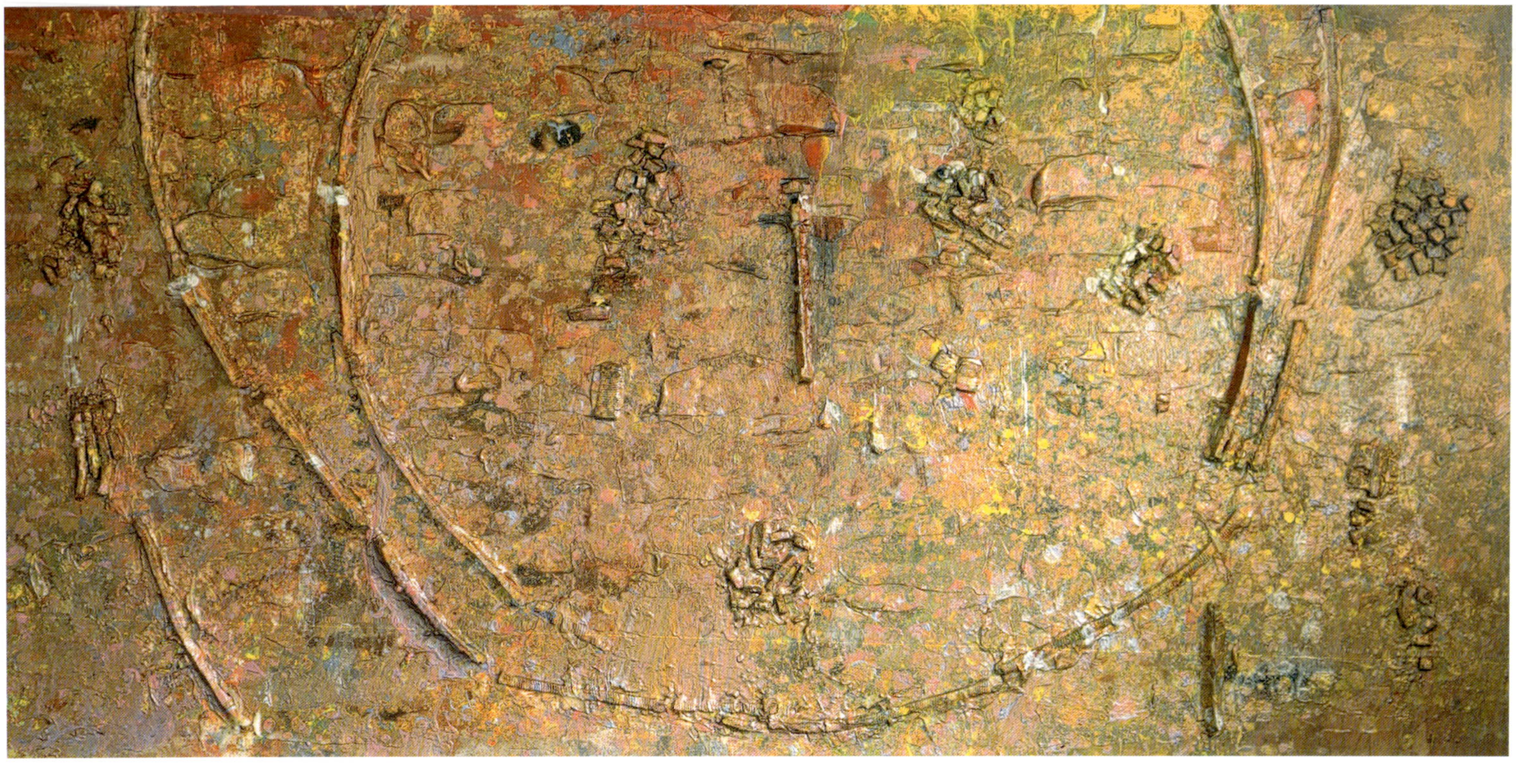

***Rockface*, 1985**
Acrylic on canvas, 179 x 363 cm

stitching or gluing on colour borders and internal framings of stained textile; the application of pigments by brush; the application by spatula or by controlled pouring of pigmented gels of various viscosities as subtle in their refinements of the image as the applications of varnish to 18th- or 19th-century landscape paintings.

Processes, on the other hand, are natural workings of energy, of gravitational dynamics, and of chemistry. The refractive and reflective layerings of acrylic gel achieve their multifarious effects by dissipations of the infused pigments and by the underlying stainings of the support; they settle and harden into faceted encrustations, with obtrusions and concavities, edges and declivities. These surface complications, catching and absorbing light with a thousand different effects, are the result of natural actions, interactions and physical contrarieties, whose outcomes are thrillingly unpredictable, bringing random, irrepressible pleasures to the eye. They allow no illusion, no pretence: means and effect are one. Such painting is the precipitation of multiple and complex micro-histories, in which artistic premeditation lies in the choice and dispositions of the materials and the release of the formative energies.

In 1986, Bowling exhibited a group of major new paintings at the Serpentine Gallery: it was the first recognition of his achievement at a public gallery in London. Among the paintings he showed was the magnificent *Wintergreens* (1986), in which the play of winter light over an indescribably rich plane of iridescent deep evergreen tones discloses a vegetal and aqueous world of fantastic complexity. The deep green and blue spaces are seen through a loose embedded grid, which might enclose the panes of a window looking on to a forest pool, or a fence against the edge of a dark wood. In the first place, however, it is a formal structure to hold the riot of colour and surface complication against optical

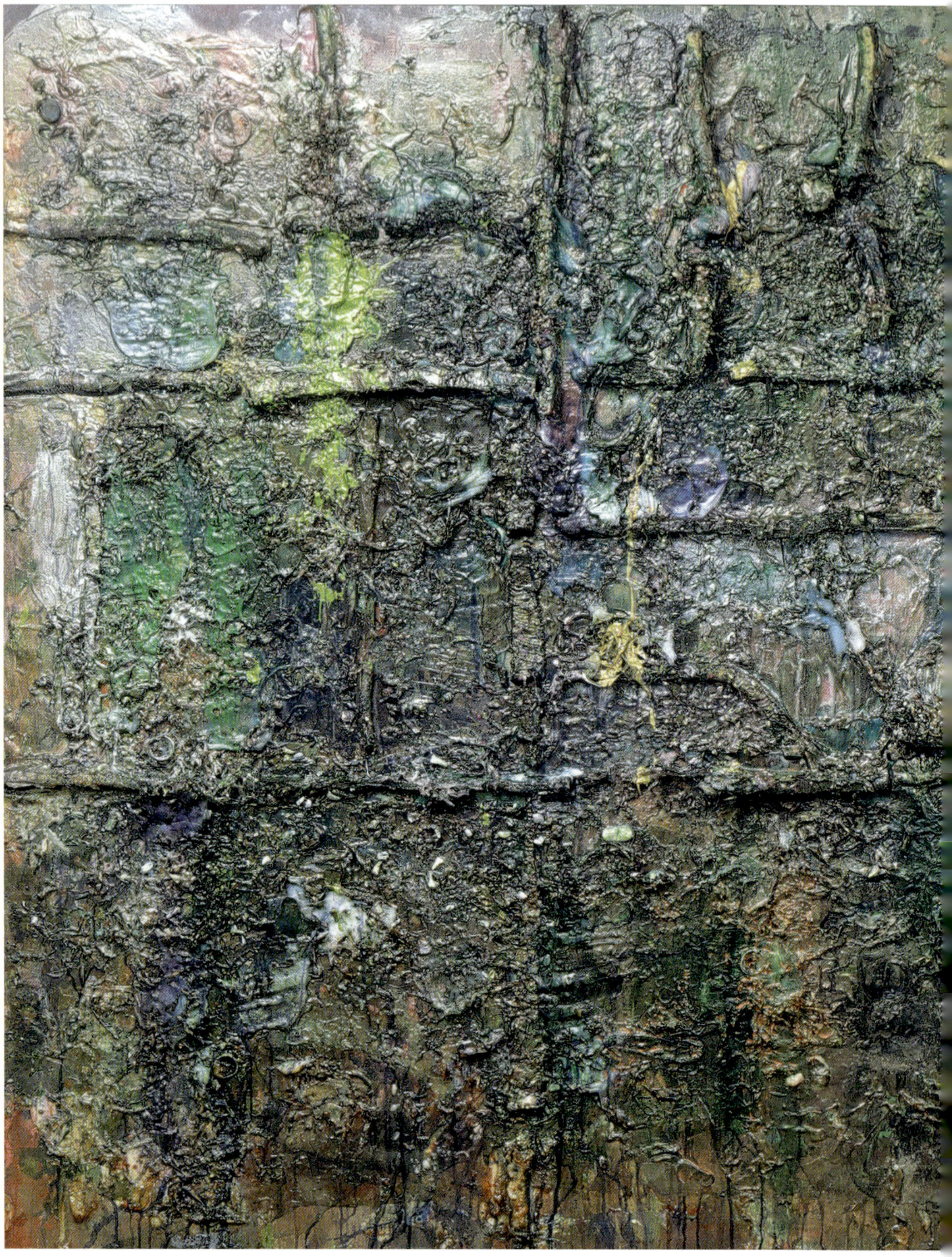

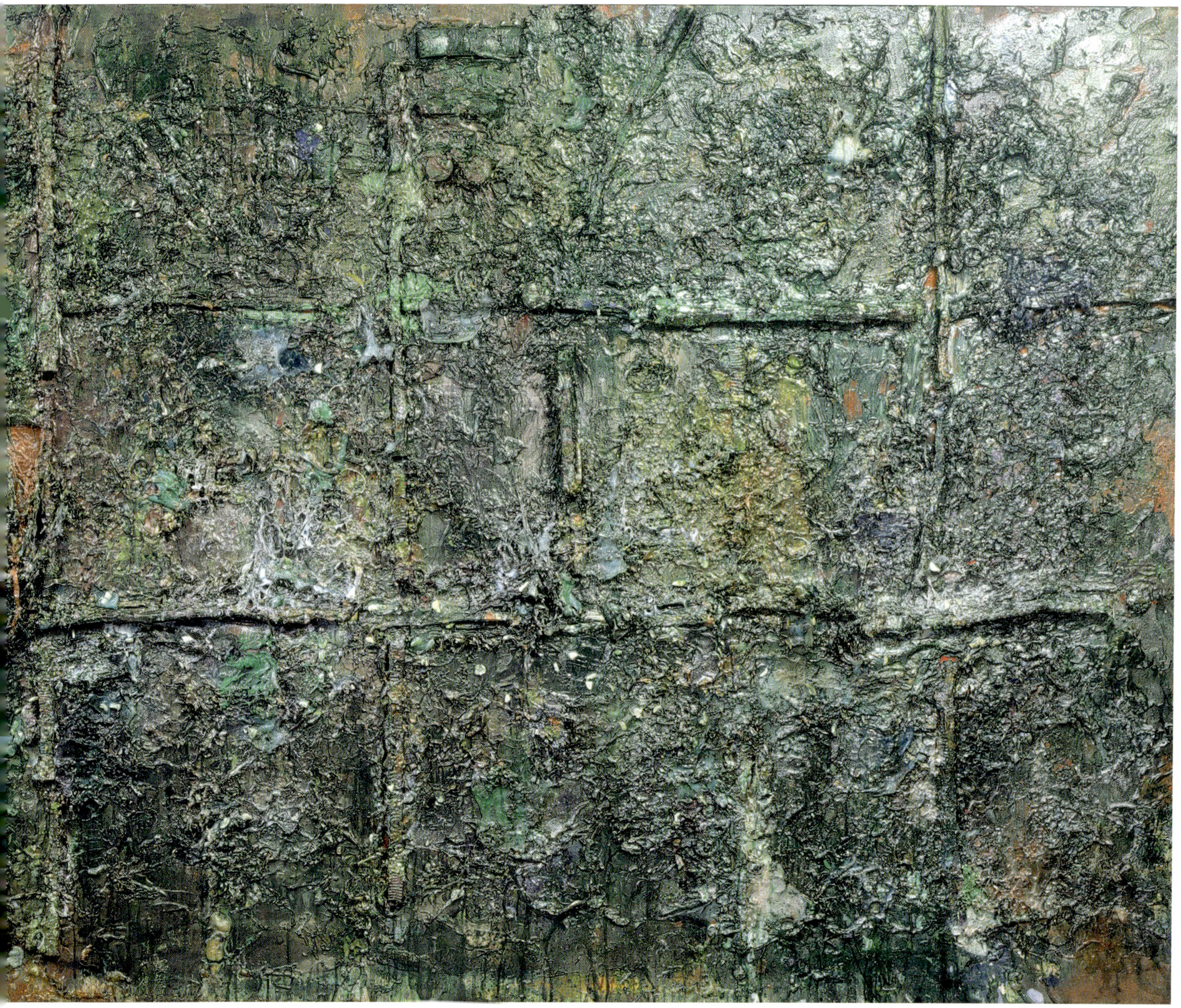

Wintergreens, 1986
Acrylic on canvas, 173 x 348 cm

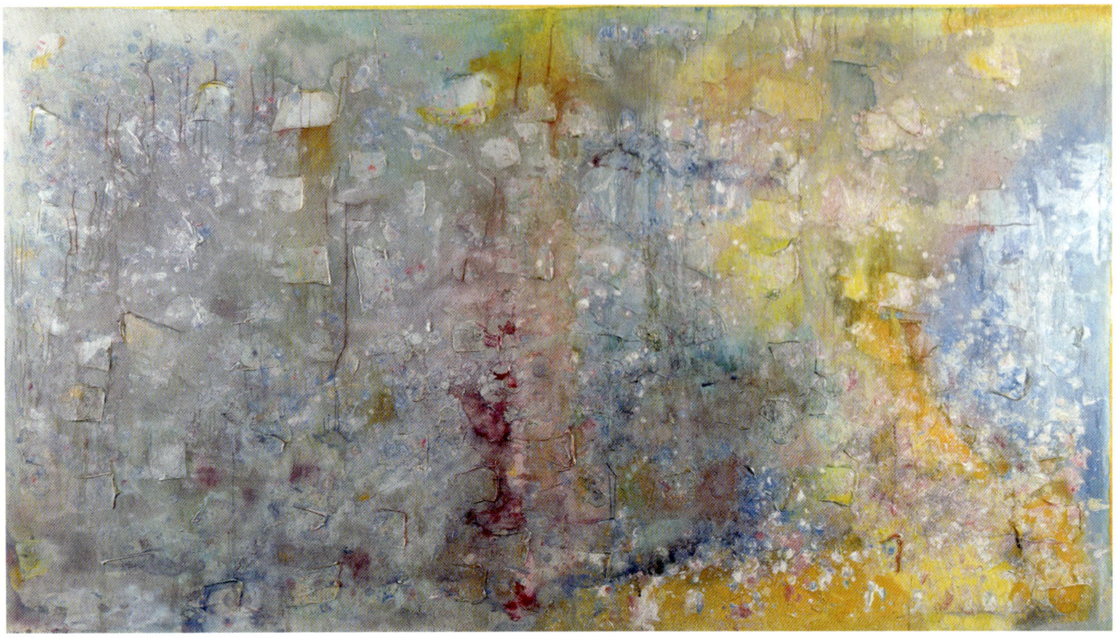

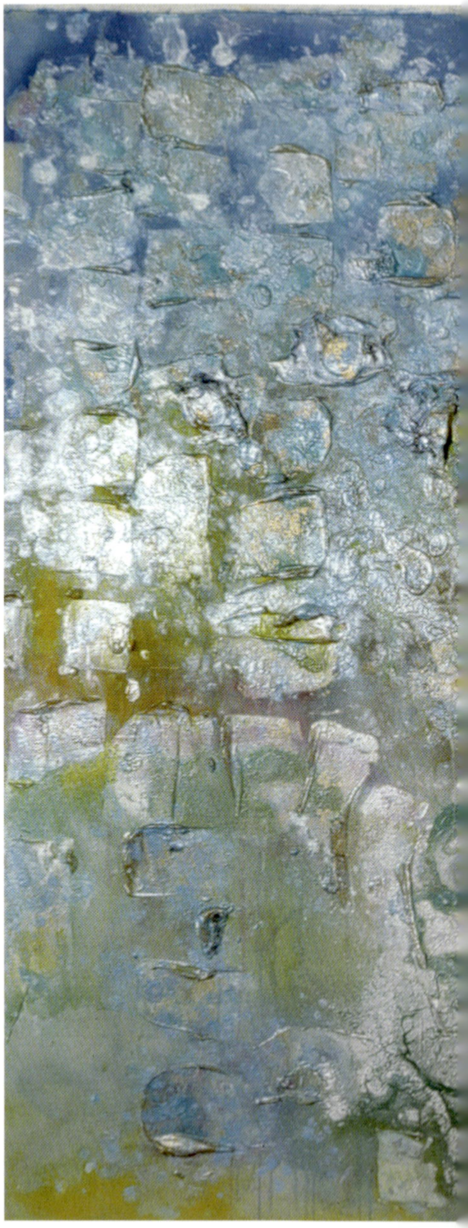

dispersal; to suggest an ordering of perception against visual dissipation and chaos. There is a range of metallic blue-greys and silvers in this painting which recall the subtle tonalities of Gainsborough's parkland and countryside settings. Close up, the chaotic surfaces bear an uncanny resemblance to those of Constable's great 'six footers', the full-scale oil sketches for his grand Academy paintings – 'the great machines', as he called them. It is peculiarly fitting that this monumental masterpiece should have been accepted as Bowling's diploma painting on his election in 2005 to the Royal Academy.

In the 1980s, Bowling became a transatlantic commuter, working in the spring and autumn in New York (from 1990 in his Brooklyn studio) and in the summer and winter in London. For a period in the late 1980s, he rented a second London studio in a disused factory in Cable Street, close to the Thames at Wapping, larger and with more light than that at Peacock Yard. Here, at the end of the '80s, he made the *Great Thames* series of paintings (1989), in which his homage to the great English painters of natural effects is extended to Turner, the master of aquatic and aerial light. It was around this time that Bowling wrote: 'The fact is, it's exciting and challenging to work in London, Turner's town, and the pressures of the weight of British tradition are exhilarating.' The *Great Thames* series consists of paintings of extraordinary grace and grandeur, quite unlike anything being made in London, or anywhere else, at the time. As with *Simon Helps* (1986), *Philoctetes's Bow* (1987), *Waiting for Samson* (1989-90), *Samson's Arrival* (1989-90) and many other works of this period, they are characterised by surfaces of reflective translucence, faceted and gleaming structures of light.

Writing to a Tate curator in 1989, two years after the Tate's acquisition of *Spreadout Ron Kitaj* (1984-86), Rachel Scott gave an invaluable account of the elaborate procedures

above left
***Great Thames I*, 1989**
Acrylic on canvas, 180.5 x 320 cm

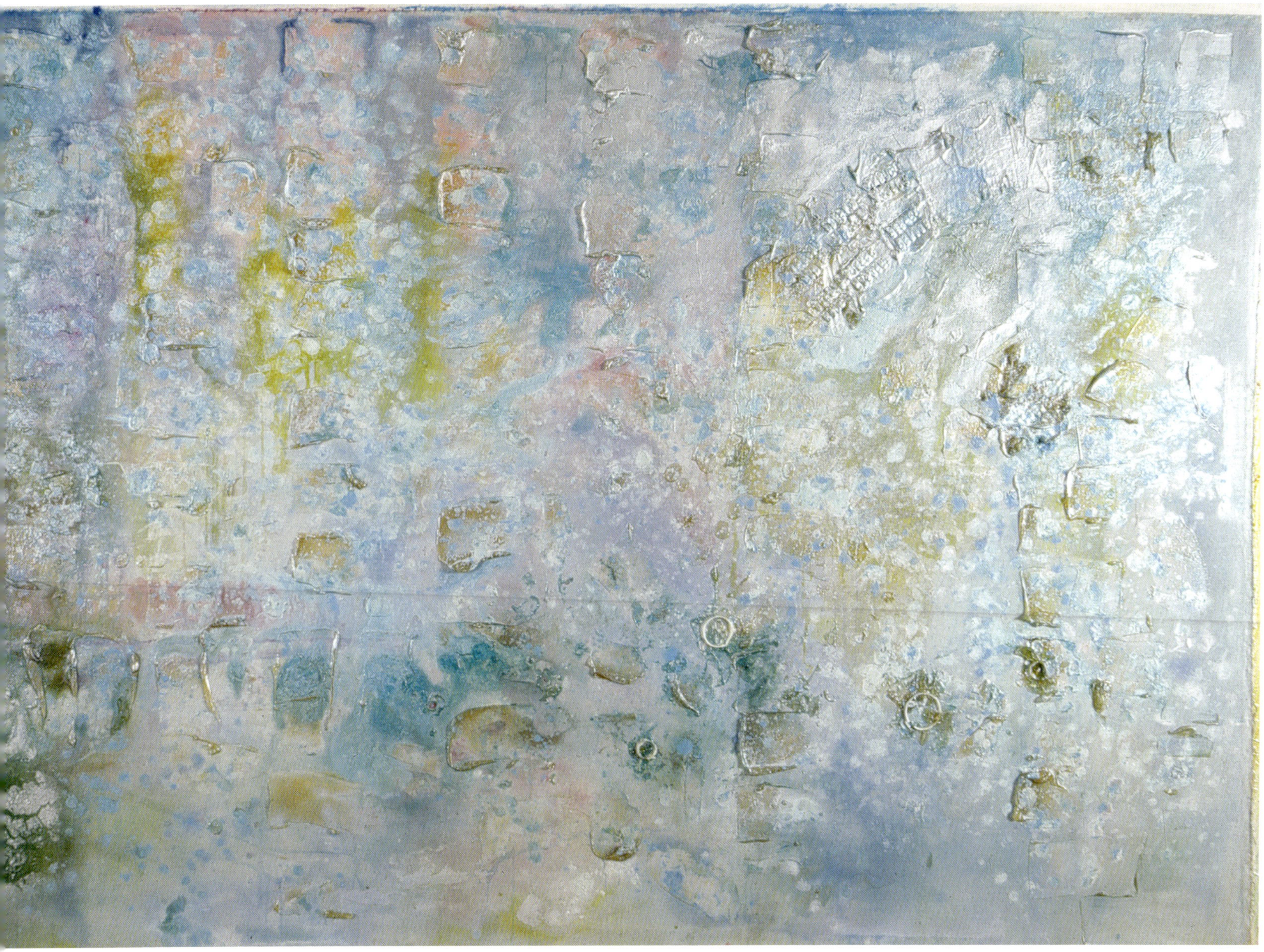

Great Thames IV, 1989
Acrylic on canvas, 180.5 x 320 cm

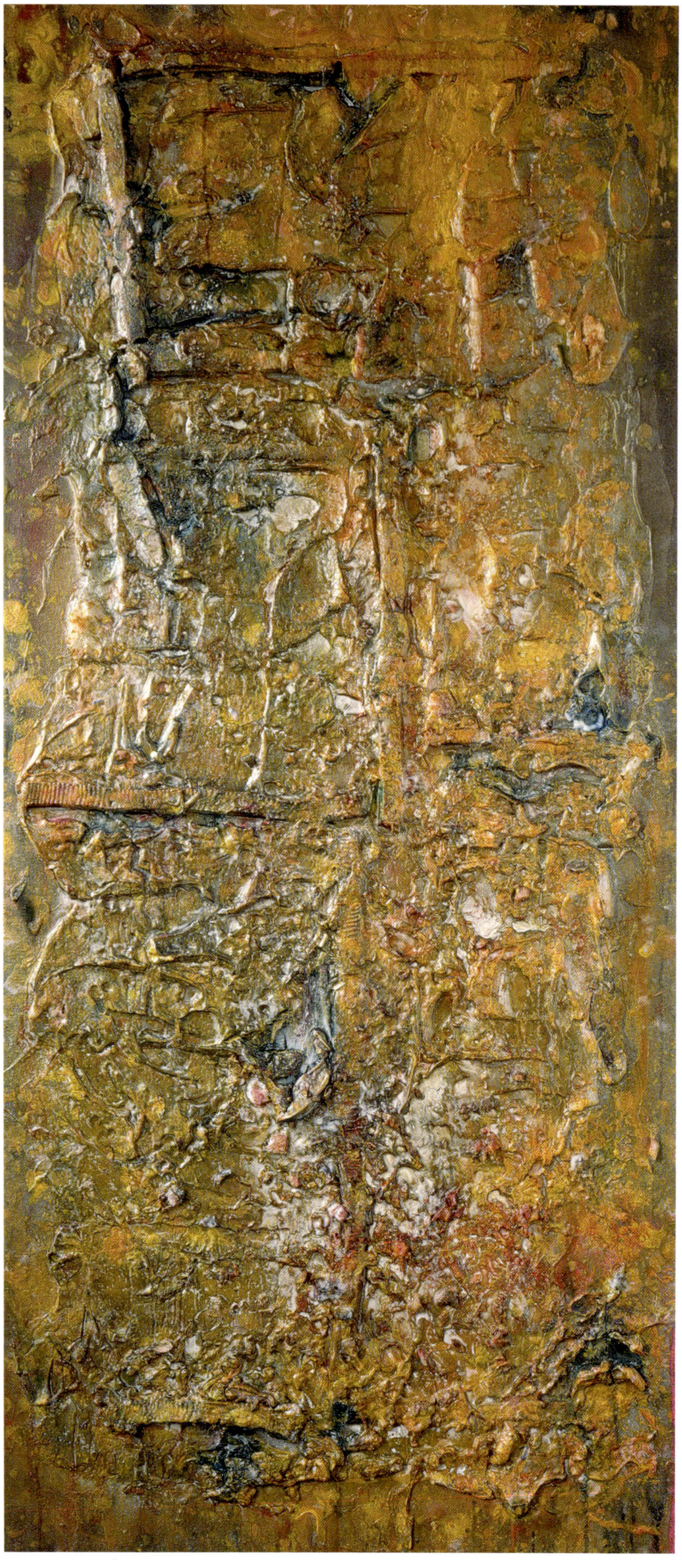

Simon Helps, 1986
Acrylic on canvas, 186.5 x 81.5 cm

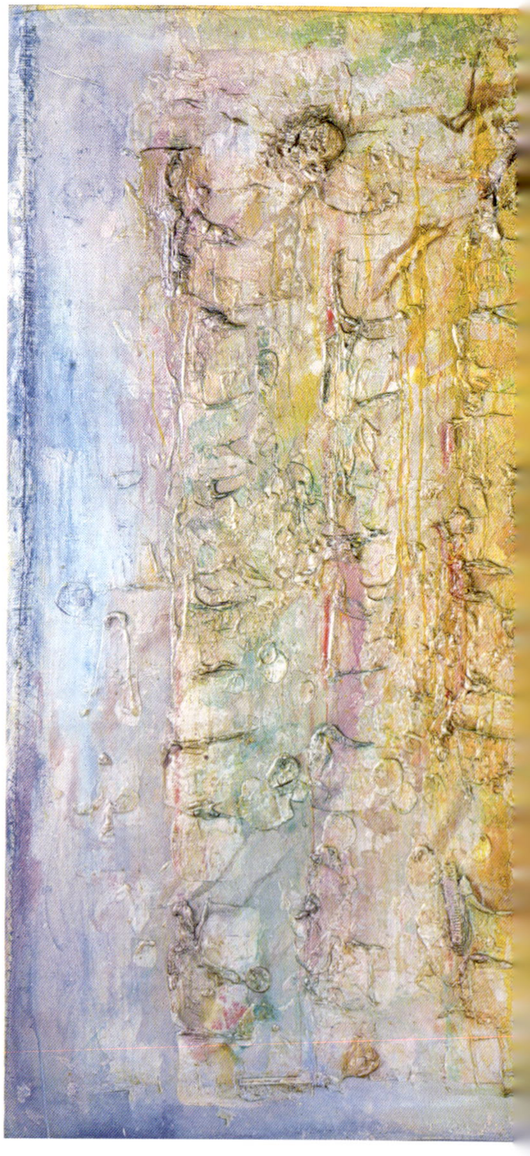

right
***Philoctetes's Bow*, 1987**
Acrylic on canvas,
183 x 360.5 cm

below
***Waiting for Samson*, 1988-89**
Acrylic on canvas,
184 x 353 cm

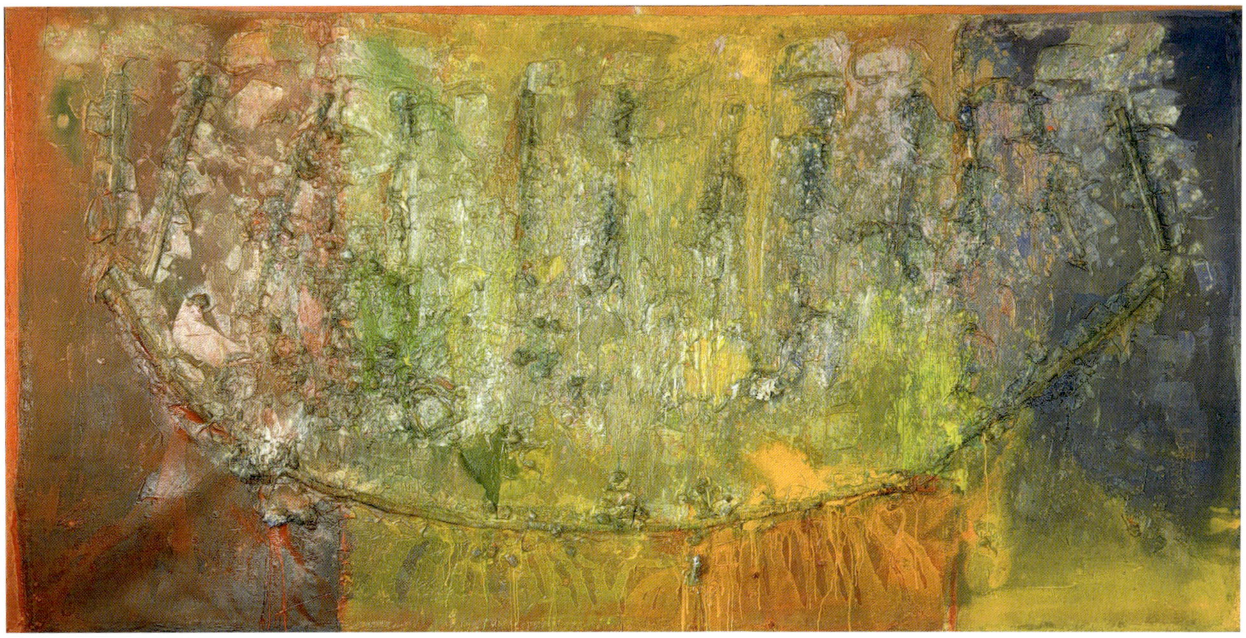

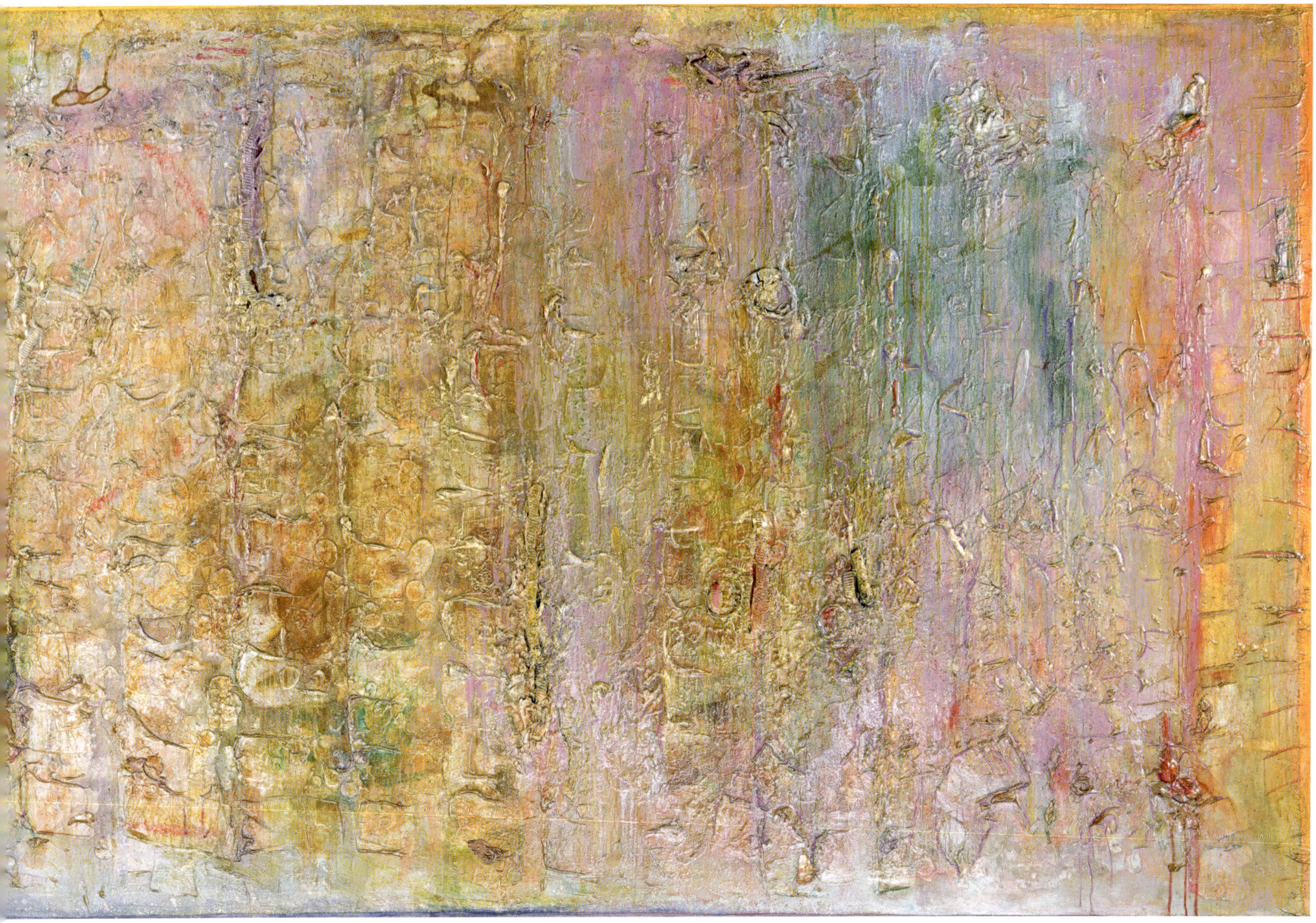

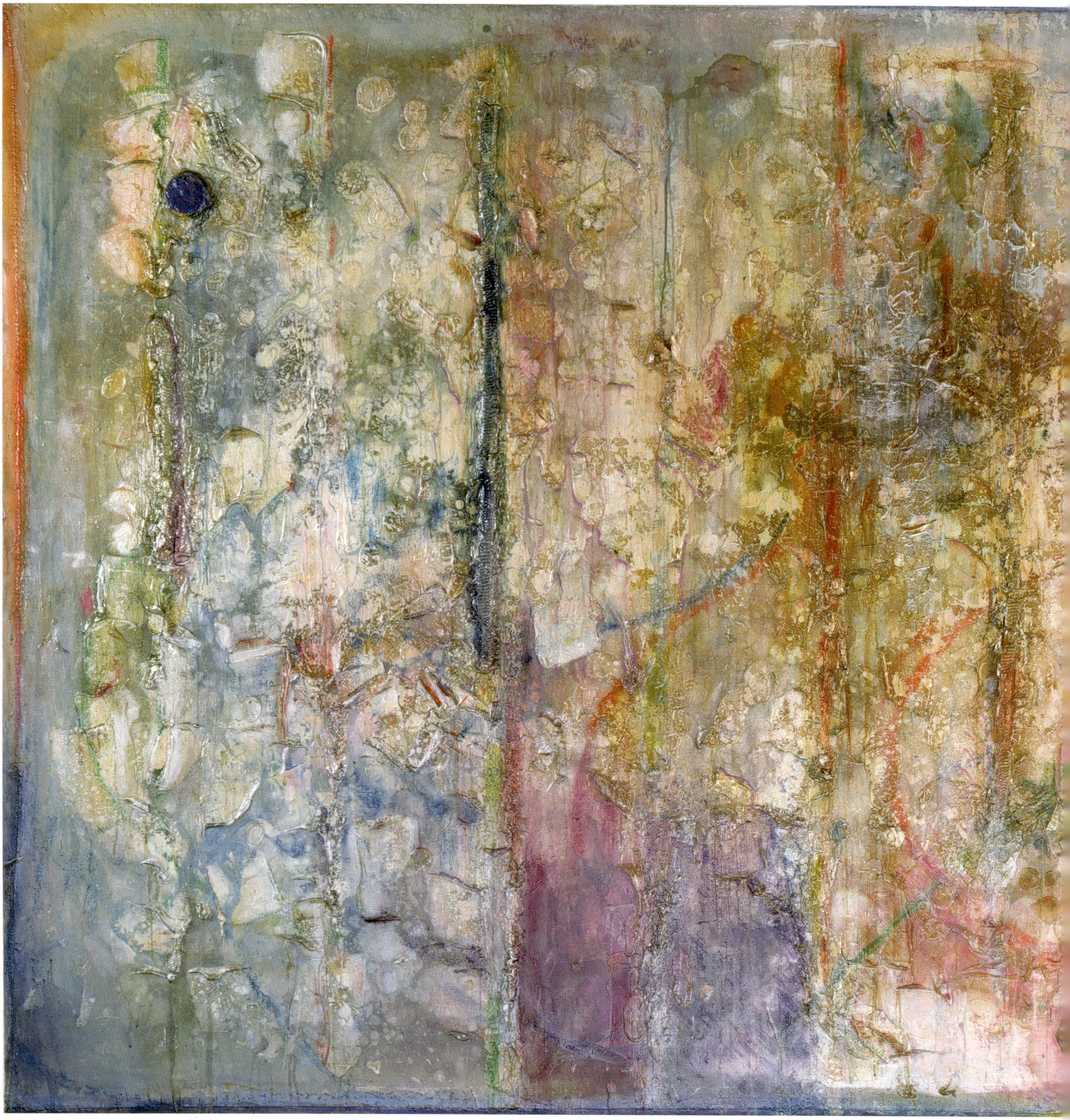

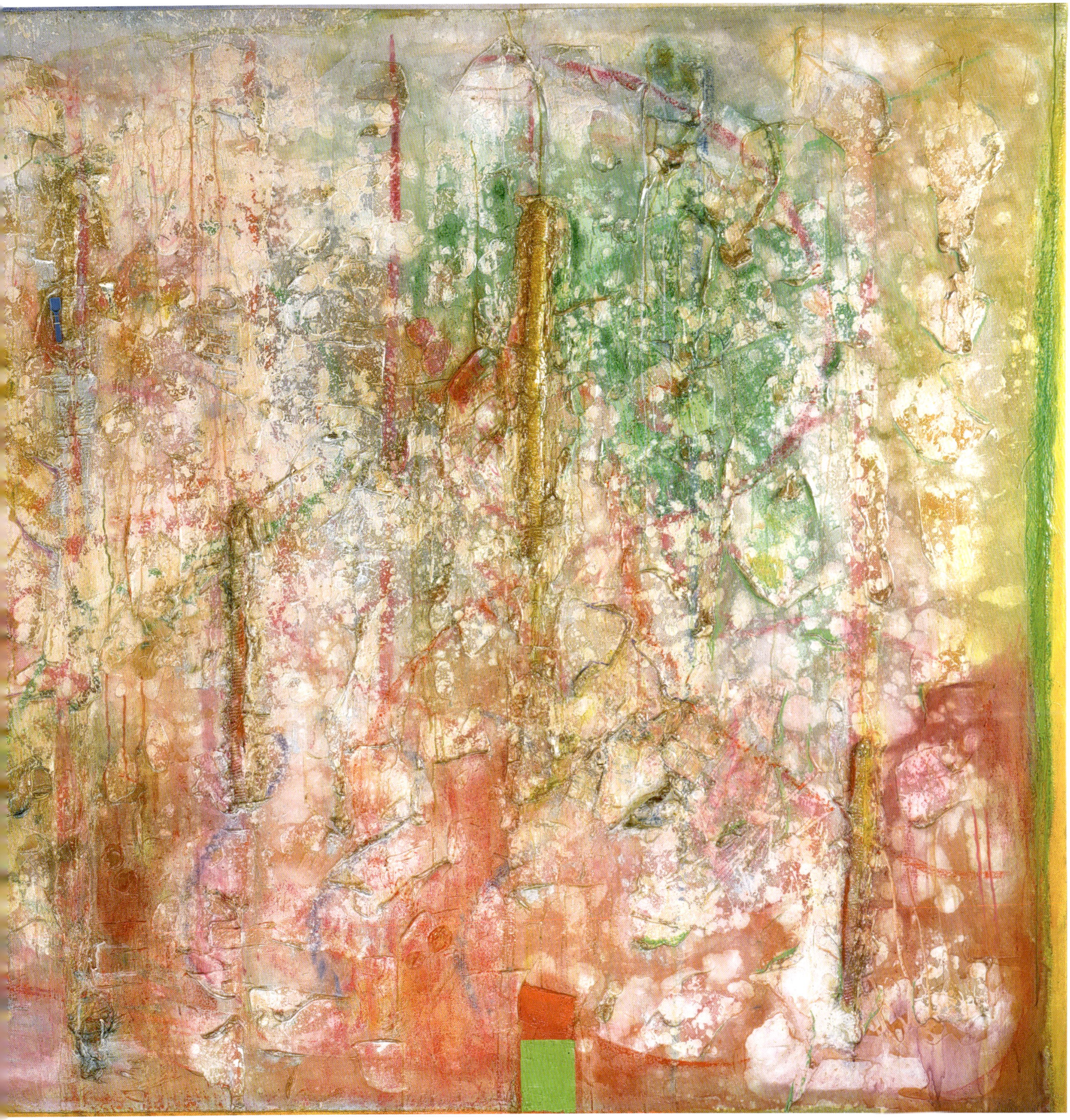

Samson's Arrival, 1989-90
Acrylic on canvas, 184 x 353 cm

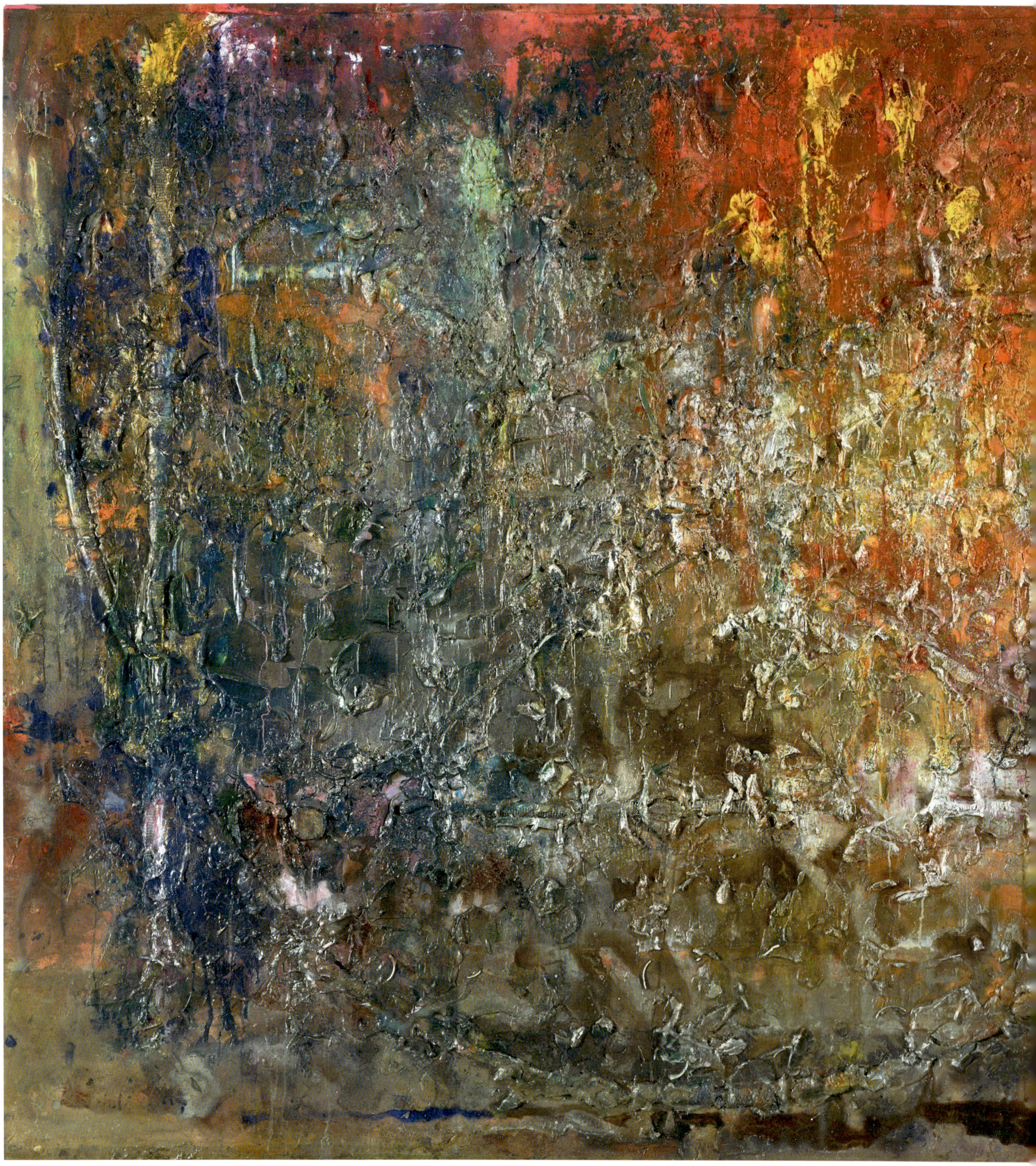

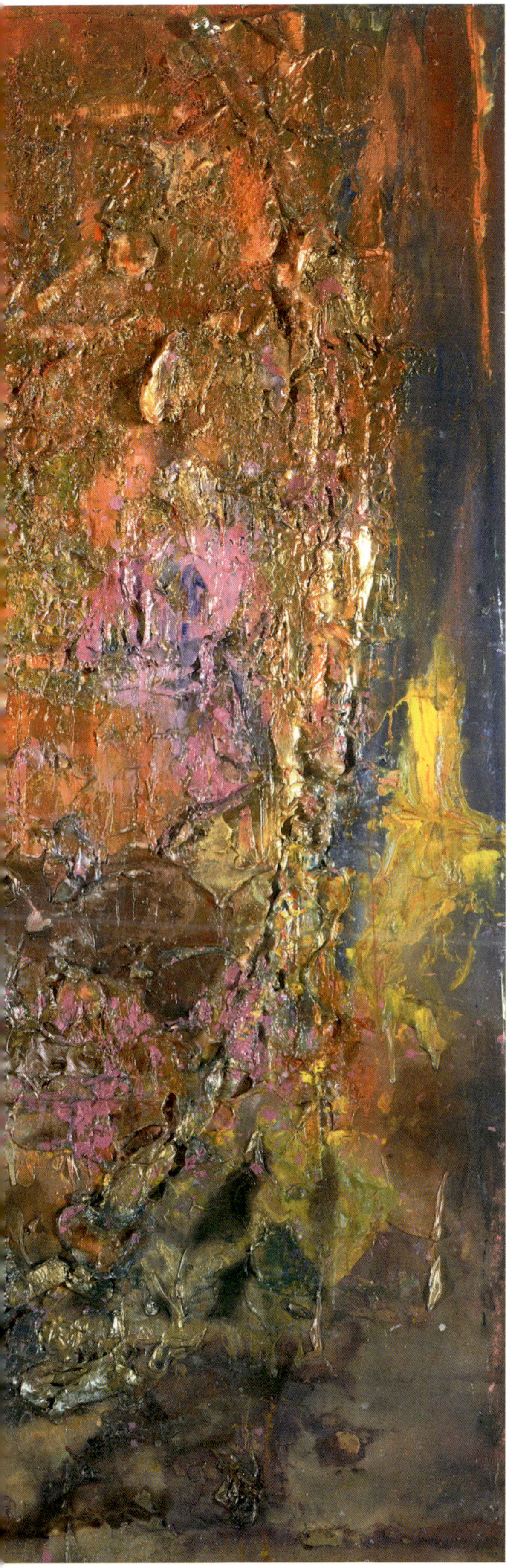

Spreadout Ron Kitaj, 1984-86
Acrylic on canvas, 228.5 x 287 cm

by which Bowling created his paintings during this period:

> The cotton duck canvas is tacked to its full length and draped on the wall.
> The polyether type foam is cut into strips and glued to the canvas.
> A colour ground is flooded into the canvas.
> Acrylic gel is applied with spatula and palette knife.
> The canvas is transferred to the floor.
> Paint and acrylic gel are mixed with ammonia and water in equal proportions in containers and then applied.
> Sometimes pearl-essence and sometimes metallic pigments are added and/or mixed in with the paint.
> The paint is applied, shells and plastic toys are embedded in the thick globular acrylic gel.
> The painting is left to dry a little for a day or two, depending on room temperature and weather conditions, influenced by the time of year.
> The canvas is pulled up and tacked to the wall in stages (low, middle, high). This allows the material on the canvas to move, drip, cascade and slither in a downward motion. More gel, paint, fluorescent chalk, metallic dust is applied as the work goes from stage to stage. When completely dry, oil paint is sometimes but not always applied.
> After the work is stretched a thinned mixture of damar crystals and distilled turps is applied. This mixture sometimes includes liquid beeswax.

Spreadout Ron Kitaj originated as one half of a vast canvas begun at Skowhegan and cut into two parts there; each of these was rolled up, conveyed to London and kept in the studio until

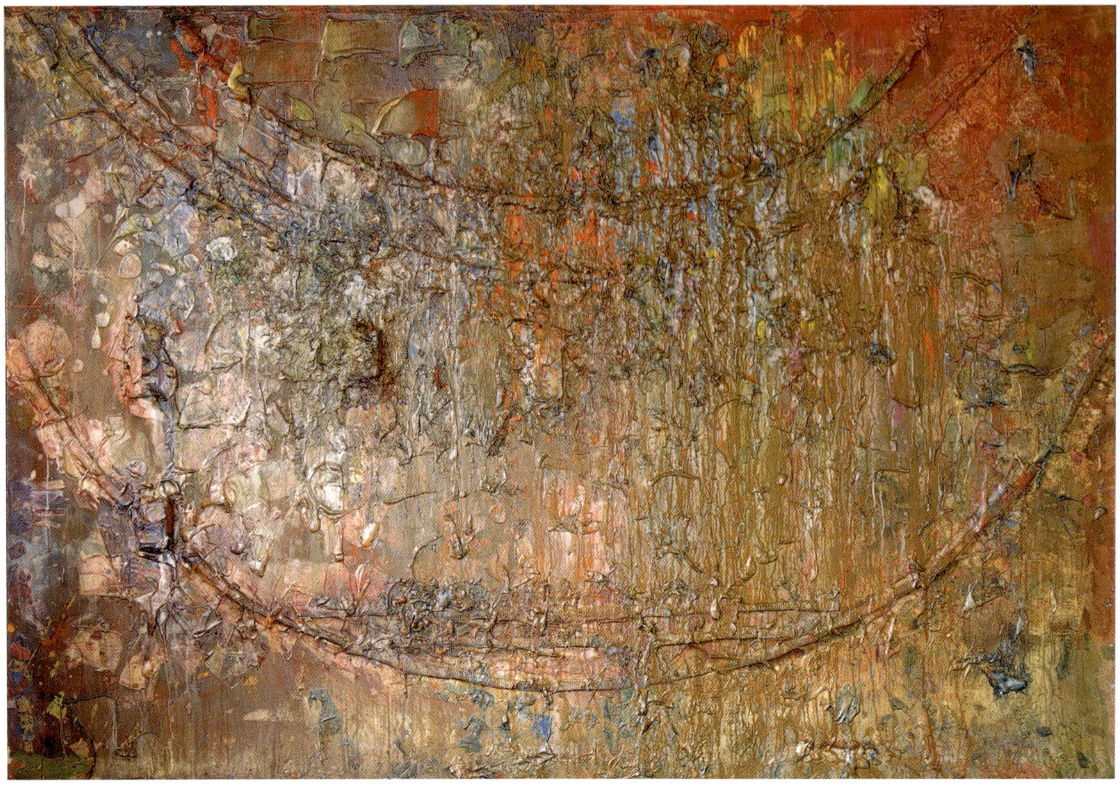

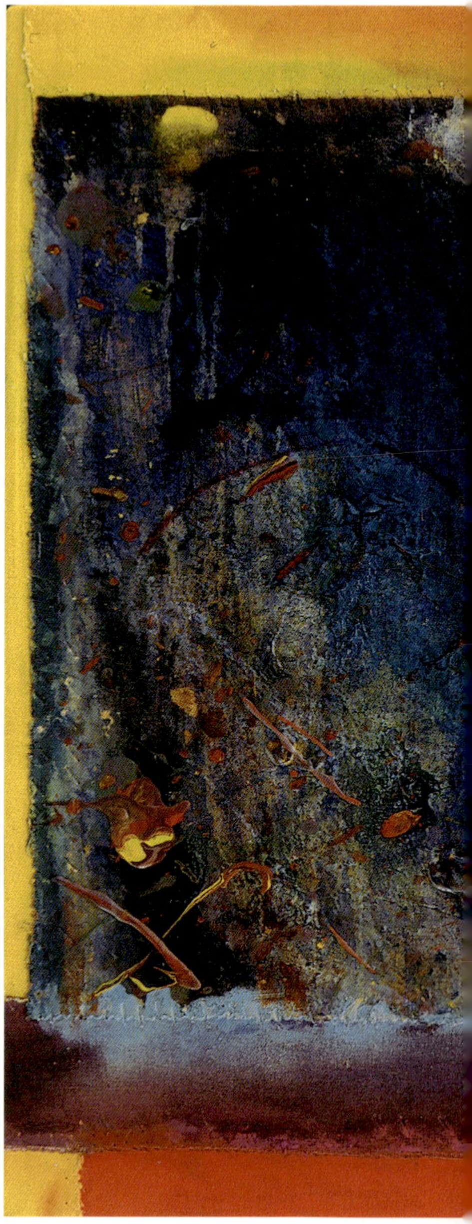

1986, when the artist began to work on them once more. It was completed that autumn, and the other portion, which became *Sacha Jason's Quail's Nest*, was finished in 1987. In each case, extra strips of canvas were attached to the cropped edges, a habitual device by which Bowling formally controls and delimits the painterly field. Sometimes such formal framing extends into the painterly area itself, as in the magisterial *Jamsahibwall* (1990) and the brilliantly chaotic *Up Against the Al Loving* (1991).

The division of the large Skowhegan canvas and its resolution as two separate paintings is, in terms of Bowling's essential creative approach, an exemplary procedure: it indicates that the outcome of any painting is unpremeditated, and that the final work is something discovered in the making of the object. As well as the procedures that Scott describes, there are numerous others, among them chemical dissipations, fusions and marbled diffusions, pooling and drying, pouring, splashing and spattering, and those that are essentially additive or collage-like (involving stitching, patching, and gluing fragments to the surface, etc.). They are components of what I have referred to as the 'controlled automatism' that constitutes Bowling's primary creative methodology, an approach to the creation of image and effect which he has used consistently since the late '70s. Bowling is not interested in autobiographical reference or personal expression; he seeks resemblance, surprise and revelation.

above left
Sacha Jason's Quail's Nest, 1987
Acrylic on canvas, 202 x 289.5 cm

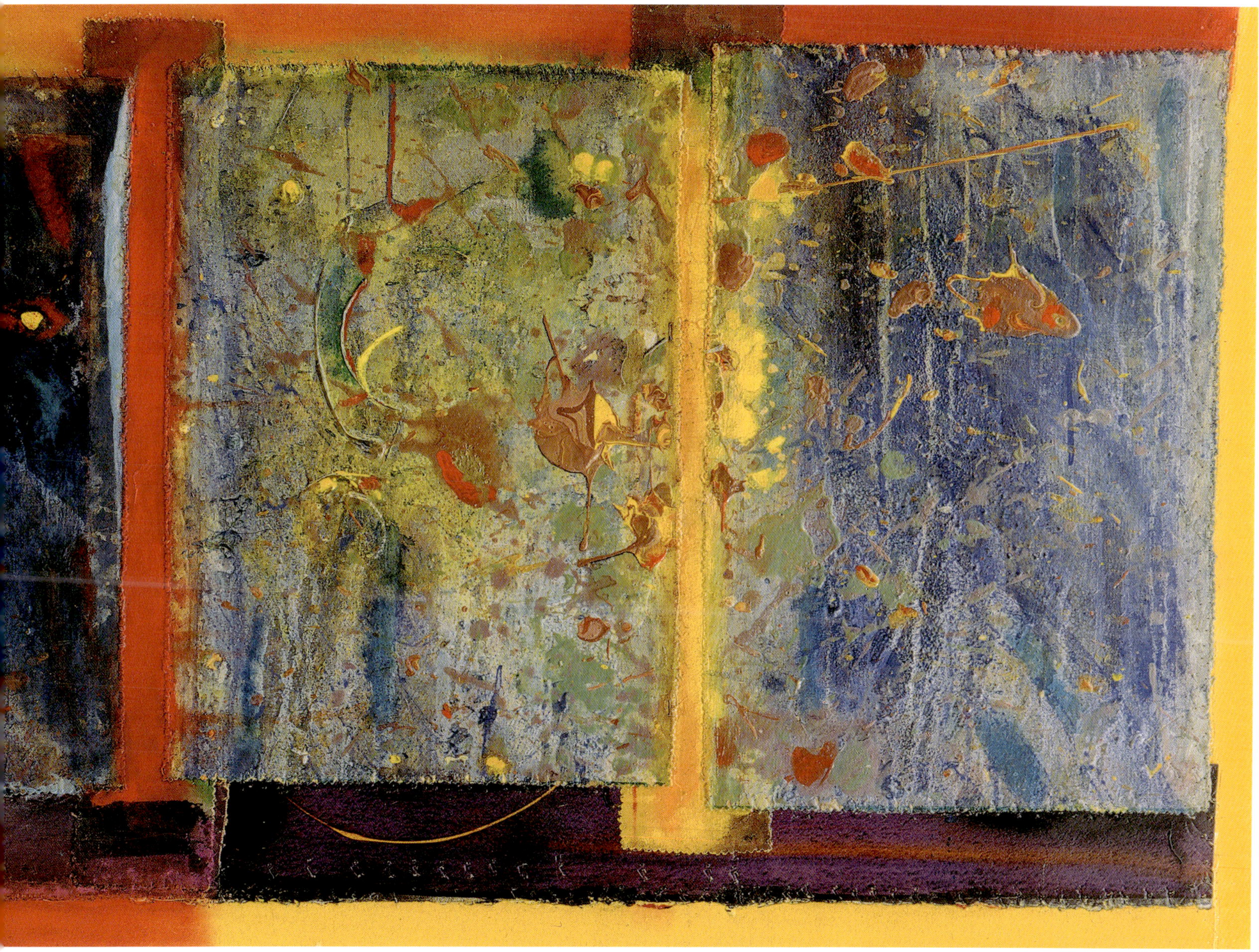

Up Against the Al Loving, 1991
Acrylic on canvas, 61 x 106.5 cm

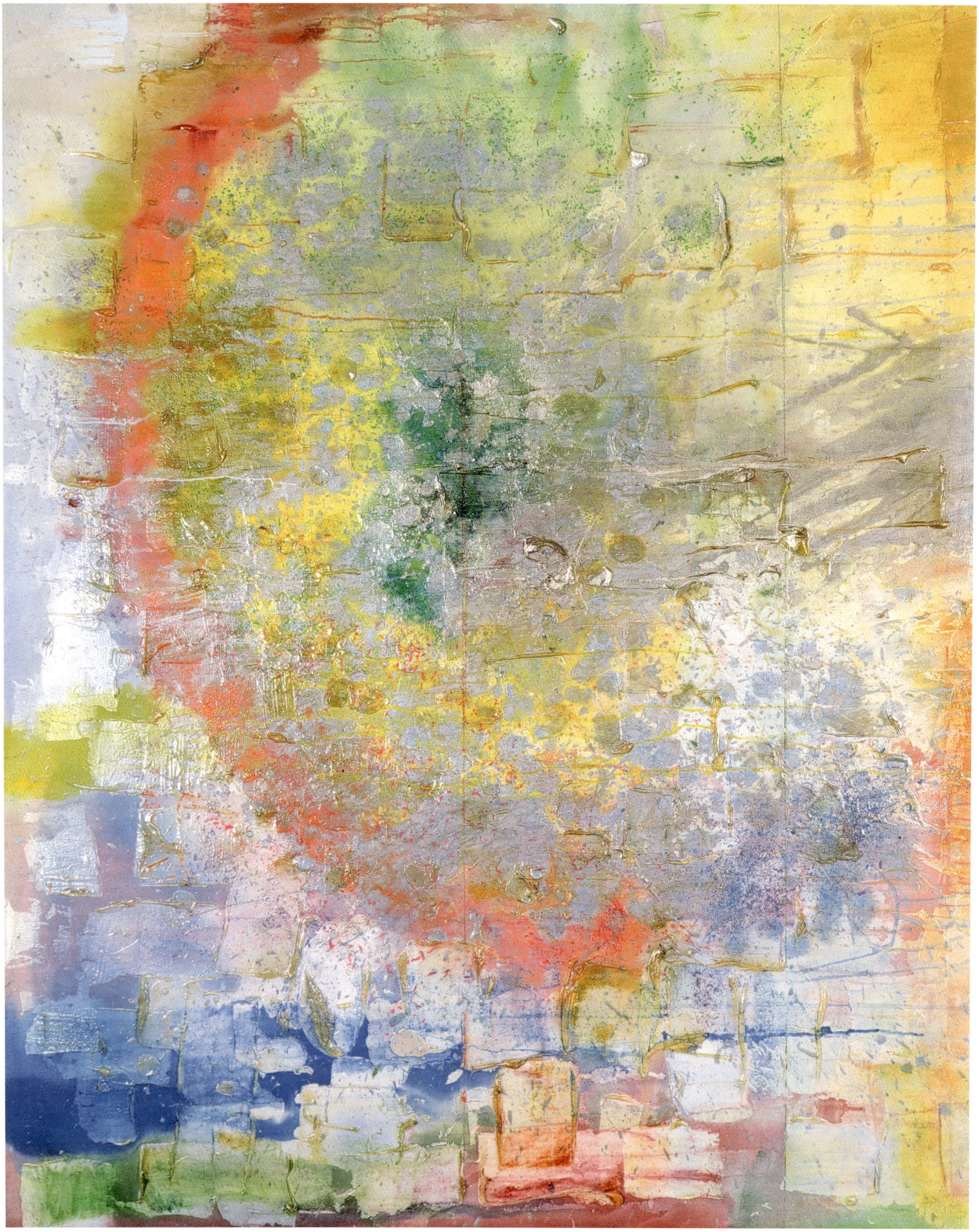

11 GUYANA DREAMS AND PERSONAL REVERIES

On a hot spring day in 1989 Bowling asked his son Sacha to look at the light over the sea and salt flats of the Demerara estuary at Georgetown: a brilliant light, an early morning white light, a marine light, refracted and flattened through the haze over salt flats and a distant glittering blue-silver sea, the flats gleaming and reflecting the sun as its light pierces the dawn mist. 'I asked Sacha to look over the sea wall', says Bowling, 'to see whether what he could see had any connection with my painting.' Sacha had not been to Guyana before, and his response confirmed for Bowling that there was indeed a correspondence. He later recalled that his son had recognised in 'this heat haze where everything looks flat, and with very little depth, what I had been trying to do in my art … There it was, visible to any ordinary eye.' Memory in painting is just such a discovery of surprising resemblances. In *SachaJasonGuyanaDreams* (1989), Bowling has produced a precise and utterly beautiful record of this moment of realisation and confirmation. Flat spatula strokes of pigmented gel, parallel with the surface, paradoxically play the part of the reflective mud-flats receding to a bright horizon, over which a pure arc of sunrise pink refracts through similar flat spatula strokes of translucent haze. It is a phenomenon at once remembered and immediate: here, now, nature becomes art.

This moment of epiphany occurred on a journey to Guyana (Bowling's first for many years) made to attend the opening of an exhibition organised by and shared with Dennis de Caires, a Guyanese painter much concerned with matters of cultural identity. De Caires's purpose was to bring the modernist son home to the place of his origin. And now, after years of resistance to the resented notion that his colour was somehow 'exotic', Bowling was at last prepared to consider that he might have carried into his painting, albeit unconsciously, qualities of the tropical light and colour that he had experienced as a child: 'Well, around that time of visiting New Amsterdam and Georgetown with my son, I began to review the situation *vis-à-vis* the difference between what I intended to do as an artist, and the way my work was received by people who I knew and people who seemed sympathetic to the work; it seemed always as though they couldn't forget I was born in the Caribbean … no one seemed to be able to look down the history of art in the terms in which I was viewing my own efforts, which [was to see them within] the Western traditions and Modernism.'

Earlier, in 1986, reviewing Bowling's exhibition at the Serpentine Gallery, de Caires, with a backward glance at the map paintings, had expressed a similar thought with eloquent and succinct force: 'They were the beginnings of Bowling's enlightening description of man and his environment, pictures that fall ahead of standard tradition; paintings that are more land than landscape. Later pictures … portray that interest in the fundamental marriage of man to his physical world which no descriptive narrative alone can reveal.' Behind this formulation lies an idea especially important to those, like de Caires, for whom cultural and historical groundings are crucial determinants of significant difference between artists. It is that we have only a limited reality – material or cognitive – without this definitive connection to the world in which we come into being, and that *being* in itself finds expression in felt relations to specific locations, their particularities of colour and light, and their abiding presence in the memory and the imagination.

The extraordinary power of Bowling's great landscape paintings of the 1980s and 1990s derives from the actuality of their imaginative connections – their vivid resemblances – to the places to which their titles sometimes refer. 'I live near water. In New York and in London, my

opposite
SachaJasonGuyanaDreams, 1989
Acrylic on canvas, 178 x 141.5 cm

studios have been on the river. In recent times, I thought my eye [was] influenced by London light. When I went home in 1989, I was staggered. When I looked at the landscape in Guyana, I understood the light in my pictures is a very different light. I saw a crystalline haze, maybe an east wind and water rising up into the sky. It occurred to me for the first time, in my fifties, that the light is about Guyana. It is a constant in my efforts.'

For de Caires, the material landscape of Bowling's paintings is the expression of a history and an identity that are, in certain important respects, specifically Guyanese: 'The question of identity [never mind the psyche] of the Guyanese is a hugely problematic area, and in relation to Bowling's work has not previously been discussed. I would maintain that it is a subject that he has long been interested in and that its investigation has been a central theme of his work over the last twenty years.' This relates to something more than the abstract and vaguely evocative use of colour and texture: 'It seems to me that one of the interesting features of Bowling's work is his interest in establishing a corresponding equivalent of [the language of such Guyanese writers as Wilson Harris and Edgar Mittelholzer] with visual language … Bowling uses pictorial language to imbue his work with a poetic charge. It is logical then, to see Bowling's commitment to formalism not as a political or ideological posturing, but as the necessary means through which the relationship between man and his history, and his immediate physical environment, can be examined.'

De Caires acknowledges that '[it] would be foolish, however, to try and place Bowling within a South American context, he should really be placed within the broader streams of Western painting, indeed within that English modernist landscape tradition, which originated with Gainsborough.' And, of course, we might add, also within the ambit of mid-century American abstraction in its diverse manifestations. But as a consequence of his close and creative friendship since the early 1990s with the Brooklyn Guyanese photographer and critic Spencer Richards, there has deepened in Bowling an abiding sense of the significance of his own Guyanese history, of the people and places of his childhood and youth. Through this long conversation with Richards, Bowling has come to recognise that culture grows within the individual consciousness, and that there are aspects of it that cannot easily be eradicated.

In a manner that evades narrative reference, or anything so specific as a Guyanese 'history', every painting, whatever its title, is in any case for Bowling a repository of experience and memories, of other people, other times, other places: '…the experience that a painting "carries" through literal and depicted shape is generally a painting experience (time, colour surface/area, peri-metric demarcation points, etc.). The point, however, is that energy is located somewhere in the subtlety of "experience": shared experience is trapped in the web of skeins and layers of the material being worked.' Certainly de Caires's emphasis on the poetic element was well-placed: Bowling has always sought to achieve something of the allusive richness and metaphorical potency of literary language. His first ambition, we should not forget, was to become a poet. Formalism was the means to a poetic visual language that was in no way descriptive or literal.

In his paintings, there is often embedded an odd and arbitrary memory-object – a button, a small toy, a needle, an eye tooth. Such arbitrary personal mementoes hint at some private experience inaccessible to the viewer: they are charms, perhaps, against the forgetful darkness. This aspect of the paintings will be missed by any reading that takes account solely of procedure and medium. In fact there is always a personal investment in the formalist process that makes

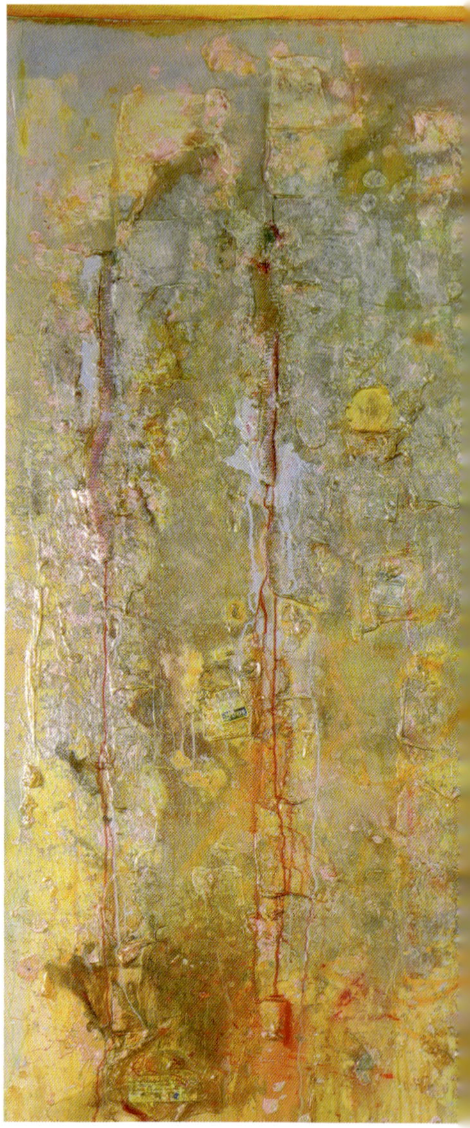

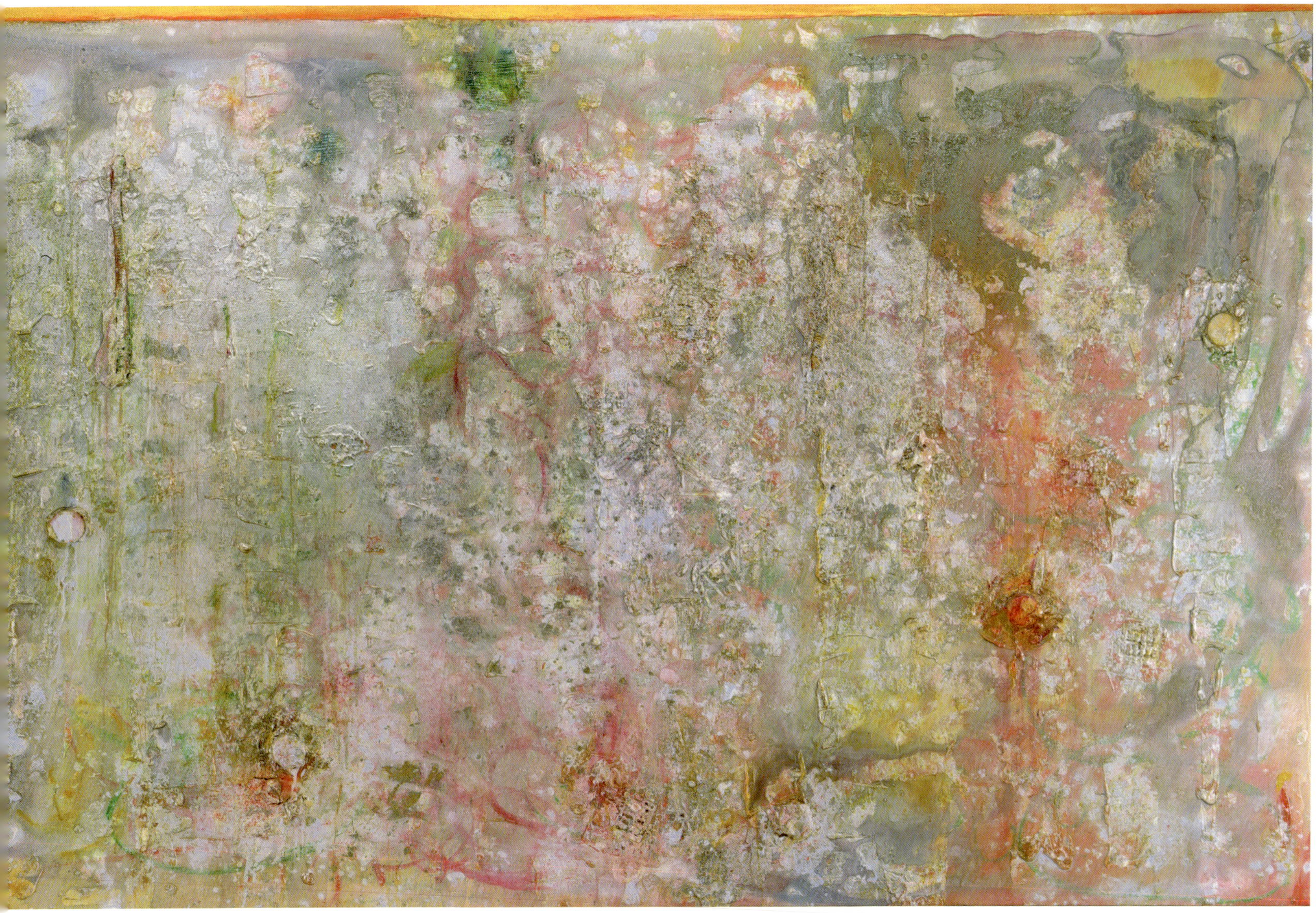

Chaguaramus Bay, 1989
Acrylic on canvas, 181.5 x 331.5 cm

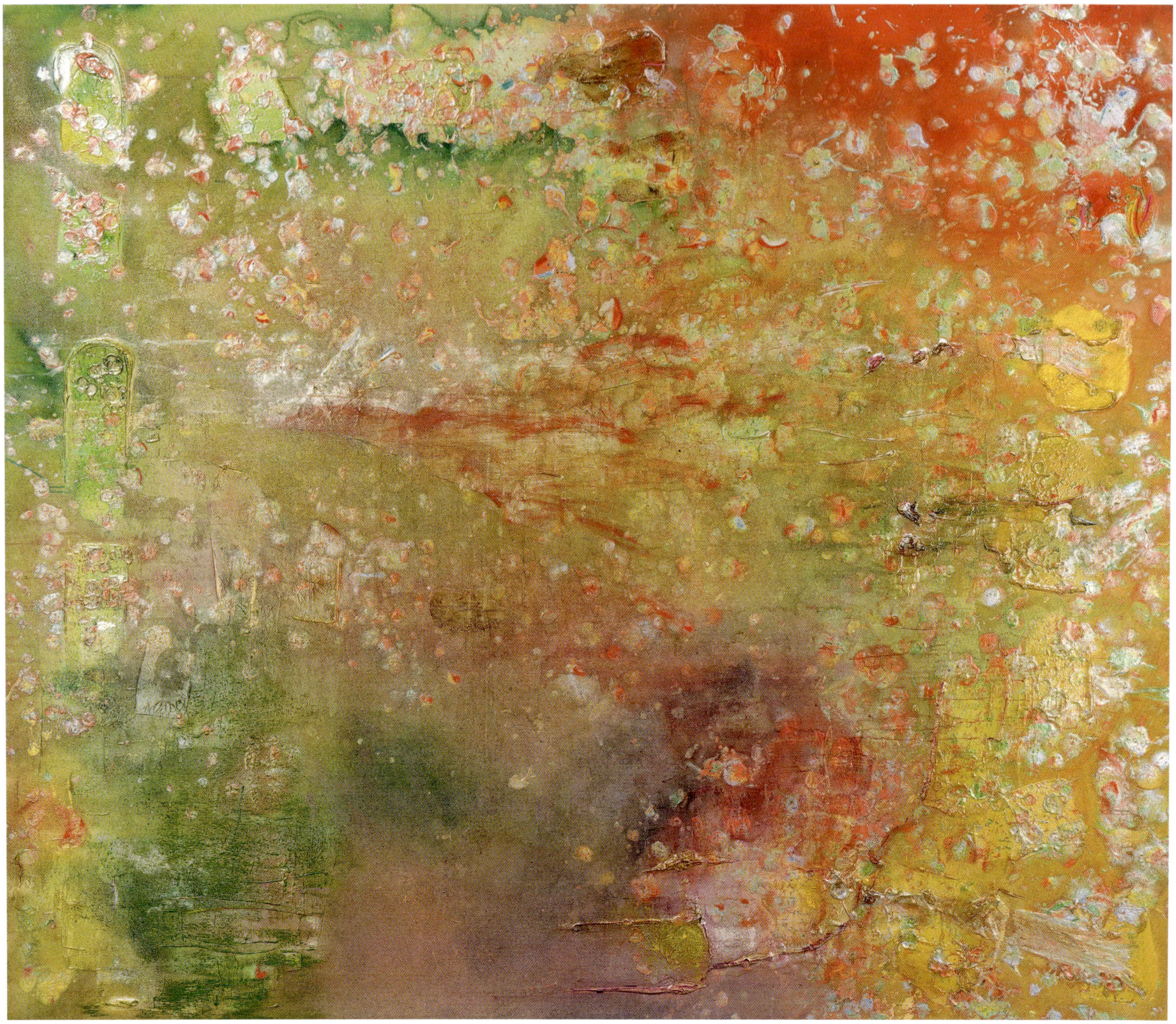

Iona to Aachen, 1990
Acrylic on canvas, 167.5 x 193 cm

Iona to Aachen II, 1990
Acrylic on canvas, 180.5 x 78.5 cm

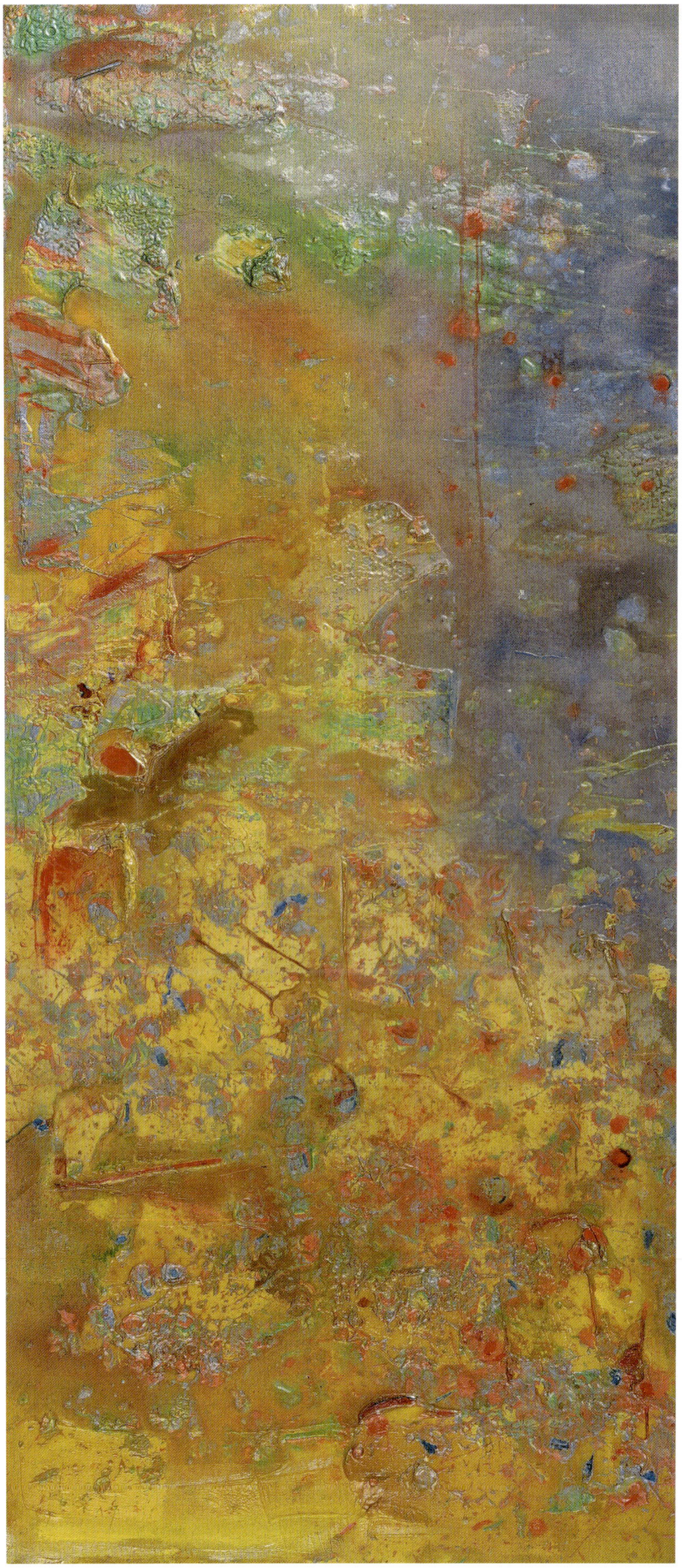

its outcomes distinctive, uniquely expressive. Bowling's beloved Gainsborough, refusing an aristocrat's commission to paint a 'view' once wrote: 'if his Lordship wishes to have anything tolerable of the name of G. the Subject altogether as well as the figures &c must be of his own Brain.' Gainsborough means that art at its highest level comes of imaginative invention that is neither amenable to convention nor susceptible to external direction. The topography in Bowling's paintings is the topography of the painting itself: it is 'more land than landscape'. Its subject is the product of his own imagination.

In fact, Bowling's later painting has always been peculiarly responsive to the places where he lives, works or travels – from Brooklyn to Skowhegan, Cable Street to Cork, Georgetown to Bartica. But his characteristic response to specific landscapes, and beyond them to the phenomenal world in all its transcendent glory, is imbricated with the most intimate personal memories rather than with abstract historical or merely topographical considerations. *Chaguaramus Bay* (1989), titled for its evocative name, grandly celebrates that momentous trip with Sacha Jason to Guyana, and their shared epiphany of sea-light; *Iona to Aachen* (1990) refers to a journey abroad of Rachel Scott's daughter; *Sasha's Green Bag* (1988) recalls an afternoon in the Peacock Yard studio when the small daughter of Dennis de Caires searched the painting for the exact colour of her toy handbag; *If Marcia's Hair* (1983) is a painterly meditation on the fiery temperament of another Scott daughter.

When Bowling remarked, 'I am not painting the view, I am painting the idea of the view', he was suggesting that his paintings might be seen as representations (albeit abstract and impressionistic) of landscapes, and certain titles – *Towards Crab Island*, *Skowhegan Green*, *Barticaflats* (1986), *Oysterbeds* (1986), the *Great Thames* (1989), etc. – underline those fruitful

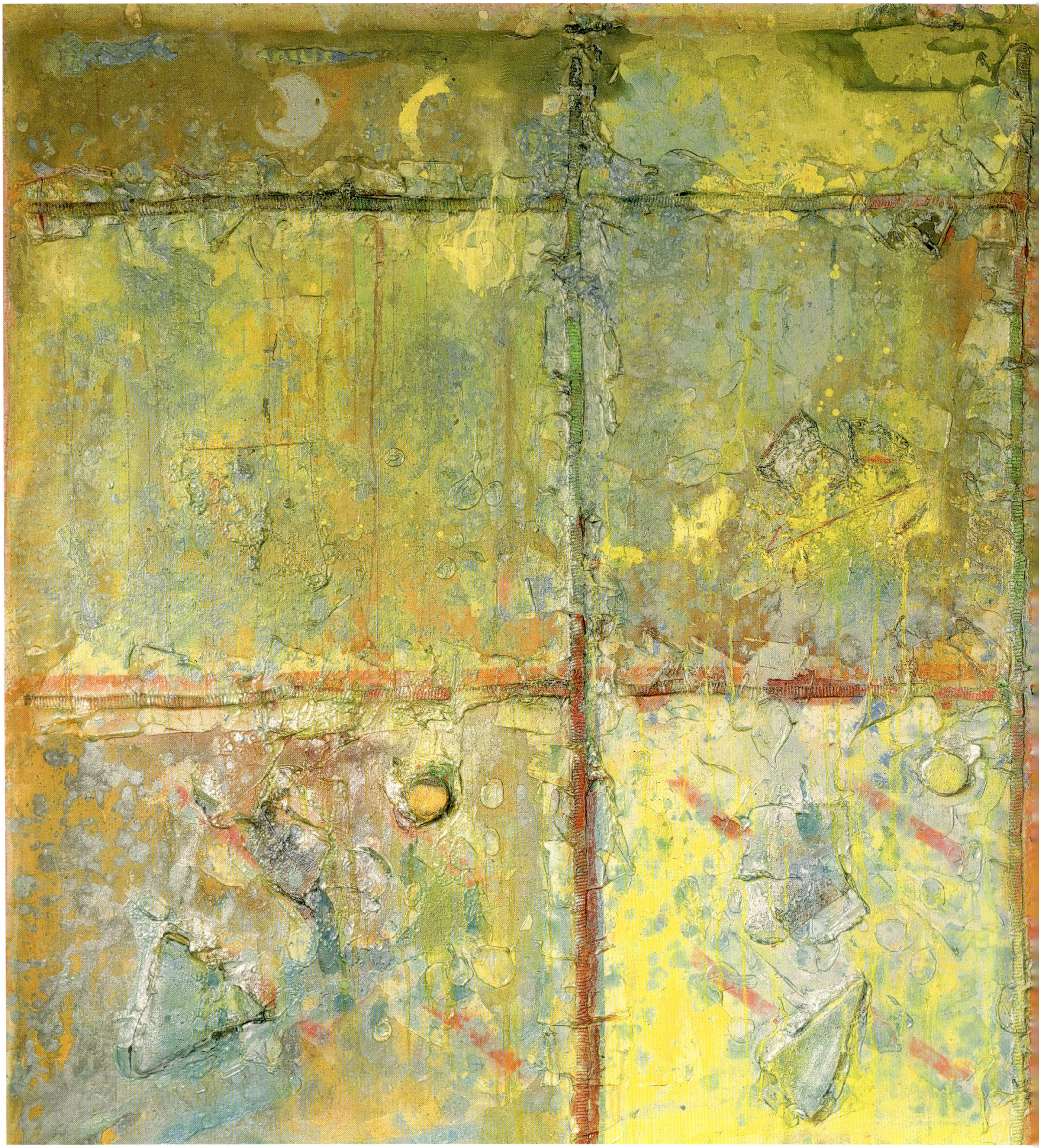

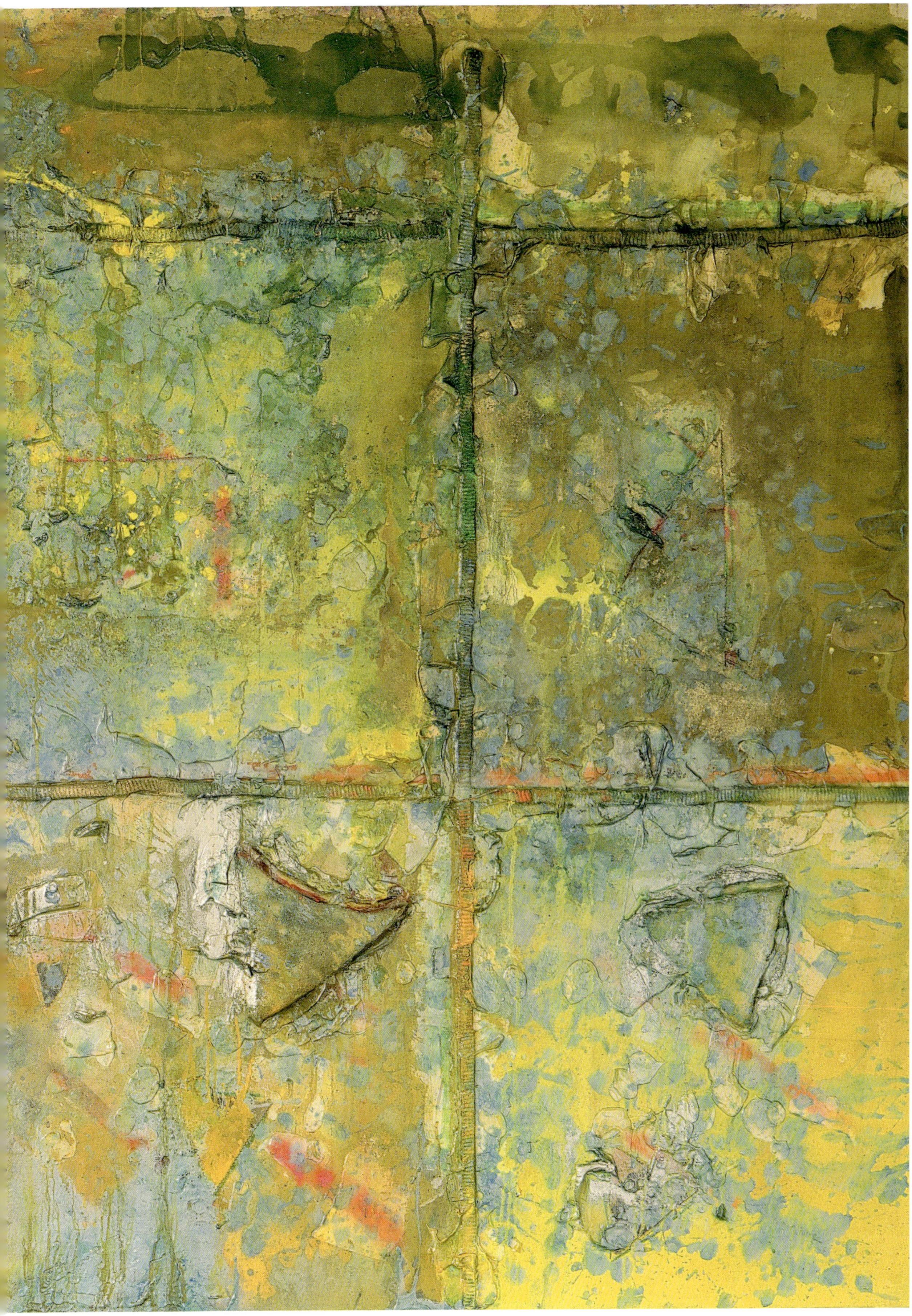

Sasha's Green Bag, 1988
Acrylic on canvas, 178 x 292 cm

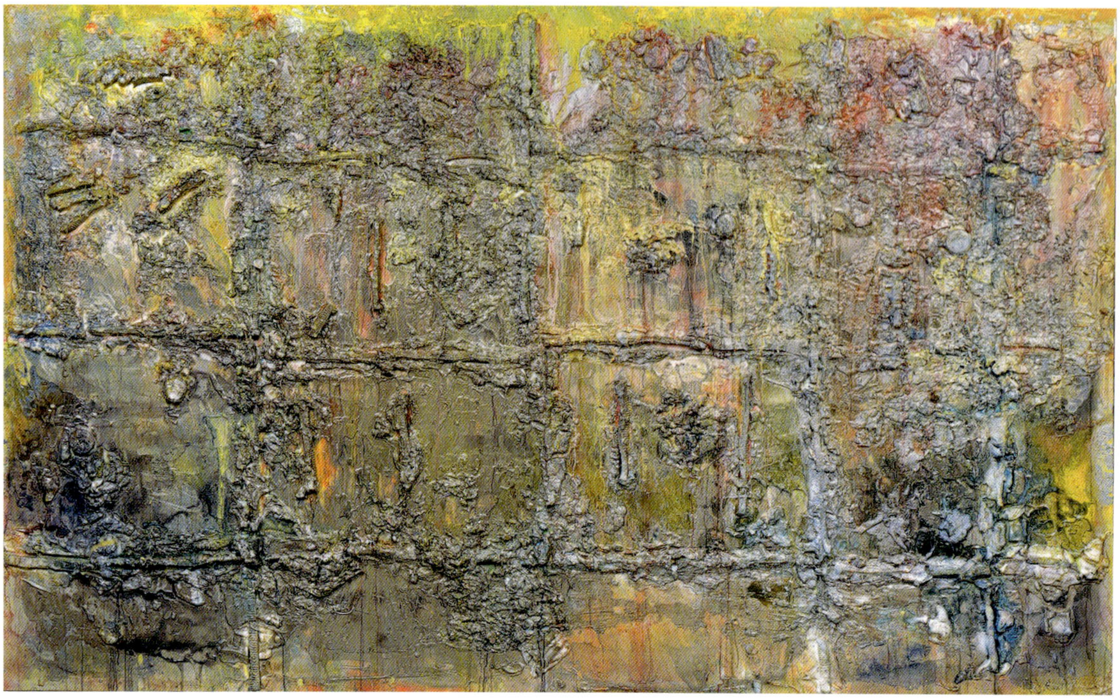

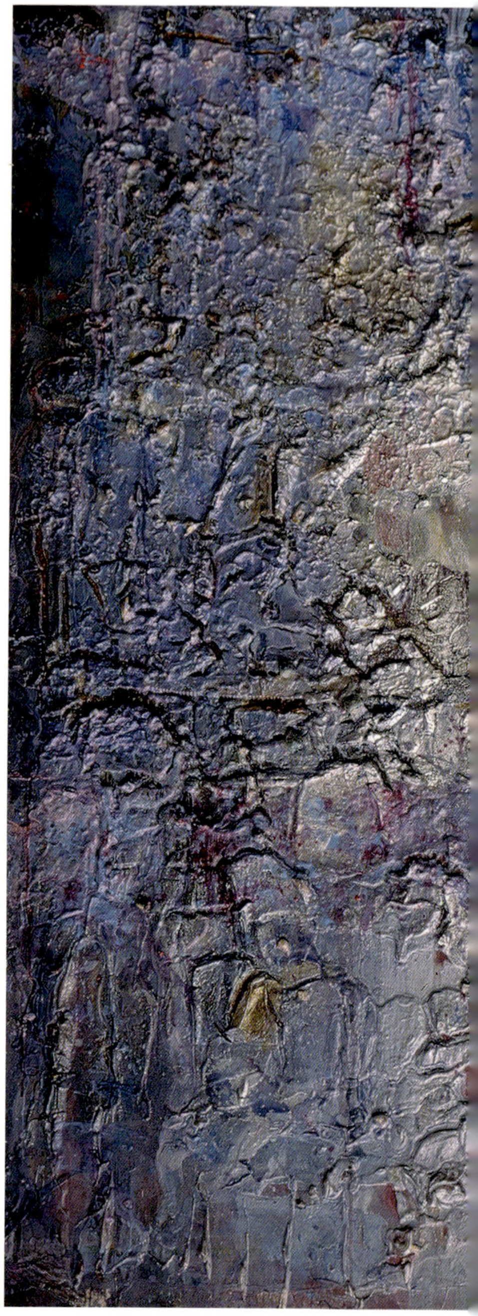

possibilities of reading. 'The task', he adds, 'is to contradict what is there; to make a picture of it.' By 'picture' here he means a work of art that must conform to the formalist laws of its own nature. It would be truer to his intentions to say that a painting by Bowling is a self-contained object incorporating into its complex physical structure both tangible and intangible components of the perceived world. Such a painting thus presents itself to the view as in itself a species of natural landscape, a portion of the spatial world crammed with material and objects, configured by energies and irradiated by light. But first of all, it is abstract.

Formalist criticism encounters this abstract language in terms of its own disciplines, taking account of relationships and rhythms, annotating generic characteristics of style and placement and specific deviations and departures from established modes. But even at its characteristic best, in the work of Greenberg and Michael Fried, it does not venture beyond cool description and assertions of value whose justifications tend to be circular and originate in arbitrary critical diktat. Formalist criticism, to put it another way, is strong on visual structure but fails to follow up visual clues in an imaginative or inventive way, and its judgments of quality are really a matter of taste. Good painting of any kind engages with experience in the world beyond the canvas edge; formalist criticism is inadequate to this insofar as that experience goes beyond engagement with materials, their disposition, and the visual facts of the painting.

Criticising Fried in an essay written as early as 1972, Bowling notes a characteristic assertive leap from description to purist judgment: 'On confronting pictures one asks oneself not only are they good? Are they bad? But now ever more critical, are they relevant, in what sense, to whom?' Bowling called for a clear articulation

above left
Barticaflats, 1986
Acrylic on canvas, 176.5 x 287 cm

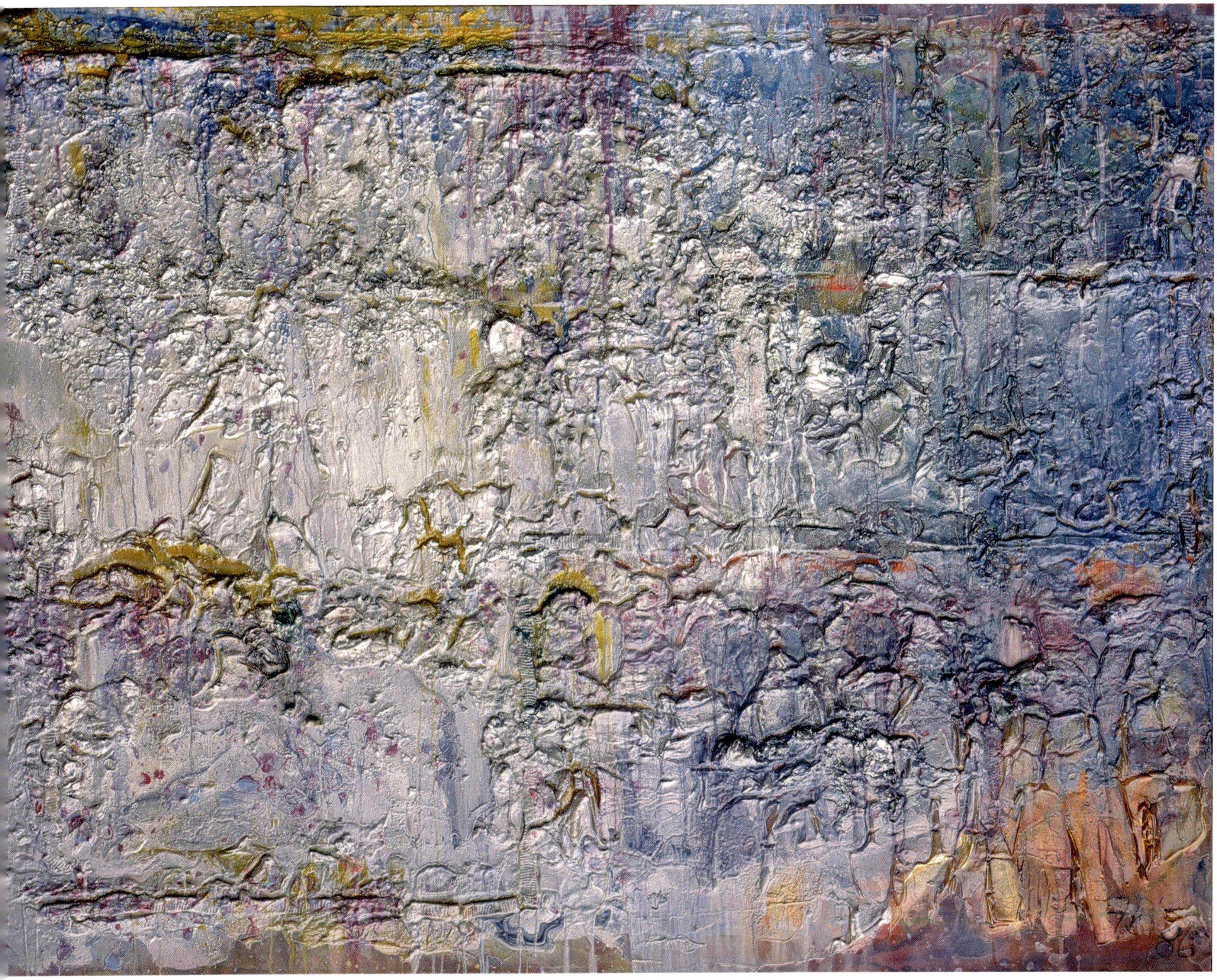

Oysterbeds, 1986
Acrylic on canvas, 178 x 292 cm

of what modernist painting was doing rather than any 'elegant description of pigment action' or 'constant reiterations and assertions about what [its] painted surfaces appear to be like.' As a writer-critic, Bowling never successfully answered to his own call, being essentially an anxious and sometimes angry polemicist, a seeker rather than a finder, a commentator without a fixed position or a settled philosophy, though he understood better than anyone the historical provenance and implicit meaning of the various abstractions of his black artist contemporaries in New York.

As an abstract painter, however, Bowling was deeply committed to formalist principles and procedures, and ever tolerant of processes that would underpin the essential objectivity of his aesthetic stance, he was happy to accept reference to phenomenal actuality, however it entered the picture, and to welcome allusions to particular places or scenes at particular moments of light. In doing so, he arrived at his own connections to material and emotional reality, to place and time, and to the kind of relevance he demanded: relevance to the spectator's experience of the living world; and relevance also to the profound aesthetic connections between time, place and events in a personal history.

12 LATE VARIATIONS AND DIVERSITIES

'I get closer and closer', Bowling said in 1995, 'to believing that as an abstract artist you are trying to unearth your whole self with maximum openness.' This may surprise, for it is easy to think that abstraction – especially abstraction created out of particular formalist ideas (whether geometric or automatic, colour field, hard-edge or free-form) is a kind of disguise, a means to objectivity. For the modernist it is axiomatic that it is not the artist that communicates, it is the work. And Bowling is far from believing in the expressionist fallacy that a stroke or mark necessarily expresses a definable personal meaning. But as we have seen, he is deeply aware that the 'awesome subtlety' of experience is somehow 'trapped in the skeins and layers of the material being worked'. But how does this work? How is the self unearthed with maximum openness?

The answer must reside in the idea of the painting as a poetic object susceptible to a constructively imaginative – i.e. creative – response. The task of the poet-artist is not to speak directly and persuasively of personal experience, it is, rather, to create the sensational object and for the viewer/critic to find in it possibilities of communicable meaning. The greatness of great art is defined by the inexhaustibility of these possible meanings: its greatness is created by the discourse of those who find and elaborate them. Of course, as Roland Barthes has pointed out, 'one does not create meanings in just any way (if you doubt that, try it): what controls the critic is not the meaning of the work, it is the meaning of what one says about it.'

The thought (consistent to Bowling's work since the late '60s) that a painting should be free to work through the senses and generate meanings in whatever way that might occur is what underlies his wonderfully idiosyncratic way with titles. Bowling's titles have always indulged his love of word-play. The title is the subtle hinge that attaches a painting to the world beyond its

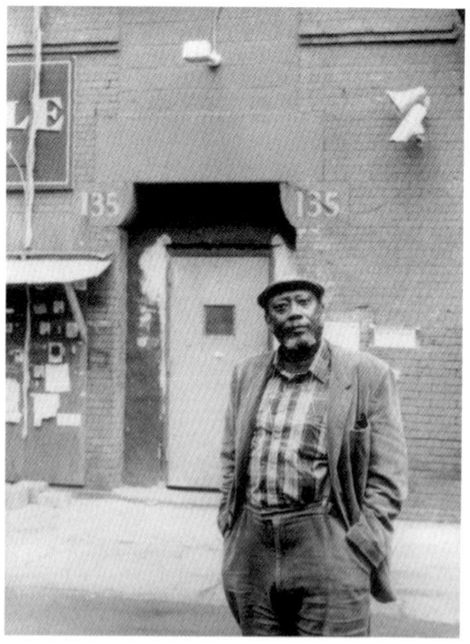

Bowling outside his Brooklyn studio at 135 Plymouth Street, 1997.

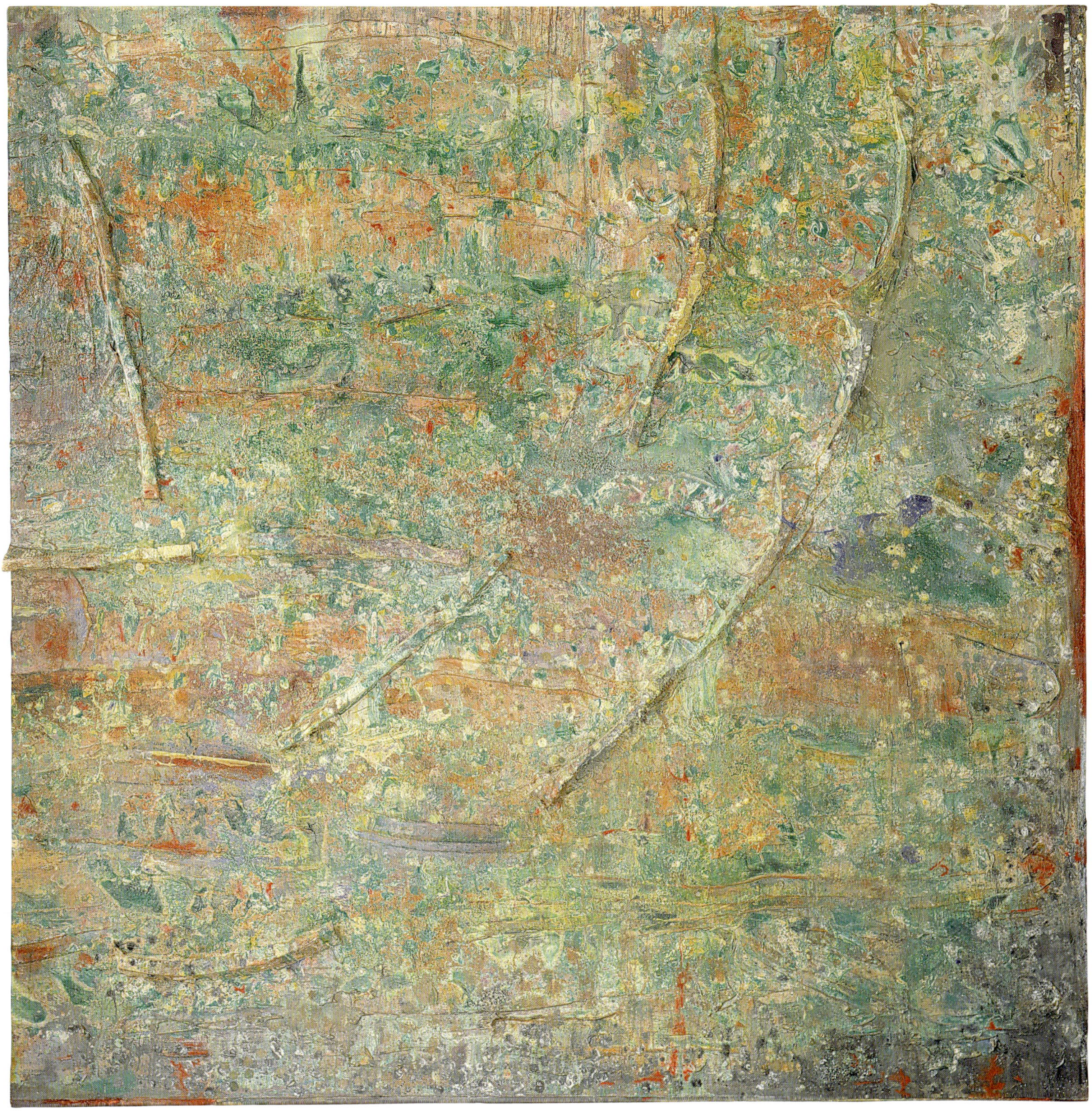

Bamboodam, 1983
Acrylic on canvas, 180.5 x 179 cm

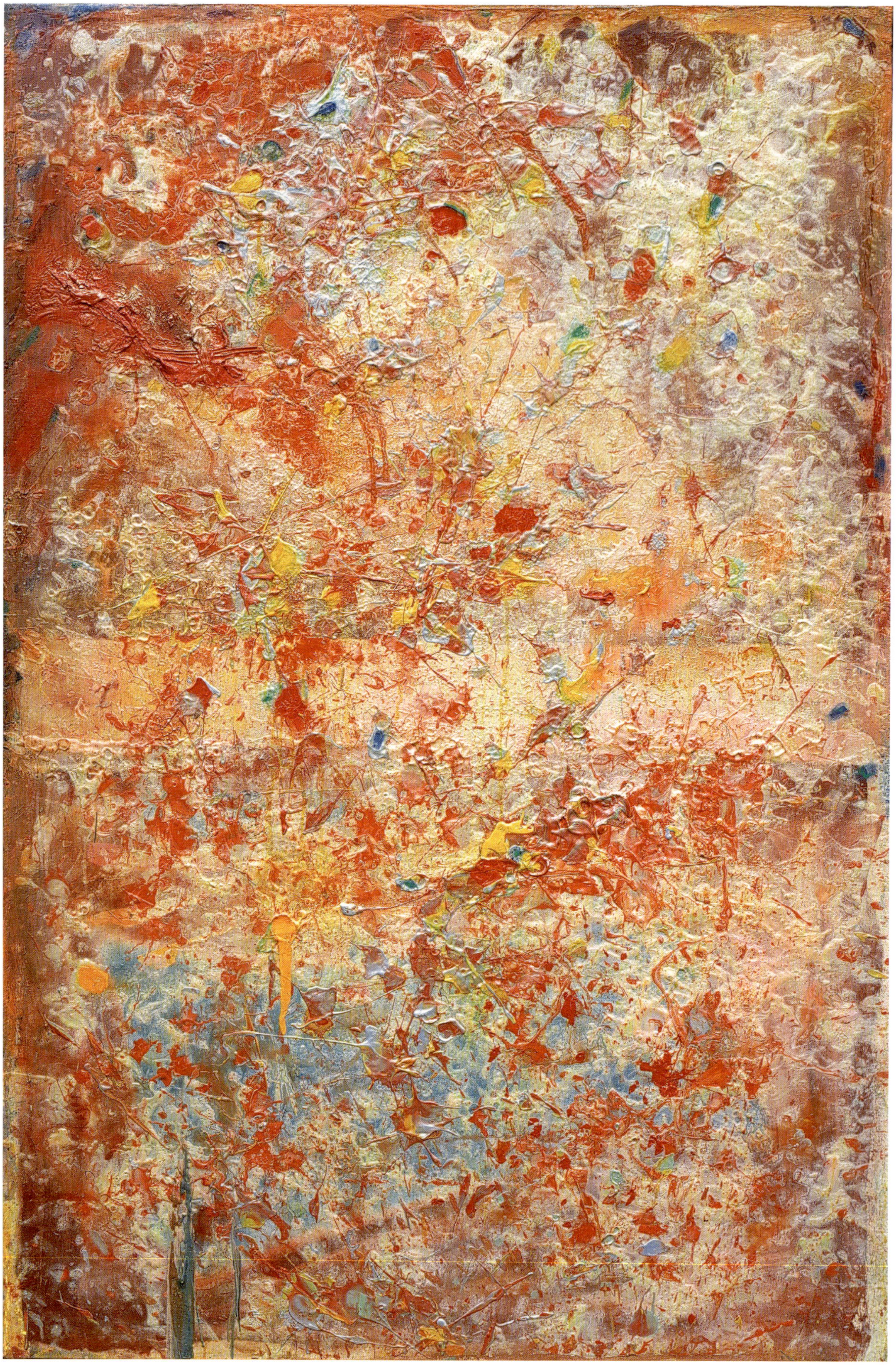

Orange Balloon
(4 Paul Adams), 1996
Acrylic on canvas, 180.5 x 118 cm

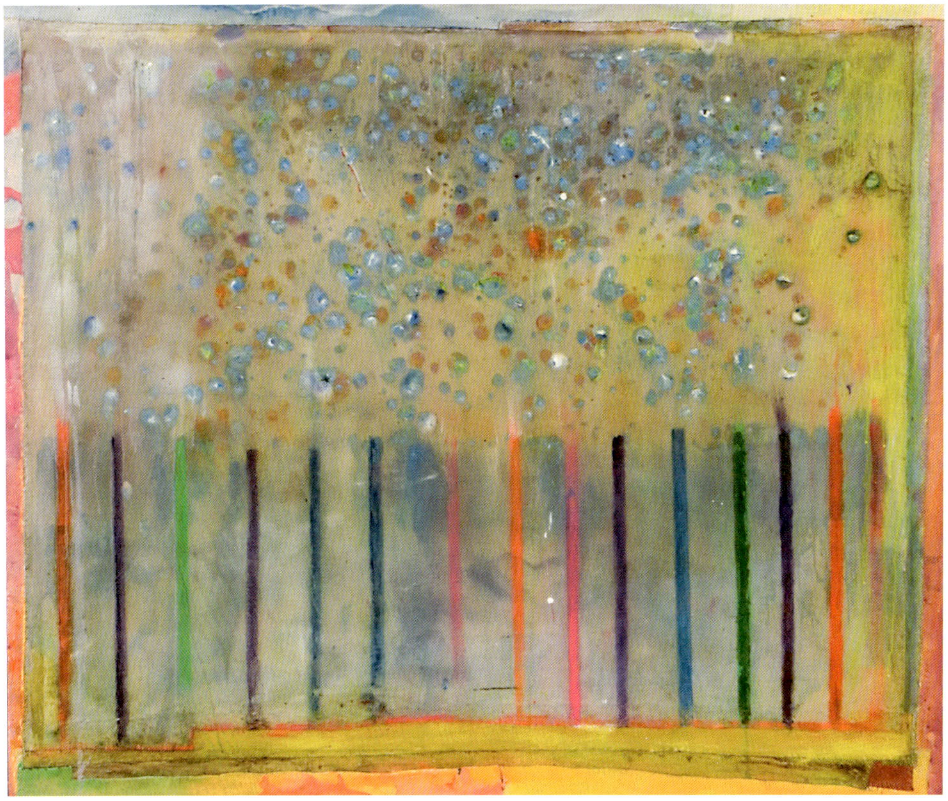

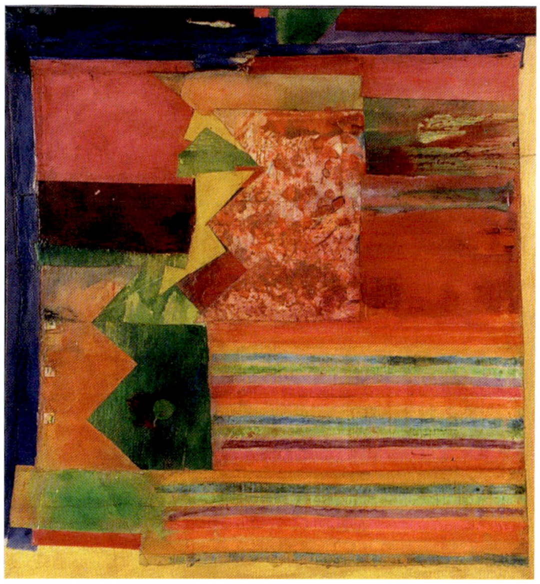

edges and surfaces – the world of imaginative response, reflective thought and natural language. In this sense, it is the first contact the painting makes with the wider critical and historical discourse. Withholding a title, as was fashionable among modernist abstractionists, who resorted to identifying works by simple descriptions (as in Rothko's *Light Red over Black*, say, or Heron's *Yellow Painting*) or by using the date of a work's completion (as in John Hoyland's *28.5.66*) or by non-committal titles such as *Untitled* or *Painting*, is itself a way of influencing aspects of the first round of critical response, besides making life difficult for historians. Bowling has never resorted to these devices.

While acknowledging that abstract painting might want to admit into its ambit of effect and affect the power of poetic allusion, Bowling has never, in his paintings after 1972, extended this to any kind of mimetic figuration or sign-making, however ghostly or subliminal. In the paintings made prior to that date – a period that culminated in his one-person show of the abstract map paintings at the Whitney in 1971 – it was just such use of the map-sign, whether it be as a bold outline, a vague emanation or a fading cipher, that had drawn critical and public attention to his paintings. For some, they carried political implications, for others, they had affinities with the iconographic aspects of pop art. Bowling had then, and still has now, mixed feelings about these associations, largely on the grounds that they might sometimes limit the range of imaginative response to the work, or inhibit the pleasures of a purely sensuous experience such as might be enjoyed by listening to music.

He has, however, always made cunning and witty use of titles: as we have seen, they may be intriguingly enigmatic or helpfully allusive. They may be anecdotal, celebrating or commemorating a person or an event, sometimes trivial, sometimes momentous; they may summon to mind a myth or legend; they may prompt recollection of things past; they may refer to a natural phenomenon, a place or an effect of light. A title may be simple or complex, obscure or obvious: *Bamboodam* (1983) borrows a Guyanese term for a simple barrier across a drainage canal; the 1996 *Orange Balloon (4 Paul Adams)* refers to a small run of paint in it resembling a collapsed balloon, but also to a young black South African spin bowler; *Hafenlicht* (2007) evokes the twinkling harbour lights referred to in its German title; *Secret Garden* (2001) is evocative, mysterious; *Old Dutch Vase*

above left
***Hafenlicht*, 2007**
Acrylic on canvas, 165 x 190.5 cm

above
***Secret Garden*, 2001**
Acrylic on canvas, 162.5 x 152.5 cm

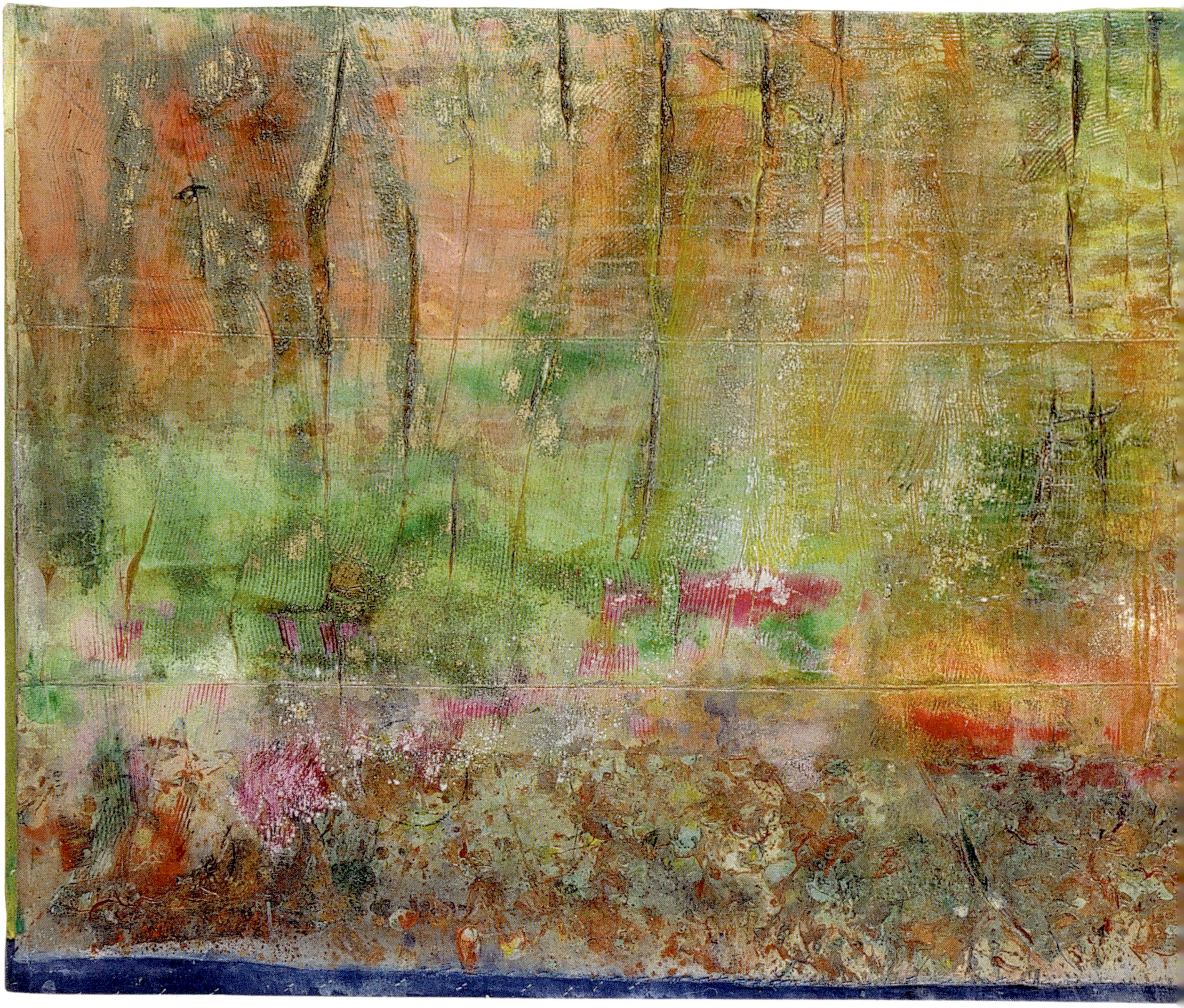

and *Vines* (both 2010) wittily acknowledge the subjects their images bring to mind. In these ways Bowling's titles – allusive, evocative, enigmatic, comical – are very like those often encountered in modern jazz, another abstract modernist art, a number of which Bowling has incidentally, knowingly and pointedly appropriated or adapted.

A title may bear multiple connotations. The 1996 *Traingone (Mahaicony Abary)*, for instance, refers to an isolated leper colony in the forest marshes, close to where two railway bridges crossed the rivers Mahaicony and Abary. Those patients who heard the whistle of the steam trains echoing over the creeks and swamplands and watched its steam rise through the trees would never be able to depart; for them, every train had gone forever. If the formal objectivity of the painting is emphasised by complex visual textural effects, and by the sharp, horizontal creases in the canvas that have been incorporated into the image, its vivid iridescent colours –

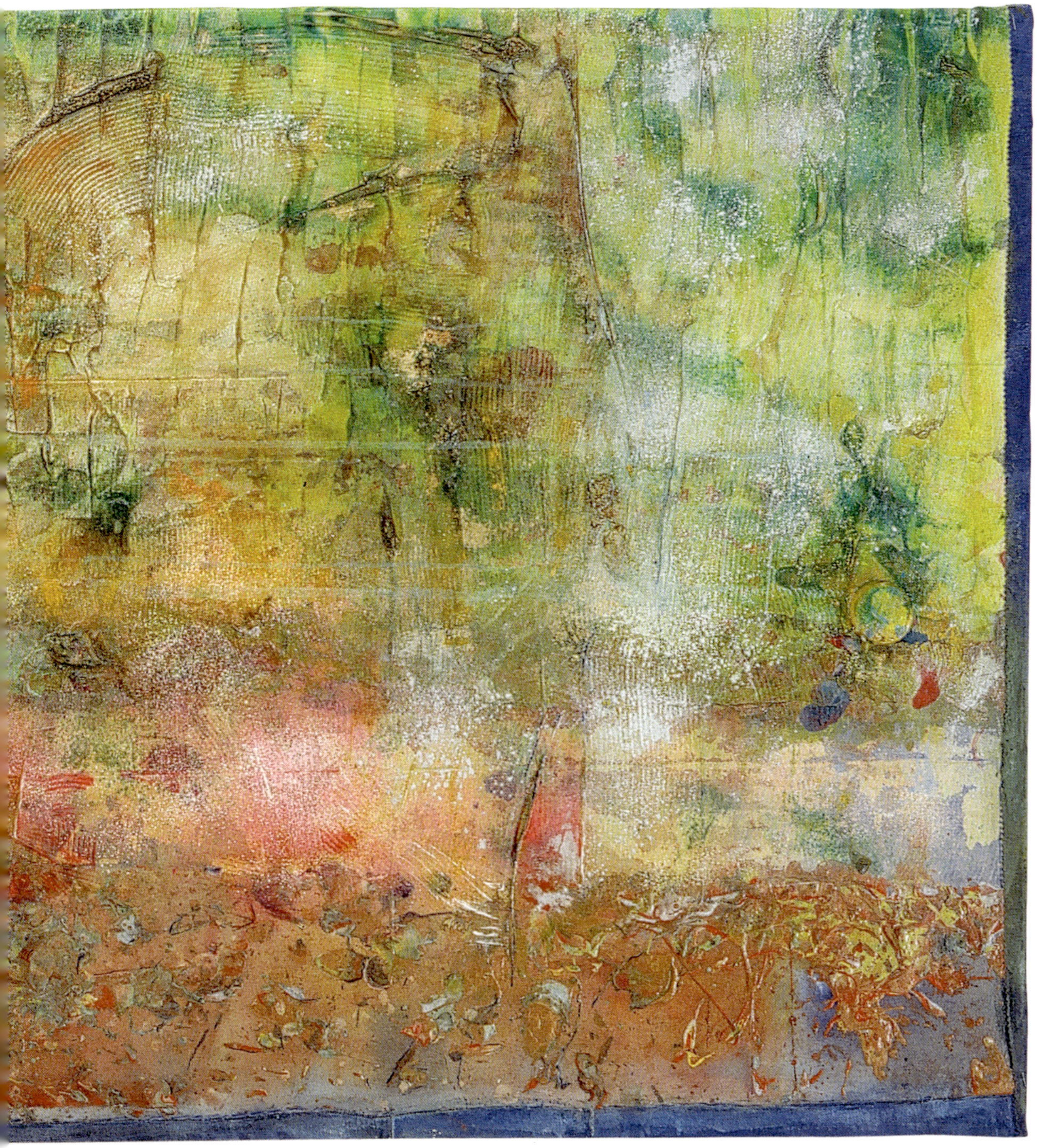

Traingone (Mahaicony Abary), 1996
Acrylic on canvas, 96.5 x 210 cm

tropical greens, yellows and magentas – are evocative of a coastal water-plain remembered from the artist's childhood, with a pink evening light that shines from the distance through deep forest glades.

There are subtle allusions in the painting to the atmospherics of Turner's *Rain, Steam and Speed* and to the elegiac sunset of *The Fighting Temeraire*. A succession of vertical strokes of transparent gel suggests, through a kind of visual pun, the rhythm of the train's sound, a rhythm that animates a thousand blues songs and jazz tunes – music that Bowling listened to all day in his Brooklyn studio. It brought to the artist's mind, especially, the great John Coltrane, whose birthday was marked, each year after his death, with a week-long programme of his music on Columbia University's WKCR. 'Trane is gone, and Bowling is creating his own complex visual music in celebration and elegy.

It is on a tightrope between such poetic associations and the objective formality of the

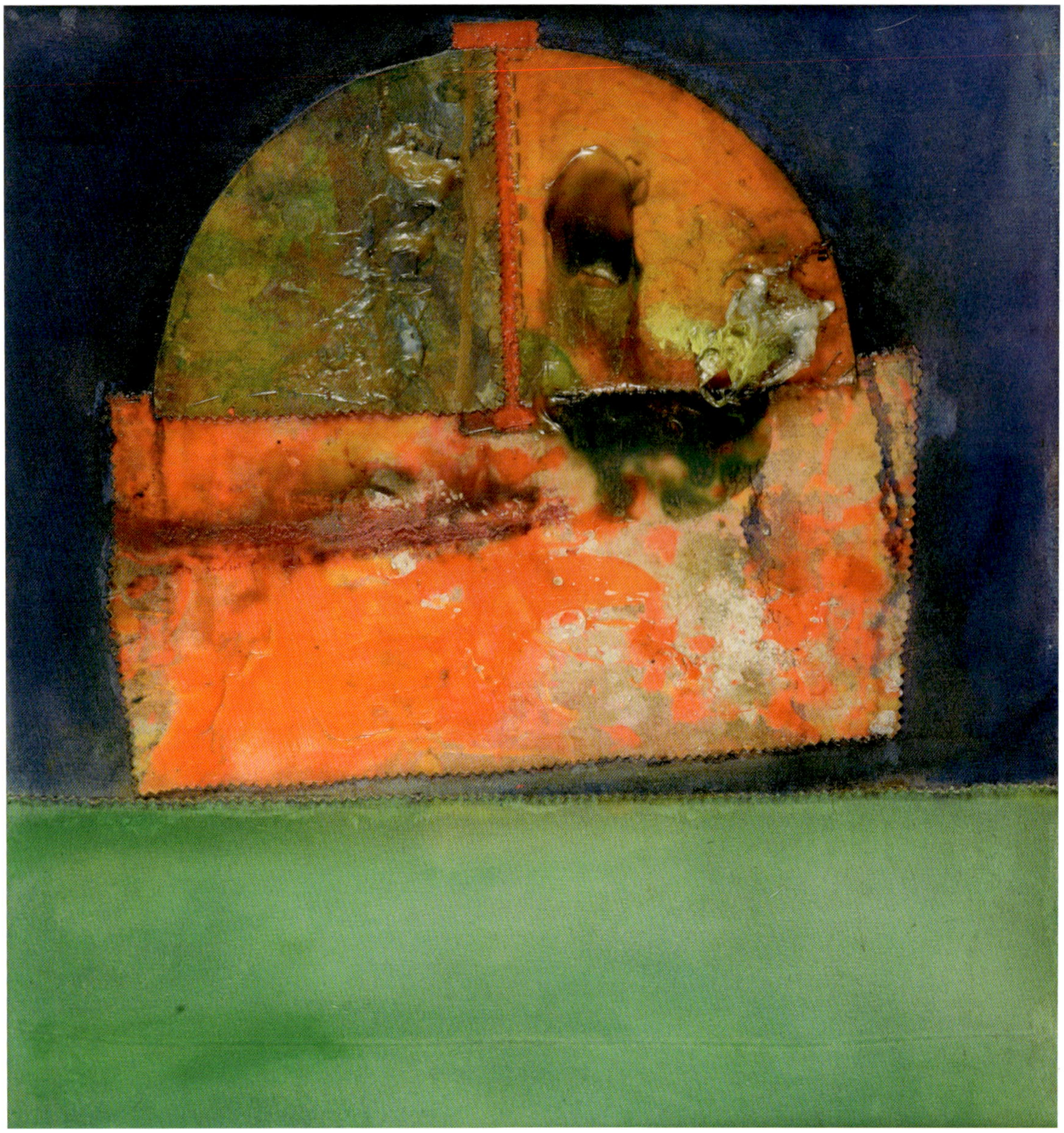

Ark, 2003
Acrylic on canvas, 47 x 44.5 cm

painting as such that Bowling achieves what he described as 'maximum openness'. In recent times, in the fullness of his years and the authority of his achievement, Bowling has not been afraid to exercise the creative freedoms that are associated with a late style. He is aware of grand precedents: 'Part of the nervousness of being an abstract painter is this notion of meaning', he told the critic Matthew Collings in 2006. 'I had been good at figurative painting and been rewarded for it when I was young, but I realised I never wanted to be that competent in the tradition of figuration. If you look at Titian's *Diana and Actaeon* in the National Gallery, the way he's drawn the trees, that flick, flick, flick of the brush – it's so encouraging. You feel that you can go and try your own thing after that. Drag the brush, and so on. You feel the whole activity is opened up.' It is typical of Bowling to have seen in the treatment of a terrible subject the extraordinary speed and freedom of the late Titian's brushstroke gestures, and to recognise in them a model for the formal focus of his own work. The conversation with Collings appeared as the introduction to the catalogue for an exhibition in 2006 of two groups of paintings made at the beginning of the new century. One group included richly worked and intensely coloured small paintings, such as *Ark* and *Two Blues (After Monticello)* of 2003, *Self Portrait as*

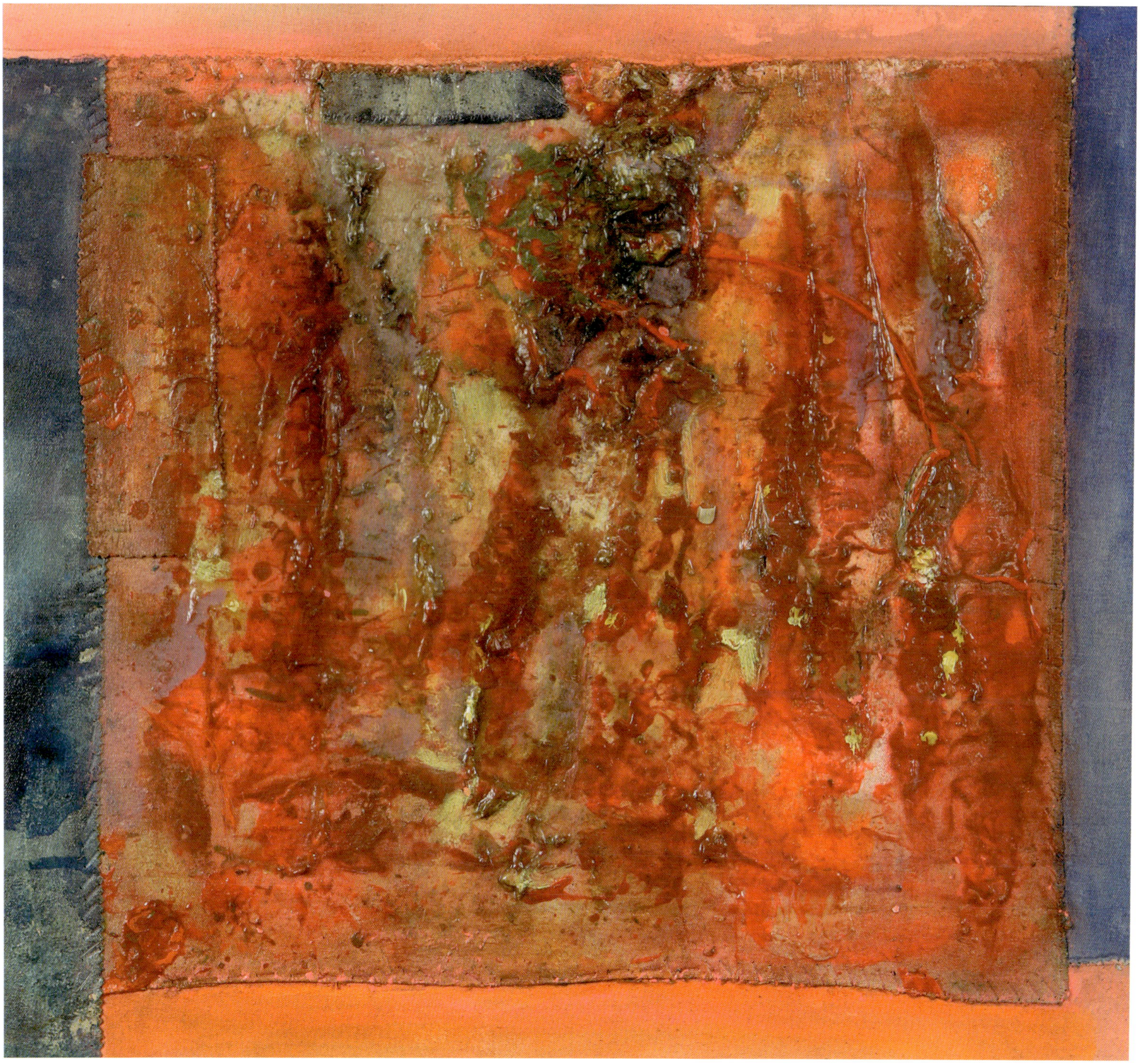

Two Blues (After Monticello), 2003
Acrylic on canvas, 53.5 x 57 cm

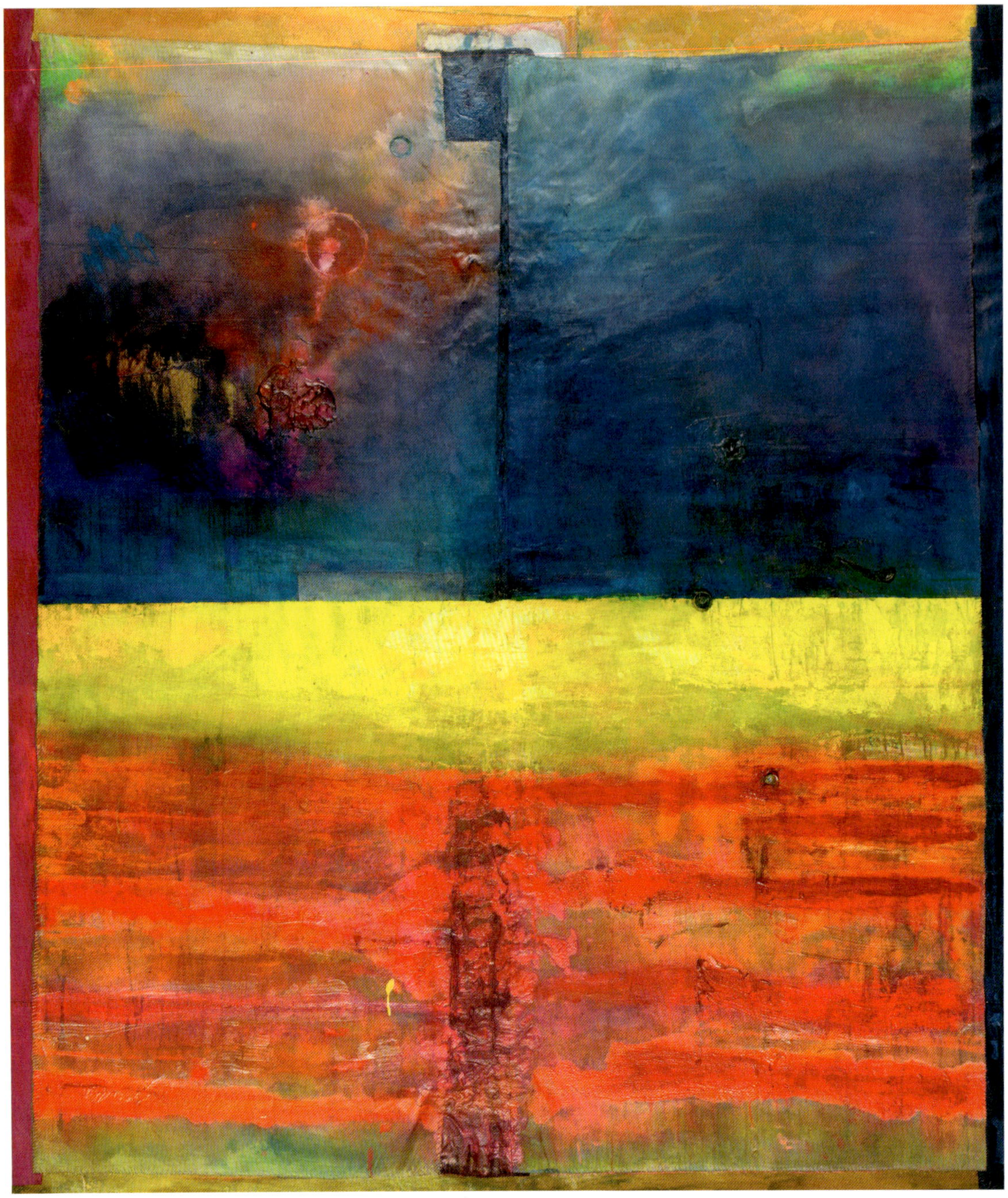

Tranegone (Who's Afraid of Red, Yellow and Blue), 2008
Acrylic on canvas, 223.5 x 188 cm

Uncle Remus (for my friend John Hoyland) and *Amelia* (both 2004) and *Rose* (2006); the other consisted of the white paintings he had made as elegies to his eldest son Dan (who died suddenly in 2001), which looked back to the white paintings of bottle still-lifes and the winter landscapes of 1962 such as *Snow Painting* that he was making at the time of Dan's birth in the January of that year.

The work of the last few years has been characterised by a wonderfully inventive diversity of formal device. The vertical and horizontal 'zippers' paintings (as Bowling calls them), such as *Epps*, *Litchfield*, *Chinese Chance* and *Kitty* (all 2009) suggest tall skies or long horizons, their combings of translucent gel inviting reveries of sunrise and sunset over watery Delft or Venice, while their collective name ironically refers to their atmospheric use of Newman's rigorously formal zip. In the 2011 *Crossings* series, Bowling returned to the format, but with a more complex treatment. The marvellous 'flower' paintings of 2010, such as *Old Dutch Vase*, *Basket* and *Vines*, with their colour-stained, stitched collage-frames and central fields of spatter and speckle, are

opposite
Self Portrait as Uncle Remus (for my friend John Hoyland), 2004
Acrylic on canvas, 100.5 x 72.5 cm

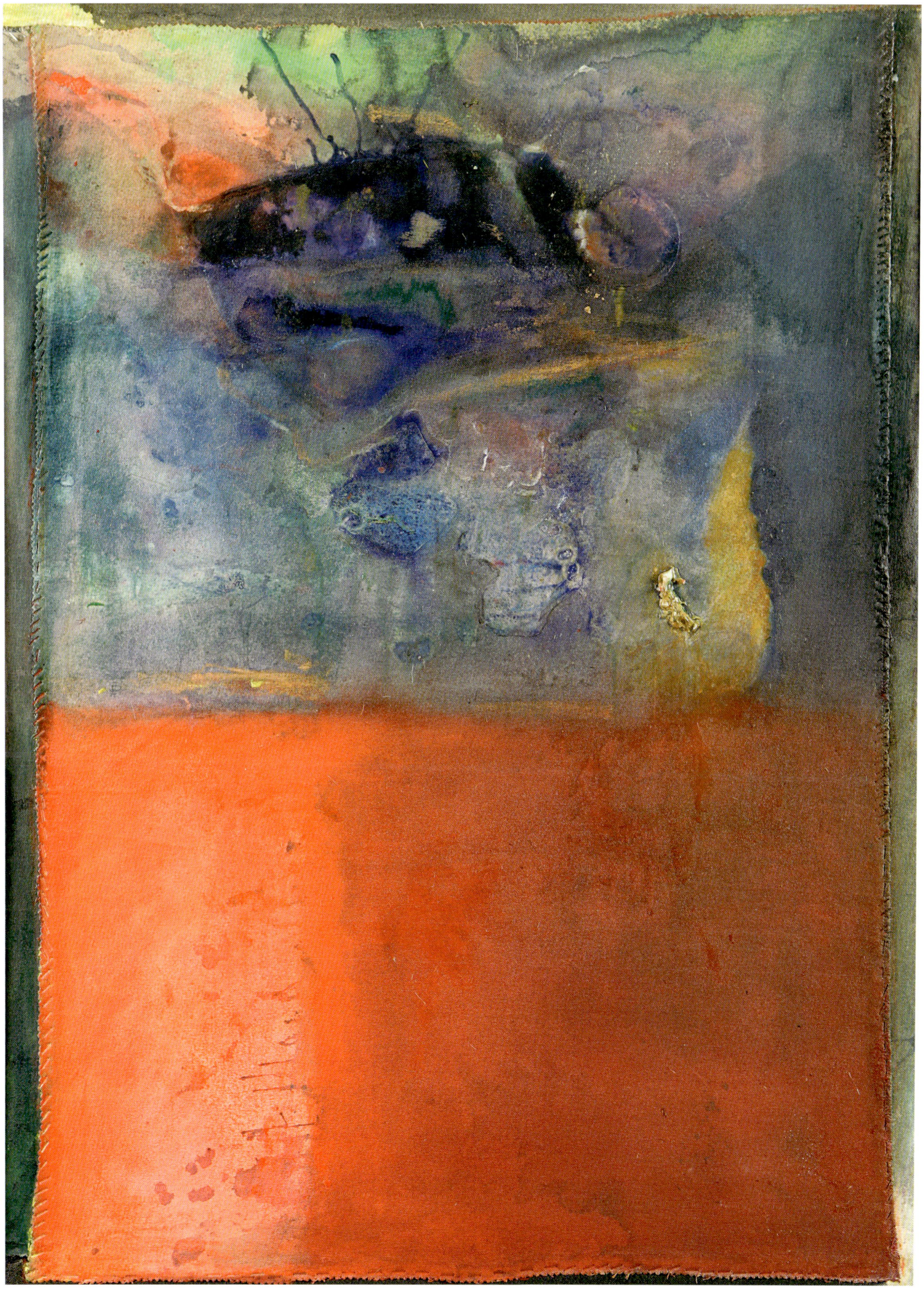

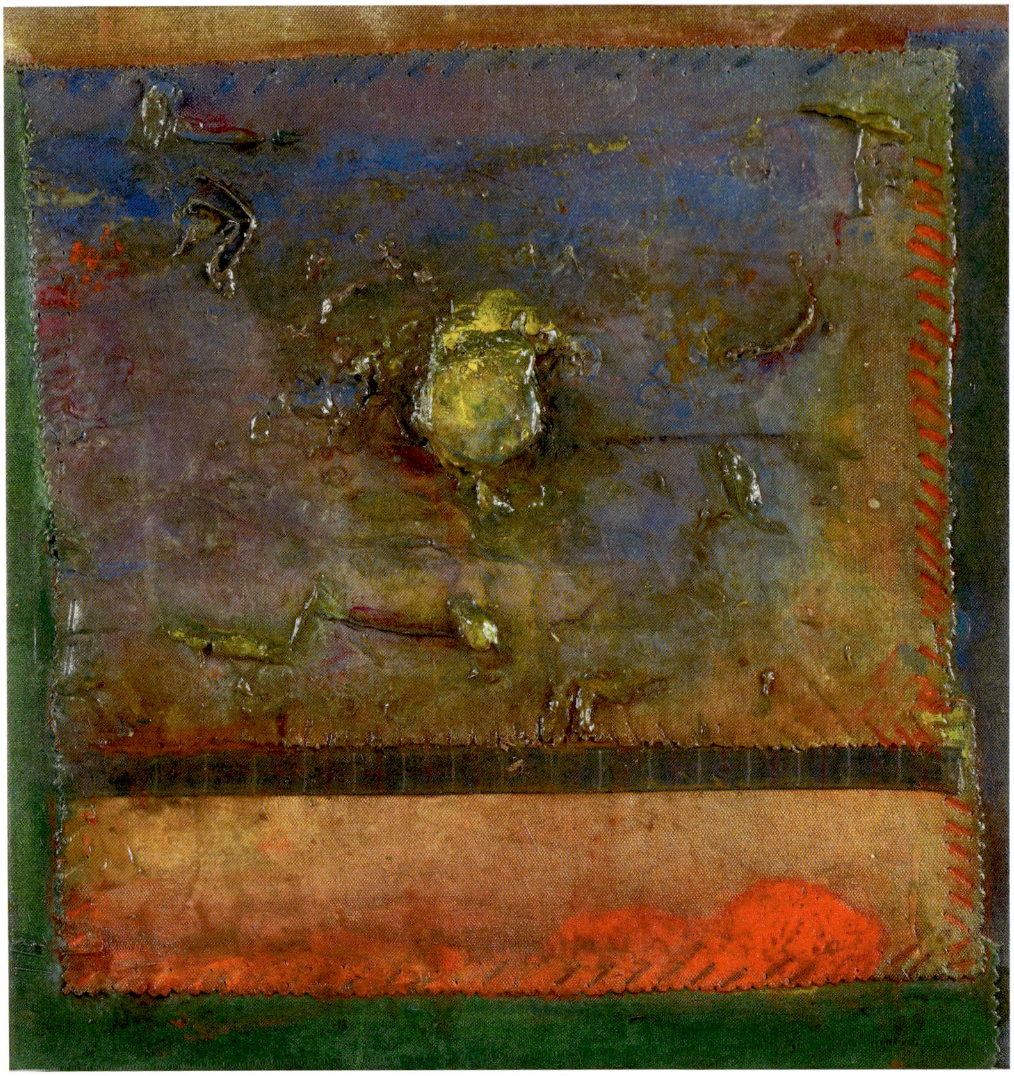

Amelia, 2004
Acrylic on canvas, 35.5 x 33 cm

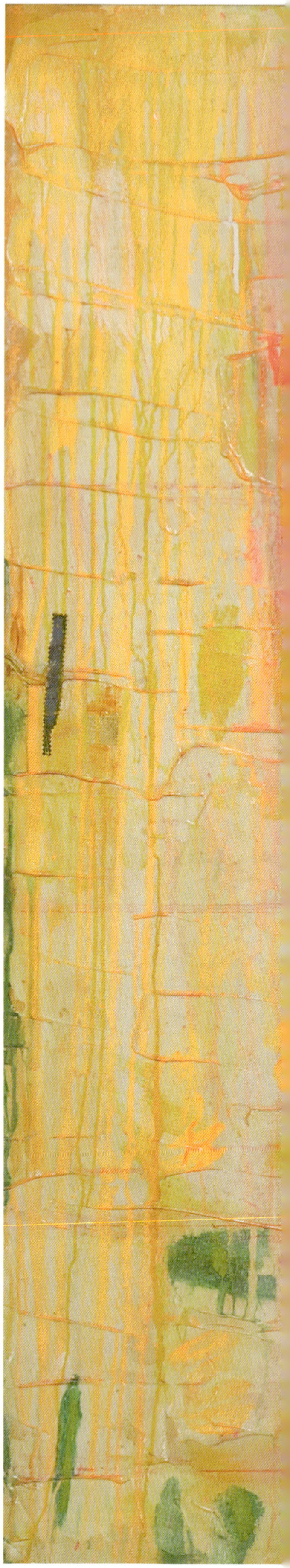

Rose, 2006
Acrylic on canvas, 176.5 x 199.5 cm

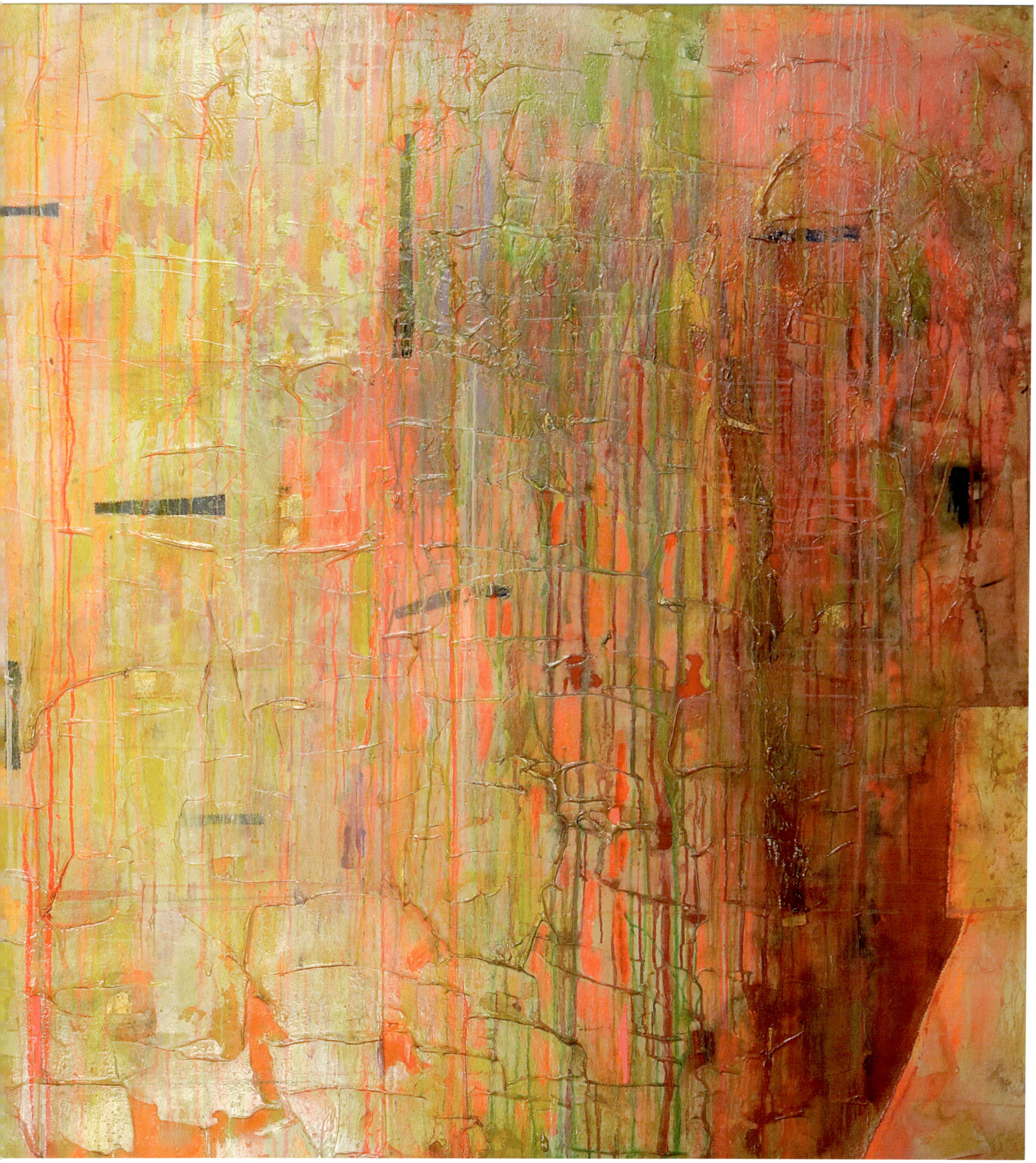

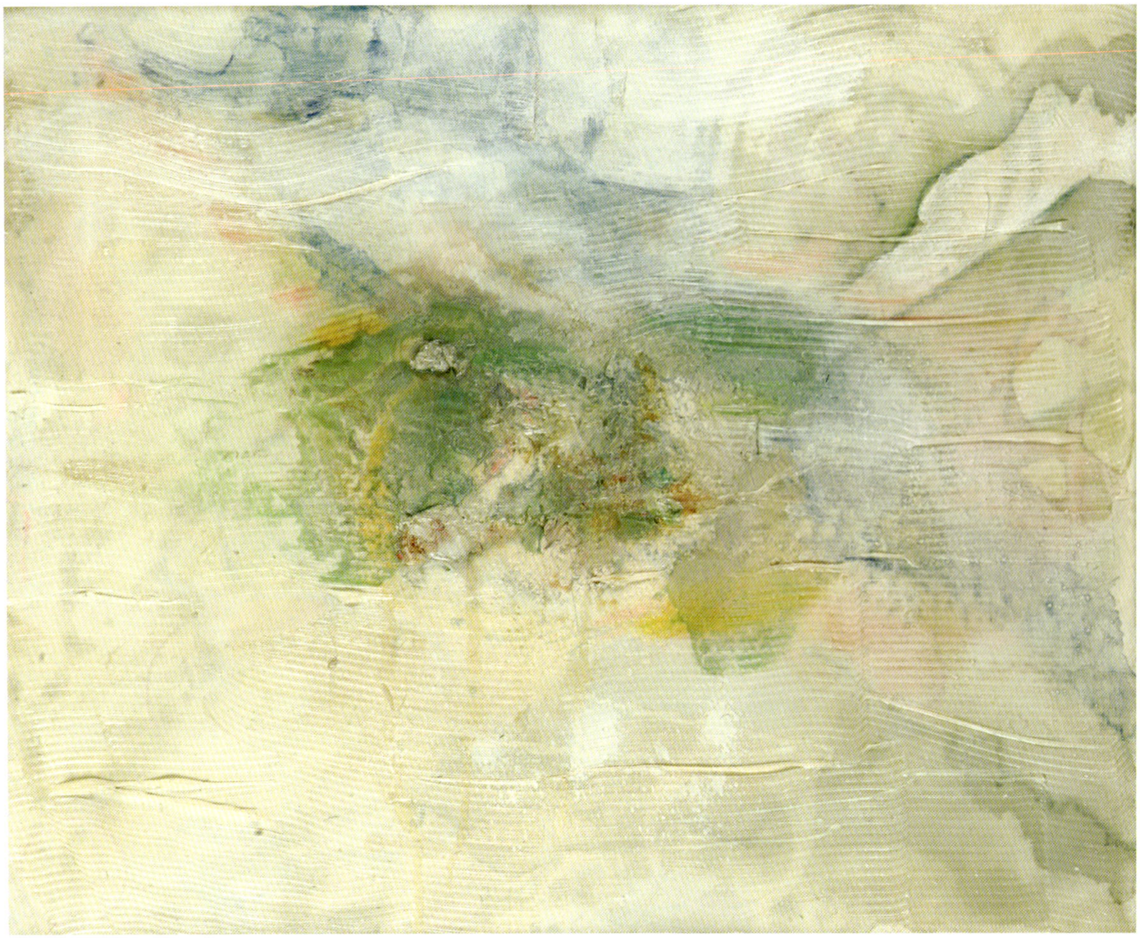

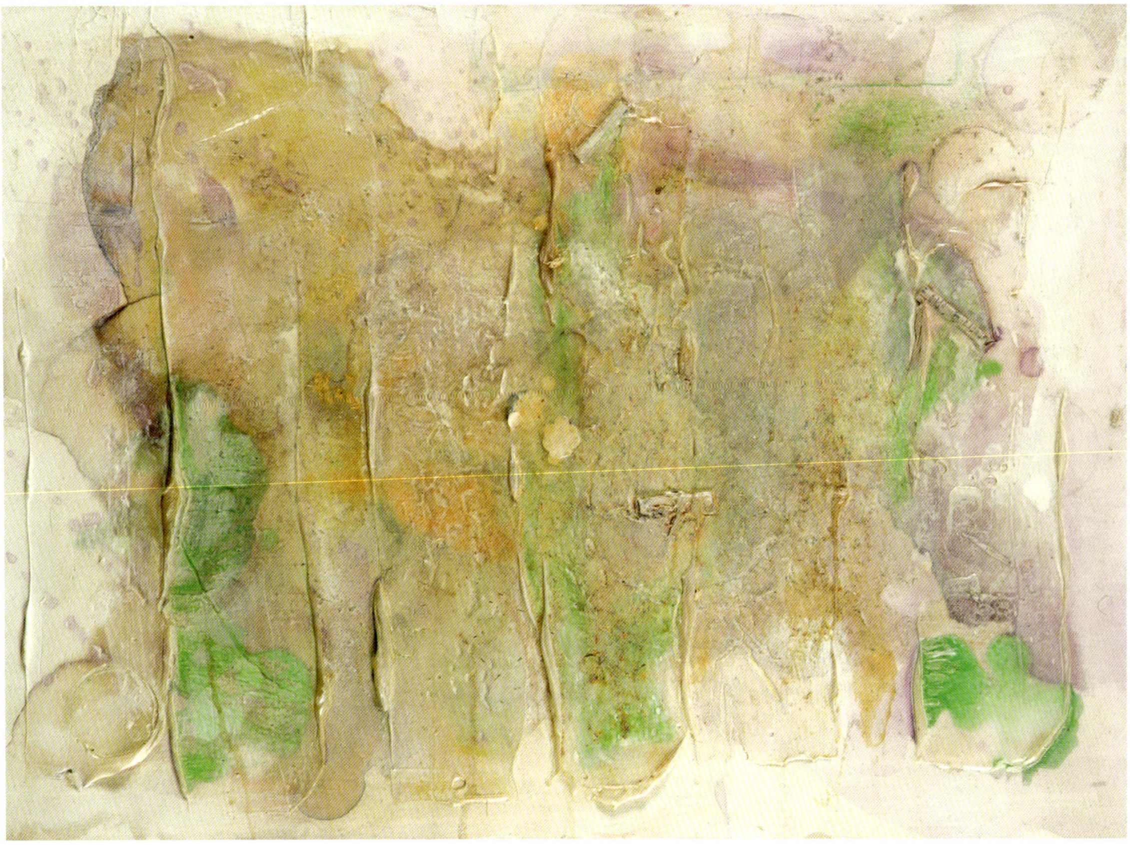

left
Icarus, 2005
Oil on canvas, 51 x 63.5 cm

below
Spring, 2005
Oil on canvas, 46 x 61 cm

opposite
Haze, 2005
Acrylic on canvas, 61 x 46 cm

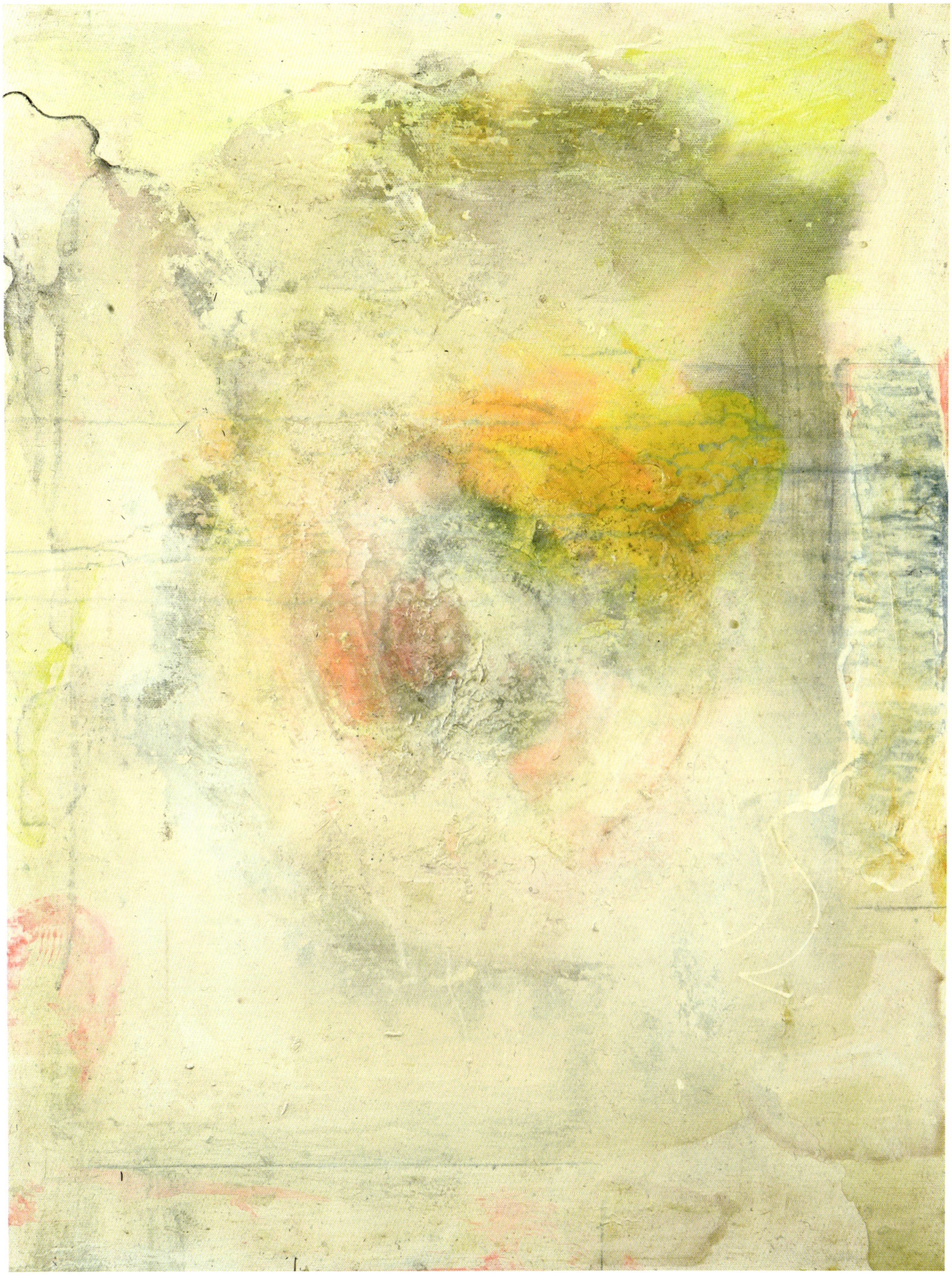

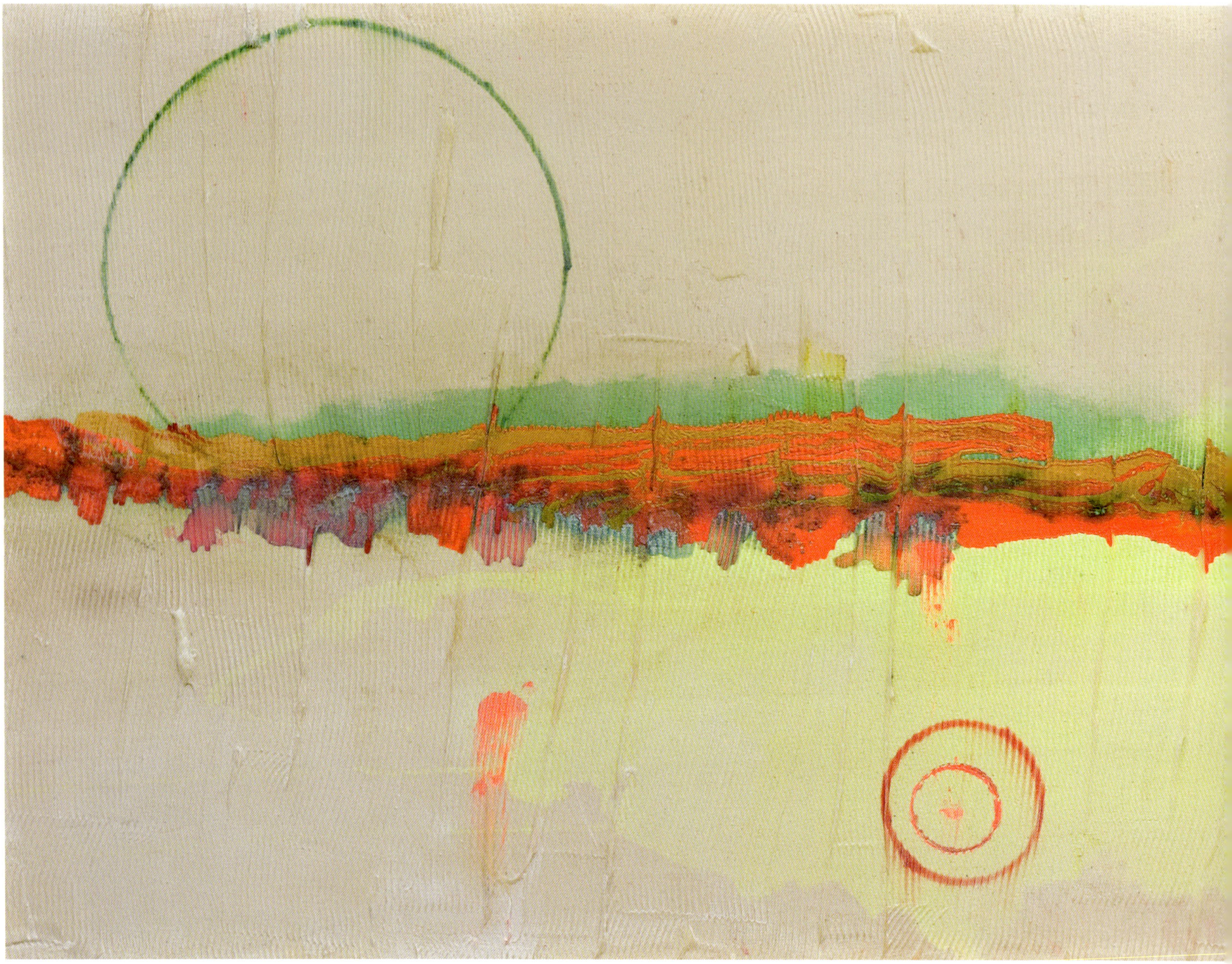

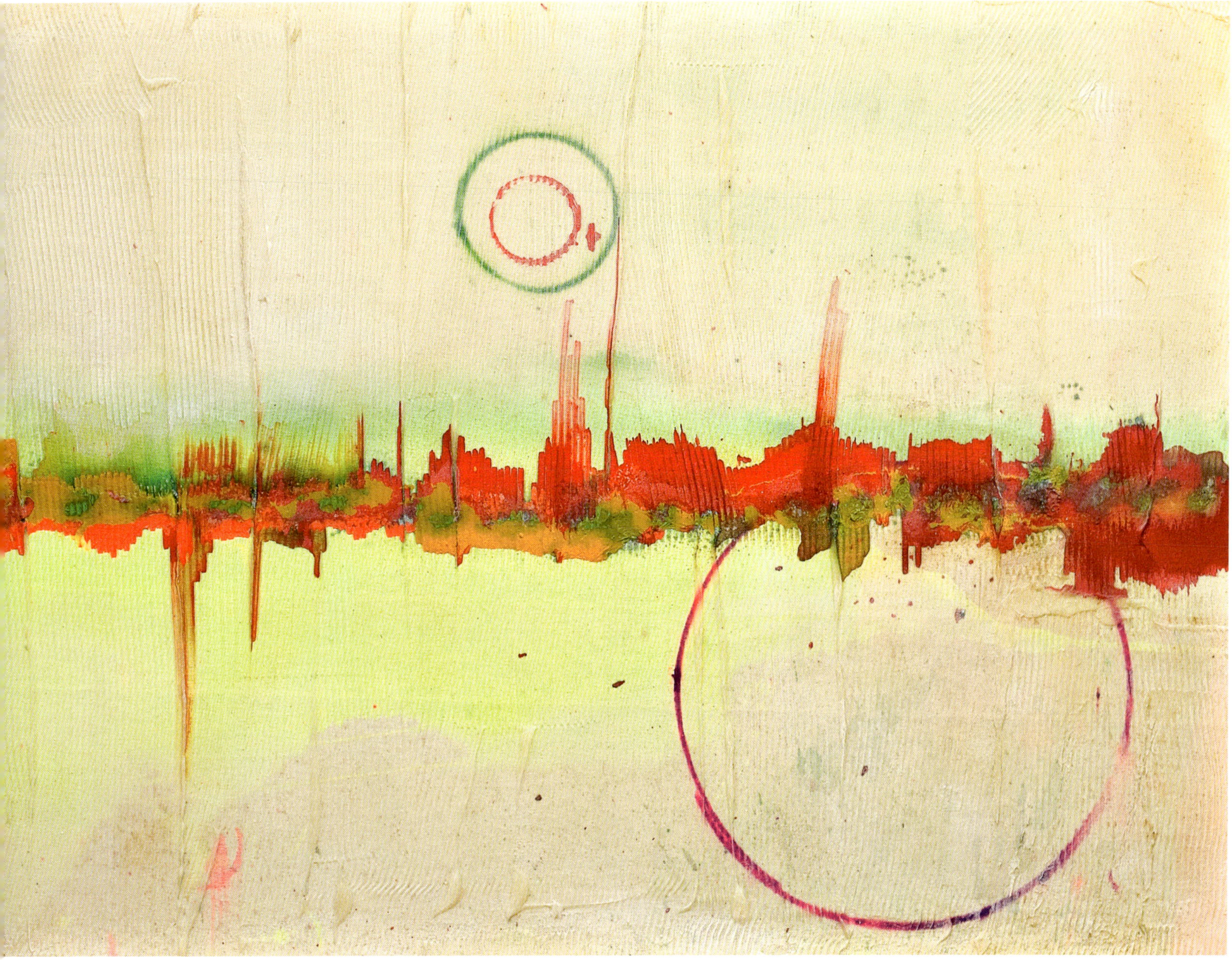

Epps, 2009
Acrylic on canvas, 66 x 173 cm

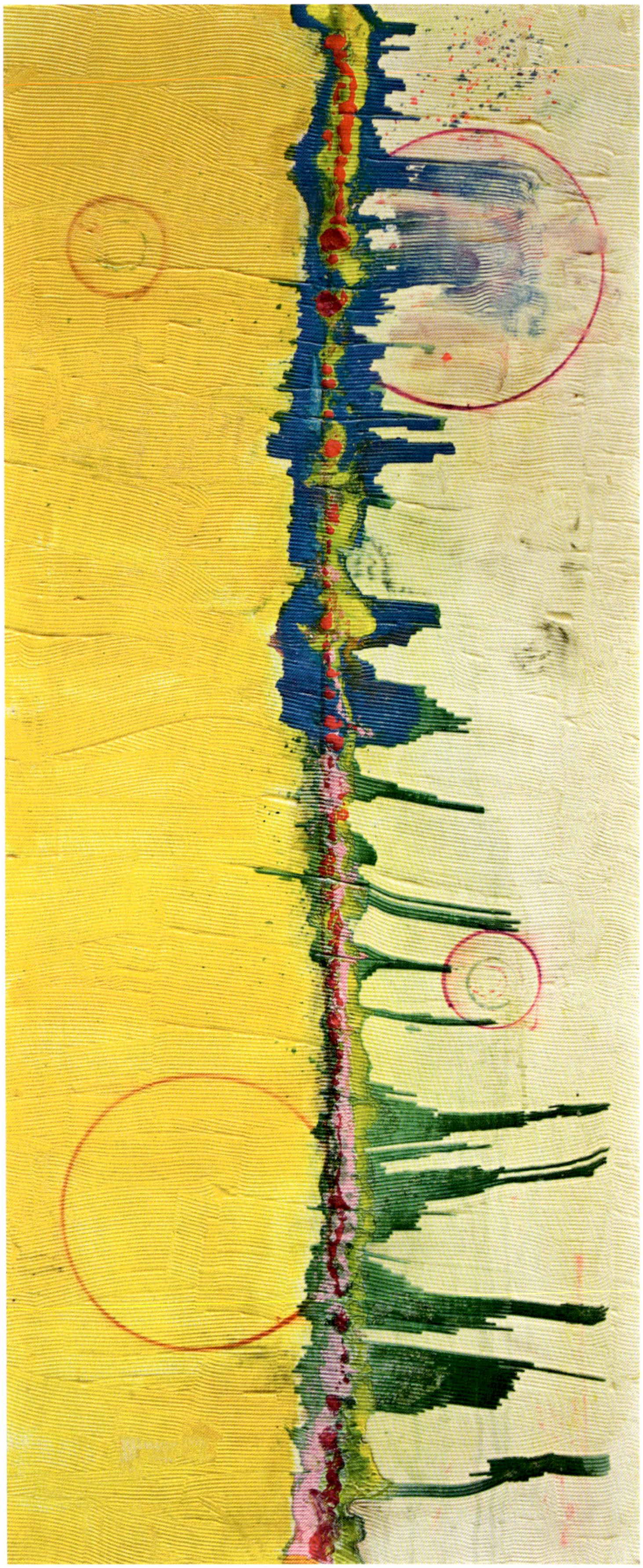

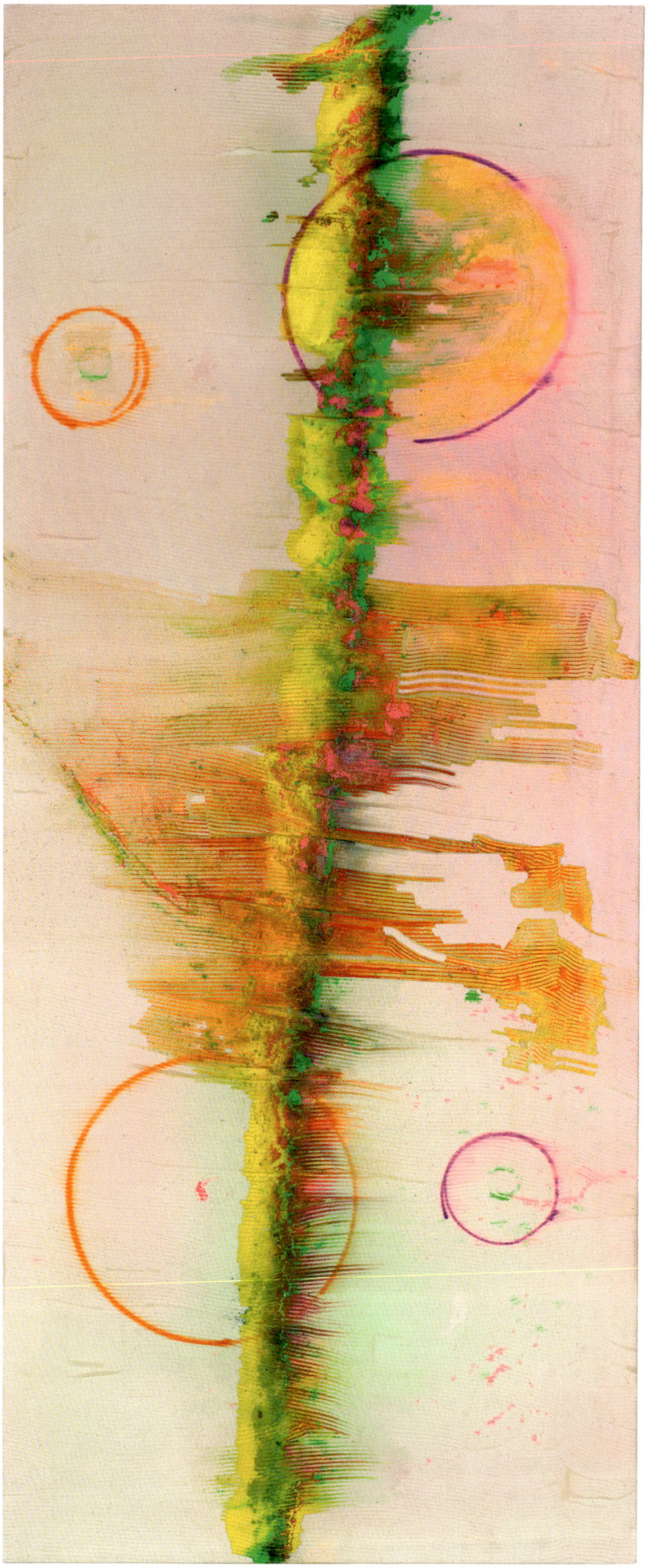

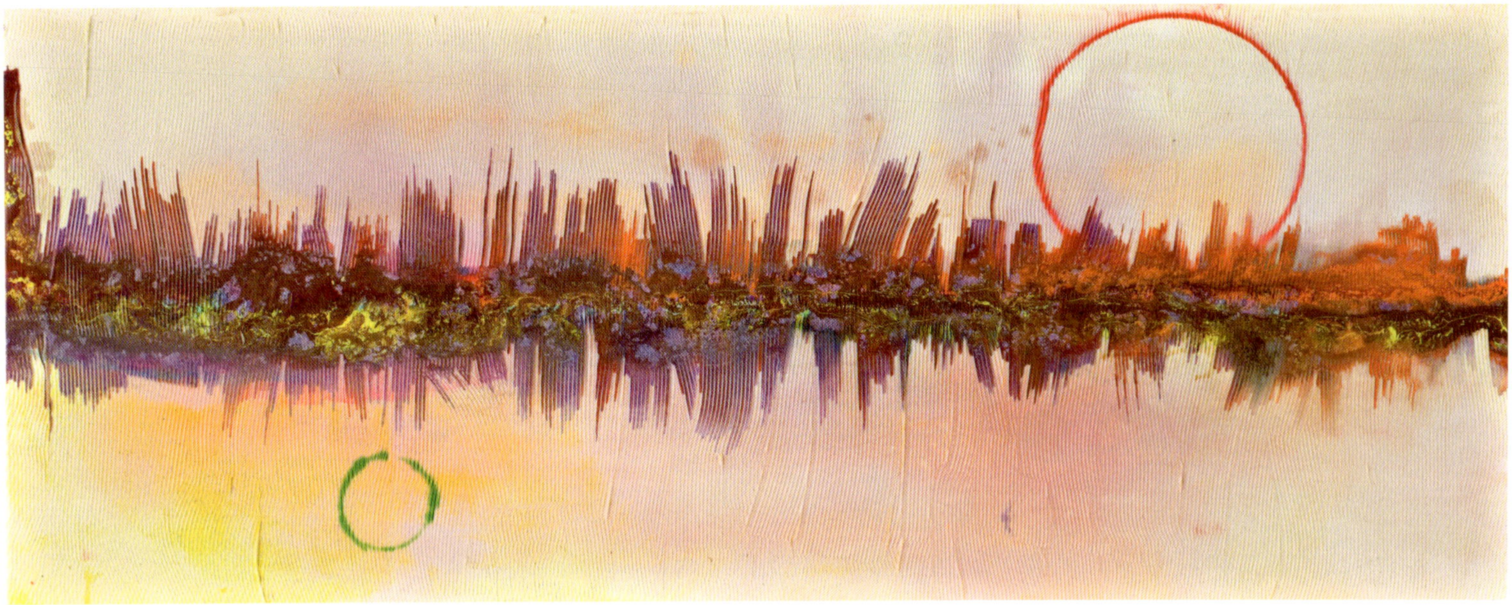

unashamedly evocative of classic still-life paintings. And in the optically reverberant blood-red sun of the disturbing late masterpiece, *Red, Yellow and Blue* (2010), Bowling returned to his long-standing interest in the geometric with renewed vigour.

Everything Bowling has made in these later years draws, with a sublime insouciance, upon the principles, procedures and processes that have been the primary elements of his art since the late 1970s. These have enabled him to continue to experiment and explore the limits of his chosen media, and to respond to diversities of experience, both remembered and immediate, to the sorrows of loss and the vicissitudes of illness, to new places and new joys in familiar surroundings, and, as ever, to the great rivers of his life, the Essequibo and the Berbice, the Thames and the East River, each with its own particular shimmer, gleam and brilliance of light.

Kitty, 2009
Acrylic on canvas, 68.5 x 173 cm

opposite, left
Litchfield, 2009
Acrylic on canvas, 173 x 63.5 cm

opposite, right
Chinese Chance, 2009
Acrylic on canvas, 173 x 70 cm

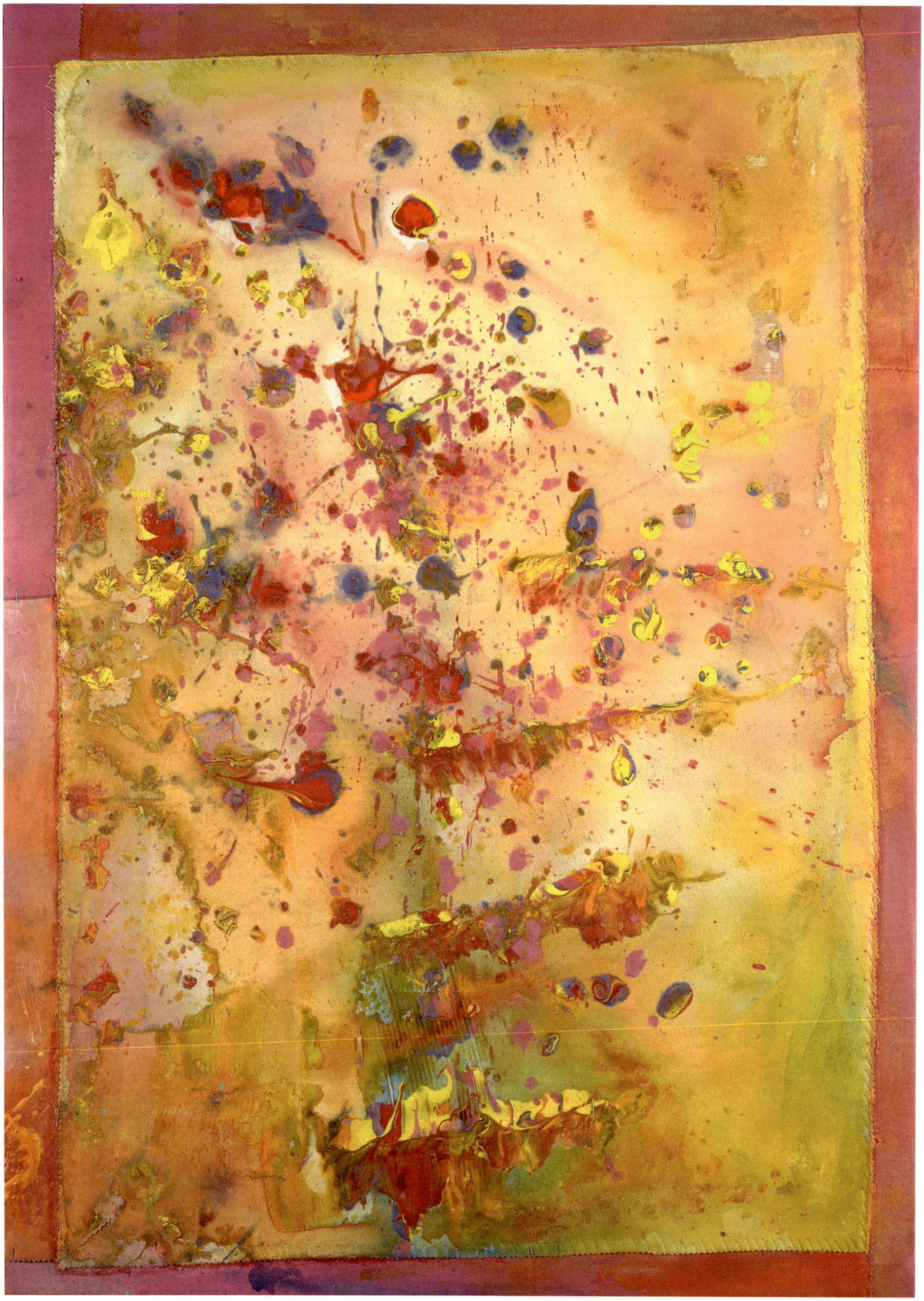

opposite
Old Dutch Vase, 2010
Acrylic on canvas, 117 x 84 cm

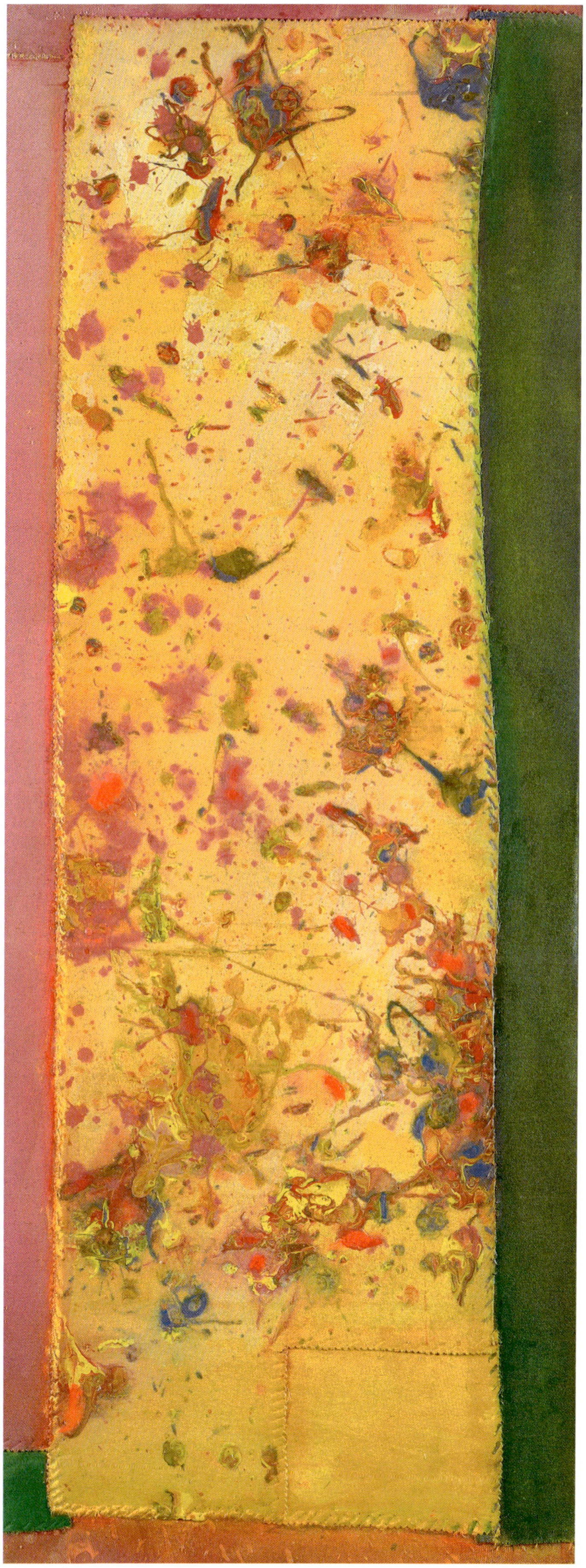

Vines, 2010
Acrylic on canvas, 117 x 43 cm

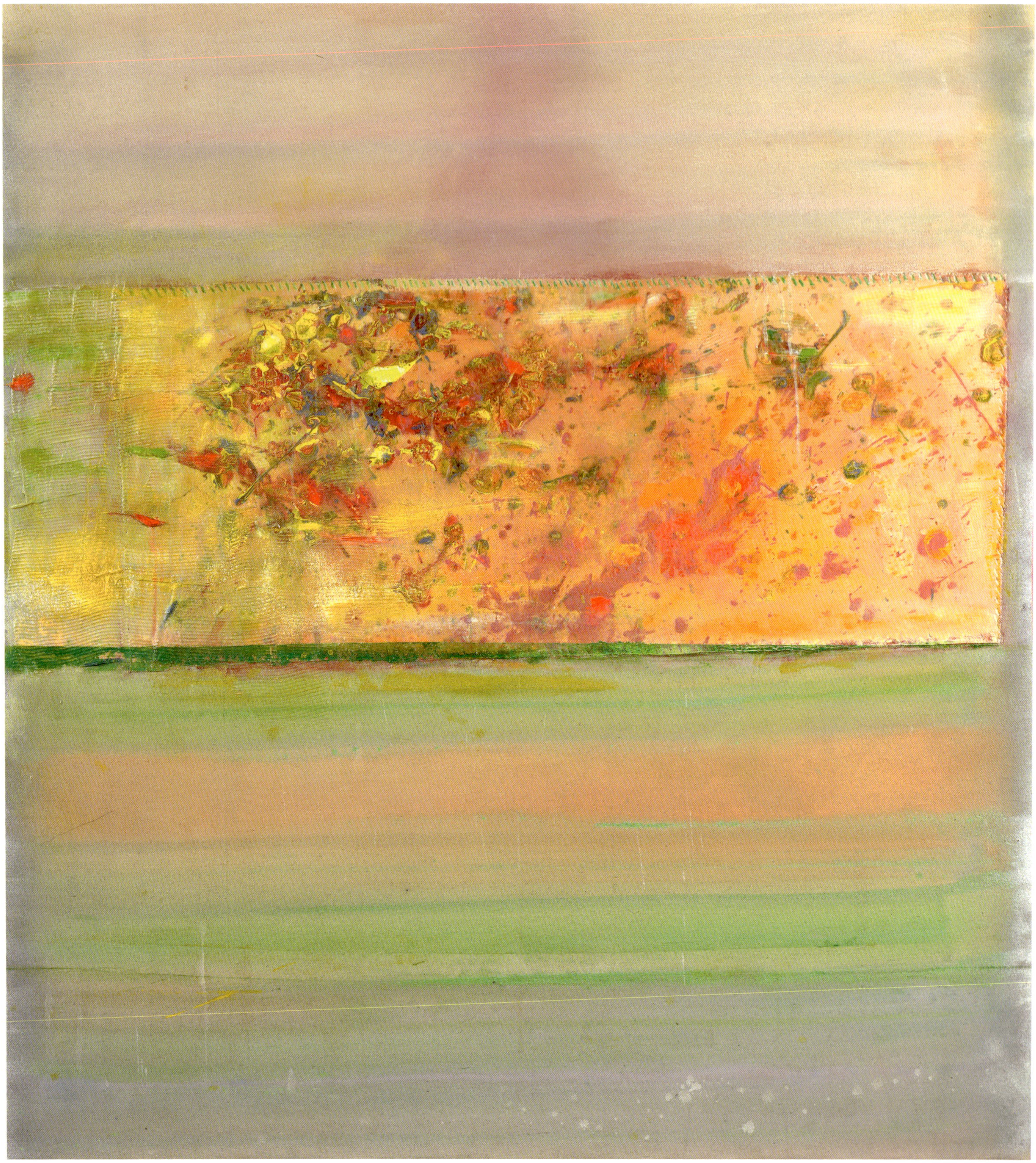

Pondlife, 2010
Acrylic on canvas, 145 x 129.5 cm

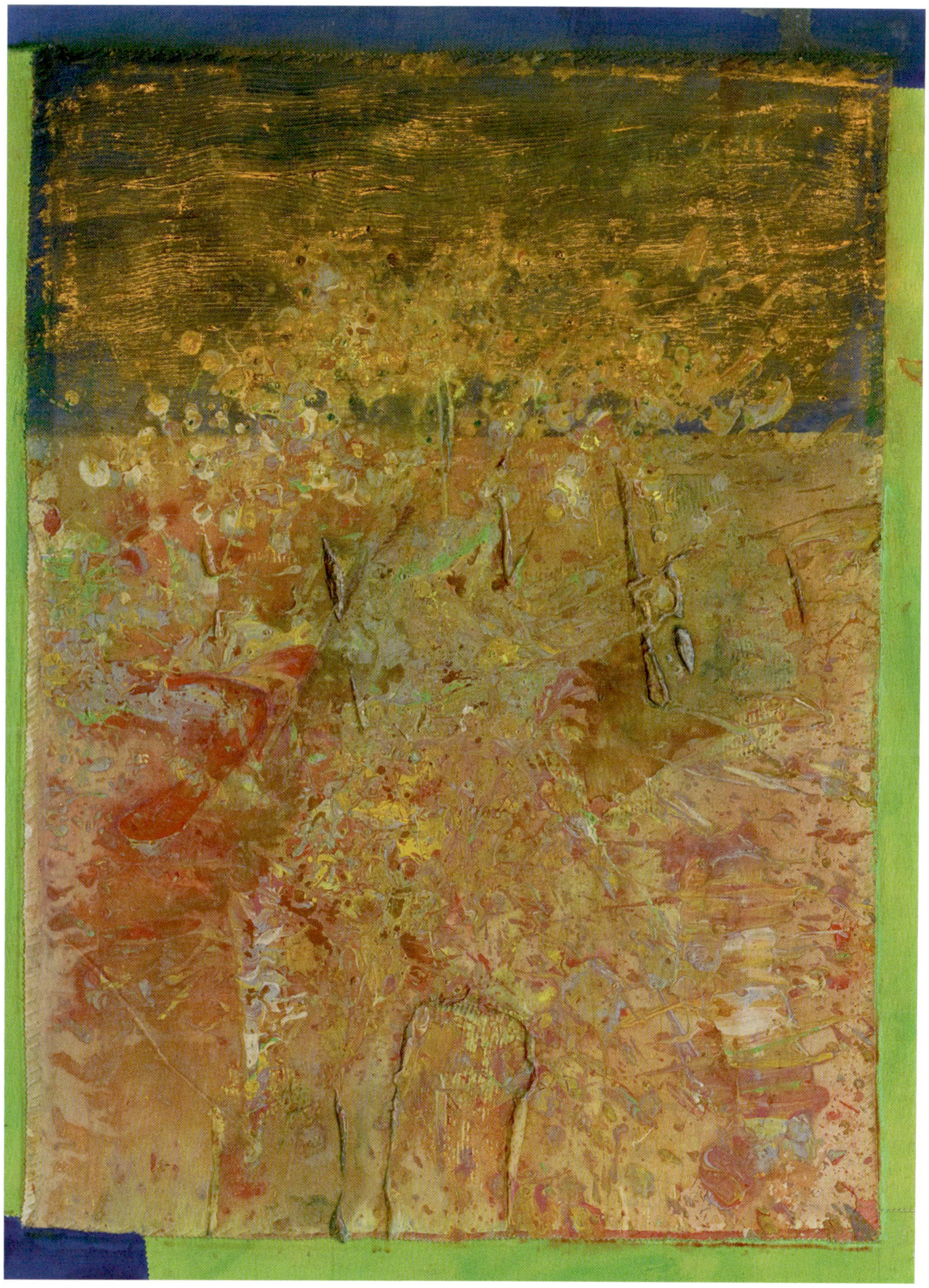

Bramble, 2010
Acrylic on canvas, 115.5 x 84 cm

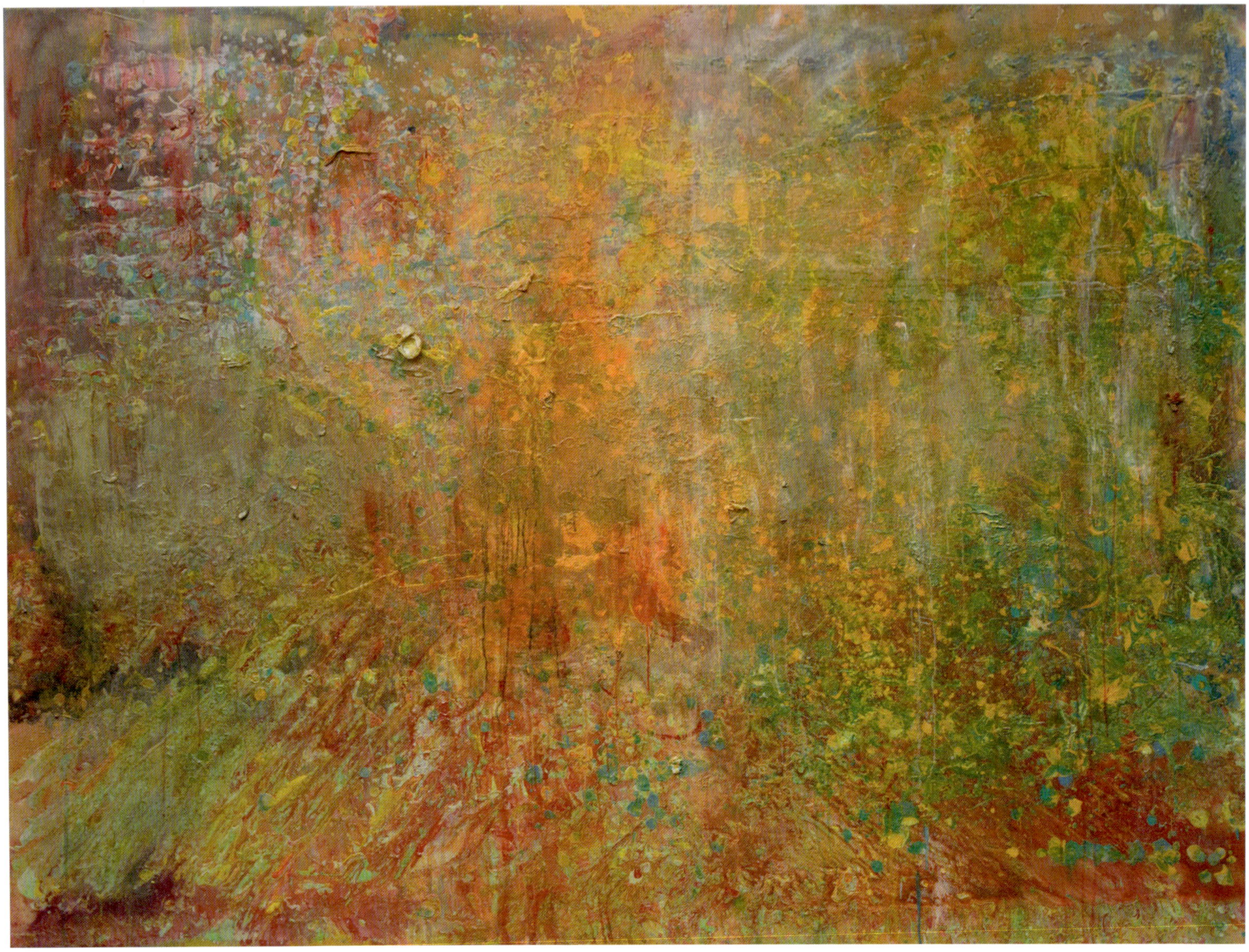

Lemongrassblackpepperbush,
2011
Acrylic on canvas, 167.5 x 221 cm

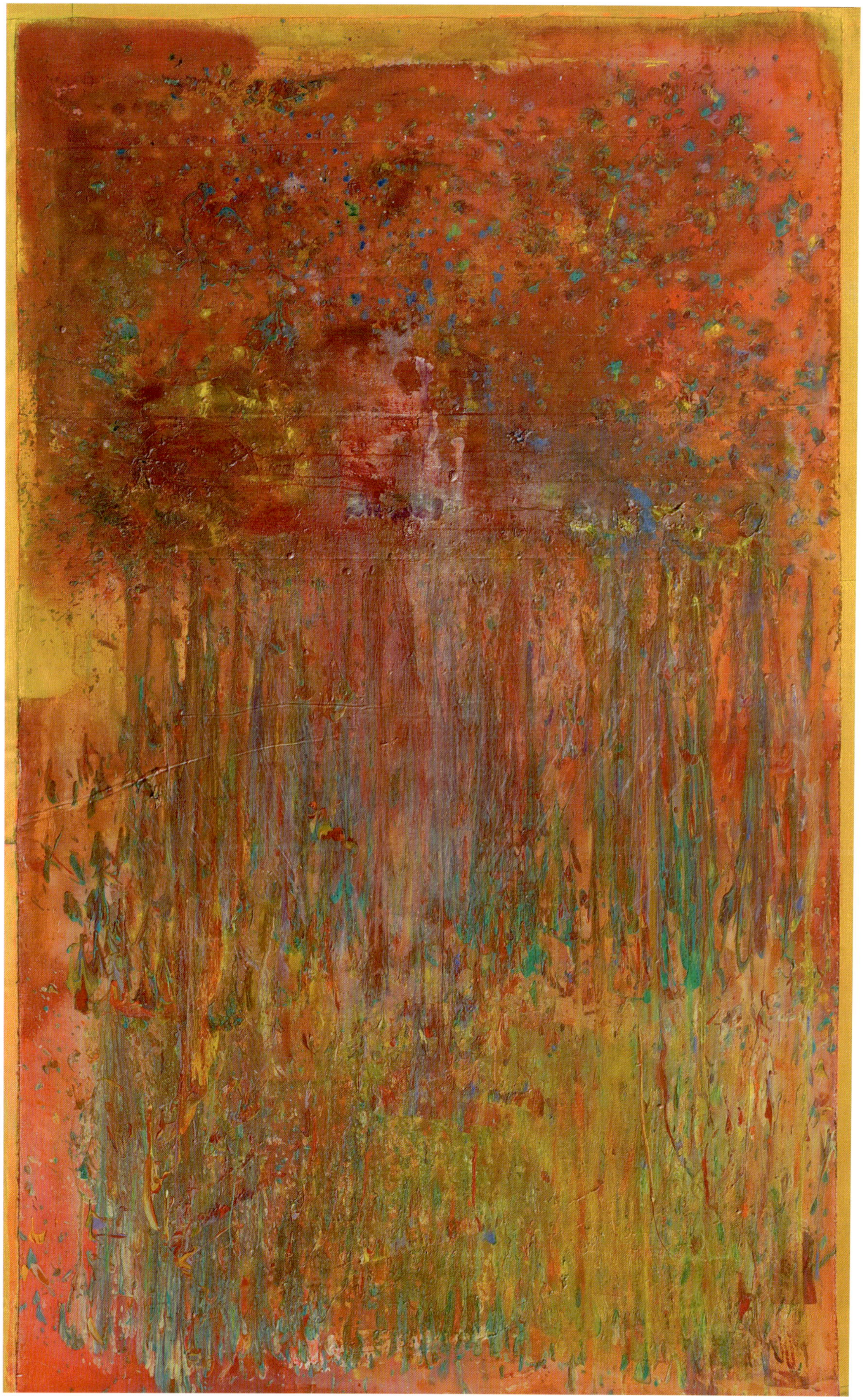

Journey along with Marcia Scott, 2011
Acrylic on canvas, 310 x 193 cm

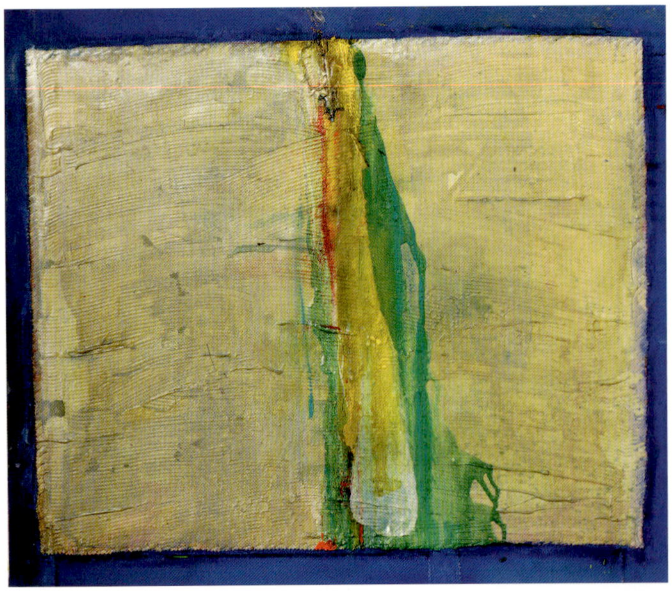

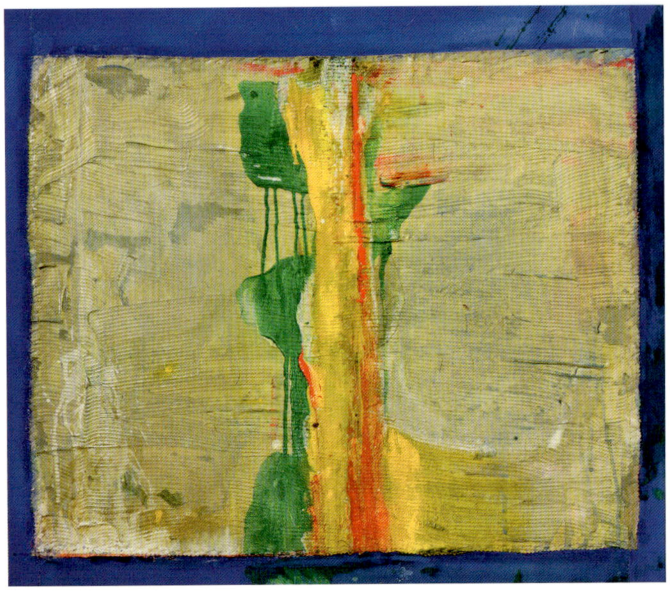

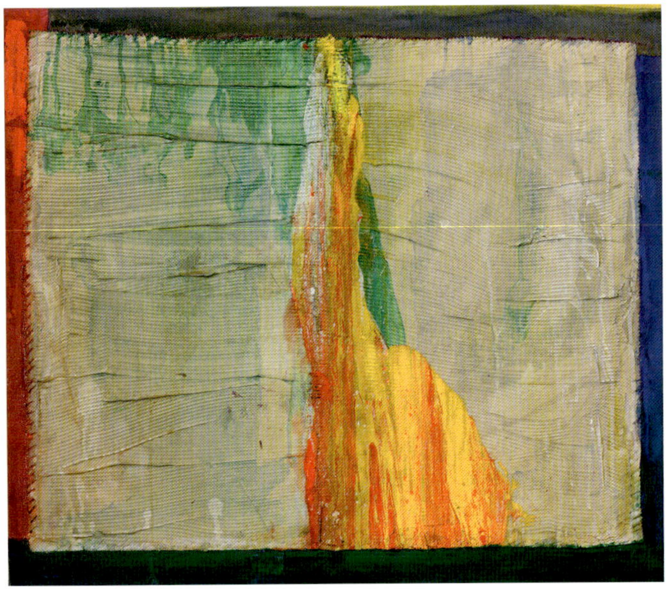

top
***Crossings: Overlooking Chaguaramus*, 2011**
Acrylic on canvas, 71 x 81 cm

middle
***Crossings: Egyptian*, 2011**
Acrylic on canvas, 71 x 81 cm

bottom
***Crossings: Towards Liberty*, 2011**
Acrylic on canvas, 71 x 81 cm

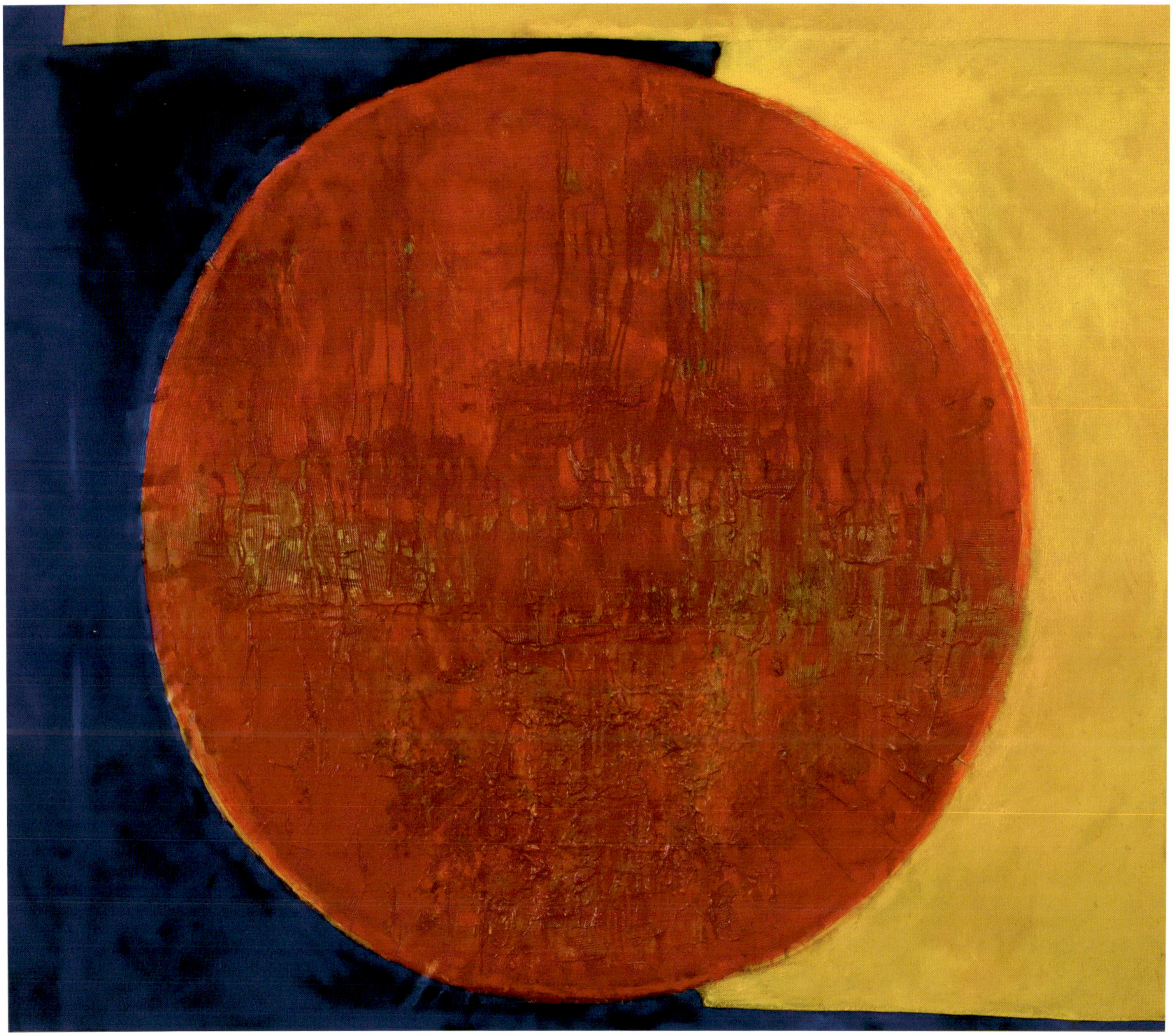

Red, Yellow and Blue, 2010
Acrylic on canvas, 189 x 216 cm

NOTES AND REFERENCES

Unless otherwise indicated, Frank Bowling is quoted from the *National Life Stories Artists Lives* recordings made with the author, 2001-07, which are accessible at the British Library and the Tate Archive. Quotations from these transcripts have been lightly edited and modified for clarity, in all cases with Frank Bowling's knowledge and permission.

In 1966 the former colony of British Guiana became independent and adopted the name Guyana. In the text I have used both appellations depending on the historical context: thus, for example, I have written that Bowling was born in British Guiana, and that in later life he visited Guyana.

PART 1

page 14
T.S. Eliot is quoted from 'East Coker' in *Four Quartets*, 1940.

page 17
'Windrush generation': The *Empire Windrush* arrived at Tilbury on 22 June 1948, carrying 492 passengers from Jamaica. This was first large group of West Indian immigrants to the UK after World War II, who were to be followed over the next few years by thousands more.

page18
Lord Kitchener was a popular post-war calypso singer from Trinidad; 'London Belongs to Me' was one of his most popular songs.

page 21
Place, an exhibition at the ICA in 1959, introduced the idea of large-scale so-called 'environmental' painting to London. Royal College graduates Richard Smith and Robyn Denny were among the artists represented.

page 33
Lonnie Donegan was a popular 'skiffle' singer in the mid- to late 1950s.

PART 2

page 47
Simon Wilson's comment is from an unpublished essay (2010) on *Mirror.*

page 48
The Elements of Dynamic Symmetry by Jay Hambidge (1926) was re-published by Dover Publications, New York in 1953.

pages 52 to 53
The reference to artists in New York 'who happened to be black', and the quotation 'I thought my career path ...' are from an interview with the present author in *Frank Bowling*, a film by Rose Jones (2011).

page 58
All quotations from Martin Heidegger are from 'The Origin of the Work of Art' in *Poetry, Language, Thought*, translated and introduced by Albert Hofstadter (Harper and Row, New York, 1971).

page 59
'[The] practice of painting...' is from 'Notes Along the Way', in the first and only issue of *Fuse* (London, Autumn 1988).

page 60
The remarks on the work of William T. Williams are from 'It's Not Enough to Say "Black is Beautiful" ' in *Art Magazine* (New York, April 1971). This essay indicates something of Bowling's extensive critical knowledge of his black American contemporaries in New York.

page 61
William T. Williams and Mel Edwards are quoted from exchanges in 'Black Artists and Abstraction: A Roundtable' in *Energy/ Experimentation: Black Artists and Abstraction 1964-1980*, the catalogue to an exhibition of that title at the Studio Museum, Harlem, New York, 5 April – 2 July 2006.

Patrick Heron is quoted from 'A Note on my Painting' in the catalogue to an exhibition of his work at Galerie Charles Lienhard, Zurich, 1963, reprinted in *Painter as Critic Patrick Heron: Selected Writings* ed. Mel Gooding (Tate Gallery Publications, 1998).

page 68
The interview with Robert Doty (dated September 1971) was published in the leaflet accompanying Bowling's solo exhibition at the Whitney Museum of American Art, November–December 1971.

page 70
Susanne K. Langer is quoted from 'Artistic Perception and "Natural Light" ' in *Problems of Art: Ten Philosophical Lectures* (Routledge and Kegan Paul, London, 1957).

Marcia Hafif's review appeared in *Arts Magazine* (New York, December 1971-January 1972).

page 71
Clement Greenberg coined the term 'Post Painterly Abstraction' to characterise a stylistic shift from the painterly abstraction of the second generation abstract expressionists of the New York School. It was the title of an exhibition he organised at Los Angeles Museum of Art (and tour) in 1964.

page 72
Bowling's conversation with William Thomson appeared in *Art International* (December 1976). 'My ambitions as a painter...' and 'My ambition for my painting...' also derive from this text.

page 77
Rimbaud is quoted from the seminal letter to Paul Demeny, 15 May 1871.

Wallace Stevens discusses 'resemblance' in the first of his 'Three Academic Pieces' in *The Necessary Angel* (Faber and Faber, London, 1960); essay first published in *Partisan Revew* (Boston, 1947).

PART 3

page 93
Louis MacNeice's poem, 'Snow' also contains the lines: 'I peel and portion/A tangerine and spit the pips and feel/The drunkenness of things being various.' Bowling's paintings can induce this feeling.

page 100
'I wanted to catch the light and movement of nature itself': from a recent conversation with the present writer.

page 101
Dan Chiasson was writing about the New York poet James Schuyler in *The New York Review of Books* (New York, 27 May 2010).

page 104
'The fact is, it's exciting... to live in London...': from 'Notes Along the Way', *Fuse* (London, Autumn 1988).

Rachel Scott's account of Bowling's working procedures is from a letter to the compiler published in *Tate Gallery: Illustrated Catalogue of Acquisitions 1986-88* (Tate, London 1996), as is the description of the technical history of *Spreadout Ron Kitaj.*

page 115
An edited version of Dennis de Caires's review of the Serpentine exhibition (entitled 'Establishing an El Dorado') appeared in *Artscribe International* No.157 (April/May 1986).

page 116
'...the experience that a painting "carries"...' is from 'Formalist Art and Black Experience' in *Third Text* 5 (London, Winter 1988-89).

page 119
The letter from Gainsborough to the Earl of Hardwick is quoted by John Barrell in 'Topography v. Landscape' in the *The London Review of Books* (13 May 2010).

page 122
'On confronting pictures...' is from 'Problems of Criticism', *Arts Magazine*, New York, May 1972.

page 124
Bowling is quoted as saying 'I get closer and closer ...' in Martin Gayford's review of an exhibition at the Cut Gallery, London, in *Modern Painters* (Autumn 1995).

Roland Barthes is quoted from *Criticism and Truth*, Part II, p.81, translated and edited by Katrine Pilcher Keuneman (The Athlone Press, London, 1987).

page 130
Bowling's conversation with Matthew Collings introduces the catalogue to *Frank Bowling RA*, an exhibition at Rollo Contemporary Art, London and Artsway, Hampshire, in 2006.

SELECTED BIBLIOGRAPHY

Ronald Alley in *Frank Bowling*, exh. cat., Serpentine Gallery, London, March 1986
Lawrence Alloway and Sam Hunter in *5 + 1*, exh. cat., Stony Brook, New York, October 1969
Michael Amy in *Art in America*, New York, May 1998
Rasheed Araeen in *The Other Story*, exh. cat., Hayward Gallery, November 1989–February 1990
Tommy Barker, 'Bowled Over by the Light', *Cork Examiner*, 9 April 1988
Janet Bloom, '5+1', *Arts Magazine*, New York, December 1969–January 1970
Frank Bowling and William Thomson, 'A Conversation between Two Painters', *Art International*, Lugano, December 1976
Frank Bowling, Paul Harrison and Jeremy Thomas in conversation, 'Formalism versus New Art', *Artscribe*, 44, London, December 1983
Robert Clark in *The Guardian*, London, 6 July 1988
Matthew Collings in *The White Paintings*, exh. cat., Rollo Contemporary Art, London, and Artsway, Hampshire, May, 2006
Jerry Cullum in *The Atlanta Journal-Constitution*, 17 October 1997
Denis de Caires, 'Establishing an El Dorado', *Artscribe International*, 157, London, April–May 1986
Denis de Caires in *Frank Bowling*, exh. cat., The Cut Gallery, London, July 1995
Dorothy Désir, 'Frank Bowling: Baku Gazin', *Bending the Grid*, exh. cat., Aljira, Center for Contemporary Art, Newark, New Jersey, September 2003
Robert M. Doty, *Frank Bowling*, interview with Frank Bowling, exh. cat., Whitney Museum of American Art, New York, September 1971
Robert M. Doty in *Colour, Material Form*, exh. cat., Currier Gallery of Art, Manchester, New Hampshire, January 1982
Christine Eccles in *Frank Bowling*, exh. cat., Castlefield, Manchester, May 1988
Sharon Fitzgerald in *One World*, Vol. 4, Issue 4, New York, January 1999
Andrew Forge, 'Alternatives', *New Statesman*, London, 14 October 1962
Martin Gayford in *The Sunday Telegraph*, London, 18 August 1991
Martin Gayford in *Modern Painters*, London, Autumn 1995
Martin Gayford in *Bowling through the Century*, exh. cat., City Art Gallery, Leicester, 1996
Martin Gayford, 'Artists on Art', interview with Frank Bowling, *The Daily Telegraph*, London, 28 July 2001
Martin Gayford in *Pondlife and other paintings*, exh. cat., Poussin Gallery, London, April 2008
Grace Glueck in *The New York Times*, 17 June 1983
Mel Gooding in *Art Monthly*, London, March 1986
Mel Gooding in *The Other Story*, exh. cat., Hayward Gallery, November 1989–February, 1990
Mel Gooding, 'Grace Abounding: Bowling's Progress', *Third Text*, 31, London, Summer 1995
Mel Gooding, 'through a door of space into memory and imagination', *Bowling through the Century*, exh. cat., City Art Gallery, Leicester, 1996
Mel Gooding, 'A Poet in New York', *Frank Bowling*, exh. cat., Spanierman Modern, New York, 2010
Marcia Hafif, 'Frank Bowling', *Arts Magazine*, New York, December 1971–January 1972
Piri Halasz in *From the Mayor's Doorstep*, New York, December 1997
Piri Halasz in *From the Mayor's Doorstep*, New York, December 1998
Gerrit Henry in *Art in America*, New York, October 1986
Sue Hubbard in *Time Out*, London, 26 March–2 April 1997
Ian Hunt in *Art Monthly*, London, December 1995–January 1996
Jim Hunter in *Big paintings*, exh. cat., text and work, Bournemouth, 2007
Jim Hunter in *Frank Bowling, Paintings*, exh. cat., The Gallery, Winchester Discovery Centre, May 2009
Maya Jaggi in *The Guardian*, London, 24 February 2007
Corrine Jennings in *A/Cross Currents: Synthesis in African American Abstract Painting*, exh. cat., Kenkeleba House, New York, 1992
Kellie Jones, 'It's Not Enough to Say "Black is Beautiful": Abstraction at the Whitney, 1969-1974', *Discrepant Abstraction*, Kobena Mercer (ed.), Institute of International Visual Arts (inVA) and The MIT Press, London and Cambridge, Massachusetts, 2006
Hilton Kramer, 'Frank Bowling', *New York Times*, 1 December 1973
Andrew Lambirth in *What's On in London*, 12–19 March 1997
Donald Locke in *Frank Bowling*, exh. cat., Camille Love Gallery, Atlanta, Georgia, August, 1997
Norbert Lynton, 'London Letter', *Art International*, Lugano, 20 December 1962
Courtney J. Martin, 'They've All Got Painting: Frank Bowling's Modernity and the post 1960 Atlantic', *Afro Modern: Journeys through the Black Atlantic*, exh. cat., Tate Liverpool, Tate Publishing, London 2010
Joseph Masheck, 'Frank Bowling', *Art Forum*, New York, February 1974
Kobena Mercer, 'Black Atlantic Abstraction: Aubrey Williams and Frank Bowling' in *Discrepant Abstraction*, Kobena Mercer (ed.), inVA and The MIT Press, London, and Cambridge, Massachusetts, 2006
Thomas Nonn in *Variations in Matter Painting*, exh. cat., Anita Shapolsky Gallery, New York, April 1987
Veerle Poupeye-Rammelaere in *Bowling through the Century*, exh. cat., City Art Gallery, Leicester, 1996
Vivien Raynor in *New York Times*, 23 May 1986
Spencer A. Richards, 'Frank Bowling: Porknockersdawn', *Dimensions of Guyana*, exh. cat., Skylight Gallery at Restoration Place, Brooklyn, New York, October 1997
Spencer A. Richards in *Frank Bowling, 4 Decades with Color*, exh. cat., Phillips Museum of Art, Franklin & Marshall College, Lancaster, Pennsylvania, September 2004
Spencer A. Richards in *Full of Light*, exh. cat., George N'Nambdi Gallery, Detroit and Chicago, 2005-2006
Carrie Rickey in *Art Forum*, New York, September 1979
Bryan Robertson, John Russell and Lord Snowdon, *Private View*, London, 1965
Frederick L. Seidel, *Frank Bowling*, exh, cat., The Acme Gallery, London, March 1977
Jeanne Siegel in *Art International*, interview with Frank Bowling, Lugano, May 1975
David Sylvester, 'No Baconians', *New Statesman*, London, 20 April 1962
John Tancock in *Frank Bowling*, exh. cat., Centre for Inter-American Relations, New York, November 1973
Tate Gallery Catalogue of Acquisitions, 1986-88, entry on *Spreadout Ron Kitaj*, London, 1989
Valentin Tatransky in *Arts Magazine*, New York, September 1983
Leon Wainwright, 'Frank Bowling and the Appetite for British Pop', *Third Text*, 9, London, March 2008
Janet Wilson in *The Washington Post*, 22 May 1993
Barbara A. Wolanin in *Art in America*, New York, November 1993

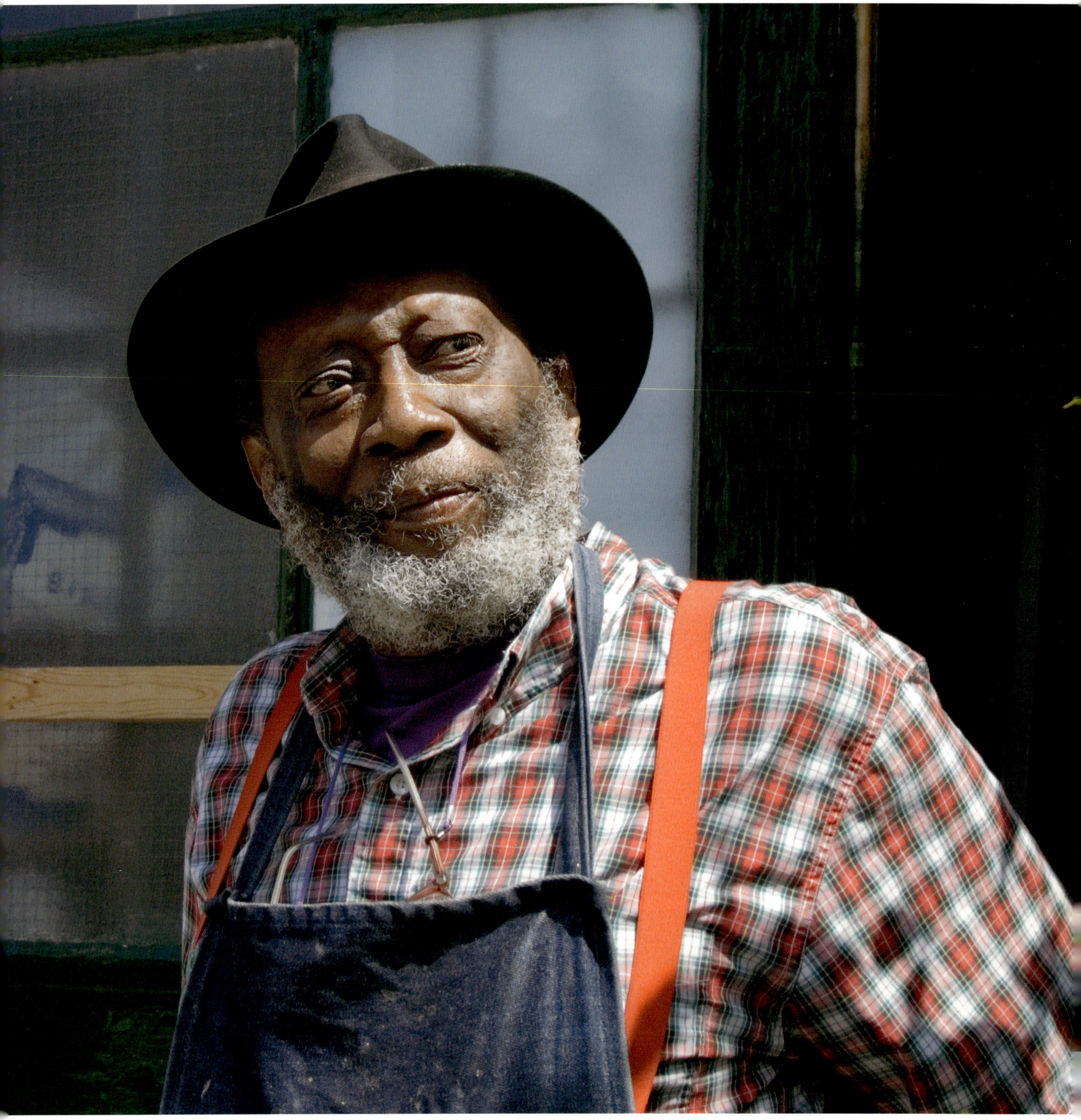

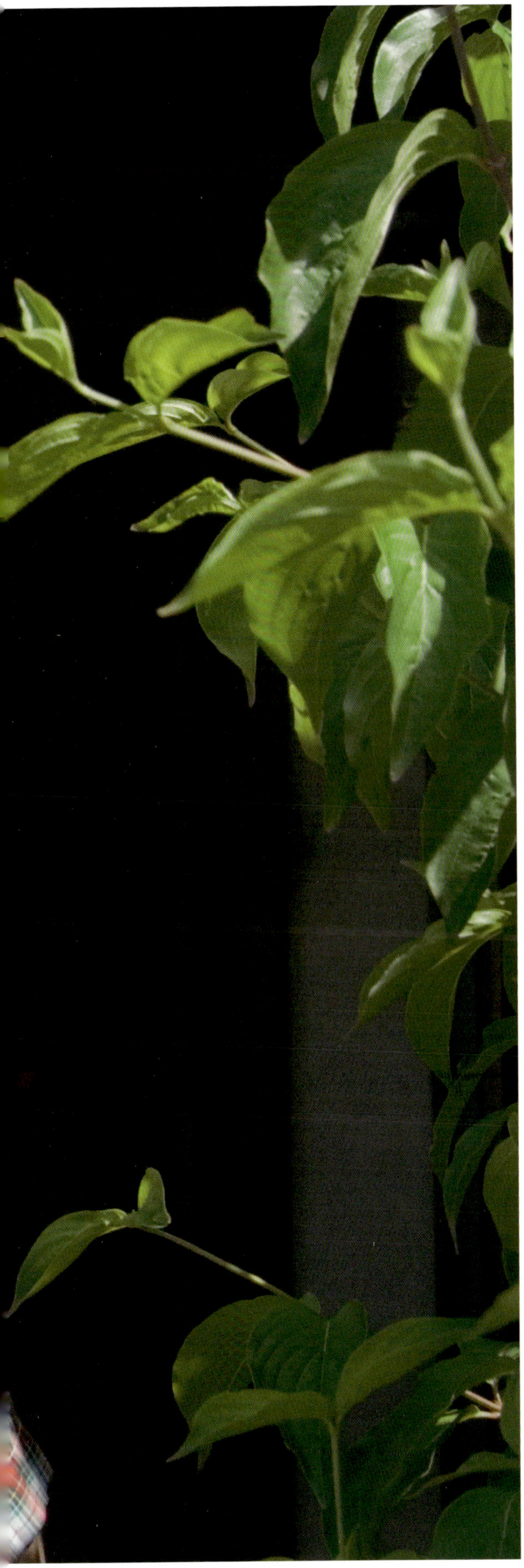

Frank Bowling outside his studio in Peacock Yard, Kennington, London, 2007.

CHRONOLOGY

1934
Frank Bowling born 26 February in Bartica, British Guiana, the eldest son of Richard Sheridan Bowling, a member of the local police force, and Agatha Elizabeth Franklin Bowling, a dressmaker and milliner. As was customary, Frank's baptismal certificate gives the date of his baptism as his date of birth.

1940
Family moves to New Amsterdam, where father becomes paymaster of local police district, and mother opens first Bowling Variety Store in Pope Street, New Amsterdam.

1945-50
Attends Catholic boys' school and then Berbice High School in New Amsterdam.

1953
Leaves British Guiana for London.

1953-56
Regular serviceman in the RAF. Meets Keith Critchlow, who becomes both friend and mentor.

1956-58
Works in various jobs, including sitting for life-classes at Chelsea School of Art and the Royal College of Art.

1958
Studies, for the autumn term, at Chelsea School of Art.

1959
Spring term at City and Guilds of London Art School, Kennington, London.

1959-62
Awarded scholarship to study at the Painting School, Royal College of Art, London. (Spring term January–March 1961 at the Slade School, University College, London.) At Royal College meets Rachel Tripp, who is to become a lifelong friend and, later, partner.

1960
Marries the novelist-to-be Paddy Kitchen; lives at 28 Cedars Road, Clapham, London.

1961
First visit to New York USA with David Hockney and Billy Apple; travels alone to Los Angeles.

1962
Eldest son, Dan, born to Paddy Bowling. Graduates from RCA; awarded Silver Medal for Painting. Travelling scholarship to the Caribbean and Guiana. Second son, Benjamin, born, to Claire Spencer. Lives 47 Lupus Street, Pimlico, London.

1963
Starts work on three paintings commissioned by Richard Buckle for Shakespeare Quatercentenary Exhibition, Stratford-upon-Avon; completed 1964.

1963-66
Teaches at Reading University and at Camberwell School of Art and Crafts.

1964
Third son, Sacha, born, to Irena Delderfield. Lives at 33 Bessborough Street, Pimlico. Creates a stock of silk-screen images on canvas in Textile Department, Camberwell, for use in future paintings.

1965
Awarded Grand Prize for Painting at the *First World Festival of Negro Arts*, Dakar, Senegal. Festival inaugurated by Leopold Senghor, but Bowling does not attend. Visits New York. Introduced by Elizabeth Frink to New York dealer, Terry Dintenfass.

1966
Takes leave from Reading University and travels to New York. Lives at the Hotel Chelsea. On return to London in December, his marriage to Paddy Kitchen comes to end. First solo exhibition in New York at Terry Dintenfass Gallery. Applies for Guggenheim Fellowship.

1967
Awarded Guggenheim Scholarship. Moves to loft studio at 535 Broadway, SoHo, New York.

1968
Travels to Guyana with photographer Tina Tranter to film in New Amsterdam for an unrealised BBC Monitor programme. Recovered footage is later incorporated by Rose Jones into her film *Frank Bowling* (2011).

1969
At invitation of critic-academics Lawrence Alloway and Sam Hunter, curates *5+1*, an exhibition of five leading black American abstract artists plus Bowling himself at Art Gallery, State University of New York, Stony Brook. The American artists were Melvin Edwards, Al Loving, Jack Whitten, Daniel Johnson and William T. Williams.

1969-72
Contributing editor for *Arts Magazine*, New York, during period of intense debate around issues of 'Black Art' in New York following the contentious Metropolitan Museum exhibition, *Harlem on my Mind*, in 1969.

1969
Assists Larry Rivers as curator for the controversial exhibition *Some American History* at Rice University,

Houston, Texas, to which he also contributes. Painting in New York.

1971
Solo exhibition of large 'map paintings' at the Whitney Museum of American Art: part of series of exhibitions showcasing black artists curated by Robert Doty at the Whitney.

1972
Painting pure abstracts in New York. Much encouraged by Clement Greenberg, who introduces him to New York dealer Noah Goldowsky.

1973-74
Receives second Guggenheim Scholarship. Exhibits at the Center for Inter-American Relations, and with the Noah Goldowsky Gallery, New York.

1975
Joins Tibor de Nagy Gallery on a retainer.

1975-82
Works in London, having returned there to look after his three teenage sons. Teaches at Camberwell and Byam Shaw.

1977
Inaugural exhibition at the Acme Gallery, Covent Garden.

1980s
Exhibits regularly with Tibor de Nagy Gallery, in New York.

1982
Meets Spencer Richards in New York – the beginning of an important friendship and valuable professional relationship.

1983
In London, moves to John Islip Street.

1984
Takes first studio in Peacock Yard, Kennington. Appointed Artist-in-Residence at Skowhegan School of Art, a summer school in Maine. Rachel Scott (*née* Tripp) joins him there.

1986
Solo exhibition of recent paintings at Serpentine Gallery, London.

1987
Tate Gallery, London, acquires *Spreadout Ron Kitaj* (1984-86).

1989
Represented in *The Other Story: Afro-Asian Artists in Post-War Britain*, an exhibition curated by Rasheed Araeen at the Hayward Gallery, London.

1990
After a protracted and draining legal dispute over the lease on the SoHo studio, which had prevented Bowling from sustaining his creative practice in New York since 1975, he takes a loft studio in Dumbo, Brooklyn. Throughout the '90s and until 2008, he spends periods during the spring and autumn working in Brooklyn.

1991
First solo exhibition for several years in New York, at the Wilmer Jennings Gallery, New York.

1992
Represented in *A/Cross Currents: Synthesis in African American Abstract Painting*, Dakar Biennale, Dakar, Senegal, touring to Abidjan, Ivory Coast; subsequently shown at Kenkeleba House, New York. Receives Pollock-Krasner Award.

1993
Solo exhibition at the National Academy of Sciences, Washington.

1994
Panel member at College Art Association Conference, New York, on 'Internationalism and the Kreole Abyss'. In London, moves to smaller studio in Peacock Yard.

1996-97
Bowling through the Century, a major British touring exhibition of paintings from the '80s and '90s, organised by Eddie Chambers, which receives one mention in British press.

1998
Receives second Pollock-Krasner Award.

2001
Death of Bowling's eldest son, Dan.

2003
Retrospective exhibition, *Frank Bowling: Bending the Grid*, at Aljira, A Centre for Contemporary Art, Newark, New Jersey, curated by Dorothy Désir and Spencer Richards.

2004
Who's Afraid of Barney Newman (1968) shown in *This Was Tomorrow: Art in the '60s* at Tate Britain; subsequently acquired for Tate collection (2006).

2005
Elected to Royal Academy, London; first black artist to receive this accolade.

2008
Awarded OBE.

2010
Represented in *Afro-Modern: Journeys through the Black Atlantic*, Tate Liverpool.

NOTE
A more detailed chronology up to 2001 can be found in the catalogue to *Frank Bowling: Bending the Grid*, at Aljira, Newark, New Jersey (2003).

EXHIBITIONS

SOLO EXHIBITIONS

1962
Grabowski Gallery, London

1963
Grabowski Gallery, London

1966
Terry Dintenfass, New York

1971
Whitney Museum of American Art, New York

1973
Gallery Center for Inter American Relations, New York
Noah Goldowsky Gallery, New York

1974
Noah Goldowsky Gallery, New York

1975
William Darby, London
Tibor de Nagy Gallery, New York

1976
Acme Gallery, London
Watson/de Nagy and Company, Houston, Texas
Tibor de Nagy Gallery, New York

1977
William Darby, London
Acme Gallery, Los Angeles

1978
Polytechnic Art Gallery, Newcastle upon Tyne

1979
Tibor de Nagy Gallery, New York

1980
Tibor de Nagy Gallery, New York

1981
Vecu, Antwerp, Belgium

1982
Tibor de Nagy Gallery, New York

1983
Tibor de Nagy Gallery, New York

1986
Tibor de Nagy Gallery, New York
Serpentine Gallery, London
Arcade Gallery, Harrogate

1988
The Senate House, University of Liverpool
Municipal Art Gallery, Limerick, Ireland and Crawford Art Gallery, Cork, Ireland
Castlefield Gallery, Manchester

1989
Tibor de Nagy Gallery, New York

1989-90
Bowling through the Decade, University Art Gallery, Reading, and The Royal West of England Academy, Bristol

1991
Wilmer Jennings Gallery, New York

1993
National Academy of Sciences, Washington
Heimatmuseum, Eckernforde, Schleswig Holstein, Germany

1995
The Cut Gallery, Waterloo, London
AFTU/Bill Hodges Gallery, New York

1996
Bowling through the Century, City Gallery, Leicester and UK tour

1997
Gallery 11, University of Bradford, Yorkshire
The YAA Asantewaa Arts Centre, Paddington, London
The Cut Gallery, Waterloo, London
South Hill Park Arts Centre, Bracknell, Berkshire
Midland Art Centre, Birmingham
De La Warr Pavilion, Bexhill-on-Sea, East Sussex
The Herbert Art Museum & Gallery, Coventry
Midlands Art Centre, Birmingham
Christiane Nienaber Gallery, New York
Center for Art & Culture, Skylight Gallery, Restoration Plaza Brooklyn, New York
Camille Love Gallery, Atlanta, Georgia

1998
Rush Arts Gallery, New York

1999
UFA Gallery, Chelsea, New York

2000
Peg Alston Fine Art Gallery, New York.
George N'Nambdi Gallery, Chicago

2001
UFA Gallery, Chelsea, New York
Rohde und Nerlich, Berlin, Germany
Georgetown Gallery of Art, Washington

2002
Peg Alston Fine Arts Gallery, New York

2003
Outfitters Gallery, Margate, Kent
G. R. N'Nambdi Gallery, Detroit
Delibar, Charterhouse Street, London
Frank Bowling: Bending the Grid, Aljira, A Center for Contemporary Art, Newark, New Jersey
Skoto Gallery, Chelsea, New York

2004
Sande Webster Gallery, Philadelphia
George N'Nambdi Gallery, Chicago
Heidi Cho Gallery, Chelsea, New York
Broadbent Gallery, London, England
4 Decades with Color, The Phillips Museum of Art, Franklin & Marshall College, Lancaster, Pennsylvania

2005
Frank Bowling: Full of Light, George N'Nambdi Gallery, Detroit
Frank Bowling Recent Works, Peg Alston Fine Arts Gallery, New York

2006
Frank's Colour: Paintings by Frank Bowling RA, Hugh Casson Room for Friends, Royal Academy of Arts, London, in collaboration with ROLLO Contemporary Art, London
Frank Bowling: The White Paintings, ROLLO Contemporary Art, London; then touring to Art Sway, Sway, Hampshire
Frank Bowling: Full of Light, George N'Nambdi, New York City and N'Nambdi Gallery, Chicago

2007
Frank Bowling Recent Works, Peg Alston Fine Arts Gallery, New York
Frank Bowling RA Poured Paintings, Arts Club London in collaboration with ROLLO Contemporary Art
Frank Bowling: Big Paintings, Art Institute at Bournemouth, The Gallery, Poole, Dorset, and Wolverhampton University Art Gallery

2008
Frank Bowling Latest Works, ROLLO Contemporary Art, London
Pond Life and Other Paintings: New Work by Frank Bowling, Poussin Gallery, London

2009
Frank Bowling: Zippers, ROLLO Contemporary Art, London
Frank Bowling, Paintings, Winchester Discovery Centre, Hampshire County Council Museums
Frank Bowling: Light and Water: Frank Bowling RA Big Paintings, Clifford Chance exhibition space, London, in collaboration with ROLLO Contemporary Art, London

2010
Frank Bowling, New Works, ROLLO Contemporary Art, London
Frank Bowling, Spanierman Modern, New York

2011
Frank Bowling, Works on Paper, Royal Academy of Arts, London
Frank Bowling: Crossings, ROLLO Contemporary Art, London

SELECTED GROUP EXHIBITIONS

1962
Young Commonwealth Artists, RBA Galleries, London, and touring to France and Germany

1968
The Obsessive Image, Institute of Contemporary Arts, London

1969
5+1, State University of New York, Stony Brook; The Art Museum, Princeton

1970
Afro-American Artists, Museum of Fine Arts, Boston
Some American History, Rice University, Houston, Texas

1971
Contemporary Black Artists in America, Whitney Museum of American Art, New York
Whitney Biennial: Contemporary American Art, Whitney Museum of American Art, New York

1972
Two Guyanese Painters: Frank Bowling & Philip Moore, Guyana Consulate, New York

1976
The Golden Door: Artist Immigrants of America 1876-1976, Hirshhorn Museum and Sculpture Garden,Washington, DC

1977
Artists' Maps, Philadelphia College of Art, Pennsylvania
25 Years of British Painting, Royal Academy, London

1978
Selected Works from Tibor de Nagy Gallery, Mint Museum, Charlotte, North Carolina

1979
Contemporary Caribbean Artists…African Expressions, Bronx Museum, New York
British Art Show, Mappin Art Gallery, Sheffield, touring to Newcastle and Bristol
Another Generation, Studio Museum, Harlem, New York

1980
Hayward Annual, Hayward Gallery, London
Maps, John Michael Kohler Art Center, Sheboygan, Wisconsin

1981-83
Mapped Art, Galleries of the University of Texas, Austin; Toledo Museum of Art, Ohio

1982
Bowling, Loving, Mohr, The Currier Gallery, Manchester, New Hampshire; The Hecksher Museum, Hartington, New York; Kresge Art Center, Michigan State University, East Lansing

1986
Caribbean Expressions in Britain, Leicester Museum, Leicester

1987
Variations in Matter Painting, Anita Shapolsky Gallery, New York, and Kingsborough Community College Gallery, City University of New York
The First American: Selections from the Nancy Sayles Day Collection of Latin American Art, Americas Society, New York; touring to El Paso Museum of Art, Texas; Boston University Art Gallery, Massachusetts, University of Florida, Gainesville; Museum of Art, Rhode Island School of Design, Providence, Rhode Island

1988
The Presence of Painting: Aspects of British Abstraction, Mappin Art Gallery, Sheffield; Hatton Gallery, Newcastle; Ikon Gallery, Birmingham
Exhibition Road: Painters at the Royal College of Art, Royal College of Art, London

1989
The Umana Yana, Georgetown, Guyana
198 Gallery, Herne Hill, London
The Other Story: Afro-Asian Artists in Post War Britain, Hayward Gallery, London, touring to Wolverhampton and Manchester
My Generation: 10 Contemporary Abstract Artists, Atkinson Art Gallery, Stockport, touring to Skelmersdale Library Art Centre, Lancashire
Jouvert, touring to Swindon, Huddersfield, Bradford & Cheltenham

1991
Frank Bowling and Graham Mileson, Painting and Sculpture, Greenwich Citizens Gallery, London, and Lanchester Gallery, Coventry Polytechnic
The Search for Freedom: African American Abstract Painting 1945-75, Kenkeleba House, New York City, and touring

1992
A/Cross currents: Synthesis in African American Abstract Painting, Dakar Biennale, Dakar, Senegal, West Africa, touring to Abidjan, Ivory Coast; subsequently shown at Kenkelaba House, New York

1993
Landscape as Metaphor: the Transcendental Vision, Fitchburg Museum, Massachusetts, and touring

1994
Dimensions of Guyana, Frank Bowling and Donald Locke, Camille Love Gallery, Atlanta, Georgia.
Caribbean Visions: Contemporary Painting and Sculpture, Center for Fine Arts, Miami, Florida, and touring

1997-98
Space, Time & Object: Black Abstractionists, IRADAC, (The Institute for Research on the African Diaspora in the Americas and the Caribbean) City University of New York, New York
A Year in the Life of Present Modernism, curated by Piri Halasz, Tribes Gallery, New York

1998
The Fanelli Show, O.K. Harris Gallery, New York.

2000
In a Marine Light, The Custom House Gallery, Mill Dam, South Shields, Tyne & Wear, England
African American Abstraction, City Gallery East, Atlanta, Georgia
19th & 20th Century: African American Art, Kenkeleba Gallery, New York

2001
Jazz and Visual Improvisation, Kantonah Museum of Art, Katonah, New York
Take Five, George N'Nambdi Gallery, Chicago

2002
Tate Unseen: living artists from Tate Storeroom, Tate Britain, London
Six American Masters: Bowling, Carter, Clark, Huston, Loving, Pindell, Sugar Hill Art Center, Harlem, New York
No Greater Love, Abstraction, Jack Tilton/Anna Kustera Gallery, SoHo, New York
Forms of Abstraction 111: Abstract works from the 60's, 70's & 80's; Bowling, Clark, Edwards, Gilliam, Hunt, Hutson, Loving, Pindell, Whitten, G. R. N'Nambdi Gallery, Detroit

2003
Not just for Christmas: Visual Art with Life and Soul, Outfitters Gallery, Margate, Kent
London Group, Woodlands Gallery, Greenwich, London
Faultlines: Contemporary African Art and Shifting Landscapes, a project for the 50th Venice Biennale

2004
This Was Tomorrow: Art and the Sixties, Tate Britain, London
A Century of African American Art: The Paul R. Jones Collection. University of Delaware

2006
Energy/Experimentation: Black Artists, 1964-1980, The Studio Museum, Harlem, New York
Unstitched, Unbound: Imprints for Change, The Nathan Cummings Foundation, New York

2007
25th Anniversary Exhibition: Forms of Abstraction – George N'Namdi Galleries, New York, Detroit, Chicago
Swinging London, Collection of Grabowski, Muzeum Aztuki, Lodz, Poland

2010
Afro Modern: Journeys through the Black Atlantic, Tate Liverpool

SELECTED PUBLIC AND CORPORATE COLLECTIONS

American Telephone and Telegraph Corporation, New York
Arts Council of Great Britain
Boca Raton Museum, Boca Raton, Florida
Calouste Gulbenkian Foundation, Lisbon, Portugal
Carmen & G.R. N'Nambdi Collection
Chase Manhattan Bank, New York
Chelsea & Westminster Hospital, London
Currier Gallery, Manchester, New Hampshire
Crawford Municipal Art Gallery, Cork, Ireland
De Menil Foundation, Houston, Texas
Herbert Art Gallery and Museum, Coventry, England
Herbert F. Johnson Museum, Cornell University, Ithaca, New York
John Simon Guggenheim Foundation
Kresge Art Center, Michigan State University
Lloyds of London
London Borough of Southwark
London Lighthouse
Metropolitan Museum of Art, New York
Museum of Fine Arts, Boston, Massachusetts
Museum of Modern Art, New York
National Gallery of Jamaica, Kingston, West Indies
New Jersey State Museum, Trenton, New Jersey
Neuberger Museum, State University of New York at Purchase, New York
Owens-Corning Fiberglass Corporation, Toledo, Ohio
Port Authority of New York, World Trade Center, New York
Rhode Island School of Design, Providence, Rhode Island
Rivercross Tenants Corporation, New York
Royal Academy of Arts, London
Royal College of Art, London
Tate Gallery, London
University of Delaware, 'The Paul R Jones Collection'
University of Liverpool
Unilever PLC, UK
Victoria & Albert Museum, London
Westinghouse Corporation
Whitney Museum of American Art, New York

INDEX

All page numbers in italic refer to information in captions